WOMEN'S EDUCATION IN THE THIRD WORLD

REFERENCE BOOKS IN INTERNATIONAL EDUCATION
(General Editor: Edward R. Beauchamp)
VOLUME 6

GARLAND REFERENCE LIBRARY
OF SOCIAL SCIENCE
(VOL. 544)

Reference Books in
International Education

Edward R. Beauchamp
General Editor

1. *Education in East and West Germany: A Bibliography*
   by Val D. Rust

2. *Education in the People's Republic of China, Past and Present: An Annotated Bibliography*
   by Franklin Parker and Betty June Parker

3. *Education in South Asia: A Select Annotated Bibliography*
   by Philip G. Altbach, Denzil Saldhana, and Jeanne Weiler

4. *Textbooks in the Third World: Policy, Content and Context*
   by Philip G. Atlbach and Gail P. Kelly

5. *Education in Japan: A Source Book*
   by Edward R. Beauchamp and Richard Rubinger

6. *Women's Education in the Third World*
   by David H. Kelly and Gail P. Kelly

WOMEN'S EDUCATION IN THE THIRD WORLD
An Annotated Bibliography

David H. Kelly
D'Youville College

Gail P. Kelly
State University of New York at Buffalo

with the assistance of

Chen Shu-Ching
Junko Kanamura
Machiko Matsui
Wu Yen-Bo

Garland Publishing, Inc. • New York & London
1989

Library of Congress Cataloging-in-Publication Data

Kelly, David H.
   Women's education in the Third World : an annotated bibliography /
David H. Kelly, Gail P. Kelly with the assistance of Chen Shu-Ching
. . . [et al.].
      p. cm. — (Reference books in international education ; v. 5)
(Garland reference library of social science ; vol. 544)
   Includes indexes.
   ISBN 0–8240–8634–1 (alk. paper)
   1. Women—Education—Developing countries—Bibliography.
I. Kelly, Gail Paradise. II. Title. III. Series: Reference books
in international education ; vol. 5. IV. Series: Garland reference
library of social science ; v. 544.
Z5815.D44K44 1989
[LC2572]   89–32058
                                                                     CIP

Printed on acid-free, 250-year-life paper
Manufactured in the United States of America

Contents

Acknowledgements   3

Introduction   5

New Directions in Research on Women's Education in the Third
    World: The Development of Women-Centric Approaches
    by Gail P. Kelly   15

I.   Bibliographies   39

II.   Research Methods   53

III.   General Studies   59

IV.   Historical Studies   99

V.   Women's Enrollment in Schools   129

VI.   Educational Processes   171

VII.   Women as Teachers and Administrators in
        Primary and Secondary Schools   193

VIII.   Women and Higher Education   199

IX.   Adult and Nonformal Education   221

X.   Women, Education and Development   249

XI.   Women, Education and the Workforce   303

XII.   Women's Education and the Family   379

XIII.   Women's Education and Fertility   401

XIV.   Women's Education and Politics   435

XV.   Women's Studies   445

Author Index by Entry Number   451

Geographical Index   475

Women's Education in the Third World

ACKNOWLEDGEMENTS

This bibliography was prepared over a three year period. In that time span, many people helped us to locate materials and assisted in abstracting materials. Without the consistent help of Interlibrary Loan at the State University of New York at Buffalo, this bibliography would not have been any where near as comprehensive as it is. Fran Abosch and the Interlibrary Loan staff located materials for us. For over two years they cheerfully accepted the many, many orders for works from obscure places and managed to find them and provide us with them in a timely fashion. Jennifer Kelly assisted in obtaining periodical and book literature and in bibliographic research.

A number of individuals helped us with abstracting. Elisa Marleny Cardova and Jennifer Newton provided assistance in abstracting some of the Spanish language materials contained in the bibliography. Zhou Nhan Zhao also assisted in abstracting works for the bibliography for several months. Sharon Hladczuk spent time for almost a year abstracting a number of articles on Africa. The indexes to this bibliography were prepared by Wang Jing.

We are grateful to the office of the Department of Educational Administration, Organization and Policy and the Comparative Education Center at the State University of New York at Buffalo and the Department of the Social Sciences and the Office of the Academic Dean at D'Youville College for their support in the preparation of this bibliography, and for the services of Maria Cotroneo who prepared the manuscript.

David H. Kelly
Gail P. Kelly
December 1988

INTRODUCTION

This bibliography focuses on women's education in the developing nations of Asia, Africa, Latin America and the Caribbean and the Middle East. It contains annotations for about 1200 published works in English, French, Spanish, Portuguese and German. Originally we had planned to cover dissertations, unpublished reports and conference papers, but we came to realize as we began this project in 1986 that the research on women and their schooling, once almost non-existent in academic journals and scholarly books, had flourished. In 1980 when we compiled a bibliography for the International Bureau of Education on the topic, we could find but 355 studies, including government reports.[1] Today, we found it hard to limit the bibliography to 1200 items. We decided early on, given the explosion of literature on the topic, to direct our efforts to locating the extensive journal, monograph and book literature, including many individual chapters hidden in books which did not have women or education as their central concern. This bibliography represents a guide only to the published research literature on women's education in the third world. It is limited to research published in five languages; we are clear that a literature on the topic exists in Arabic, in Chinese, and in languages other than the five in which we worked.

Women as a center of research concern is a relatively new phenomenon and the study of women's education in the third world is even more recent. "Oldies but goodies" in this field date back to the 1960s--Ester Boserup's 1970 book, **Women's Role in Economic Development**, was the work that marked the beginnings of serious scholarship on the topic.[2] Before that date, but a few histories and fragmentary descriptions of women's education in the third world as a whole and in a couple of specific third world nations had been written. Our bibliography is primarily a bibliography of works published in the 1970s and 1980s. In a few instances earlier scholarship is included. We deleted a few earlier works if they had been superceded by a more recent literature. For example, studies providing enrollment statistics appearing in the 1950s or early 1960s were excluded if studies were published in the 1980s which included and went beyond the earlier works.

We focused this bibliography on women's education in third world countries. We confined the bibliography to developing countries in Africa, Asia, the Caribbean, Latin America and the Middle East. We thus did not include works on third world women in the industrialized

5

countries of North America and Western Europe, despite the fact that a rich research literature has emerged on Turkish women migrants in Germany, Indian and West Indian women in Great Britain, Algerian and Middle Eastern women in France, and Asian-American, Afro-American and Hispanic-American women in the United States. A guide to this scholarship is an important undertaking that remains to be done and we felt that we could not do justice to the research published on third world women in Western Europe and North America, given the limitations of space and time.

Not only have we chosen to limit the bibliography to research on women residing in third world nations, we have also chosen to limit this bibliography to developing countries of the third world. The problems of education and of women are vastly different in highly industrialized nations and in nations where most of the population is rural, the GNP per capita falls below $500, and where production still remains agricultural and in the main dependent on manual labor. Some countries of Asia and the Middle East have emerged in the post World War II era industrialized nations. The problems confronting the school systems, the economies and women are more akin to those of Western Europe and North America than they are to countries like Zaire, Bolivia, Guatemala, Turkey, Algeria or Morocco. Thus, we have limited the studies in this bibliography to developing countries and have not focused on the literature on industrialized societies like Japan or Israel. We have done this with full realization that there is a literature on women and their education in these countries.

We take our mission to be one of listing the published literature on women's education in the developing nations of the third world quite seriously, and we have listed works only if they pertain to education and the uses to which women put that education. Thus, we have included studies of educational access and processes as well as the outcomes of education in the public spheres of the workforce and polity and in the private, domestic spheres of family life. We have taken education broadly--listing works on non formal education as well as formal age specific schooling. What we have not covered in this bibliography is the vast research literature on women in the third world, for there are a number of histories of women in individual third world countries, particularly countries like India and China, ethnographic studies of women's role in society, biographies of prominent women, studies of women's organizations, women in multinational corporations, women in the workforce, etc. These studies are undeniably important for understanding the context in which women are educated. However, if education is not a major concern--and in many of these studies education is not treated even in passing--we have not listed them here. Guides to such studies do exist. There are, for example, a number of bibliographies on women in development, women in China, women in India, women in Latin America and the Caribbean. We have not attempted to duplicate them. Rather, we see our contribution as providing a guide to the literature on

women's education and its outcomes in third world countries of Latin
America, Asia, Africa and the Middle East.   In some of the literature
we have included, education is a background variable; in most, however,
women's education is the central concern--and most look at women's
education in the context of women's lives in the family, as producers
or reproducers of the laborforce, in the economy, in production, in
the political system and in the context of struggles for women's
rights.

Just as we have limited this bibliography to the study of women's
education and not included research on women in general, we have also
chosen to ignore the vast literature on education in third world
countries which has systematically refused to acknowledge women and
their access to schools and to acknowledge the differences between
male and female experiences both in and out of school.   The literature
on education in third world countries is extensive.   Unfortunately
most of it has and continues to ignore women.   Most of the main line
journals have run but a token article or two on women.   It is striking
how little gender issues have found their way into the many, many
studies of education and development, education and social equality,
and educational reform and options in third world countries.   Indeed,
many of the studies we have listed in this bibliography stand as
critiques of the mainstream education, sociology, economics and
political science literature on third world countries.   It is our hope
that our delimitation of this bibliography to women's education will
help scholars of the third world pay attention to women's experience
with the schools, with informal and nonformal education and the uses
to which women put their knowledge and skills--which are often not the
same as found among men.

Finally, this bibliography is not a comprehensive guide to the
literature on women's education in the third world.   It is a guide to
published works, and attempts have been made to include research
studies and not to include advocacy, polemical literature.   We also
tried to list only those works which are substantial research studies.
We eliminated most one and two page articles in favor of including
lengthier, substantive studies.   In addition, we did give priority to
works published after 1970, since the vast flourishing of the
literature has occurred after 1975.   The works that have appeared more
recently have gone beyond the descriptive studies of women's
enrollment patterns or gender based disparities in educational access
which characterized most of the initial work in the field.   We have
placed greater emphasis on listing studies that looked at educational
processes, the role of women's organizations and women's studies in a
school reform and the outcomes of education in both the public and
private spheres of life.   Finally, we have attempted to provide a
comprehensive guide to the English language literature.   While we
tapped into the Portuguese, Spanish, French, and German literature, we
relied heavily on indexes to that literature and are not all that
clear that we have provided as comprehensive a guide to book chapters

in those languages as we have in the case of English.

This bibliography was developed over a three year period. We used our earlier bibliography, published by the International Bureau of Education in 1980, as the basis for our listing of the literature which appeared in the 1960s and 1970s. To locate the more recent literature, we searched all major English language general bibliographies, including the standards like the Social Science Index and the British Humanities Index. We also searched Canadian, British and American education indexes. Non English language periodical literature was located through a survey of the Handbook of Latin American Studies, and Hispanic American Periodical Index, and the French Bulletin Signaltique and less comprehensive indexes like the International African Bibliography.

In searching for book literature we consulted international indexes like the Bulletin Signaltique, the Australian National Bibliography, and the African Book Publishing Record. However, our major source was the American National Union Catalogue, published by the U.S. Library of Congress. In using these indexes we excluded obvious dissertation materials, items published only in microfiche or microform formats and most government documents and reports. In the attempt to locate as many studies as possible, we searched these indexes with a very broad net. We read all the materials included in this bibliography and often we excluded works because they lacked any focus on women's education or were not research studies. Throughout the time span we worked on this bibliography we kept an eye out for new books in publishers' brochures and in publishers' journals like Choice that might be of interest. All indexes indicated here were checked through the summer of 1988. We completed our work by scanning current issues of about twenty journals which published research in the past on women and/or education.

Despite our care to search the literature and provide a current annotated listing of the literature, we are acutely aware that this bibliography will be out of date before it is published. The research literature on women's education in third world countries possesses a vitality and dynamic less evident in research in other subspecialities. The literature has grown dramatically in a very short time and continues to expand.

The Organization of the Bibliography

The 1200 or so citations in this bibliography are organized topically. Within each topic, we have provided geographical divisions. For the most part the geographical divisions are regional: Sub-Saharan Africa, Asia, Latin America and the Caribbean, and the Middle East. If we could locate five or more works on a given country on a specific topic we developed country listings within the region. There is a country as well as regional index to the bibliography which should help the reader locate works on a given country iregardless of how we categorized them topically or whether a separate subsection for that country was organized. For the most part, there is a large literature on India and in most of the 15 topics, if there are any country subdivisions, that subdivision is likely to be on India.

We have divided the literature into 15 topics. Not all of them are of equal length. There are, for example, very few studies of educational processes women experience including textbooks and curriculum or socialization in the schools. There are, on the other hand, a vast number of studies on the relation of women's education to their workforce participation, the relation of female education to development and education and fertility control. There are a handful of studies that focus on women, schools and the political system or the impact of female education on women's lives.

The division of the literature into the 15 topics was not always easy, since many research studies tend to focus on a number of issues affecting women's education and its outcomes. Many studies, for example, of women and development are really studies of women's participation in the workforce. Often studies of education and fertility tend to also be conceptualized as development studies. Similarly many of the studies of women in the workforce often are studies of how women combine life in the family with life in the workforce. There is, in short, little discretion at times among topics. We have tried to get around this problem by extensive cross-listing.

The 15 topics we selected are common sense ones and are organized around access to education, educational processes and societal outcomes of women's education. We begin with a presentation of bibliographies and resources on the topic and move to a discussion of research methods. We have chosen to highlight research methods because much of the research on women's education was begun as a corrective to male-centric scholarship which simply ignored women or presumed the male experience stood for the female experience. The literature quickly emerged into a discussion of research strategies and questioned whether women could be studied the same way as men. It explored and continues to explore whether new conceptual schemes, new theories, indeed, new methods of conducting inquiry are necessary in order to place women at the center of scholarship. Questions of interpretation, of data collection and of the uses of scholarship are important and we chose to highlight these issues by devoting a separate section of the bibliography to them.

Part III of the bibliography includes general works. We have included here those studies which focus on women's status and women in society and which for the most part include education as a substantial part of that discussion.   We have divided this section into three parts: the first presents anthologies and collections on women's education which cover a range of topics on women's education in the third world.   Included here as well are anthologies on individual countries or regions of the third world which also contain a substantial number of articles on women's education.   We list the collections here, but many of the chapters contained in them have been abstracted individually elsewhere in the bibliography.   The second part of Section II contains statistical compendia.   These statistics are not confined to education (those which are limited to enrollment statistics are placed elsewhere in the bibliography).   Rather, they include statistics on health, workforce participation, income and the like as well as on education.   The third part relates to overviews of women's education and society.   These studies tend to describe inequalities in education, what types of institutions are open to women and relate educational patterns to women's political, social, familial and economic roles.

The fourth section of the bibliography annotates histories of women's education.   Some of these works are general histories, others focus on individual institutions, or they are biographies of important women, such as Rajen Kartini, an Indonesian feminist and nationalist who lived in 19th century Java.

Part V of the bibliography presents the literature on female enrollment patterns in third world countries.   Many of these studies not only detail how many women, relative to men, are enrolled at each level of schooling, they also dwell on factors affecting access to education.   We have also included as a subsection a number of studies on general factors affecting female access to education, including parental income and attitudes and the sex role divisions of labor in production and the use of female child labor.   Given the sudden increase in studies on the impact of religion, mainly of Islam, on female education, we have devoted a separate subsection to this literature.

While there may be a number of studies that focus on women's enrollment in schools and the factors that affect it in third world countries--we have annotated over 130 such studies--there are precious few studies on educational processes and on female achievement patterns and the curriculum which prepares women for subordinate roles in society.   Nonetheless, we see the study of the schools--what goes on in schools, what kind of knowledge about gender roles schools transmit and the relation of that knowledge to educational and social outcomes of schooling--a key research area and one which is in desperate need of attention.   We could locate fewer than 70 studies in all of the third world on sex role socialization in the schools, the classroom, the curriculum and the achievement of girls.   We have, nonetheless, devoted Part VI to such studies.

Part VII underscores the sparsity of studies on women as teachers and administrators in the schools. It annotates the few studies we have of women as teachers and their in-class behavior. Much of this literature focuses on teachers' attitudes more than it does on the gendered nature of teaching as a profession.

Higher education is the topic of Part VIII of this bibliography. We have included here institutional studies, studies of women's enrollment in higher education, studies of the attitudes and expectations of female college students and studies of women academics. Several studies of women's higher education and the workforce are included here. There is extensive cross listing to Part XI which is on women in the workforce.

Most women in third world countries do not go to school and a persistent problem in the literature is how to provide education to adult women. Adult and nonformal education has become an important part of the literature on women in third world countries. This literature has focused not only on how to provide educational services to adult women, but it has turned to questions of empowerment and how women can design educational programs to meet their needs in the context of patriarchial institutions which oppress women. Part IX of this bibliography lists the rich and diverse literature on adult and nonformal education for women in the third world.

Women and development is the tenth topical division of this annotated bibliography. We include here studies which seek to use education as a means to maximize women's contribution to development, those which are critical of the impact of development on women and those which hope to provide women via education the benefits of development. We identified two subsections of this literature which have emerged of late: one is the role of international agencies; the other focuses on women's access to science and technology.

By far the largest literature on women's education in the third world is the literature which links educating women with their participation in the paid laborforce. Part XI of this bibliography lists over 200 works on this topic. We have included as a subsection the literature on women and the professions.

Part XII of this bibliography turns to the impact of education on the domestic sphere--on women, marriage and the family. It surprised us how few studies there were on the topic. Annotated here are a range of studies which ask about education and marriage choice, about education and childrearing practices, about the impact of mothers' education on children's schooling and on children's nutrition and health care.

While the literature on women and the workforce dominates

research on women's education in the third world, a literature which also accounts for a very large share of the research has been the literature on the relation between female education and fertility reduction. This literature is annotated in Part XIII of the bibliography.

A neglected part of the literature on women's education in the third world is the focus of the fourteenth section of this bibliography—the study of the relation between women's education and their access to political power in society. We have included here not only the study of women and the political system but also the studies of women's organizations and the women's movement in third world countries and their roles in agitating for women's education.

We end the bibliography with a listing of research on women's studies in third world countries. The development of women's studies is a new phenomenon and an important one, and its appearance in the 1980s bodes well both for the continued flourishing of scholarship on women's education and issues of importance to women, as well as for the development of new voices and perspectives in the research community on this topic.

David H. Kelly
D'Youville College

Gail P. Kelly
State University of
New York at Buffalo

NOTES

1. David H. Kelly and Gail P. Kelly. "Education of Women in Developing Countries." Educational Documentation and Information, Bulletin of the International Bureau of Education 56 (no. 222, 1982).

2. Ester Boserup, Women's Role in Economic Development (New York: St. Martin's Press, 1970).

NEW DIRECTIONS IN RESEARCH ON WOMEN'S
EDUCATION IN THE THIRD WORLD:
THE DEVELOPMENT OF WOMEN-CENTRIC APPROACHES

Gail P. Kelly
State University of New York at Buffalo

Women's education as a research concern is relatively new to academic scholarship as well as to policy makers and planners. Before the rebirth of the women's movement in the late 1960s, academic research and policy studies focusing on women were virtually non-existent. Most disciplines be that discipline education, anthropology, sociology, history, political science, economics or literature ignored women or assumed that their roles were marginal to public life.[1] There were but a handful of scattered individual studies which remained outside of the mainstream of research and all but ignored. This was the case in North America and Europe as well as in the third world. Studies of education and its outcomes were, when all is said and done, studies of males. Gender was rarely acknowledged, even as a background variable. Few studies even explored the existence of sex differences. In research on schooling in the third world, scholars may have focused on education and equality, but the only forms of equality of interest were based on class, ethnicity or race.[2] Most were mute when it came to gender.

The 1960s witnessed the rise of a research and policy literature on development which initially ignored women while focusing on how a country might modernize via the schools. Inkeles and Smith's book, Becoming Modern, for example, was a study of males' attitudes and how they contributed to development. That study, and many like it, became the basis for policy prescriptions about education.[3] In 1981 the International Bibliography of Comparative Education was published.[4] It covered the research literature written between 1960 and 1975. Out of the 3080 works listed on education worldwide (excluding the United States), 33 were on women. A bibliography of published and unpublished research on women's education in the third world compiled for the International Bureau of Education which included materials issued to 1979, yielded but 355 citations.[5] The annotated bibliography contained in this volume consists of approximately 1200 published books, book chapters, monographs and journal articles on the subject. Research on the education of women in the third world has flourished in the past decade. We now have a rich and diverse research literature on a wide range of topics.

15

This essay focuses on how the research has evolved. It looks at the questions that have framed the study of women's education in the third world and shows how those questions changed over time. Research on the topic began using modernization as a starting point for viewing women's education. It tended to ask how women could contribute to development via education rather than   how education might serve women. Over time, as the community of scholars involved in scholarship on women's education in third world countries extended beyond North American and West European academics and policy analysts, scholarship became increasingly female-centric. As it did, new strategies for conducting research arose which challenged those which had hitherto guided study. The development of new research strategies in the long run meant that new research interests arose and considerable revision of and debate about earlier studies on a range of issues emerged. In the 1980s the research on women's education in the third world has become diverse in its approach, underlying theoretical assumptions, topics covered and the community of women who contribute to its development. These trends are traced in the pages that follow.

Research on women's education in the third world is not evenly distributed among countries and regions. This essay also explores this distribution and how national and regional contexts have shaped questions asked about women's education.

Tentative Beginnings

In 1980 the **Comparative Education Review** published a special issue on women's education in the third world. This issue contained four review essays, commissioned by the Ford Foundation in 1978.[6] The four--one on women's educational enrollment patterns, another on school processes and achievement outcomes; a third on women and the laborforce and the fourth on maternal outcomes of women's education--underscored the fragmentary nature of the literature. Bowman and Anderson's article, which charted educational enrollment patterns, noted the very incomplete statistical basis for making any comparisons. Many third world countries in the past have not provided educational enrollment statistics broken down by gender--some not until 1978. When they did, these statistics tended to focus exclusively on access to primary school. Little systematic data had been collected on survival rates, on access to secondary and higher education broken down by region, race, ethnicity and by type of school attended. Bowman and Anderson's very excellent analysis relied entirely on illustrations drawn from but a few countries.

While the data base for charting women's educational enrollments may have been fragmentary in the late 1970s, that literature was massive when one compares it with research on educational processes and outcomes. Jeremy Finn, Janet Dulberg and Lorretta Reis, in their review article, cited primarily sources on the United States and Western Europe, simply because there were almost no studies of curriculum, of teacher/student interactions, of students and their expectations or of how girls relative to boys achieved in school conducted in the third world. Rai Ram's review essay on the labor force rested on a very narrow data base--there simply were few studies that related women's education to the workforce in third world countries. Robert LeVine's review on the maternal outcomes of women's education quite tellingly relied on a few ethnographic studies. He pointed out that the literature on fertility reduction was not conclusive, mainly because most of those studies had asked how educating men related to controlling women's fertility; they had not bothered to look at the impact of educating women.

The review articles that appeared in the 1980 special issue of the Comparative Education Review did not cover the full spectrum of the research literature. By that time a literature on women and development had begun to surface which investigated the impact of modernization policies and educational policies designed to bring about modernization on women.[7] Additionally, a number of studies which did not use modernization as their[8] frame appeared which linked education to changes in women's status.[8] A few studies of[9] women in the professions made their way into the literature as well.[9] Despite the fact that some of the research was not included in the four review articles in the Comparative Education Review special issue, these literature surveys illustrated, by and large, the very fragmentary nature of the research base at that time. They demonstrated how little we knew and how under-researched women's education in the third world was. In the 1980 bibliography on the subject, Kelly and Kelly listed 355 published and unpublished works; of these 50 were overviews consisting of general descriptive studies; 132 focused on women and development; while another 41 were on women and the workforce. In 1988 when we compiled this bibliography the volume of the literature had increased over four fold, it had diversified and it had begun to develop a solid research base on a number of issues, many of which had not even been considered in the 1960s and 1970s.

One further point deserves mention before turning to an analysis of how the literature on women's education in the third world has emerged in the past decade. In the 1960s, for the most part, the literature on women in third world countries was written predominantly by women in the United States and Western Europe working in universities and in public and private national and international agencies. In the 1980s the literature is no longer dominated by scholars from the industrialized world. While their voices remain strong, increasingly studies have been generated by women in Latin America, Africa, Asia, the Caribbean and the Middle East. The nature of those contributing to the research literature has changed in large part because of the emergence of the women's movement in third world countries like India and because of the United Nations Decade for Women, begun in 1975, which tried to bring women's issues to the forefront of national agendas and which stimulated and made research on women legitimate. Funding agencies like the Rockefeller and Ford Foundations, the International Development Research Centre of Canada, and the Swedish International Development Agency encouraged research on the topic by assisting in the development of women's studies centers in third world countries and by supporting individual third world women to engage in research on the topic. The growing presence of women from third world countries in the research community has meant research directions have shifted and new debates have emerged.

Women's Education for Development

The research on women's education in the third world began as a descriptive literature. For the most part, scholarship in the 1960s and mid-1970s tended to provide fragmentary glimpses into women's educational enrollment patterns, the history of women's education and the relation between schooling and women's status in society. For the most part, that literature argued that third world countries in the post World War II expansion of schooling were, for the most part, neglecting female populations. Much of it urged that governments educate women, linking female education to economic development and to other national priorities. Ester Boserup's Women's Role in Economic Development, first published in 1970, is typical of this sort of work--and it is also one of the best within its genre.[10] In that work, Boserup argued that the key to modernization is the unleashing of productive labor via schooling. Women, Boserup pointed out, traditionally constituted productive labor in agriculture in much of the third world and she argued that as modernization occurs, women are removed from productive activities. They cannot enter the modern workforce because they lack skills male laborers possess by virtue of the males having received schooling. Boserup contended that modernization will be stalled unless women are enabled to continue to contribute to production. Thus, she links the modernization of society to the education of its women.

Boserup and much of the literature of the late 1960s and early 1970s linked female education to production and others followed in her steps, asking about the relation of education to women's participation in the paid laborforce. The workforce became the major focus of research, along with studies of women and development. These two research foci remain. Research on the workforce is the single most researched topic when it comes to the study of women's education in the third world.

The early and continuing concern of the scholarship on women's education in third world countries about constructing an argument that would convince national governments they ought to educate women did not always focus on women as producers, either in past or future economies. A second stream in the literature linked women's education to national development via women's roles in reproduction. Broadly stated, this literature argued that a key impediment to modernization was population growth and that women could contribute to modernization by limiting family size. It was claimed that women's education had a strong impact on declines in birth rates.[11]

The initial literature on women's education in the third world, thus, provided a rationale for educating women, and it did so by showing how women's schooling could benefit states controlled by men. The literature on women's education began to emphasize educational access. It looked at factors affecting access and tried to show policy makers how women could be brought into the educational mainstream. This literature tended to establish that educational access for women equal to men's could be achieved without special effort. It argued that class, ethnicity and urban/rural residence were the major factors which prevented girls from attending school.[12] A few scholars, like Marjorie Mbilinyi, focused on sex role divisions of labor in the family and how that affected girls' schooling.[13] Very few studies, as Kelly and Elliott pointed out in 1980, sought to understand how the nature of school provision, the content of education, school quality or the uses to which women could put their education once they receive it, influenced educational access.[14] The access literature which emerged in the 1970s assumed that governments had accepted the necessity of educating females. It thus sought ways to extend preexisting educational provisions to females. One innovation thought to be effective in delivering educational services to women was nonformal education. Nonformal education was seen as a way for females to catch up with males without taking them away from production or their household tasks while they learned skills that would presumably enable women to contribute more to national economic development.

Toward a Female Centric Approach

In the mid-1970s a new strand appeared in the research literature which questioned the premise on which education for women had been based. It rejected modernization as both a strategy for improving women's lives and as a rationale for educating women. Some of this came from third world scholars as well as from feminists in North America who argued that modernization served to further oppress women, even if women were given access to work in the modern sector of the economy.   Norma Chinchilla and Glaura Vasquez de Miranda, among others, pointed out in the special issue of Signs which appeared in 1977 that the entry of women into the paid laborforce, via education, in fact served to marginalize women.[16] Women with education often were unemployed because the workforce was sex segregated and women, while qualified to take up positions among skilled workers, managers, technicians and professionals, could not find work in these fields, which men dominated. Additionally, the work women did find--as domestics, as clerks and in sales as well as in light industry--made women more dependent on male structures for their sustenance. While Latin American scholars were quite vocal in pointing out that modernization was not always in women's best interests, scholars of Africa also came to similar conclusions. The phrase "modernization means more dependency" was coined by Judith Van Allen in reference to Africa in 1970.[17] Claire Robertson's and Deborah Pellow's respective studies of Ghanaian women pointed out that while more women were entering the modern sector of the economy via education and earning a wage, women gave up economic autonomy and their female economic networks.[18]

When Norma Chinchilla in her study of women, education and work in Guatemala published in 1977 argued that modernization tended to marginalize women, she insisted that the marginalization was not necessarily intrinsic to the modernization process, but rather resulted from capitalist forms of modernization.[19] Implicit in Chinchilla's work is the notion that socialist modernization proceeds differently. Such an assumption has been challenged in the 1980s by studies of women in China. Phylis Andors, Margarey Wolfe and Elizabeth Croll, each of whom has written on women in China during the Four Modernizations' Policy, point out that development policies have ended up fostering and exacerbating inequalities between males and females.[20] Under socialism, as well as capitalism, the emphasis is on production. Issues relating to women's work in the household and in child bearing and rearing are ignored. Socialist governments have been, in fact, more effective in driving women into wage labor than have nonsocialist governments. At the same time, women continue to lag behind men in income and they continue to lose political power because they work two jobs: one for a wage in the laborforce and the other without a wage in the family. Socialist modernization, Croll, Andors and Wolfe all point out, does not benefit women all that much.

The criticism of the modernization rationale for educating women also signaled a shift in questions undergirding research. Initially the question scholars asked was how women could contribute to development via schooling and education; by the late 1970s the question had changed to how education improves women's lives. Initially it had been thought that development meant improving women's lives; by the 1970s there was a debate about whether the two went hand in hand and whether improvement in the material conditions of women's lives represented progress toward equality or liberation. This shift was evident in the growing literature on women and development which began to see modernization as oppressing rather than liberating women and leading to the further erosion of the material conditions of women's lives.[21] Such trends were also apparent in the research on women's education and the workforce as well as in the literature emerging on nonformal education. Eleonora Cebotarev, for example, in her landmark 1980 article, "Toward A Non-Oppressive Framework for Adult Education Programs for Women in Latin America", asserted that most nonformal programs tended to allocate women to gender specific roles in the household.[22] These programs, she asserted, were designed to bring women into new forms of patriarchy, they were not designed to liberate women. Similarly, Barbara Rogers in her 1981 book, damned UNDP programs for women, not because they excluded women, but because most development projects were designed exclusively to teach women how to become better mothers through dissemination of childcare techniques, nutrition and health programs and through emphasis on fertility control.[23] Bringing women into development, she pointed out, had meant making the domestic sphere female and exacerbating inequalities between males and females in access to science, technology and the modern workforce.

Works such as Rogers' and Cebotarev's raised the question of whether emphasis on access to education was beneficial to women because of the relation of schools and educational programs offered by the state and by international agencies to sex gender systems that oppress women. They argued that education allocated women to narrowly defined and subordinate roles in the family and in the workforce. In the 1960s most scholars had assumed that schools would benefit males and females similarly. By the 1980s attention began to turn to the nature of what schools and educational programs taught and how that represented either the reinforcement of existing gender based inequalities or the development of new ones. Works in this genre took a range of forms--from Biraimah's on a Togolese secondary school to Kalia's study of Indian textbooks.[24] A number of studies looked at how schools prepared women for predominately female professions and for predominately female unskilled labor in the workforce.[25] The literature began to turn from access issues, to issues of how to reform schools and educational programs so that they could open rather than close women's options. By the 1980s "participatory" planning became almost a buzz-word in some of the literature. Some scholars asserted that programs that would not allocate women into narrowly defined, subordinate roles would only be those programs that women themselves planned and controlled.[26] The nonformal education literature began to focus on women organizing themselves for their own needs, irrespective of the state and of the needs of the economy to develop.

Increasingly, women, rather than state policy or development, became the starting point of study and the goals often were not

development, but women's liberation, equality or empowerment.   The
terms of research had changed--engendering a great deal of debate and
controversy.   This change also led to the development of new research
strategies.

New Research Strategies Emerge

Initially research on women's education in the third world had
been conducted on data sets generated for the study of male
populations.   Quickly scholars realized the limitations of such data
sets.   D'Souza, for example, pointed out that these data sets
consistently devalued women.[27]   The clearest examples were workforce
statistics.   Those gathered in most third world settings counted only
individuals employed as wage labor; they did not count those who were
engaged in agriculture and petty trade or crafts--female populations
in much of Africa, Latin America and parts of Asia.   Thus, research
which used as a basis the very idea that wage labor was the only form
of productive labor and interpreted entry of women into such labor as
their entry into production denied productive processes in most third
world countries.   D'Souza and others have pointed out that the
statistical bases for conducting research on women are simply
unreliable and misrepresent women's work and role in the economy.

Increasingly in the 1980s scholars began relying on qualitative
forms of inquiry--open-ended interviews, ethnographic techniques,
participant observation, life histories and participatory research
strategies.   The focus was on trying to understand the reality of
women's lives as a basis for understanding why and how women chose the
forms of education they do for themselves and for their daughters.
Such studies began to focus on how much time women have during the day
to study, the perceptions of women about the values of programs the
state and international agencies offer them and the reasons women have
for educating themselves.   Research shifted from preconceived analytic
categories, established on the basis of the study of male populations,
to new ones that stemmed from women's experience.   Such studies led
scholars away from exclusive interest in the relation between
education for women and development, education and workforce entry and
education and fertility control to a more diverse range of questions
which reflected women's concerns.   Some of these involved studies of
the family and power relations in it; women's control over their
bodies and access to resources independent of their husbands; income
and equality.   Sometimes these studies looked to how women could
organize to help themselves.

The Study of New Questions and the Revision of Old Questions

New studies appeared in the 1980s on topics which heretofore had barely been considered or which substantially revised the scholarship on topics which had been the center of considerable research attention like the workforce. The family, for example, was rediscovered in the 1980s as a research focus. Before that time, the family--or domestic sphere--was deemed unimportant and there were few studies on the topic. In 1980, in the Kelly and Kelly bibliography on women's education in the third world, only 31 studies, published and unpublished, could be located.[28] Of these, most were on fertility and the remainder asked how education could enable women to better bear and rear children. In the current bibliography, we have listed over three times that number of studies--all of them published--on the family exclusive of studies of women's education and fertility reduction (there are over 100 studies on education and fertility listed separately in this bibliography).

The works on the family that have appeared since 1980 are different from earlier works. They did not see women's roles as determined by nature; rather they viewed the family as a patriarchial institution characterized by unequal power relations. Scholars began to focus not only on whether education helped women to perform their roles as wives and mothers more efficiently; but rather they began to ask whether education changed power relations between males and females in the family. Soraya Altorki's work on Saudi Arabia is an excellent example of such scholarship.[29] Altorki looked at changes in how women assert their use of space in the household and their relations with their husbands and basic social life. Her study suggests that education's impact on the day to day life of women does affect a woman's ability to enter into social relations independent of her husband, to make decisions about herself and her children and to exert her right to space within the household.[30] A number of studies conducted on India make a similar point. They find that educated working women have greater control over their income than do working women who have little or no education and that educated women, iregardless of whether they work, are able to make a wider range of decisions concerning the household, the community and the disposal of family income than their lesser educated sisters.

The shift toward women as the starting point of research also led to an increasing realization that much of the scholarship on women's education in third world countries had been guided by a mistaken isolation of domestic life from public life. Many studies conducted in the 1960s and 1970s tended to look at the relationship between women's education and the workforce presuming that the domestic sphere--of marriage, the family and the child bearing and child rearing--had no impact on that relationship or, if it did, the impact was the same on women as on men. Studies of women in the family, similarly, assumed that women played no role in public life in the

workforce or in the political system. The bifurcation of the public
from private spheres increasingly came under question--and it came
under question because scholarship on women which focused on women's
lives came to see that from women's perspective, the two are
inextricably intertwined. This renewed attention to women's education
and the family began to show that workforce participation influenced
on women's roles in the family just as women's roles in the family
affected their workforce participation.   Catalina Wainerman, for
example, in 1980 studied the relation between education and women's
workforce participation by looking at how marriage, child bearing and
child rearing affected whether a woman would enter the workforce and
how long she would sustain her participation in the workforce.[31]
Wainerman's was a study of Paraguay and Argentina. She argued
forcibly that education mediates the impact of marriage, child rearing
and child bearing on the workforce life of women but pointed out that
unless one studied in greater depth education and the family and
relations within it, one could not understand why this was the case.

Wainerman's work is not the only one to look at how the domestic
and public spheres interact in looking at the impact of education on
women's workforce participation patterns.   Increasingly, the
scholarship on Indian women has turned to this question and looked at
how marriage and the family affects educated versus uneducated women
in the workforce in terms of their incomes, their role conflicts,
their career patterns, their social status and their power within the
family. Some of these studies focus exclusively on elite women and
focus on women's attitudes toward work as well as toward their
families and their perceptions of the impact of one on the other.[32]

Placing women at the center of research has also led the
literature to consider unequal power relations not only in the family,
but also in the society at large and how education either changes
those relations or empowers women to struggle to change them. Studies
of the workforce increasingly ask not if education increases women's
workforce participation rates, but rather if education changes the
jobs at which women work, women's income relative to men's and the
pattern of sex segregation--both horizontal and vertical--which[33]
characterizes the workforces of most third world countries.   The
focus is on whether education changes women's inferior status in the
workforce, and lack of power and autonomy relative to men and, if it
does not, why this is the case. Attribution does not stop in the more
recent research as it did in the literature of earlier decades with
women's qualification.   Rather, it centers on discriminatory
structures within the workforce, the nature of public policy and the
relation of family structures to workforce structures.

As the workforce literature witnessed new currents which
challenged the old, so also did the research on education and
fertility. That literature in the 1960s and early 1970s simply looked
at national educational levels and fertility rates, or male

educational levels and fertility rates. In the 1970s it began to look
at women's educational levels and fertility rates, presuming that
women controlled their reproduction independent of the power relations
in the family. Scholarship began to study those relations and whether
education changed them in such a way that women sought to assert
reproductive rights. Some studies looked at the fertility behavior of
educated women who, because they were educated and were in the paid
labor force, had incomes independent of their husbands.[34] Others began
to look at women's versus men's attitudes toward and knowledge of
birth control and how women versus men make decisions about family
size, relating female education to how decisions about child bearing
are made.[35]

     Women-centric studies have also led to the development of a
research literature, small though it is at the current time, on
women's education and access to power in society. That literature
arose, for the most part, from the study of women in societies which
had undergone revolution, like China. In these countries, educational
extension for women has been dramatic and in the case of socialist
societies, the extension of education was marked by unprecedented
entry of women into the workforce. Margarey Wolfe's 1982 study of
women in China as well as Phylis Andor's and Elizabeth Croll's
respective works on China, Peter Knauss' on women and revolution in
Algeria and Maxine Molyneux's on women in the People's Republic of
Yemen were among those studies which began to question whether entry
into the workforce signaled changing relations in women's access to
public policy making.[36]

     Access to power in society and in the family via education has
been one of the strands to enter the research literature in the 1980s.
It has led to a renewed focus on women's organizations and the role of
women in organizing for change.[37] This literature is but a small part
of the overall literature, but it reflects an important development.
The growing research on women's studies in the third world is related
to the understanding that education may not, as currently constituted,
liberate women, provide women with equality, modify power relations in
society or the family or even improve women's lot. However, this does
not mean that education cannot be changed to work in the interests of
women. The studies which are listed in the last section of this
bibliography reflect such a hope.
     While new research orientations and concerns have emerged, they
have not displaced those which characterized scholarship on women's
education in the third world in earlier decades. The majority of
studies remain studies on women's education and its contribution to
development. The emphasis remains on enhancing women's productivity
or controlling reproduction rather than on empowering women and
changing gender relations. Much of the research continues to study
women as if they were men and assume the schools, institutions like
the family, the political system and the work place are gender neutral
and devoid attachment to sex gender systems. There are still

relatively few studies that focus on educational processes and how they
relate to the outcomes scholars ascribe to schools, universities and
nonformal education programs.   There are still but a handful of
studies that look at the power relations in the family and how
education of women affects them.   Even rarer are those studies which
look at how education affects women's access to power and authority in
society.   Despite this, the growing presence of studies which take
women as their starting point and focus on new topics and concerns,
have engendered a lively set of debates and new directions and trends
for future scholarhsip.

This essay has looked at the research on women's education in the
third world as a whole.   However, it should be pointed out that the
forms that research has taken and the questions it has addressed vary
by geographic region and by country.   Without question, national
concerns and the concerns of international agencies, governments and
the women's movement often shape not only the volume of research on a
particular country or region, but also what kinds of questions about
women's education are posed.

Regional and National Variation

The bibliography which follows illustrates all too clearly the
fact that while research on women's education in the third world,
taken as a whole, is voluminous, it is uneven in terms of the nations
and regions on which research has been conducted.   There is, for
example, more research on women's education in India than in any other
third world nation.   This reflects in large part the strength of the
Indian feminist movement, the presence of a number of professional
women scholars working in universities and in research institutes and
the development of a large indigenous publishing infrastructure.
There are few countries which rival India in terms of the volume of
research on women's education.

Not only are there differences in volume of scholarship among
countries and regions, there are differences in the types and
diversity of questions research addresses.   While there are a number
of studies on countries like Bangladesh, Ghana, Kenya, Brazil, Chile,
Columbia, China, Turkey, Malaysia and others, research on those
countries tends to focus almost exclusively on one or two
questions--like the relation of the education of women to fertility
reduction and female education and workforce participation; or women
and development and women's education and the professions.   India is
one of the few national contexts in which research has covered a full
range of questions.

In the next few pages I will explore the regional and national variation in the research literature. It should be clear, however, that the statements made here need to be taken as tentative ones since they are based exclusively on published research published in English, German, French, Spanish and Portuguese. There may be, for example, a substantial research literature in Arabic or in Chinese which I have neglected. In addition, statements can be made only about the relative emphasis of scholarship on a country or region. Why scholarship has focused on some questions and not others is a topic for future research. Here I can only speculate.

The research on women's education in the Middle East is a fine example of how a regional context has shaped the scholarship. The research as a whole tends to focus on the impact of religion, particularly Islam, on educational opportunities and outcomes and on the family. Indeed, some of the most interesting studies of women and the family are situated in Middle Eastern countries. This literature, except in the case of Iran before the Shah was deposed and Turkey, tends to avoid issues of fertility control. There are but a handful of studies on nonformal education in the countries of this region.

There are of course variations among countries. Research is stronger on Egypt and Turkey than on any other countries. And the research on Egypt tends to be a workforce literature, more so than elsewhere in the Middle East. Studies of Algeria are studies of women in politics and of the role of revolutionary movements in changing women's status.

While, as I have already pointed out, studies of women and the workforce are relatively few in the Middle Eastern countries, those that are available tend to focus on women in the professions. This is the case of research on Turkey, Egypt and Kuwait where the increases in women's education have led to the formation of a female professional elite which for the most part serves women.

Research on women's education in Latin American and the Caribbean tends to emphasize topics different from those found in the literature on women in Middle Eastern countries. The research on women's education in Latin America is heavily oriented toward the workforce outcomes of women's education. It has tended to look at how modernization processes have displaced and marginalized women's labor in both the wage and non-wage economy. Indeed many of the studies criticizing modernization processes for undermining women's role in production arose from the Latin American context. Research on women's education in Latin America has also focused on nonformal education. These have been studies which are critical of government sponsored nonformal education. Such studies have increasingly turned to the development of participatory research and participatory projects with the aim of empowering women. This work has been heavily influenced by Paulo Friere's theories of expressed in his book **The Pedagogy of the**

Oppressed. There are a number of fertility studies that have been conducted in the region; more of these have been on the Caribbean than on other parts of the region.

There are, as in the Middle East, some countries in which there has been a great deal of research and other countries where scholarship on women's education is almost non-existent. There is more research on Brazil, Argentina, Columbia and Chile than there is on Mexico, Bolivia or Peru. There are variations by country in the topics studied. The literature on Brazil and Columbia is heavily weighted to studies of the workforce, more so than is the case elsewhere. Most of the studies of education and fertility control are situated in Barbados, Jamaica, Trinidad and Tobago where the Catholic church's influence tends to be weaker than it is in the very heavily Catholic nations of Peru, Columbia or Brazil.

The research on women's education in Africa is perhaps stronger in historical studies than is the case elsewhere (with the exception of India). There are a number of published works tracing the history of women's education in Zaire, Nigeria, Senegal and, to a lesser extent, Ghana. Most focus on the impact of colonialism on women. In much of Africa, perhaps more so than elsewhere, the past century has been a time of erosion in women's economic roles and social status. Accounting for that process and the role of education in it has been a consistent strand in research. The tension between women's roles in African society and the ones offered women in newly emergent urban modern nation states is ever present in the research literature. The few studies of school processes—the curriculum in use, teacher/student interactions, etc.—are from African settings. The research on women's education in Africa has tended to look at women's goals and aspirations in opposition to those of the school system.

The research on Africa is not, for the most part, a workforce literature, but it is a literature which focuses on development and women's access to and contribution to that process. Education and fertility control is a stronger element in the literature on Africa than is research on education and workforce participation. The study of nonformal education in Africa is not the same as that generated in Latin American contexts. It tends to focus on women's basic needs and uses terms like "income generation", reflecting again the obvious erosion in women's economic position in the past three decades.

There are national variations in research emphasis in Africa as there are elsewhere. Overall there is more scholarship on Nigeria, Ghana and Kenya than there is on other countries in the region. Some of the research on Nigeria focuses on the impact of Islam on women's educational opportunities, reflecting concern about the deeper inequalities between males and females in education in the Islamic north versus the Christian and animist south. The research on Ghana, on the other hand, has focused on education's role in the erosion of women's autonomy and power in the workforce and community.

The literature on women's education in Asia, when taken as a whole is diverse, and covers a very broad spectrum of issues. In large part this is because of the overwhelming volume and diversity of studies of women in India. Yet, within Asia there appears to be specialization among countries, just as there is unevenness between countries in the amount of research available. There is, as the bibliography which follows shows, considerable research on Bangladesh, Pakistan, the Philippines, China and, to a lesser extent, Malaysia. Very little scholarship has been done on women in Sri Lanka, Indonesia (aside from a number of studies on Kartini as a historical figure and feminist), Burma, Thailand, Hong Kong, Singapore, Vietnam or Korea.

While the literature on India is diverse, the literature on other countries tends to specialize. The research on Bangladesh tends to focus on fertility control and nonformal education and development, almost exclusively so, perhaps reflecting the demographic strains of that nation and its place among the poorest of the poor countries of the world. The literature on Pakistan is also a women and development literature, but it also, like the research on a number of Middle Eastern countries, focuses on the role of Islam and the impact of Islamicization policies on women's status. Scholarship on China is a scholarship on women's liberation under socialist revolution and the impact of current modernization policies on the progress women have made since the revolution. The scholarship on China barely looks at the impact of education on the family or on fertility reduction and, aside from a discussion on women's entry into production, there is little analysis of women in the professions or in technological, managerial positions. The studies that have been conducted on women in Indonesia tend to be historically based studies. Kartini, who lived at the turn of the 20th century, as a feminist and educator, has received much attention in the research literature, even more so than any analysis of women's educational enrollment patterns, their participation in the workforce or the impact of education on their status in the family, the community or the economy.

The research literature on India, as I have pointed out repeatedly, is a very rich and perhaps most innovative literature that has emerged today on women's education in any third world setting. The literature on India has not only provided a very detailed analysis of women's educational access patterns and a description of women's fields of studies and their attitudes, it has explored curricular issues and has sought to develop and assess reform strategies aimed at bringing women into education. The literature on India in this regard is not only rich in its consideration of nonformal education, but also in experimental programs designed to reach working girls of school age and daughters of the rural poor.

The Indian literature has also focused on curricular reform, the textbooks and the development of women's studies. It has also looked at a range of outcomes of education, increasingly focusing on the interrelation between private, domestic and public, economic and political outcomes of education. In India study has centered on women's organizations and the women's movement and their roles in extending educational and economic opportunities for women and in empowering women.

An Agenda for the Future

This essay has described research trends that have emerged in the past decades on women's education in the third world. While that scholarship has grown remarkably both in the range of questions explored and the diversity of perspectives guiding research, it is also notable for what it has neglected. Some of the questions that remain unexplored in that scholarship are discussed below.

There is, as this essay has repeatedly pointed out, a literature on female access to education. However, there are almost no studies of educational processes and how they affect the cognitive, social and economic outcomes of education for women. This is a shortcoming of most educational studies; but it is an even greater lack in the scholarship on women's education conducted in third world contexts. Increasingly studies have shown that access patterns constitute only one of several reasons why the social, economic and political outcomes of women's education are what they are. There are but a handful of studies which have explored the gendered nature of knowledge entering the classroom via texts, tests and the hidden and formal curriculum. Those few studies generated to date have yet to distinguish between gendered knowledge in the primary school from that present in secondary and higher education. Left unexplored for the most part are questions focusing on differences between subject matter and the implications of the ways in which knowledge in a particular subject is structured for female educational outcomes. Even less explored are peer group relations and how male and female students socialize one another and make some forms of knowledge female friendly and other forms not. Educational achievement of females is another area about which many assumptions have been made but little solid research has actually been carried out. We know very little about not only how girls achieve in schools of the third world, much less and about the national and regional variations in those patterns. We are equally in ignorance about the relation between school policies and practices and female achievement and the relation between school achievement and the social, political and economic outcomes of women's education.

This bibliography has underscored the paucity of studies on

teachers and the teaching process and how both relate to present and future female educational outcomes. The literature is silent on how women enter teaching, despite the fact that teaching professions worldwide have become increasingly female. Teachers' attitudes toward and interaction with female students is a topic research has, for the most part, avoided. Most of the studies that we have of teachers in third world settings are studies that deal with teachers' ability to balance home and family with teaching. Teaching, however, as gendered labor and its relation to changing the obvious differences in the outcomes of schooling between males and females are topics for future research.

There is, as the bibliography makes quite evident, a vast literature on the public outcomes of women's education. For the most part that literature has focused exclusively on issues related to production. A small stream has arisen that seeks to understand how the domestic sphere affects the public sphere, and that stream needs to be encouraged to grow. Research is just beginning to look at the impact of child bearing and child rearing on participation in paid labor and how education changes that impact. However, it has yet to relate education to women's access to power and authority in the workforce and look at the relation between women's economic autonomy and her access to power and authority. Additionally, the workforce has been almost the exclusive aspect of the public sphere covered by research. There are almost no studies of education, women and the political system and the relation between changes in women's educational pattern and their role in societal governance. The assumption that entry into paid labor—symbolic of the public sphere—signals changes in women's roles in other aspects of public life has been implicit in much of the research. Whether that assumption is warranted is a question that future scholarship should investigate.

Much of the recent literature on women's education sees education as empowering women or at least having the potential to do so. The concept of empowerment needs further elaboration and empirical study. The role of education in women's access to and use of power and authority in society is an area which stands in need of careful scholarship. The extent to which the content of education, as well as the mode of education—educational methods, who teaches, etc.—affects education's role in giving women greater control over their lives is certainly a topic that future research might address. Under what circumstances does education translate into power in what spheres of life is certainly a question for scholarship to pursue.

Research on the private domestic sphere has moved away from exclusive focus on fertility regulation and from women's roles as mothers and wives. The impact of public policies and women's roles in public life, however, is barely touched upon in the research. Additionally, as in research on women's education and the public domain, issues of power and authority have been for the most part neglected. The extent to which education changes power relations in the family needs to be looked at more carefully. Research on women's education and its impact on daughters' education has begun to appear; however, that research has yet to look at women's role in that decision making.

Finally, most of our research on women's education in the third world has lacked a comparative dimension. As the bibliography which follows so well demonstrates, most of the research consists of one country studies. The impact of differing education, economic and social policies on women's education and the uses to which women put their education has not been thoroughly explored, nor has research looked systematically at how experimental programs, initiated in one national, political and economic context aimed at improving women's education and its outcomes, might be transferred and applied in differing contexts.

While there are many questions noted briefly here that scholarship has yet to explore, the fact that such an array of questions has arisen testifies to the richness and vibrancy of the research literature which has developed in a very short time period. There is much that we have yet to learn, but we do know more today than we did two decades ago about women's educational pattern, the factors that affect it, and the uses to which women put the education that they do receive.

NOTES

1. See Ellen DuBois et al. **Feminist Scholarship: Kindling in the Groves of Academe** (Urbana and Chicago: University of Illinois Press, 1985), chapters 1-3, especially.

2. See, for example, the State of the Art Issue of the **Comparative Education Review**, published in October 1977 (vol. 21, nos. 2/3). Women were not even mentioned in the 15 review articles on research in the field. Two articles in particular, Philip J. Foster, "Education and Social Differentiation in Less-Developed Countries" and Rolland Paulston's "Social and Educational Change: Conceptual Frameworks" focused exclusively on the third world and simply ignored women as well as gender relations.

3. See Alex Inkeles and David Smith. **Becoming Modern: Individual Change in Six Developing Countries** (Cambridge, Mass.: Harvard University Press, 1974).

4. Philip G. Altbach, Gail P. Kelly and David H. Kelly. **International Bibliography of Comparative Education** (New York: Praeger, 1981).

5. David H. Kelly and Gail P. Kelly. "Education of Women in Developing Countries." **Educational Documentation and Information, Bulletin of the International Bureau of Education** 56 (no. 222, 1982) 110 pp.

6. See, **Comparative Education Review** (Volume 24, June 1980). The four review articles discussed were commissioned initially by the Ford Foundation which underwrote the costs of the special issue as well. See Mary Jean Bowman and C. Arnold Anderson, "The Participation of Women in Education in the Third World." **Comparative Education Review** 24 (1980): S13-S31; Jeremy Finn, Loretta Dulberg and Janet Reis. "Sex Differences in Educational Attainment: The Process." **Comparative Education Review** 24 (1980): S33-S52; Robert LeVine. "Influence of Women's Schooling on Maternal Behavior in the Third World." **Comparative Education Review** 24 (1980): S78-S105; Rati Ram, "Sex Differences in the Labor Market Outcomes of Education." **Comparative Education Review** 24 (1980): S53-S77.

7. See, for example, the 1977 special issue of **Signs**. Norma S. Chinchilla, "Industrialization, Monopoly Capitalism and Women's Work in Guatemala." **Signs** 3 (1977): 38-56; See also, E. Chaney and J. Schmink, "Women and Modernization: Access to Tools." in **Sex and Class in Latin America**. Edited by June Nash and Helen Safa. (New York: Praeger, 1976), pp. 160-182.

8. For a listing of these studies, see Kelly and Kelly "Education of Women in Developing Countries." op cit., pp. 17-26.

9. Ibid., see pp. 63-65.

10. Ester Boserup, Women's Role in Economic Development. (New York: St. Martin's Press, 1970).

11. The best single review of this scholarship can be found in: Susan H. Cochrane. Fertility and Education: What Do We Really Know? (Baltimore: Johns Hopkins University Press, 1979).

12. See, for example, Bowman and Anderson, op cit.

13. See Marjorie Mbilinyi. The Education of Girls in Tanzania. (Dar Es Salaam: University of Dar-Es-Salaam, 1969): Marjorie J. Mbilinyi "Education, Stratification and Sexism in Tanzania: Policy Implications." African Review 3 (no. 2, 1973): 327-340.

14. Gail P. Kelly and Carolyn M. Elliott. "Orientations Toward the Study of Women's Education in the Third World." Women's Education in the Third World: Comparative Perspectives. Edited by Gail P. Kelly and Carolyn M. Elliott (New York: SUNY Press, 1982) pp. 1-10.

15. See, for example, Judith Van Allen, "Modernization Means More Dependency," The Center Magazine 7 (no. 3, 1974): 60-67.

16. Chincilla, op cit.; Glaura Vasques de Miranda. "Women's Labor Force Participation in a Developing Society: The Case of Brazil." Signs 3 (1977): 261-274. For other articles see Wellesley Editorial Committee, Women and National Development: The Complexities of Change. (Chicago: University of Chicago Press, 1977). (This book reprints the special issue of Signs on the topic.)

17. Van Allen op cit.

18. Claire C. Robertson. Sharing the Same Bowl: A Socioeconomic History of Women and Class in Accra: Ghana. (Bloomington: Indiana University Press, 1984); Deborah Pellow, Women in Accra: Options for Autonomy (Algonac, Michigan: Reference Publications, 1977).

19. Chinchilla, op cit.

20. Phyllis Andors, The Unfinished Liberation of Chinese Women, 1949-1980. (Bloomington: Indiana University Press, 1983); Margarey Wolfe. Revolution Postponed: Women in Contemporary

China (Stanford University Press, 1985); Elizabeth Croll. **Chinese Women Since Mao** (London: Zed Books, 1983).

21. An excellent summary of this literature can be found in Sue Ellen Charlton, **Women in Third World Development** (Boulder: West View Press, 1984), Chapter 1. See also Elsie Boulding, "Integration into What? Reflections on Development Planning for Women." **Convergence** 13 (nos. 1-2, 1980); 50-58.

22. Eleanora A. Cebotarev, "Non-oppressive Framework for Adult Education Programs for Rural Women in Latin America." **Convergence** 13 (nos. 1-2, 1980): 34-49.

23. Barbara Rogers. **The Domestication of Women: Discrimination in Developing Societies** (London: Tavistock, 1981).

24. Karen C. Biraimah. "The Impact of Western Schools in Girls' Expectations: A Togolese Case." **Comparative Education Review** 24 (1980): S196-S208; Karen C. Biraimah. "Different Knowledge for Different Folks: Knowledge Distribution in a Togolese Secondary School." **Comparative Education.** Edited by Philip G. Altbach, Robert Arnove and Gail P. Kelly. (New York: Macmillan, 1982) pp. 161-175. N.N. Kalia **Sexism in Indian Education: The Lies We Tell Our Children** (New Delhi: Vikas, 1979).

25. This literture is vast. See for example, Audrey Chapman Smock, "Sex Differences in Educational Opportunities and Labor Force Participation in Six Countries." **Comparative Education.** Edited by Philip G. Altbach, Robert Arnove and Gail P. Kelly (New York: Macmillan, 1982) pp. 234-251; Siok-Hwa Cheng, "Singapore Women: Legal Status, Educational Attainment and Employment Patterns." **Asian Survey** 17 (1977): 358-374; Earl L. Sullivan. "Women and Work in Egypt." **Women and Work in the Arab World.** Edited by Earl L. Sullivan and Korima Korayen. (Cairo Papers in Social Science, Monograph 4, December 1981) pp. 1-44; Lucy M. Cohen "Woman's Entry into the Professions in Colombia: Selected Characteristics." **Journal of Marriage and the Family** 35 (1973): 322-330; Keziah Awosika. "Women's Education and Participation in the Labour Force: The Case of Nigeria." **Women, Power and Political Systems.** Edited by Margherita Rendel (London: Croom Helm, 1981) pp. 81-93.

26. See Cebotarev, op cit.; Margaret Gayfer, "Women Speaking and Learning for Ourselves." **Convergence** 13 (nos. 1-2, 1980): 1-13; M. H. G. Igoche, "Integrating Conscientization into a Program for Illiteracy, Women in Nigeria." **Convergence** 13 (nos. 1-2, 1980): 110-117; Anne K. Bernard and Margaret Gayfer. "Women Hold Up More than Half the Sky: Report of the ICAE Women's Project." **Convergence** 14 (no. 4, 1981): 59-71.

27. Stan D'Souza. "The Data Base for Studies on Women: Sex Biases
     in National Data Systems." **Women in Contemporary India and South
     Asia.** Edited by Alfred d'Souza. (New Delhi: Manohar
     Publications, 1980) pp. 31–60. See also L. Beneria.
     "Conceptualizing the Labor Force: The Underestimation of Women's
     Economic Activities." **Journal of Development Studies** 17 (1981):
     10–28.

28. Kelly and Kelly, "Education of Women in Developing Countries."
     op cit.

29. Soraya Altorki. **Women in Saudi Arabia: Ideology and Behavior
     Among the Elite.** (New York: Columbia University Press, 1986).

30. Examples of such scholarship are Rhoda Lois Blumberg and Leela
     Dwaraki. **India's Educated Women: Options and Constraints.** (New
     Delhi: Hindustan Publishing Corporation, 1980); Kala Rani. **Role
     Conflict in Working Women** (New Delhi: Chetana Publications,
     1976); A. Ramanamma. **Graduate Employed Women in an Urban Setting**
     (Poona: Dastane Ramchandra, 1979); Karuna Ahmad. "Studies of
     Educated Working Women in India: Trends and Issues." **Economic
     and Political Weekly** 14 (no. 33, 1979): 1435–1440.

31. See Catalina Wainerman. "Impact of Education on the Female Labor
     Force in Argentina and Paraguay." **Comparative Education Review**
     24 (1980): S180–S195. See also Zulmal Recchini de Lattes and
     Catalina Wainerman. **La Medición del Trabajo Feminino.** (Buenos
     Aires: Centro de Estudios Publación, 1981).

32. Some of these works are listed in footnote 30. Other examples
     include Maithreyi Krishnaraj. "Women, Work and Science in
     India." **Women's Education in the Third World: Comparative
     Perspectives.** Edited by Gail P. Kelly and Carolyn Elliott.
     (Albany: SUNY Press, 1982) pp. 249–263; Devi D. Radha and M.
     Ravindran. "Women's Work in India." **International Social
     Science Journal** 35 (1983): 683–701; Vinita Strivastava.
     "Professional Education and Attitudes to Female Employment: A
     Study of Married Working Women in Chandiagarh." **Social Action** 27
     (Jan.–March 1977): 19–30.

33. Examples of such studies are Francine D. Blau and Carol L.
     Jusenius. "Economic Approaches to Sex Segregation in the Labor
     Market: An Appraisal." **Signs** 1 (1976): 181–199; M.C. Aranha
     Bruschini "Sexualização dos Ocupaçoes: O Caso Brasileiro."
     Cadernos de Pesquisa (no. 28, 1979): 5–20; Myrna Blake
     "Education and Research. Mobilization Needs of Women's
     Employment Trends in Asia." **Convergence** 13 (nos. 1–2, 1980):
     65–78; Bruce J. Chapman and J. Ross Harding. "Sex Differences in
     Earnings: An Analysis of Malaysian Wage Data." **Journal of
     Development Studies** 21 (1985): 362–376.

34. See, for example, R.H. Chaudhury. "The Influence of Female
     Education, Labor Force Participation and Age at Marriage of
     Fertility Behavior in Bangladesh."   Social Biology   31
     (Spring/Summer 1984): 59-74; Akbar Aghajanian, "Fertility and
     Family Economy in the Iranian Rural Communities." Women in the
     Family and Economy: An International Comparative Survey. Edited
     by George Kurian and Ratna Ghosh (Westport, Conn.:   Greenwood
     Press, 1981) pp. 297-305.   M.A. Khan and I. Sirageldin,
     "Education, Income and Fertility in Pakistan."   Economic
     Development and Cultural Change 27 (1979): 519-547; Helen Ware,
     Education and Modernization of the Family in West Africa.
     (Canberra: Department of Demography, Australian National
     University, 1981) (Changing African Family Project Series,
     Monograph no. 7).

35. See, for example, Eugene B. Brody.   Sex, Contraception and
     Motherhood in Jamaica (Cambridge: Harvard University Press,
     1981).

36. See, for example, Andors, The Unfinished Liberation of Chinese
     Women, op cit.; Margarey Wolfe Revolution Postponed, op cit.;
     Elizabeth Croll.   Chinese Women Since Mao, op cit.; Peter R.
     Knauss.   The Persistence of Patriarchy: Class, Gender and
     Ideology in Twentieth Century Algeria.   (New York and Westport:
     Praeger, 1987); Maxine Molyneux.   State Policies and the Position
     of Women Workers in the Democratic Republic of Yemen, 1967-1977
     (Geneva: International Labour Office, 1982).

37. See, for example, M.F. Katzenstein. "Toward Equality: Cause and
     Consequence of the Political Prominence of Women in India."
     Asian Survey 78 (1978): 473-486; June H. Turner. Latin American
     Women: The Meek Speak Out (Silver Springs, Maryland:
     Educational Development, Inc. 1980); A.S. Seetharamu.   Women in
     Organized Movements.   (New Delhi: Ambika Publications, 1981);
     Hanna Papanek.   Women in Development and Women's Studies (East
     Lansing: Office of Women in International Development, Michigan
     State University, 1984).

I. BIBLIOGRAPHIES

We have limited the citations here to bibliographies which are specifically on women and which contain a sizeable number of citations on women's education. Not included here are general bibliographies on education in the third world, in specific countries of the third world or general bibliographies on women.

1. General Works

Books and Monographs

1. Ballou, Patricia K. **Women: A Bibliography of Bibliographies.** 2nd Edition. Boston: G.K. Hall, 1986. 268 pp.

   Includes 906 items organized by geographical region and subject. Lists and annotates about 30 items on education. A larger number of bibliographies on women in Asia, Africa, Latin America and the Middle East are annotated.

2. Bickner, Mei Liang. **Women at Work: An Annotated Bibliography.** Los Angeles: University of California Manpower Research Center, 1974. 437 pp.

   Includes published articles and books focusing solely on working women, particularly non-professional and minority women and women in the labor movement. The bibliography is cross indexed and divided topically as follows: general, historical studies, education and training, working women, occupations, women's groups, public policy and bibliographies.

3. Buvenic, Mayra et al. **Women and World Development: An Annotated Bibliography.** Washington: Overseas Development Council, 1976. 162 pp.

   Includes published and unpublished materials appearing before 1975 on women and development. The bibliography is divided into nine subject areas and is organized geographically.

4. Byrne, Pamela R. and Suzanne R. Ontiveros (eds.) **Women in the Third World: A Historical Bibliography.** Santa Barbara,

California: ABC-CLIO, 1986. 152 pp.

Contains 600 abstracts and citations of journal articles taken from ABC-CLIO's history data base. The data base includes over 2,000 periodicals from 90 countries. Articles and book chapters included were published between 1970 and 1985. The articles are listed alphabetically by region. Contains a subject and author index.

5. Cismaresco, Françoise. **Education and Training of Women. Educational Documentation and Information.** Geneva: UNESCO, International Bureau of Education, 1975. 46 pp.

Lists 233 items on women's education. Includes a large number of UNESCO reports as well as national government documents. The material all appeared between 1970 and 1975. Arranged by continent and contains an author index.

6. Danforth, Sandra C. **Women and National Development.** Monticello, Illinois: Vance Bibliographies, 1982. 35 pp. (Public Administration Series, Bibliography no. P916)

Lists English-language academic literature on women and development, most of which has appeared after 1960. Divides the work into eight sections which include bibliographies and reviews of the literature, original source materials, general works, politics, education, work, ethnographic and rural case study literature and family and cultural contexts. No indexes are included.

7. Eskamp, C. **Inequality of Female Access to Education in Developing Countries: A Bibliography.** The Hague: Centre for the Study of Education in Developing Countries, 1979. 42 pp.

Includes studies on the formal and informal education of women in developing countries produced prior to 1978 and published by the United Nations and UNESCO, the ILO, FAO, WHO, and UNICEF.

8. **Formation et Emploi des Femmes.** Abidjan: Centre Interafricain pour le Développement de la Formation Professionnelle, 1982. 16 pp.

Lists 67 articles, books and government reports published between 1978 and 1981 on women and development, women's professional training and women's employment in the Third World. The bibliography is annotated and represents the materials held in the library of the Interafrican Center for the Development of Professional Training of women in Abidjan, Ivory Coast.

9. Jacobs, Sue Ellen T. (ed.) **Women in Perspective: A Guide for Cross Cultural Studies.** Urbana: University of Illinois Press, 1974. 299 pp.

Lists a substantial literature on women in Africa, Middle East and Asia published before 1974. The bibliography, which is unannotated, is arranged geographically. There is a topical listing and the materials included on education are for the most part on the U.S. and, to a lesser extent, western Europe.

10. Kelly, David H. and Gail P. Kelly. **Education of Women in Developing Countries.** Geneva: International Bureau of Education, 1982. 114 pp. (Bulletin, Educational Documentation and Information, 56, no. 22)

Provides an annotated bibliography of 355 items published after 1975 on women's education in the third world. Includes published and unpublished works as well as government reports. Divided into 14 topics which include: histories of women's education, studies pertaining to the status of women's education, women's educational access, higher education, non-formal education, women's education and development, education and the workforce, women and the professions and education and the family. Contains reports from the 1980 International Congress on the Situation of Women in Technical and Vocational Education, the 1980 International Seminar on the Opening-up to Women of Vocational Training and Jobs Traditionally Occupied by Men held in Frankfurt and the International Seminar on Women's Education, Training and Employment in Developed Countries held in Tokyo in 1980. Contains an author index.

11. Kohen, A. I. et al. **Women and the Economy: A Bibliography and Review of the Literature on Sex Differentiation in the Labour Market.** Columbus: Ohio State University, Center for Human Resource Research, 1975. 88 pp.

Divides the literature on women in the labor market into 27 categories including: historical perspective, the supply of female labor in the labor market, women workers' earnings, occupations, unemployment, women and trade unions, working women and the law and attitudes toward women working. Contains a review of the theoretical and empirical literature as well.

12. Nwanosike, Eugene. **Women and Development: A Select Bibliography.** Buea, Cameroon: Regional Pan African Institute for Development, 1980. 33 pp.

Lists a number of works intended for the staff and students of the Regional Pan African Institute for Development. The works consist primarily of periodical articles from over 30 journals in African, women's and development studies. Is arranged alphabetically by authors' surnames.

13. Parker, F. and Betty June Parker (comps.) **Women's Education, A World View:** Annotated Bibliography of Doctoral Dissertations. Westport Conn.: Greenwood Press, 1979. 470 pp.

Includes doctoral dissertations in English from U.S. and Canadian universities on women's education, primary through university level. Provides a subject index to the theses which focus on the third world as well as on industrialized nations.

14. Rihani, M. **Development as if Women Mattered:** An Annotated Bibliography with a Third World Focus. Washington, D.C. Overseas Development Council, 1978. 137 pp.

Includes 287 annotated works on women and development published before 1977. Categorizes the studies topically and by geographical areas. Subject categories include formal, non-formal education, women's access to education and education and employment. Contains cross-referencing.

15. Saulniers, Suzanne Smith and Cathy A. Rakowski. **Women in the Development Process:** A Select Bibliography on Women in Sub-Saharan Africa and Latin America. Austin: University of Texas Institute of Latin American Studies, 1977. 287 pp.

Lists 2844 works on women and the development process in Africa and Latin America published between 1900 and 1978. Major topical divisions include: women and society, women and the law, women and the family, women and religion, women's education, women and the polity, women's organizations, women and the economy, women and social change and women and development.

16. Tinker, Irene et al. (eds.) **Women and World Development with an Annotated Bibliography.** New York: Praeger, 1976. 382 pp.

Includes 12 essays prepared as background papers for the 1975 World Conference of the International Women's Year which was held in Mexico. The essays are followed by an annotated bibliography concentrating on the effects of development and social change on women and a summary of the workshops held at the conference. One of the workshops was on education.

17. **Women and Development:** Articles, Books and Research Papers Indexed in the Joint World Bank-International Monetary Fund **Library, Washington, D.C.** Boston: G.K. Hall & Co., 1987. 181 pp.

Lists articles, books and reports held at the Joint-World-Bank-International Monetary Fund Library. Works are listed by author's last name, first word in the title by subject and by country. The materials were all produced after 1960.

Articles

18. Danforth, Sandra. "Women, Development and Public Policy: A Select Bibliography." **Women in Developing Countries: A Policy Focus.** New York: Haworth Press, 1983, pp. 107-124.

    Contains academic literature in English published since 1960 on women in developing countries. Topical divisions include: bibliographies and literature reviews, status of women, women's roles in development, ethnographies and rural case studies, public policies toward women, politics and political participation, employment and economic roles and family and domestic life.

19. Feinberg, Renee. "Select Bibliography on Women: Their Education and Employment, Both National and International, 1973-1976." **Journal of Research and Development in Education.** 10 (no. 4, 1977): 77-87.

    Lists books, monographs and articles in the following categories: resources and bibliographies, education, sex role stereotyping in schools, employment and international studies.

20. Kelly, David H. and Gail P. Kelly. "Women and Schooling in the Third World: A Bibliography." **Women's Education in the Third World: Comparative Perspectives.** Edited by Gail P. Kelly and Carolyn M. Elliott. Albany: SUNY Press, 1982, pp. 345-398.

    Lists materials, both published and unpublished, on women's education in the third world. The works covered appeared between 1975 and 1981 although several works published prior to 1975 are included. The bibliography is organized topically and contains works in English, French and Spanish. Topics include: histories of women's education, the status of women's education, women's education and the workforce, women's education and the family, higher education, women and the professions.

21. Kelly, David H. and Gail P. Kelly. "Women's Education: A Select Bibliography of Published Research." **International Handbook of Women's Education.** Edited by Gail P. Kelly. Westport, Conn.: Greenwood Press, 1989.

    Lists over 950 works on the education of women. While the focus is worldwide, close to half the references are to the third world. Includes only published books, monographs, and journal literature which, for the most part appeared in the 1970s through mid-1980s. The citations are arranged topically and a country index is included.

2.   Africa

Books and Monographs

22. Atkiewicz, Susan and M. Shimwaayi Muntemba. **Women and Development in Zambia: An Annotated Bibliography.** Addis Ababa: United Nations Economic Commission for Africa, African Training and Research Center, 1983. 98 pp.

Annotates 194 published and unpublished articles, conference papers, theses, monographs and books on women and development in Zambia. Divides the annotations into the following categories: education, health and nutrition, ideology, production, social organization and change, socio-economic position and research in progress. Contains an author index as well as a six page overview essay on research on women and development in Zambia.

23. Fortmann, Louise. **Tillers of the Soil and Keepers of the Hearth: A Bibliographic Guide to Women and Rural Development.** Ithaca: Rural Development Committee, Center for International Studies, Cornell University, 1979. 53 pp.

Contains 45 references on education. Most are on development projects and informal education. The majority of the works are from the mid-to-late 1970s and are primarily on Africa.

24. Hafkin, Nancy. **Women and Development in Africa.** Addis Ababa: United Nations Economic Commission for Africa, 1977. 172 pp. (Bibliography Series no. 1)

An annotated bibliography of 568 items produced by or held by the African Training and Research Center for Women of the United Nations Economic Commission for Africa. Organizes citations under the following topics: General Women in Development, Population, Education and Training, Urban Development, the Situation of Women (including women status and their role in the labor force) and Women's Organization. The entries are listed alphabetically by author within the major subject categories. Contains a cross-reference by country and by author's last name.

25. Mascarenhas, Ophelia and Marjorie Mbilinyi. **Women and Development in Tanzania**. Uppsala: Scandanavia Institute of African Studies, 1983. 256 pp.

Presents a 400 item annotated bibliography of English, Swahili, and German works on women and development in Tanzania. Topical divisions include peasants, women's projects and cooperatives, ideology, education, legal questions, political participation, biological reproduction and sexuality, family and domestic labor, and health and nutrition. Each section is introduced by a critical essay on the literature on the topic. Works included go up to 1978.

26. Selassie, Alesebu Gebre. **Women and Development in Ethiopia: An Annotated Bibliography**. Addis Ababa: United Nations Economic Commission for Africa, African Training and Research Center for Women, 1981. 58 pp.

Annotates 169 published and unpublished materials (leaflets, conference papers, organization reports, M.A. and Ph.D. theses, feasibility studies) on Ethiopian women. Contains nine topical divisions including women in development, employment and education, rural women and agriculture, health and family planning, women and the law, urbanization and social problems and women and the press. Provides an author index.

27. Wadsworth, Gail M. **Women in Development: A Bibliography of Materials Available in the Library and Documentation Centre, Eastern and Southern African Management Institute. Supplement to the Second Edition**. Arusha, Tanzania: Eastern and Southern African Management Institute, 1982. 26 pp.

Lists 104 items on women and development in Africa. Many of the items are unpublished documents appearing between 1978 and 1982 and acquired by the Eastern and Southern African Management Institute between January and September 1982.

Articles

28. Kerina, J.M. "Women in Africa: A Select Bibliography," **Africa Report** 22 (no. 1, 1977): 44-50.

Samples materials published since 1970 on African women's roles in society, including education. The author provides an essay that summarizes and highlights items in the bibliography. Appends a list of fiction, poetry and drama by and about African women.

29. Westfall, Gloria D. "Nigerian Women: A Bibliographical Essay." *African Journal* 5 (1974): 99-138.

    Reviews the research on women in Nigeria written before Fall 1972. Focuses on research studies in anthropology, sociology, history, political science, economics, law and education. Includes books, articles, government documents and Ph.D. dissertations.

3.   Asia

Books and Monographs

30. Chung, Betty Jamie. *The Status of Women and Fertility in Southeast and East Asia: A Bibliography.* Singapore: Institute of Southeast Asian Studies, 1977. 167 pp.

    Lists books and articles relating to fertility and aspects of women's status including education, employment and the family. Most of the items are in English although efforts were made to include Chinese language citations on women and fertility in Taiwan.

31. Fan, Kok-Sim. *Women in Southeast Asia: A Bibliography.* Boston; G.K. Hall, 1982. 415 pp.

    Lists 3865 items on women in Southeast Asia (Burma, Brunei, Indochina, Indonesia, Malaysia, Philippines, Singapore, Thailand) topically. The topics covered include: economic conditions, employment, role in development, education, marriage and divorce, religion, legal status, health and welfare, family planning, and feminism and women's rights. Contains an author index.

32. Fry, Gerald W. and Rufino Mauricio. *Pacific Basin and Oceania.* World Bibliographical Series, Vol. 70 Santa Barbara: CLIO, 1987. 468 pp.

    Lists over 1100 works on the Pacific Basin and Oceania, providing abstracts for most of the books, monographs, articles and unpublished manuscripts cited. Topical categories include: history, prehistory, culture and social change, politics and government, economic development (including the role of women in socioeconomic development), education, languages, sports and recreation, bibliographies and a listing of works by geographical area (The Islands of Melanesia, Micronesia, Polynesia, the Pacific islands, etc.).

33. Islam, Mahmuda.   **Bibliography on Bangladesh Women with Annotation.** Dacca: The Women for Women Research and Study Group, 1979.   58 pp.

Lists 197 items on women in Bangladesh all of which were published in Bangladesh.   The entries, which are annotated, are presented under the following topics: general studies, status of women in family and society, women and education, women and health, nutrition and fertility, women in productive and social work, women's organizations and programs for women and bibliography.   There is an author index.

34. Koh, Hesung Chun.   **Korean and Japanese Women: An Analytic Bibliographic Guide.** Westport: Greenwood Press, 1982.   904 pp.

Contains some 40 references directly on the education of Korean women, primarily in Asian languages.

35. Simmons, Donita Vasiti and Sin Jran Yee.   **Women in the South Pacific: A Bibliography.** Suva: The University of the South Pacific Library, 1982.   124 pp.   (Selected Bibliography no. 10)

Provides a listing of materials relating to women in the South Pacific up to February 1982.   These countries include American Samoa, Cook Islands, Fiji, Guam, New Caledonia, Solomon Islands, Tonga, Tuvalu and Western Samoa.   The works are divided into the following topics: roles and status, sociology, anthropology, economics and employment, law and politics, medicine and health, religion, education and training, literature and the arts, sports, biography, appropriate technology, technology, communications, women's associations and bibliographies.

36. Wei, Karen T. **Women in China. A Bibliography.** Westport, Conn.:   Greenwood Press, 1984.   250 pp.

Lists and annotates over 1000 items in English published before 1978 on women in China.   Includes dissertations done at American universities as well as materials from the 1920s and 1930s.   The bibliography is divided into the following topics: education, economics and employment, family planning, female roles, the women's movement, legal status, literature and the arts, marriage and the family, philosophy and religion, politics and government.

37. **Women and Development in Asia: A Selected Bibliography.** Bangkok: Population Education Clearinghouse, UNESCO Regional Office for Education in Asia and Oceania, 1979.   25 pp.

Lists 86 published and unpublished sources on women and development, with a focus on fertility and population control in

Asia.   The   bibliography   is   geographically   organized   and
descriptors are provided for each entry.

3 a. India

Books and Monographs

38. Aggarwal, J.C. Indian Women: Education and Status. New Delhi:
Arya Book Depot, 1976. 106 pp.

Provides a guide to the literature on the education of Indian
women to 1974. Topics covered include history of education,
philosophical   foundations   and   educational   statistics.
Selections from the Report of the National Committee on the
Status of Women in India, issued in 1974, are reprinted as well.

39. Anant, Suchitra et al. Women at Work in India: A Bibliography.
New Delhi: Sage Publications, 1986. 238 pp.

Covers book, periodical, dissertation, research monographs and
unpublished papers produced on Indian women in the workforce
between Indian independence and December 1985. The material is
primarily produced in India. Focuses on the problems of women
workers   and   is   divided   into   topics   such   as   employment
statistics, women in industry, women in the informal sector,
women   workers   in   distinct   occupations,   including   teachers.
There is a section on the education and training of women.

40. Das Gupta Kalpana. Women on the Indian Scene: An Annotated
Bibliography. New Delhi: Abhinav Publications, 1976. 389 pp.

Consists of an annotated bibliography of published works in
English on women in India. Contains 822 items arranged under
the   following   topics: general   studies,   studies   on   social
problems, economic studies, political studies, legal studies,
educational   studies   and   studies   on   art   and   culture   and
biographies.   Includes an author index as well as a subject
index. Appendix 1 is a list of theses on the topic; appendix 2
is a chronological list of legislative materials.

41. Mukerjee, A.K. and F.C. Katyal (comps.) Education of Indian
Women: A Bibliography. New Delhi: National Council of
Educational Research and Training, 1979. 62 pp.

Provides a listing of books, booklets, reports and journal
articles on women's education in India. Includes author and
subject indexes.

42. Sahai, S.N. **Women in Changing Society: A Bibliographical Study**. Delhi: Mittal Publishers, 1985. 441 pp.

Presents over 5200 items on women in India. Most of the works listed were published before 1981, and include books, Indian dissertations on the masters and doctoral levels as well as journal and monograph literature. The bibliography is divided into the following sections: women in general (which is predominantly the history of women); women and the family, women and marriage, women and education, women and employment, women and health, women and family planning, women in fashion, women at work, women in rural areas, women in the professions and in occupations, women's status, women and the media, women and their liberation, legislation for liberating women and biographies of women.

43. Pandit, Harshida. **Women of India: An Annotated Bibliography**. New York and London: Garland Publishing, 1985. 278 pp.

Annotates over 1000 articles, theses and books on women in India. Arranges the citations under the following topics: general historical surveys, the role and status of women, economic participation, educational status, legal status, social problems, women's movement and political participation, women in art and culture, psychological studies, eminent women, women in different communities, bibliographies and English language periodicals containing articles about women.

4.   Latin America and The Caribbean

Books and Monographs

44. Cohen-Stuart, Bertie A. **Women in the Caribbean: A Bibliography**. Leiden: Department of Caribbean Studies, Royal Institute of Linguistics and Anthropology, 1979. 163 pp.

Lists and annotates over 650 items on women in the Caribbean written prior to 1977. The bibliography is arranged topically including the following topics: family and household (including fertility and family planning, sexual inequality and migration), cultural factors, education, economic factors and politics and law. Contains an authors index and a subject cross-index.

45. Feijoó, Maria del Carmen. **La Mujer, el Desarrollo y las Tendencias de Población en América Latina. Bibliografía Comentada**. Buenos Aires: El Centro de Estudios de Estado y Sociedad (CEDES), 1980. 59 pp.

Annotates 86 studies on women, the workforce and migration in
Latin America written between 1974 and 1979.   Includes both
published and unpublished works in Spanish and in English.
Contains an author index and introductory essay.

46. Fundação Carlos Chagas.   **Mulher Brasileira: Bibliographa
    Anatada.** Vol. 2. São Paulo: Editora Brasiliense, 1981. 393 pp.

    Contains a section on education of 150 book and 50 journal
    references--with the book references annotated.   All material
    listed is in Portuguese and it covers material from the late
    19th century through the early 1970s.

47. Knaster, Meri.   **Women in Spanish America: An Annotated
    Bibliography from Pre-Conquest to Contemporary Times.** Boston:
    G.K. Hall, 1977. 696 pp.

    Contains 2524 entries on women in Spanish-speaking countries and
    ethnic groups of South and Central America as well as the
    Caribbean published before 1974.   Includes author and subject
    indexes as well as cross-referencing.

48. Massiah, Joycelin.   **Women in the Caribbean: An Annotated
    Bibliography.** Cave Hill, Barbados: University of the West
    Indies, Institute of Social and Economic Research, April 1979.
    133 pp. (Occasional Bibliography Series, no. 5).

    Lists books, book chapters, articles in professional and
    literary journals, unpublished masters and doctoral theses and
    official government documents as well as pamphlets, newspaper
    articles and official addresses on women in the Caribbean.
    Divides the citations into the following topics: role and status
    of women, law and politics, family and fertility, economics and
    employment, education, literature and the arts, religion,
    women's organizations, biography and autobiography and general
    reference works. Contains an author index.

49. Potter, Robert B. and Graham M. S. Dann.   **Barbados.** Santa
    Barbara, California: CLIO Press, 1987.   356 pp.   (World
    Bibliographical Series, Vol. 76)

    Lists 958 works on Barbados, including published and unpublished
    studies. Materials are divided into topics including geography,
    travelers' accounts, history, population, social conditions,
    women's studies, education and science, statistics, periodicals
    and bibliographies.   Most items are annotated.   Includes an
    index of authors, titles and subjects.

50. UNESCO.   Officinia Regional de Educación para América Latina y
    el Caribe.   Servicio de Biblioteca y Documentacion.

Bibliografia sobre Educación de la Mujer en Areas Rurales.
Santiago: Cursa Regional de Formacion para los Responsables de
la Educación de la Mujer en Areas Rurales de América Latina y el
Caribe Patzcurao, 1980.   5 pp.

Contains references to about 50 books and journal articles
published between 1974 and 1980 on women's education in rural
areas, women and national development and equality of
opportunity in education.

Articles

51. Knaster, Meri.   "Women in Latin America: The State of Research,
    1975."   **Latin American Research Review** 11 (1976): 3-74.

    Presents a bibliography of research on Latin American women
    since 1970.   Indicates that cooperation in research on women is
    emerging through women's networks.

52. Leon de Leal, M.   "Personas intersados en la problemática
    femenina en Perú, Argentina, Brasil y Venezuela."   Latin
    American Research Review 14 (no. 1, 1979): 134-44.

    Lists individuals and organizations, including addresses, who
    are conducting research on women in Peru, Argentina, Brazil and
    Venezuela.

5.   Middle East

Books and Monographs

53. Al-Qazzaz, A.   **Women in the Middle East and North Africa: An
    Annotated Bibliography.**   Austin: University of Texas Center for
    Middle Eastern Studies, 1977.   178 pp.

    Includes English-language, Arabic, Turkish and Persian materials
    on women in the Middle East which appeared before November,
    1976.   Contains subject and country indexes.

54. Meghdessian, Samira Rafidi.   **The Status of the Arab Woman: A
    Select Bibliography.**   Westport, Conn.:   Greenwood Press, 1980.
    176 pp.

    Lists 1616 published and unpublished works (seminar papers,
    Ph.D. and M.S. theses) on women in the Arab Middle East.   The
    bibliography is arranged geographically and the works are listed

alphabetically by author within each region. Contains an author
as well as subject index. Most of the references are for the
years 1960-1976, but there are some references to earlier works.
Covers the English, French and Italian language literature only.

55. Otto, Ingeborg and Marianne Schmidt-Dumont.   **Frauenfragen im
Modernen Orient: Eine Auswahlbibliographie.**   Hamburg:
Deutsches Orient-Institute im Verbund der Stiftung Deutsches
Ubersee-Institut   Dokumentations-Leitstelle   Modernen   Orient,
1982. 247 pp.

Lists 1242 works in English, Arabic and German on women in the
Middle East and North Africa. Includes books, journals, theses
and unpublished papers which were written from 1960 and 1980.
Topical divisions include Islam, the family, politics, and
economy. Most of the bibliography lists the materials by
country. Contains cross-references.

56. Raccagni, Michelle.   **The Modern Arab Woman: A Bibliography.**
Metuchen, New Jersey: Scarecrow Press, 1978. 262 pp.

Lists books, articles, reports and dissertations in English and
French as well as in Arabic. Includes dissertations in progress
through 1976. The bibliography is arranged by country and
includes subject and author indexes.

Articles

57. Al-Qazzaz, A. "Current Status of Research on Women in the Arab
World." **Middle Eastern Studies** 14 (1978): 372-380.

Lists a number of studies on women in middle eastern nations and
argues that further research is needed on education in relation
to politics, marriage, divorce and rural-urban migration.

II. RESEARCH METHODS

The study of women's education began with a critique of assumptions of many studies in education and the social sciences. We have included in this section many of these critiques as well as discussions of research methods appropriate to the study of women's education in general and in the third world in particular.

1. Books and Monographs

58. DuBois, Ellen Carol et al. **Feminist Scholarship: Kindling in the Groves of Academe.** Urbana and Chicago: University of Illinois Press, 1985. 227 pp.

   Focuses on the rise of women's studies in the 'American academy and focuses on feminist criticisms of traditional scholarship conducted in academic disciplines, including education. Chapter 3 explores the women and development literature as well as the scholarship seeking to link education to changes in women's status in the third world.

59. Elahi, K. Maudood. **Anthropogeographic Approaches to Population Studies: Indepth Survey Guidelines for Bangladesh.** Dacca: Centre for Population Studies, 1981. 32 pp. (Occasional Paper no. 2)

   Discusses anthropogeographic approaches to studying women and fertility and provides a detailed guide to conducting an anthropogeographic study in Bangladesh on women in rural areas.

   Pananek, Hanna. **Women in Development and Women's Studies: Agenda for the Future.** East Lansing: Office of Women in International Development, Michigan State University, 1984. 18 pp. (Working Paper no. 55)

   See item #668

60. Recchini de Lattes, Zulina and Catalina H. Wainerman. **La Medición del Trabajo Femenina.** Buenos Aires: Centro do Estudios de Población, 1981.

   Discusses the problems in studying women and the workforce. Points out that the distinctions made in the literature between "employed" and "unemployed" lack validity in the study of women's work in Latin American countries. Argues that new research strategies and tools are necessary.

61. Umea Universitet Pedagogiska Institutionen Weed-Projectet. **The Life-History Approach: A Tool in Establishing North-South Education Cooperation.** Umea, Sweden: Author, 1986.

Outlines the life-history approach to conducting research on women in third world settings and explains the development of this research strategy in the Swedish Idea vs. Reality in Reforming Higher Education Project. Advocates the usefulness of this approach in understanding why women take or do not take advantage of education opportunities offered under current development projects through analysis of data obtained in Thailand, Bangladesh and Zambia.

Articles

62. Acker, Sandra. "Feminist Theory and the Study of Gender and Education." International **Review** of **Education** 33 (1987): 419-435.

Discusses feminist theoretical frameworks applicable to the study of women and their education and provides examples of research guided by liberal, socialist and radical feminist perspectives.

63. Allaghi, Farida and Aisha Almana. "Survey of Research on Women in the Arab Gulf Region." **Social Science Research and Women in the Arab World.** Edited by UNESCO. London and Dover, New Hampshire: Frances Pinter, 1984, pp. 14-40.

Considers the research methodologies and theories used to guide research on women in the Gulf region.

Benería, Lourdes. "Conceptualizing the Labor Force: The Underestimation of Women's Economic Activities." **Journal of Development Studies** 17 (1981): 10-28.

See item #806

Blau, Francine D. and Carol L. Jusenius. "Economic Approaches to Sex Segregation in the Labor Market: An Appraisal." **Signs** 1 (1976): 181-199.

See item #807

64. Davies, Lynn. "Research Dilemmas Concerning Gender and the Management of Education in Third World Countries." **Comparative Education** 23 (1987): 85-94.

Discusses the following research problems in studying women and the management of schooling in the third world: ethnocentrism, sex stereotyping and how educational management is defined. Argues that the definition of educational management as well as the logic of research and model building in educational administration should be reassessed.

65. Joshi, Vibha and Geeta Menon. "Research on Women's Education in India: A Review." **Perspectives in Education** 2 (1986): 77-98.

Points out, in a review of 131 socio-psychological studies of women's education in India, that most research lacks a well articulated theoretical framework. Educational research has retained a male-centric bias and the few studies there are on women in India focus on urban women in secondary and higher education and neglect the vast majority of women who live in rural areas and receive at best primary schooling.

66. D'Souza, Stan. "The Data Base for Studies on Women. Sex Biases in National Data Systems." **Women in Contemporary India and South Asia.** Edited by Alfred D'Souza. New Delhi: Manohar Publications, 1980. pp. 31-60.

Maintains that there is sex bias in most statistics used in studies of the third world. This bias derives from how economic activity is measured as well as the staffing patterns of many nations' statistical offices. Points out that most census data fail to show that while there are gains in women's literacy over the past decades, women are segregated within the educational system.

67. Ellis, Pat. "Methodologies for Doing Research on Women and Development." **Women in Development: Perspectives from the Nairobi Conference.** Ottawa: International Development Research Center, 1986, pp. 136-165.

Argues that theories and models of development over the past decade have exclusively focused on economic activity and have neglected the study of the quality of life. Suggests that research alternatives be developed and explores participatory action research methods.

68. Giele, Janet Z. "Introduction: Comparative Perspectives on Women." **Women: Role and Status in Eight Countries.** Edited by Janet Z. Giele and Audrey Smock. New York: John Wiley, 1977. 3-31 pp.

Presents a framework for relating women's status to economic development and culture. Argues that with devlopment, women have more freedom and self-expression. Family structures also make a difference in women's statuses.

69. Kelly, Gail P. "Failures of Androcentric Studies of Women's Education in the Third World." For **Alma Mater: Theory and Practice in Feminist Scholarship**. Edited by Paula A. Treichler et al. Urbana and Chicago: University of Illinois Press, 1985, pp. 292–306.

Reviews the trends and literature in studies of women's education in the third world. Points out the weaknesses in the androcentric studies of women and why this approach failed. Argues that traditional research acknowledges different gender roles but not hierarchical gender systems; women are not at the center of the research but the traditionally defined family is; schooling is treated as a neutral institution that makes no distinction between males and females; educated women and their work and family lives are not studied and traced, and comparative analysis of the impact of education on women's position in socialist and nonsocialist countries is neglected. Posits that future research should recognize fully that patriarchy is an institution that can and ought to be changed, and research should start from women's lives and realities.

70. Krishna Raj, Maithreyi. "Research on Women and Career: Issues of Methodology." **Economic and Political Weekly** 21 (October 25, 1986): (WS) pp. 67–74.

Critiques role theory as applied to the study of educated, employed women on the basis that the theory neglects the complexity of gender relations and tends to bifurcate the study of public and domestic spheres. Argues that there is a need for integrated methodologies which can incorporate the experiences of women from different social classes.

71. Leonard, Karen. "Women in India: Some Recent Perspectives." **Pacific Affairs** 52 (1979): 95–107.

Discusses some of the major problems for women in India today and reviews current research on them. Argues that women's continuing inferior status in Indian society, seen in such facts as high fertility and mortality, declining female to male sex ratio, early age at marriage, low literacy, declining labor force participation, etc. is serious not only for women but also for all citizens of the country. Points out that current research concentrates on problems of middle- and upper-class educated, urban women and neglects the problems of survival faced by most Indian women.

72. Palabrica-Costello, Marilou.   "Measurement Issues in the Study
    of Working Women: A Review of the Philippine Experience."
    Women in Development: Perspectives from the Nairobi Conference.
    Ottawa: International Development Research Center, 1986,
    pp. 166-185.

    Argues that most of the research on women and the workforce in
    the Philippines and in the third world for that matter neglect
    the economic contribution of women who are usually engaged in
    family farms, business, petty trade or part-time handicraft
    production outside of the wage sector.   Urges that more
    sophisticated data collection techniques be developed for labor
    market surveys that will be sensitive to women's labor.
    Explores the use of "time allocation" research strategies.

73. Papanek, Hanna.   "False Specialization and the Purdah of
    Scholarship: A Review Article." Journal of Asian Studies 44
    (1984): 127-149.

    Reviews literature on women and education in South Asia,
    especially in India. Points out that there is a sex segregation
    in scholarship which she calls false specialization. This false
    specialization imposes a kind of purdah on scholarship.
    Identifies three main strands in the new scholarship on women in
    South Asia, 1) complementary studies that highlight forgotten
    women and the social action affecting these unrepresented
    constituencies, 2) stock-taking assessments that provide
    "complementary" data but also point to possible government
    interventions, and 3) studies that take the integration of
    gender into social theory and methodology as their deliberate
    goal. Argues that successful future scholarship on gender
    differences and gender relations will not be possible if false
    specialization and the purdah of scholarship continues.

74. Schmukler, Beatriz and Mauta Savigliano.   "Authority
    Relationships Among Women: Lower Class Women and Female
    Researchers in the Field." Women in Development: Perspectives
    from the Nairobi Confernce. Ottawa: International Development
    Research Centre, 1985, pp. 1-39.

    Investigates how authority relationships among women,
    particularly those between researchers and lower class women,
    affect research, particularly qualitative, participatory
    studies. Argues that some research methods imply authoritarian
    relations and claims that qualitative methods avoid the
    "objectification" of lower class women.

III. GENERAL STUDIES

Included in this part of the bibliography are studies which provide overviews of women, education and society. Studies of women's educational pattern and of the workforce and family outcomes of women's education are not included here; rather, they are presented separately in other parts of the bibliography.

We have divided the works included in general studies into three parts: 1) Anthologies and Collections, 2) Statistical Compendia, and 3) General Overviews of Women, Education and Society.

A. Anthologies and Collections

While there are many anthologies about women, there are relatively few that are on women's education or devote considerable space to considering schooling and its impact on women and society. We have included here only those collections which are solely on women's education or which devote considerable attention to women's education. These collections are general works and cover a range of issues. There are a number of anthologies which focus on a specific issue--like education and fertility or women's education and the workforce. These are not listed here but appear elsewhere in this bibliography under the appropriate topics.

1. General

75. Acker, Sandra, et al. (eds.) **World Yearbook of Education. 1984. Women and Education.** London: Kogan Page, 1984. 358 pp.

Contains a series of essays which address the following questions: how far has equality for women been achieved in education? What problems still remain to be solved? Is there a continuing need for further studies of women's education? Part I offers essays on the theories underlying education's relation to women's status from the perspectives of philosophy, psychology, sociology and socio-linguistics. Part II contains case studies of women's education from countries such as

59

Australia, Great Britain, Malaysia, Jamaica and Canada. Some essays focus on the education of women in the context of the family, the labor market, religious traditions and technological change.

76. Giele, Janet Z. and Audrey C. Smock (eds.) **Women: Roles and Statuses in Eight Countries.** New York: Wiley, 1977.

Contains essays on women's status in a number of nations including Mexico, Egypt, Pakistan, Kenya, Ghana and Japan. Sees education as related to status improvement.

77. Kelly, Gail P. (ed.)   International Handbook of **Women's** Education. Westport, Conn.: Greenwood Press, 1989.

Presents 25 country case studies of women's education in various countries including Peru, Iran, Vietnam, Egypt, Senegal, Chile, China, India, Nigeria, Kenya, Botswana and Zaire. Each essay focuses on the history of women's education in a specific country, current enrollment patterns, the relation between education and women's participation in the workforce and in political life, and education and women's lives in the domestic sphere. Contains a chapter detailing world-wide trends in the education of women and a 950 item bibliography of published works on the education of women.

78. Kelly, Gail P. and Carolyn M. Elliott (eds.) **Women's Education in the Third World: Comparative Perspectives.** Albany: SUNY Press, 1982. 406 pp.

Contains 18 articles on women's education in the third world. Part One focuses on factors affecting women's access to education; Part Two on educational practices and differential male/female educational outcomes; Part Three looks at women and work while Part Four focuses on women's educational outcomes in the family. A bibliography of selected works on women's education in the third world is included.

79. Lindsay, Beverly (ed.) **Comparative Perspectives of Third World Women: The Impact of Race, Sex and Class.** New York: Praeger, 1980. 319 pp.

Contains 14 essays on third world women, most of which are on women in African and Asian nations. The essays all touch on education as an aspect of women's status improvement. Four of the essays are on U.S. minorities.

80. Thomson, Aisla (ed.) **The Decade for Women.** Toronto: Canadian Congress for Learning Opportunities for Women, 1986. 187 pp.

Compiles articles and reports assessing the impact of the United
Nations Decade for Women. Seven of the essays are directly on
education and deal with nonformal education, women in
international development agencies, women and the workforce and
enrollment patterns.

81. Wellesley Editorial Committee (ed.)   **Women and National
    Development: The Complexities of Change.** Chicago: University
    of Chicago Press, 1977. 346 pp.

    Contains a number of papers which were presented at a conference
    on Women in Development held in 1976 and sponsored by the
    Wellesley Center for Research on Women. Several of the papers
    focus directly on education. They are on women and the
    workforce and explore the impact of international markets on the
    linkages between education and employment for women. (These
    papers are abstracted elsewhere in this bibliography.) Other
    papers focus more generally on women and development.

2.   Africa

82. "Femmes, Éducation, Avenir."   **Recherche, Pédagogie et Culture** 4
    (no. 19, 1975): 1-72.

    Contains a number of short articles written by African women on
    the problems confronting women in Africa. Two of the articles
    in this special issue focus on education and provide an overview
    of enrollment patterns and factors affecting access to the
    schools. Other articles are on images of women in Africa,
    women's role in development and women and literature.

83. Hafkin, Nancy J. and Edna G. Bay (eds.)   **Women in Africa:
    Studies in Social and Economic Change.**   Stanford: Stanford
    University Press, 1976.

    Contains essays on women and change in Nigeria, Ghana, Kenya,
    Sierra Leone and Mozambique. Several focus on the role of
    education in bringing about social change and are abstracted
    elsewhere in this bibliography. Others are on the development
    of women's organizations and education is not a central topic.

84. Pala, Achola et al. (eds.) **The Participation of Women in Kenya
    Society.** Nairobi: Kenya Literature Bureau, 1978. 235 pp.

    Presents papers from a 1975 conference held in Nairobi sponsored
    by the Ford Foundation. Papers include a discussion of the
    functions of African Research Center on women; women in the

rural economy, women and employment, the legal system,
educational programs and the image of women in East African
society. The papers are predominantly on Kenya, but a few focus
on Tanzania.

85. Ware, Helen (ed.) **Women, Education and the Modernization of the
Family in West Africa.** Canberra: Australian National
University, Department of Demography, 1981. 178 pp. (Changing
African Family Project Series Monograph no. 7)

Contains eight essays about women in Africa, five of which focus
directly on women's education, the family and the workforce and
are abstracted individually within this bibliography.

3.   Asia

86. D'Souza, Alfred (ed.) **Women in Contemporary India and South
Asia.** New Delhi: Monohar, 1980. 326 pp.

Contains 12 articles that focus directly on women, including the
methodology of conducting research on women, and the link
between research, policy and programs to serve women. Seven
articles are on education and deal with issues like education
and women's labor force participation, the relation between
education and women's lives in the family and education and
women's status improvement. These individual essays are
abstracted elsewhere in this bibliography.

87. Futehally, Laeeq (ed). **Women in the Third World.** Bombay:
Jaico Publishing House, 1980. 155 pp.

Contains papers delivered at a conference in Madras in 1979.
Articles on Bangladesh, Sri Lanka, Singapore, China, Korea and
Indonesia refer to education.

88. Jahan, Rounaq and Hanna Papanek (eds.) **Women and Development:
Perspectives from South and Southeast Asia.** Dacca: The
Bangladesh Institute of Law and International Affairs, 1979.
439 pp.

Contains 21 essays on women and development. Part I presents a
report of the regional South and Southeast Asian Seminar on
Women and Development; Part II contains a series of essays on
public policies, including several which link women's education
to development policies and argue that without incorporation of
women into the school systems, women's status will continue to
erode and development will be stalled. The essays in Part II

focus on women's work and development. These essays are directly on education, linking education to rising expectations in Indonesia, rural development in Bangladesh and to fertility in Pakistan. Part IV focuses on women's programs and contains two essays on nonformal education.

89. Jesus-Viardo, Alma de (ed.) The Educational Dilemma of Women in Asia. Manila: Philippine Women's University, 1969. 509 pp.

Brings together papers and proceedings from the Golden Anniversary Conference of the Philippine Women's University on the education of women in developing countries held February 15-20, 1969. The essays are divided into four sections. Part I consists of background papers on population, human rights and the education of women. In Part II the focus is exclusively on the Philippines. The essays in Part II are regional studies on women's education in Mindanao, Visays, Manila, etc. Part III presents summaries of panel discussions on women's education in Pakistan, Thailand, Singapore, Japan, Korea, Vietnam and Israel. Part IV consists of a number of general papers urging the extension of women's education in third world countries.

90. Legaspi, Leonardo Z. (ed.) The Role of Women in Development: Seminar Papers and Statements. Manila: University of Santo Tomas Press, 1976. 259 pp.

Presents the proceedings of the December 1975 meeting of the Association of Southeast Asian Institutions of Higher Learning on women and development. A number of the papers focus specifically on women's education and development in Thailand, Hong Kong, Singapore, the Philippines, Malaysia and Indonesia and are abstracted elsewhere in this bibliography. Several papers call for specific reforms in higher education for women to promote national development.

91. Nanda, B.R. (ed.) Indian Women: From Purdah to Modernity. New Dehli: Vikas Publishing House, 1976. 187 pp.

Contains essays by historians, political scientists, psychologists, sociologists and lawyers on Indian women's struggle for equality. The essays trace social reform movements against sexual discrimination led by Jawaharlal Nehru and the attempts to introduce gender equality into the Indian Constitution. Some of the essays focus on Islamic law and the Hindu code as they affect women's right to hold land.

92. Rhim, Soon Man. Women of Asia: Yesterday and Today (India, China, Korea, Japan). New York: Friendship Press, 1983. 141 pp.

Presents a series of lectures developed for a course on marriage and the family. Sees education as a factor in the change of status of women. However, the author views legal change in India, the communist revolution in China and North Korea and modernization in Japan as more central.

93. Sen, N.B. (ed.) **Development of Women's Education in New India.** Delhi: New Book Society, 1969. 304 pp.

Contains a series of short essays by eminent Indian women on girls' education. Several of these are lectures which focus on educational progress for women since Indian independence; others focus on women as teachers, dancers, women as mothers, home science, divorce and women as doctors and cinematographers.

4.   Latin America and the Carribean

94. Braslavsky, Cecilia (ed.) **Mujer y Educación: Desigualdades Éducativas en América Latina y el Caribe.** Santiago de Chile: Oficina Regional de Educación de la UNESCO Para America Latina y el Caribe, 1984. 136 pp.

Presents summaries of a UNESCO regional meeting held in Panama in 1983. Provides data on women's literacy rates, enrollment in higher education, women's access to distinct levels of schools. While most of the data is for Latin America as a whole, Argentina and Brasil are presented as case studies representing women's educational pattern in the continent. Special attention is given to the relation of women's education and access to the professional, nonformal education. The volume ends with a discussion of new strategies taken by Cuba, the Dominican Republic, Mexico, Nicaragua, Panama and Venezuela to extend education to women. The recommendations of the Panama meeting are affixed.

95. Comisión Interamericana de Mujeres. **El Pensamiento Feminino en El Ecuador.** Quito: Editorial Publitencia, 1986. 183 pp.

Contains a series of speeches given in Quito in 1985 at the end of the U.N. Decade on Women. Some of the subjects covered are women in the family and in the labor force, government initiatives for women during the decade, the influence of television on women's roles, the image of women in the press, women and politics and women's education.

96. Covarrubias, Paz and Rolando Franco (eds.) **Chile: Mujer y Sociedad.** Santiago: Alfebeta Impr., 1979. 876 pp.

Surveys the economic and social status of women in Chile.
Includes chapters on women's work in factories as well as in
rural areas, female migration patterns, fertility and population
policies, images of women in novels and in the media, family
life, machisma, women as victims, the legal status of women,
women's labor legislation and the women's movement.   Several
chapters focus directly on women's education.   Five other
chapters deal with education's relation to women's work, income
and fertility patterns.

97. Forde, Norma (ed.) **Report of the Barbados National Commission
on the Status of Women.** Bridgetown: Government Printery, 1978.
Vol. 1, 438 pp., Vol. 2, 780 pp.

Constitutes the Report of the Barbados National Commission on
the Status of Women which was begun on November 1976.   The
report covers education, the law, employment and the family.
Part I covers the commission's deliberations and recommendations
on   traditional   attitudes   toward   women's   legal   provisions
(marriage,   divorce,   inheritance,   labor   and   criminal   law),
education   (curriculum,   primary   and   secondary   education,
coeducation, non-traditional subjects, higher education, and
women as teachers and administrators), women and employment, and
women   and   health,   the   family   and   the   church.   The
recommendations on education are far-reaching and include
measures to provide equal access for women to vocational and
technical training, to sports and to non-traditional subjects.
Volume II includes background papers, two of which deal directly
with   education   and   are   abstracted   elsewhere   in   this
bibliography.

98. Guerra-Cunningham, Lucia (ed.)   **Mujer y Sociedad en América
Latina.**   Irvine: Universidad de California and Editorial del
Pacifico, 1980.   261 pp.

Contains a number of essays on the condition of Latin American
women and on women in the arts and literature on the continent.
The seven articles on women and society in Latin America do
touch very briefly on education.

99. Luz, Madel T. (ed.) **O Lugar da Mulher.** Rio de Janeiro: Ediçoes
Graal, 1982. 146 pp.

Contains a series of articles on sex segregation in Brazil in
social life, in schools, in the work place and in the family.

100. Nash, June and Helen I. Safa (eds.) **Sex and Class in Latin
America.** New York: Praeger, 1976. 330 pp.

Documents female subordination and exploitation in Latin America in family life, at work and in politics. Several of the essays are critical of social science research on development for failing to recognize women's roles in economic, political and social life. Argues that models of development have proven, as a result, to reinforce sex and class inequalities.

101. Wainerman, Catalina et al. **Del Deber ser y al Hacer de las Mujeres. Dos Estudios de Caso en Argentina.** México: El Colegio de México, 1983.

Contains articles written by Catalina Wainerman, Elizabeth Jelin and Maria de Carmen Feijoo on sex role divisions of labor in various institutions including the law, the church and the academy.

5.   The Middle East

102. Beck, Lois and Nikki Keddie (eds.) **Women in the Muslim World.** Cambridge, Mass.: Harvard University Press, 1978. 698 pp.

Contains essays on women and the law, fertility, women and social change, education and employment, working women and women in the domestic sphere. Several essays deal directly with education and are abstracted in this bibliography.

103. Fernea, Elizabeth Warnock (ed.) **Women and the Family in the Middle East: New Voices of Change.** Austin: University of Texas Press, 1985. 356 pp.

Contains essays written, for the most part, by women from Middle Eastern countries about women's experiences. Many of the essays, short stories, poems and life histories are translations from Arabic, French and Persian sources. There are 31 chapters in the volume which touch on issues including the family, health and education, revolution, religion, identity and work. Part IV contains a number of chapters on women's education and these are abstracted elsewhere in this bibliography.

B.   Statistics

The works included here are general statistical surveys of women's status and their workforce participation and fertility rates. Some of them contain educational statistics as well as general

demographic data. Studies which are limited to enrollment statistics
are not listed here. They appear in Part V of the Bibliography which
is devoted to women's educational patterns.

1.   Asia

Books and Monographs

104. Acharya, Meena. Statistical Profile of Nepalese Women: A
     Critical Review.   Kathmandu, Nepal: Centre for Economic
     Development and Administration, Tribhuvan University, 1979.
     102 pp.

     Presents statistics on the general demographic features of
     Nepalese women (age structure, sex ratio, ethnic composition,
     population growth, life expectancy, fertility rates), social
     characteristics (including marital status and education) and
     women's economic activity rates, their industrial and
     occupational work, and the like. The statistics are mainly from
     the 1971 Nepal census, although there are some time-lag data
     from the 1960s and 1950s. The statistics on schooling include
     literacy rates for 1952, 1961 and 1971, a regional breakdown of
     literacy rates for 1977 and enrollment levels for 1965, 1971 and
     1976.

105. Alamsir, Susan Fuller. Profile of Bangladeshi Women: Selected
     Aspects of Women's Roles and Status in Bangladesh. Dacca:
     USAID Mission to Bangladesh, 1977. 82 pp.

     Provides basic statistics on women in Bangladesh, including
     statistics on literacy rates, school enrollments, fertility and
     workforce participation. General demographic data is included
     as well.

106. Mitra, Asok. The Status of Women: Literacy and Employment.
     Bombay: Allied Publishers, 1979. 74 pp.

     Provides an overview of women's literacy rates and employment
     between 1901 and 1971. Statistics include breakdowns of women's
     educational levels according to urban/rural residence and by
     state.   Data demonstrate a decline in women's workforce
     participation since 1901. This decline is most evident between
     1951 and 1971.

107. Siraj-ul-Haq, Mahmud. Statistical Profile of Females of
     Pakistan.   Islamabad: Government of Pakistan, Health,

Demography and Social Welfare Section, Planning and Development Division, 1980. 89 pp.

Presents statistics on basic demographics, education, health, food and nutrition, housing and water supply, social welfare, and employment for both men and women in Pakistan for 1972.

Articles

108. Bose, Ashish. "A Demographic Profile." **Indian Women.** Edited by Devabi Jain. New Delhi: Publications Division, Ministry of Information and Broadcasting, Government of India, 1975, pp. 125-184.

     Provides statistics on female mortality rates, marriage ages, fertility, employment and education. Contains 39 tables concerning population structure, marriage, fertility, education, work force participation, migration and political participation.

109. Rana, Kamal. "Status and Role of Women in the Organized Sector." **Sub-regional Seminar on Status and Role of Women.** Bangkok: International Labor Organization, 1978, pp. 1-33.

     Presents background paper for an ILO seminar which was held in Dacca in 1977. Focuses on the status of women in Nepal and argues that one of the reasons women's status is low is because of their lack of schooling. Despite increases in education, women's share of enrollments at all levels remains low. Reviews the government's efforts to encourage female education. Women's employment rates remain stagnant or have declined. In part this is due to persistent unemployment as well as women's lack of skills gained via education. Includes a number of tables detailing illiteracy rates and school enrollments for 1971.

Latin America and the Caribbean

Books and Monographs

110. Báez, Clara. **La Subordinación Social de la Mujer Dominicana en Cifras.** Santo Domingo: Dirrección General de Promoción de la Mujer, Instituto Internacional de las Naciones Unidas para la Investigación, Capacitacion y Promoción de la Mujer, 1985.

     Provides basic statistics detailing women's subordination in the Dominican Republic. Statistics cover the workforce, basic demography, marriage, fertility and education.

111. Cathelat, Marie-France and Teresa Burga. **Perfil de la Mujer Peruana 1980-1981.** Lima: Editorial Ausonia-Talleres Graficos S.A., 1981. 340 pp.

Presents statistics on women in Peru in 1980-81. The statistics focus on health, workforce participation, education according to race and gender and include wastage rates, culture, religion and legal status.

112. Centro de Estudios de Población y Desarrollo. **Diagnostico Social y Juridico de la Mujer en el Perú 1979.** Lima: Editoria Italperu S.A. 1979. 204 pp.

Provides detailed statistics on women's education, occupation, health and legal status in Peru in 1979. Includes a discussion of women's organizations in Peru, the special problems of peasant women, and recent research on Peruvian women. The educational statistics include breakdowns between male and female educational levels as of 1961, detailed statistics on the school population in Lima metropolitan area in 1979, comparisons between male and female enrollment patterns in rural areas, illiteracy rates for 1970 and 1972 broken down not only by gender but by region and department. Detailed statistics on higher education by gender and area of specialization are also presented for the early 1970s.

113. **Estadística sobre la Mujer.** México: Secretaría de Programción y Prepuvesto, 1980. 332 pp.

Gives a complete statistical picture of Mexican women drawn from the national census of 1970, an inquiry into fertility rates in 1976, a survey of the urban work force in 1978 and a general inquiry on employment in 1979. Statistics are given in all geographic areas on enrollment in all levels and types of education and in all teacher training.

114. Fundação Instituto Brasileiro de Geografia e Estatistica. **Perfil Estatistico de Crianças e Maes no Brasil: Caracteristicas Socio-demograficas 1970-1977.** Rio de Janeiro: Instituto Brasileiro de Geografia e Estatistica, 1982.

Presents statistical abstract and analysis which compares figures from 1970 to those of 1977. Covers Brasil as a whole with separate figures for the Northeast, Sao Paulo, and metropolitan region of San Paulo. Contains statistics relating education to birth rate. Gives sex breakdowns by age group for school attendance and relates years in school to number of children and marriage.

115. Perez, Magaly and Noemi Pascual.   Estadisticas Sobre la Mujer Cubana.   Habana: Editorial Letras Cubanas, 1985.

Provides basic statistics in French, Spanish and English on Cuban women. These include: sex, age and educational levels of the workforce, women as leaders in the trade union, the enrollment of women in higher education and the medals won by Cuban women in international competitions. The statistics are for the years 1978, 1982 and in some instances 1983.

116. Trinidad and Tobago, Republic of.   Final Report of the National Commission on the Status of Women.   Port of Spain: Government Printery, 1978.   79 pp.

Provides an overview of women's status in Trinidad and Tobago, including fertility rates and women's workforce participation rates. Argues for greater education for women and provides a number of statistics on women's education for the 1970s.

C.   Overviews of Women, Society and Education

The works included here are general ones which do not have education of women as their central focus, but none the less do consider education either as a background variable or as a means of status improvement for women.

1.   General

Books and Monographs

117. Ali, Parveen Shaukat.   Status of Women in the Muslim World: A Study in the Feminist Movements in Turkey, Egypt, Iran and Pakistan.   Lahore: Aziz Publishers, 1975.   248 pp.

Provides an overview of women in Islamic thought and then reviews cultural status of women. Chapter 3 is on education and provides an overview of educational statistics for all levels up to about 1960.

118. Newland, Kathleen.   The Sisterhood of Man.   New York: W.W. Norton, 1979.   242 pp.

Focuses on women's subordination worldwide and contains a 17 page chapter which deals with worldwide trends in women's enrollment. Points out that while there has been a rise in female literacy and in school attendance, this has not translated into increasing women's workforce participation or enhancing women's income or political power.

119. United States. Department of Commerce. **Women of the World**. Washington: Government Printing Office, 1984-1985. 5 volumes.

Consists of a five volume work on the status of women worldwide. Four of the volumes cover regions: Latin America, Sub-Saharan Africa, North Africa and the Middle East and Asia. In each, basic data on demographics, women's roles in society and education are presented. The statistics are for the most part from the mid-1970s although occasionally data for the 1980s are included. The fifth volume summarizes the first four volumes and compares the status of women across regions.

Articles

120. Farrell, Joseph P. "Educational Expansion and the Drive for Social Equality." **Comparative Education**. Edited by Philip Altbach et al. New York: Macmillan, 1982, pp. 39-53.

Assesses whether educational expansion has resulted in equality. Argues that while in many third world countries gender based equality in access to school may have been achieved, equality of survival, outcomes and output remains elusive.

121. Lindsay, Beverly. "Perspectives of Third World Women: An Introduction." **Comparative Perspectives of Third World Women: The Impact of Race, Sex and Class**. Edited by Beverly Lindsay. New York: Praeger, 1980, pp. 1-20.

Provides an overview of women's status in the third world, focusing primarily on Africa. Argues that colonialism eroded women's traditional statuses and denied women access to new statuses by denying them education. Maintains that education is key to status improvement and for women's entry into political and modern economic life.

122. Mead, Margaret. "The Position of Women Around the World." **The Educational Dilemma of Women in Asia**. Edited by Alma de Jesus-Viardu. Manila: The Philippine Women's University, 1969, pp. 89-106.

Surveys women's status around the world and looks at changing sex role divisions of labor in the family and the economy. Warns that industrialization may deepen the boundaries between male and female labor, confining women to childbearing and childrearing. Believes that education can and has led to changes in women's roles that might offset those that are set in motion by urbanization and industralization.

123. Molyneux, Maxine. "Strategies for the Emancipation of Women in Third World Socialist Societies." **Women and Education World Yearbook of Educations, 1984.** Edited by Sandra Acker et al. London: Kogan Page, 1984, pp. 268-278.

Explains why women in socialist third world countries have experienced greater gains in their legal, economic and social status than their sisters in capitalist third world countries. Points out that socialist countries have adopted policies aimed at family reform, mobilizing women to participate in the workforce and increasing educational opportunities. Many non-socialist societies have done little for women other than provide access to schooling. Argues that in socialist countries, women's emancipation is still limited because the state has not been concerned as much with liberating women as with economic development and the construction of socialism.

124. Molyneux, Maxine. "Socialist Societies Old and New: Progress Toward Women's Emancipation." **Monthly Review** 34 (July/August 1982): 56-100.

Analyzes progress in abolishing gender based inequalities in socialist societies. Points out that despite efforts to bring women into the workforce and into the schools, inequality persists. Argues this is the case because socialist societies have been concerned less with liberating women and providing them with equality than with mobilizing women's labor for development programs.

2.   Africa

Books and Monographs

125. Hall, Marjorie and Bakhita Amin Ismail. **Sisters Under the Sun: The Story of Sudanese Women.** New York: Longmans, 1981. 264 pp.

Charts the changes in women's status in Sudan since independence. Argues that lack of education is the main obstacle to women's employment but that major gains in education have been made for women in Sudan, particularly in the northern part of the country. Much of the volume is based on anecdotal evidence. Two chapters are devoted to education, charting the historical bases of the evolution of education for women with the advent of British colonialism.

126. Max-Forson, Margaret. **Progress and Obstacles in Achieving the Minimum Objectives of the World and Africa Plans of Action: A Critical Review.** Addis Ababa: United Nations Economic Commission for Africa, 1979. 56 pp.

Asks whether the status of women in Africa in employment, economic roles, education and training, health and nutrition, the legal system and in politics has changed. On the basis of a survey sent to 49 countries (only 18 replied) points out that there has been little progress toward meeting the goals set out by the UN in 1975, the International Women's Year. Believes that education could play a major role in the future in terms of improving women's status in Africa.

127. Newman, Jeanne S. **Women of the World. Sub-Saharan Africa.** Washington, D.C.: U.S. Department of Commerce, 1984. 200 pp.

Presents an overview of the status of women in sub-Saharan Africa, covering education, women in the economy, women in marriage and the family, fertility rates and women's health and mortality rates. Chapter 4 focuses exclusively on literacy and education and presents literacy rates for women and men by age, rural/urban residence as well as school enrollment rates broken down by gender and by urban/rural residence.

128. Powdermaker, Hortense. **Coppertown: Changing Africa.** New York: Harper and Row, 1962. 391 pp.

Looks at Rhodesian copper belt. Contains five chapters on women--one is partially concerned with both the desire for and the extent of female education.

129. Robertson, Claire C. **Sharing the Same Bowl: A Socioeconomic History of Women and Class in Accra, Ghana.** Bloomington: Indiana University Press, 1984. 299 pp.

Studies women in Central Accra and argues that with capitalism, women have experienced increases in economic dependence on men, evident in the residential system, as well as in a decline in the autonomy of women's trade. This has been accompanied by a decline in women's access to capital and in women's apprenticeship system. Chapter 5 focuses on education. Maintains that women have been denied access to education equal to that of men, and thus have not been able to gain control of new resources which are replacing women's trade (such as parastatal industries). Also reports surveys among school girls involved in trade and finds that girls with schooling have a

greater knowledge of trading networks and possibilities than
girls with little schooling. From this concludes that
deterioration of women's educational status also serves to
reinforce women's allocation from the middle levels to lower
levels of the trading occupation.

130. Urdang, Stephanie. **Fighting Two Colonialisms: Women in
Guinea-Bissau.** New York and London: Monthly Review Press,
1979.   320 pp.

Focuses on the role of women in Guinea-Bissau and how the
African Party for the Independence of Guinea and Cape Verde has
integrated women's liberation into the revolution. Much of the
book discusses Marchel's theories of revolution and reports
Urdang's visits to the liberated zones. Chapter 7 is on
education and describes efforts on the part of the African Party
for the Independence of Guinea and Cape Verde to extend
education to females. Despite these efforts, about 25 percent
of girls of school age attend school. Points out that political
cadres have urged families to send their daughters to school,
but that traditional attitudes, especially among Muslim parents,
combined with poverty which brings girls into production at an
early age, have kept female enrollment stagnant. Discusses
curricular reform and schools' attempt to promote new sex role
divisions of labor.

131. Weinrich, A.K.H. **Women and Racial Discrimination in Rhodesia.**
Paris: UNESCO, 1979.   143 pp.

Focuses on the eroding status of women under British colonialism
and white rule in Rhodesia. Particular emphasis is given to
changes in economic life with the introduction of capitalism and
changes in family life. Chapter 2, which is on the economy,
points out that women are discriminated against in the workforce
and clustered in low-paying service occupations. African women
are paid less than African men and considerably less than white
women and white men. Part of women's low status is due to lack
of education. Chapter 2 presents enrollment statistics that
illustrate women's low literacy levels and their relatively low
participation in the school system. Statistics in this chapter
also provide urban/rural as well as tribal breakdowns in
male/female access to education. Argues that once majority rule
is introduced, the disparities between male and female will
erode.

Articles

132. Gupta, Anirudha.   "Illusion of Progress--The Women of Kenya."
Women of the World: Illusion and Reality. Edited by Urmila

Phadnis and Indira Malani. New Delhi: Vikas Publishing House,
1978, pp. 245-260.

Argues that, despite government policies in Kenya to provide
women equality, women are absent from positions of power and
authority in the country except in two government ministries
which serve predominantly female clientele.   Concludes that
while many promises were made to provide women with equal access
to education and to political and social life, most have
remained unfulfilled.

133. Greenstreet, Miranda. "Notes and Documents: Social Change and
     Ghanaian Women." Canadian Journal of African Studies 6 (1972):
     351-355.

Describes the position of Ghanaian women in education, work,
politics and women's organizations.   Although there are equal
educational facilities for boys and girls, girls are encouraged
less to attend school, especially among the lower income groups.
As the educational level goes up, there are less and less girls
enrolled in school.   Argues that it is necessary to provide
women with vocational guidance, new types of employment and part
time work, day care services, knowledge of birth control and
family planning centers to improve their status in society.

134. Obbo, Christine.   "Stratification and the Lives of Women in
     Uganda." Women and Class in Africa. Edited by Claire Robertson
     and Iris Berger. New York: Africana Publishing Company, 1986,
     pp. 178-196.

Surveys stratification systems in Uganda and Ugandan women's
perceptions of that system.   Points out, through biographical
sketches of a female pediatrician, a nurse, a business woman, a
market trader, a dressmaker and a farmer, that education brings
women high social status.

135. Rousseau, Ida Faye.   "African Women: Identity Crisis? Some
     Observations on Education and the Changing Role of Women in
     Sierra Leone and Zaire." Women Cross-Culturally: Change and
     Challenge.   Edited by Ruby Rohrlick-Leavitt.   The Hague:
     Mouton, 1975, pp. 41-51.

Argues that in pre-colonial Africa women's roles were different
from men's but not necessarily inferior.   With the advent of
colonialism, sex   roles   changed   and
increasingly unequal roles have deepened since Independence.
Argues that educational inequality has been one way in which sex
role divisions have increased women's subordination.

136. Steyn, Anna F. and J.M. Uys. "The Changing Position of Black
     Women in South Africa." The Changing Position of Women in
     Family and Society. Edited by Eugen Lupri. Leiden: E.J.
     Brill, 1983, pp. 344-370.

     Describes the changes in the position of black women in South
     Africa in terms of family and marriage, education, work, etc.
     Unlike iñ traditional society, where girls are taught to help
     their mothers at home, formal schooling has become increasingly
     important in changing society. More girls are enrolled in
     school now, but fewer girls than boys are found as the level of
     education goes up. Points out that, while urban black women
     have gained more freedom and independence, they have at the same
     time lost the security and protection which traditional society
     had secured them, and that women often find themselves in
     conflict between old and new norms.

137. Sudarkasa, Niara. "The Status of Women in Indigenous African
     Societies." Feminist Studies 12 (1986): 91-103.

     Examines the roles of women in families and descent groups, in
     the economy and in the political process in West Africa. Points
     out that in contemporary Africa the relationship between women
     and men has become hierarchical.

138. Van Allen, Judith. "African Women, 'Modernization' and National
     Liberation." Women in the World: A Comparative Study. Edited
     by Lynne B. Iglitzin and Ruth Ross. Santa Barbara: American
     Bibliographical Center, CLIO Press, 1976, pp. 25-54.

     Contrasts the regressive effects on women's status of
     'western-style' modernization with the effects on women from
     revolutionary movements in Angola, Mozambique, Guinea-Bissau,
     Tanzania and Zambia. Argues that in these revolutions, leaders
     have moved beyond focusing on women in production to focusing on
     women's liberation and social justice. Points out that women's
     groups have launched campaigns against traditional women's roles
     and, through political education and consciousness-raising
     programs, have promoted women's participation and leadership in
     politics.

3.   Asia

     Books and Monographs

139. Abbasi, M.B. Socioeconomic Characteristics of Women in Sind. Karachi: Sind Regional Plan Organization Economic Studies Center, 1980. 126 pp.

Asks whether women's status relative to men's has improved in Pakistan by sampling women in Sind Province. Provides data on the employment of women, women's educational levels, women's health and how geographical factors affect women. Shows that female laborforce participation is low as are women's educational levels and argues that social attitudes prevent women from contributing fully to the country's economic and social development.

140. Bennett, Lynn. Tradition and Change in the Legal Status of Nepalese Women. Kathmandu: Center for Economic Development and Administration, Tribhuvan University, 1979. 107 pp.

Reviews the legal status of women in Nepal focusing on land and property ownership, inheritance, divorce and family law as well as laws affecting women's ability to enter into business contracts. Examines also labor legislation and attempts to improve women's status. Points out that the gap between legality and reality is due to high rates of illiteracy especially among rural women.

141. Chaudhury, Rafiqul Huda and Nilufer Raihan Ahmed. Female Status in Bangladesh. Dacca: The Bangladesh Institute of Development Studies, 1980. 176 pp.

Focuses on the status of women in Bangladesh. Looks at the civil rights of women, their educational achievement, women's workforce participation rates, conjugal roles and women's organizations. Chapter 4 is devoted specifically to education. It covers literacy and adult education, school attendance and achievement, hígher education and educational expenditures devoted to women. Points out that girls are undereducated relative to boys. Urges the opening of girls schools, the reallocation of monies to primary education and the development of more nonformal education programs for adult women. The educational statistics in chapter 4 are quite detailed.

142. Chiang, Lan-hung Nora and Yenlin Ku. Past and Current Status of Women in Taiwan. Taipei: Population Studies Center, National Taiwan University, 1985. 50 pp.

Surveys briefly all aspects of women's lives in the post-World War II era. Points to tremendous decrease of illiteracy and improvement of women's educational level from half that of men to only one and one half years less. Women's educational level has risen faster than men's as parents invest more resources in

fewer children. Women still have only half the university
enrollment and are generally in liberal arts fields.

143. Eisen, Arlene. **Women and Revolution in Vietnam.** London: Zed
Books, 1984. 289 pp.

Focuses on the changes in women's status resulting from the
revolution in Vietnam. Points out that women's status under
Confucianism was low and women had no opportunity to improve
their status since they were officially denied access to
education. Colonial rule, which began in the 1860s, further
eroded women's status and the war in Vietnam that lasted until
1975 in the South continued that trend. Claims that women are
moving toward liberation; they have entered the workforce in
unprecedented numbers, the legal barriers to women's equality
have been removed and the communist government is committed to
women's equality. Chapter 13 focuses on education and the
literacy crusade which followed the 1946 revolution in Vietnam.
Illiteracy has been eradicated and women have entered higher
education in increasing numbers. However, sex segregation still
remains within the professions and in the workforce and women
are poorly represented in government and in the Communist Party.

144. Khiang, Mi Mi. **The World of Burmese Women.** London: Zed Books,
1984. 193 pp.

Surveys women's roles in post-independence Burma. Focuses on
kinship patterns, family law, women's roles in the household
throughout the life cycle, women and religion, women in
agricultural labor and in factory work and women's political and
professional participation. The author notes the lack of
nationally aggregated statistical data on Burma and presents few
herself. The chapter on the household contains case studies of
rural women, urban professional women and urban traders.
Chapter 7 is on education. Chapter 9 presents fragmentary data
on women's workforce participation. In chapter 10 the low
participation of women in politics forms the focus and there is
some discussion of women in higher education. The enrollment
statistics for 1975/76 in higher education indicate that women
predominate in education and in economics programs. The book
ends with profiles of a number of Burmese professional women
which focus on their education, work and marriage. These women
include a university professor, a doctor and a military officer.

145. Strange, Heather. **Rural Malay Women in Tradition and
Transition.** New York: Praeger, 1981. 264 pp.

Explores, through an enthnographic study of the village of
Rusilia in Malaysia, whether strategies for improving women's
status and achieving equality through development have

succeeded.   The strategies studied are in the areas of
employment, land ownership, health services and education. The
book is organized around chapters on the village setting,
women's life cycle, education, marriage and the family, polygamy
and divorce, and the economy. Chapter 3 on women's life cycle
in Rusilia points out that education and literacy levels have
risen appreciably since 1952.   The chapter also focuses on
socialization of girls to be docile.   Chapter 4 deals
exclusively with education and, unlike the section in Chapter 3
on education which focuses on the village of Rusilia, looks at
the school system of Malaysia as a whole and presents nationally
aggregated educational statistics for all levels.   Chapter 4
also presents a detailed statistical analysis of women's
educational enrollment patterns in Trennganu State.

146. Thapa, Krishna B. **Women and Social Change in Nepal, 1951-1960.**
Kathmandu: Ambikathapa, 1985. 200 pp.

Focuses on changes in women's status in Nepal between 1951 and
1960 and argues that many of these changes were a result of
foreign contact and educational expansion.

147. Whyte, Robert Orr and Pauline White. **The Women of Rural Asia.**
Boulder: Westview Press, 1982. 262 pp.

Focuses on women's status in Asia looking at religion, family,
marriage, fertility patterns, the division of labor between
males and females, agricultural modernization and female
employment. Chapter 4 is devoted to women's status in public
life. Literacy and education are taken as indicators of women's
advancement. Surveys gains in educational enrollment patterns
and their lack of impact on the status of women in the
professions. Chapter 9 focuses on education and fertility.
Sees the major gains for women in Asia stemming from increases
in education.

3.   Asia

Articles

148. Arittin, Rohana.   "The Exploitation of Women: An Overview."
Sojourn 1 (1986):   133-154.

Surveys the status of Malaysian women who have been kept in
subordination by an interplay of feudal tradition, colonialism
and neocolonialism and lack of educational opportunity. Points

out that by 1980 more than 70 percent of women over the age of 35 were illiterate and that the gap between male and female illiteracy was very wide. Shows that the number of females enrolled in secondary and higher education is proportionately less than that of males despite the increases in female enrollment rates over the past decade. Argues that socialization patterns which stress female subordination begin in the home and are reinforced in the schools, the media and prevalent ideology. These socialization patterns explain why women in higher education are enrolled in "feminine" courses and employed in predominately female fields upon graduation from school.

149. Don, Fatimah Hamid. "The Status, Roles and Achievements of Women in Malaysia." The Role of Women in Development: Seminar Papers and Statements. Edited by Leonardo Z. Legaspi. Manila: University of Santo Tomas Press, 1976, pp. 23-38.

Surveys changes in women's roles in Malaysia by focusing on women's educational levels and their labor force participation. Argues that women have made major gains in education; in higher education, however, they are segregated by field from their male peers. The smallest gains for women have been made in the political sphere.

150. Hwa, Cheng Soik. "The Status, Roles and Achievements of Women in Singapore." The Role of Women in Development. Seminar Papers and Statements. Edited by Leonardo Z. Legaspi. Manila: University of Santo Tomas Press, 1976, pp. 57-77.

Surveys women's legal, educational and workforce status in Singapore. Points out that while there have been major changes in the law and increases in women's educational pattern, women remain subordinate to men in the family and in the workforce.

151. Ihromi, T. Omas. "Social and Cultural Background of Concepts of Roles of Women: Reflections on the Indonesian Scene." Ecumenical Review 27 (1975): 357-365.

Describes the role and status of women in Indonesia. Argues that the position of women is affected by the three types of family structures: matrilineal, patrilineal and bilateral. Progress has been slow and argues that Christian churches have contributed to more secure marriages, more stable family systems and equal opportunity of education to boys and girls.

152. Khan, Nighat S. "Women in Pakistan: Position, Status and Movement." Journal of Social Studies (Dhaka) (no. 30, October 1985): 27-40.

Describes the low status of women in Pakistan and argues that it is due to traditional Islamic interpretations of women's roles, government lack of policies to emancipate women and the portrayal of women as subordinate in the media.

153. Lee Hyo Chae and Kim Chu-Suk. "The Status of Korean Women Today." Virtues in Conflict: Tradition and the Korean Woman Today. Edited by Sandra Mattielli. Seoul: Royal Asian Society, 1977, pp. 147-155.

Focuses on the changing status of Korean women. Points out that women have greater freedom in their families and that women have greater access to primary and secondary school. Despite these changes, women's political participation remains low.

154. Neher, Clark D. "Sex Roles in the Philippines: The Ambiguous Cebuana." Women of Southeast Asia. Edited by Penny Van Esterik. Normal: Northern Illinois University Center for Southeast Asia Studies, 1982, pp. 154-175.

Analyzes the roles of women in Cebu Province in the Philippines in terms of their role images and their educational, economic and political participation levels.

155. Suryochondro, Sukanti. "The Status, Roles and Achievements of Women in Indonesia." The Role of Women in Development: Seminar Papers and Statements. Edited by Leonardo Z. Legaspi. Manila: University of Santo Tomas Press, 1976, pp. 82-96.

Finds that status improvement for women in Indonesia is hindered by traditional attitudes and lack of employment opportunities. Argues that education is a critical means for women to gain the skills necessary to enter the paid workforce and thereby improve their social status.

156. Szanton, M. Christina Blanc. "Women and Men in Iloilo, Philippines: 1903-1970." Women of Southeast Asia. Edited by Penny Van Esterik. Normal: Northern Illinois University Center for Southeast Asia Studies, 1982, pp. 124-153.

Discusses changing male/female relationships in the Philippines. Argues, through analysis of the 1903 and 1970 national censuses for Iliolo province, that women, while they have increasingly been brought into the workforce, still remain inferior to men because of institutionalized inequalities in salary structures.

3a.   China

Books and Monographs

157. Andors, Phyllis. **The Unfinished Liberation of Chinese Women,**
     1949-1980. Bloomington, Indiana: Indiana University Press,
     1983.   212 pp.

     Argues that while the Chinese revolution has meant real progress
     for women in education, in entering the workforce and in changes
     in the family; development strategies have often been in
     conflict with women's liberation.   The government has often put
     development first and has been reluctant to provide women with
     the enabling conditions of liberation.   In addition, the
     government has sought to control women's reproduction as part of
     development policy without providing women with alternative
     means of social security besides children.

158. Croll, Elisabeth. **Chinese Women Since Mao.** London: Zed Press,
     1983.   129 pp.

     Charts the changes in women's status in Chinese society since
     the Four Modernizations' policies which followed the Cultural
     Revolution.   Points out that changes in the organization of
     production which focus on increasing productivity have tended to
     further the sex segregation of the workforce and to make the
     household rather than the collective the basic unit of
     production.   In so doing, women have become more rather than
     less dependent on the family unit.   The relegation of women to
     household production has occurred despite rising educational
     levels among women.   Concludes that while women's status in
     China has improved since the Revolution, problems of child care,
     domestic work, sex segregation of the labor force, low income
     and educational disadvantage still remain and are likely to get
     worse as the government pursues policies aimed at rapid
     industrialization.

159. Wolfe, Margery. **Revolution Postponed: Women in Contemporary**
     China. Stanford: Stanford University Press, 1985.

     Surveys the changes in women's status in China since the
     Cultural Revolution in China.   Based on field work in a number
     of sites in China, including Beijing, Shaoxing and several rural
     areas, points out that gender asymmetry remains despite
     education.   In Beijing men with middle school education earn 22
     percent more than women with similar education; in Shoaxing men
     earn 18 percent more than similarly educated women.   Men with
     primary education or less earn 39 percent more than similarly
     educated women in Beijing, the differential is 37 percent in
     Shoaxing.   Points out that education improves women's earnings,
     but only relative to the earnings of other women, not relative
     to the earnings of men.   Believes that the policies introduced

under the Four Modernizations in China will not improve women's status at all. Most of those changes have in the rural areas substituted the nuclear patriarchial family for the extended patriarchial family as the regulator of women's labor; in the urban areas the patriarchical state, rather than the family, has come to play the same role.

Articles

160. Bernstein-Tarrow, Norma and Douglas Ray. "Assessing A Rolling Policy Reform: Rights for Women and Children in Modern China." **Canadian and International Education** 15 (1986): 53-87.

Analyzes reform for women and children in China and finds that while reforms have brought about greater access to education on the primary and secondary level, women remain under-represented in higher education. Women are paid less for their labor than are men and they have not attained elected or appointed office in government. Finds also that a national network of peer pressure and legal reform has eliminated the exploitation of children.

161. Croll, Elizabeth J. "Social Production and Female Status: Women in China." **Race and Class** 18 (Summer 1976): 39-52.

Examines Maoist strategies designed to provide women with equal access to and control over China's strategic resources. Describes the programs of the 1960s launched to trace the origin and development of ideologies which oppressed women.

162. Link, Beulah M. "Holding Up The Sky Is A Shared Responsibility." **Delta Kappa Gamma Bulletin** 47 (1980): 14-19.

Describes progress made in China after the revolution in 1950. Argues that the Communist Revolution liberated Chinese people from poverty, starvation, illness, exploitation by foreigners as well as national and local rulers, etc., gave women full citizenship and that women extensively participate in the social and economic process of the country.

163. Robinson, Jean C. "Of Women and Washing Machines: Employment, Housework and the Reproduction of Motherhood in Socialist China." **China Quarterly** (no. 101, 1985): 32-57.

Argues that the social and economic policies adopted since the Third Plenum of the Central Committee of the Chinese Communist Party have created conditions which reinforce patriarchy and sex inequality in employment and benefits and ignore the need to provide goods to ease domestic labor.

164. Wang, Bee-Lan Chan. "Chinese Women: The Relative Influences of Ideological Revolution, Economic Growth and Cultural Change." *Comparative Perspectives of Third World Women*. Edited by Beverly Lindsay. New York: Praeger, 1980, pp. 96-122.

Compares the changes that have occurred in women's roles among Chinese in Mainland China, Taiwan and Malaysia. Argues that the type of political and economic system does make a difference in women's social, educational, and occupational aspirations and opportunities.

3b. India

Books and Monographs

165. Mehta Sushila. *Revolution and the Status of Women in India*. New Delhi: Metropolitan, 1982. 278 pp.

Describes the changes in women's status as a result of decolonization in India. The first four chapters focus on women's oppression in India in the 19th and early 20th centuries, including Sati, child marriage, purdah and polygamy. Points out that western influences were key in questioning such practices and that the western educated elite tended to argue for women's emancipation. Chapter 6 focuses on women in the Congress Party and the Nationalist movement while chapter 7 reviews legislation on marriage, property and work which was supposed to give women rights and status equal to those of men. Points out that such legislation was nothing more than "paper tigers." Women remain oppressed and subordinate to men. Attributes this to lack of education. In chapters 8 and 9 reviews women in the workforce as university teachers and in sex-segregated professions like engineering, law and architecture.

166. Usha Rao, N.J. *Women in a Developing Society*. New Delhi: Ashish Publishing House, 1983. 180 pp.

Focuses on the status of women in Karnataka State (formerly British Mysore) in India. Chapter 2 is on the history of women in India between 1880 and 1981; chapter 3 is devoted exclusively to women and education. The chapter, which contains literacy statistics and school enrollment data for the 1950s through 1970s, broken down by state, caste and urban/rural residence, argues that despite considerable improvement in girls' school attendance, girls still lag behind boys. While girls may have better access to education, the drop-out rates in the primary grades indicate that they will relapse into illiteracy. The data presented indicate that rural girls have less of an opportunity to be educated than do urban girls, scheduled castes less of an opportunity than unscheduled castes. The remaining chapers of the book are devoted to women's employment. Points out that despite educational advances for women, over time women's workforce participation rates have dropped. Attributes this decline to development policies which have encouraged the displacement of female labor in rural areas with male labor and which have encouraged industries which compete directly with women's household production. Argues that education, both formal and nonformal, is key to incorporating women into the development process.

167. Vohra, Roopa and Arun K. Sen. **Status, Education and Problems of Indian Women.** Delhi: Akshat Publications, 1986. 148 pp.

Argues that education is key to changing women's status in India. Provides data on changes in women's literacy rates to 1981 and reviews women's workforce participation patterns and rates and enumerates problems facing working women and women in general.

Articles

168. Desai, Neera. "Changing Status of Women: Policies and Problems." **Women and Society: The Developmental Perspective.** Edited by Amit Kumar Gupta. New Delhi: Criterion Publications, 1986, pp. 71-100.

Presents a broad perspective on women. Points out the urgent need for women's education, but notes that according to the 1971 census India had an increase of illiterate women from 162 million to 215 million. According to 1981 figures, 80 percent of the children in the 6 to 14 year old age group who were not in school were girls. In higher education women do not achieve equality at any level or type of education—even in teacher training institutes they constituted only 49 percent of enrollment.

169. Jones, Connie A. "Observations on the Current Status of Women in India." **International Journal of Women's Studies** 3 (1980): 1-18.

Discusses the demographic, legal, political, educational, economic and social position of women in India. Argues that women's status remains low and proposes that women be resocialized to challenge present authority structures and change traditional values.

170. Leonard, Karen. "Women in India: Some Recent Perspectives."
Pacific Affairs 52 (1979):   95-107.

Describes the social and educational status of women in India.
Points out that women from upper economic strata have made
substantial achievement in gaining access to university
education and government employment.   Women from low SES
backgrounds, however, have experienced little progress in terms
of basic health status, workforce participation rates and in
gaining literacy.

171. Minattur, Joseph. "Women and the Law: Constitutional Rights
and Continuing Inequalities."   Women in Contemporary India and
South Asia.   Edited by Alfred D'Souza.   New Delhi: Manohar
Publications, 1980, pp. 165-178.

Examines Indian legislation designed to improve women's lives,
including marriage law, employment and education law.   Finds
that despite the legislation, there remains undereducation of
women and the resultant inequalities in the workforce.
Concludes that legislation alone will not bring about
change--India has compulsory education laws and still girls do
not attend school.

172. Srinivas, M.N.   "The Changing Position of Indian Women."   Man 12
(August 1977):   221-238.

Discusses changes in women's status in rural society before,
during and after British colonial rule in India.   Notes the
effects of modernization, urbanization, education and other
actions of social reformers which have benefitted women.

4.   Latin America and the Caribbean

Books and Monographs

173. Carmen Regueiro, Maria del, et al.   La Mujer en sus Actividades.
México: Secretaria de Programación y Presupuesto, Coordinación
General de los Servicios Nacionales de Estatistica, Geografia et
Informatica, 1981.   40 pp.

Discusses the changing status of women in Mexico.   Provides
statistics on women's enrollment in primary and secondary school
and women's workforce participation.   Illustrated.

174. Forde, Norma Monica.   The Status of Women in Barbados: What Has
Been Done Since 1978.   Cave Hill, Barbados: Institute of Social

and Economic Research, University of the West Indies, 1980.   53
pp. (Occasional Paper no. 15)

Assesses progress made for women since the National Commission
on the Status of Women was issued in 1978.   Interviews
government employees and reviews reports and government
documents. Finds that many of the recommendations remain to be
acted upon. Points out that 56 recommendations were made in
education and while they resulted in the teaching of home
economics, agriculture and technical subjects to both sexes,
more needs to be done to provide women with agricultural and
technical training.

175. Grande, Humberto. A Educação Cívica Dos Mulheres. Rio de
Janeiro: Reper Editura, 1967. 172 pp.

Presents a debate from all areas of social foundations of
education on the value and reasons for special consideration of
civic education for women. From history, the author tries
economic motivation; from sociology, a way to meet family needs;
from political science, the need to include women within the
community. Looks briefly at how ideas of civic education for
women fit into feminism.

176. Jiménez de Vega, Mercedes. La Mujer Ecuatoriana: Frustraciones
y Esperanzas. Cubierta: Banco Central del Ecuador, 1981.
123 pp.

Surveys the status of women in politics and education.   The
major focus is on urban women in relation to education and
statistics on education from the last 1970s on primary,
secondary and higher education are provided.   Particular
attention is given higher education showing a growing number
of students (the majority in higher education are women) but
they are segregated into the arts, letters and a lesser though
strong representation in medicine and economics, but there are
almost no women in engineering or the sciences.

177. Klimpel, Felicitas. La Mujer Chilena: El Aporte Femenino al
Progreso de Chile 1910-1960. Santiago de Chile: Editorial
Andres Bello, 1962.

Provides an overview of women's status in Chile between 1910 and
1960, with emphasis on women in the workforce as well as women's
legal status, women in international organizations and the
health and educational status of women. Argues that women's
status along all these dimensions has improved as Chile has
undergone modernization.

178. Lafosse, Violeta Sara et al. **Problematica de la Mujer** en el **Perú.** Lima: Editorial Mendez, 1983. 45 pp.

     Demonstrates gender based inequalities in Peru in the workforce, in education and in sex role ideologies. Uses the 1972 Peruvian census as a data source.

179. Mauras, Marta and Josefina Ossandon. **The Situation of Women in Latin America and the Caribbean and Its Impact on Children.** Mucato, Venezuela: United Nations Children's Fund, Regional Office for the Americas, 1979. 82 pp.

     Focuses on the status of women in Latin America and the Caribbean and reports on a second regional conference on the Integration of Women into the Economic and Social Development of Latin America.   Reviews women in poverty, women's education, health and employment as well as family life.   Presents statistics on educational enrollments and literacy rates for 1960 and 1970.   These figures show gains in literacy rates for women which exceed those for men in Brazil, Costa Rica, Chile, Dominican Republic and Uruguay (there are no similar gains in Guatemala and Peru).   Points out that despite this progress, women's schooling and literacy rates still lag behind men's.

180. Naciones Unidas.   Comisión Economica para América Latina y el Caribe.   **El Decenio de la Mujer en el Escenario Latinoamericano.** Santiago: United Nations, 1986. 86 pp.

     Provides an overview of women's participation in the family, the work place and in mass organizations, focusing on rural women. Presents a number of statistics on educational enrollments for 19 countries and discusses the effect of social class on women's access to education.

181. Rama, Germán W.   **Educación y Sociedad en América Latina y el Caribe.**   Santiago: UNICEF, Projector Desarrollo y Educación en Américan Latina y el Caribe, 1980. 276 pp.

     Focuses on the relation between education and the social structure in Latin America with some information about gender based inequalities in schooling.

182. Rosales, Sara Elisa.   **Consideraciónes Preliminares sobre la Situación de la Mujer in Honduras.** N.P.:   Ediciones SITRAUNAH, 1980. 43 pp.

     Describes women's position and exploitation in Honduras. Contains information on political participation, laws and commitments to the United Nations.   Gives figures on education from 1973 that show women teachers were 73 percent of primary

school teachers and 24 percent of those at the university level.
In 1974 women were 12 percent of the enrollment in professional
training programs and 13 percent of the graduates. Looking at
the time span from 1847 to 1978 shows that at the university
women graduates formed 18 percent of the lawyers but less than 1
percent of the administrators or engineers.

183. Sievent, Maria Teresa.   La Mujer y el Proyecto Principal de
Educación en América Latina y el Caribe.   Santiago: UNESCO
Oficina Regional de Educación, 1983.

Surveys women's educational needs in Latin America and sets
three goals: 1) extension of literacy to rural women; 2)
development of programs which will facilitate women's workforce
entry; 3) improvement of nutrition and health care via
nonformal education.

184. Thomson, Marilyn. Women of El Salvador: The Price of Freedom.
Philadelphia: Institute for the Study of Human Issues, 1986.
166 pp.

Focuses on women in El Salvador. Part 1 is on women and work in
rural areas, health and family planning; part 2 is on women in
struggle against the U.S. backed regime and includes chapters on
the popular church, trade unions and market women.   Chapter 10
is on the new education and describes the ANDES 21 de junio
(Associacion Nacional de Educadores Salvadorenos) which is a
predominantly female teachers' association. Part 3 focuses on
women's organizations, both right wing and progressive; and part
4 is on women in controlled zones and the FMLN education
programs run by ANDES 21.

Articles

185. Bazante, Julia.   "Notas para un Planteamiento de la Educación de
la Mujer Ecuatoriana."   Revista Ecuatoriana de Educación 54-55
(1964-1965): 168-180.

Provides a general overview of the status of women in Ecuador.
Argues that women's low status is due to both underdevelopment
and women's lack of education. Urges that schooling be extended
to women and that workforce opportunities be opened to them as
well.

186. Conde, Maryse.   "L'Image de la Petite Fille."   Recherche
Pédagogie et Culture 8 (no. 44, 1979): 39-93.

Summarizes three novels, Sapotille et le Serin d'Argile by
Michele Lacrosil, Pluie et Vent sur Telume'e Mirale by S.

Schwarz-Bart and **Le Temps des Madras** by Francoise Ega. The novels deal with both the psychological and physical realities of intra-family relations, growing up, education and race of women in the Antilles over several generations.

187. Drayton, Kathleen. "Introduction: Women and Education." **Women and Education. Women in the Caribbean Project. Vol. 5.** Edited by Joycelin Massiah. Cave Hill, Barbados: Institute of Social and Economic Research, University of the West Indies, 1982, pp. vii-xv.

Provides an overview of women's education in Barbados and relates education to changes in women's status over time. Argues that the expansion of education, particularly secondary education, has reinforced class divisions among women.

188. Guarin de Vizcaya, Delina. "Normas Legales que Afectan a la Mujer en la Salud, el Trabajo y la Educación." **La Mujer y el Desarrollo en Colombia.** Edited by Magdalene Leon de Leal. Bogota: Asociación Colombiana para el Estudio.de la Población, 1977, pp. 229-272.

Summarizes the laws affecting women in education from 1819 to 1976. Covers all levels of education and teachers as well as students at those levels.

189. Lipeovich de Querol, Tamara and Esther Romero San Martin. "Panorama de la Educación Femenina en el Perú." **Convergence 2** (Nov. 1969): 37-48.

Provides an overview of women's educational opportunity and status in Peru.

190. Sara-Lafosse, Violeta. "La Condición Femenina en el Perú." **Rikchay** 2 (1972): 32-35.

Surveys women's status in Peru and points out that women are discriminated against in both the workforce and in the schools. Women's workforce participation levels are relatively low and argues that the women's movement and increasing educational levels will help both to increase that participation and, through that, improve women's status.

4a.   Cuba

Books and Monographs

191. Sejourne, Laurette. **La Mujer Cubana en el Quehacer de la Historia.** México: Siglo XXI Editores, S.A., 1980. 412 pp.

Focuses on women and revolution in Cuba. Points out that the revolution placed a high priority on women's education. Not only did the government provide school places, it provided job training for women as well. Provides data on women's participation in the workforce, broken down by occupation, and argues that, despite the progress made, women are still discriminated against.

Articles

192. Casal, Lourdes. "Revolution and Conciencia: Women in Cuba." **Women, War and Revolution.** Edited by Carol R. Berkin and Clara M. Lovett. New York: Holmes and Meier, 1980, pp. 183-206.

Examines the status of women in prerevoluntionary Cuba and the changes the Revolution has provoked in such fields as laborforce, education, politics and ideology. In prerevolutionary Cuba, equality for both sexes was guaranteed in legal terms but significant discrimination against women remained in all other areas. The revolution has brought increases in the participation of women in the paid workforce, in the highest levels of the educational system, especially high-status technical fields, and in the political system, although women are underrepresented in the party. Argues that the primacy of economic development and socialist construction has allowed the coexistance of new egalitarian norms and the old sexual ideology and a conservative view of the role of the family, but that the transformations at the cultural and ideological level concerning the status of women are still continuing.

193. Cole, Johnnetta. "Women in Cuba: The Revolution Within the Revolution." **Comparative Perspectives of Third World Women.** Edited by Beverly Lindsay. New York: Preager, 1980, pp. 162-178.

Shows that women's status in Cuba dramatically advanced after the revolution. The 1960 literacy campaign eradicated illiteracy and government policies have brought more women into the schools than ever. The increases in woman's education have been accompanied by increases in women's participation in politics and in cultural activities.

194. Franco, Zoila. "Women in the Transformation of Cuban Education." **Prospects** 5 (1975): 387-390.

Maintains that discrimination against women in education has been removed since the Cuban Revolution. Traces reforms in the schools and the literacy campaign. While participation of males and females has not been achieved, women's enrollments have increased and a multitude of training courses have provided women with skills necessary to enter the workforce. Despite this, women's participation in the workforce lags behind men's and women are employed in female dominated fields. Sixty-five percent of Ministry of Education management, technical staff and employees are women. Government plans to increase the participation of women in the workforce, include the construction of childcare facilities and the further expansion of education.

195. Ramos, Ana. "La Mujer y la Revolución en Cuba." **Casa de las Américas** 65-66 (1971): 56-72.

Describes the Cuban government's programs after the revolution designed to bring women into the workforce via the schools.

5.   Middle East

Books and Monographs

196. Altorki, Soraya. **Women in Saudi Arabia: Ideology and Behavior among The Elite.** New York: Colombia University Press, 1986. 183 pp.

Focuses on change among elite women in Jiddah, Saudi Arabia, by comparing the behavior and ideology of three generations of women in 13 families. The study is based on field work conducted in 1971, 1974 and 1984. Two generations of women studied did have some education. In Saudi society education of women has little to do with a family's elite status although in the 1940s some elite families began to have their daughters tutored at home. In the 1950s girls from these elite families began to board and attend schools in Lebanon and Egypt. Most of the initiative for girls' education came from their mothers. A central argument of the book is that the elites have taken the lead in changing life styles and although Saudi society is sexually asymmetrical, changes in relations between males and females have occurred and are most obvious in family life. The changes in the life styles of elite women noted are the movement from extended to nuclear family, less seclusion for women within the household, greater social networking for women outside of the family group, less strict veiling practices, more social mixing with men and changes in pilgrimage participation. Women of the middle and younger generation who have more education are less willing to grant men unrestrained authority in the household. Women do assert their autonomy more. Younger generation women tend to spend more time with their husbands and take greater interest in promoting their children's education. They take on the role of teachers and mothers. Changes in ideology have accompanied the changes in behaviors and attitudes of these elite women and their educated husbands.

197. Fürst, Alduild. **Bildungs—und Berufsmöglichkeiten der Frau in Vorderen Orient.** Wein: Institut fur Bildungs—und Entwicklungsforschung (IBE): 1976. 130 pp. (IBE Forschungsdokumentation 7)

Presents a short overview of women in Islam and a slightly more detailed picture of the process of building a school system amid fears of colonial control and a legacy of the Koranic schools. Presents detailed pictures of women in the Egyptian and Syrian education systems. Stresses the youthfulness of the population and the very traditional place of women (confined to the home) even in the countryside—advocating nonformal technical training as a means of reaching such women. For Syria, there is an even greater stress on occupation and training. Indicates almost 80 percent of working women are in agriculture but even in agriculture they form less than one third of the workforce. In most other work areas, including banking, communications and service women are less than one tenth the workforce and they work predominantly in non-Muslim areas.

198. Ingrams, Doreen. **The Awakened: Women in Iraq.** London: Third World Centre for Research and Publishing, 1983. 173 pp.

Provides an overview of the changing status of women in Iraq and argues that since the Ba'th Socialist Party has come into power, women have been emancipated. Provides a history of Iraq and an overview of childrearing practices and discusses the Ba'th literacy campaign, government policies towards women and the development of the Iraqi Women's Federation. The book ends with a chapter on women in the professions and women in arts and literature. There are few or no statistics presented in this book. Much of the book accepts at face value the claims of the Iraqi government and those of the Women's Federation, which is an arm of the government.

199. Lebner, Dietlinde. **Zur sozialen Lage der Frau in Entwicklungslandern: Eine Fallstudie: Algerien.** München: Tuduv-Verlagsgessellschaft, 1978. 201 pp.

States a general theory of patriarchy in developing countries and then considers the special case of Algeria in its Muslim and

revolutionary context.   Uses the overall concept of
socialization to consider women's roles in the family, the
formal educational sphere, the work place and politics.   There
has been some improvement for women in primary education, a five
fold increase (slightly greater than that for men) in secondary
education and a rise from 20 percent to 25 percent of university
enrollment for women from 1962 to 1975.   Women have also had
tremendous gains in legal and medical education.   In 1970, 56
percent of 10 to 14 year old girls were illiterate as were 97
percent of women 40 to 59 years old.   Does not relate education
level to the job market or political participation in a
statistical manner but implies higher participation in both for
the educated.

200. Maher, Vanessa. **Women and Property in Morocco. Their Changing
Relation to the Process of Social Stratification in the Middle
Atlas.** Cambridge: Cambridge University Press, 1974. 238 pp.

Presents an ethnographic study of Berber women in the Akhdar
region of Morocco.   Most of the study is irrelevant to
education.   Chapter 5 alone focuses on education as part of the
system of stratification which keeps women subservient to men.
Points out that the distribution and content of modern education
prevents most Akhdaris, including women, from becoming socially
mobile.   Educational attendance declines with distance from
towns, urban schools are far superior to rural schools, the
content of education is still very French influenced and
irrelevant to the bulk of the rural population.   In rural areas,
there is ambivalence toward the schools, given it is an
intrusion of the state.   In Akhdar only 8 percent of the girls
are in school, most of these girls live in the town.   Most
parents believe that education is irrelevant and may be a
corrupting influence.   Girls who receive secondary education,
who are few in number, become nurses, teachers and monitors in
schools.

201. Rashedi, Khorram. **Les Femmes en Iran Avant et Après la
Révolution.** n.p.: Nouvelles Editions Rupture, 1983. 198 pp.

Contains far more information about Iran before than after the
revolution.   This information stresses the patriarchial values
of Iranian culture and is caustic about the role of westernizing
women of the middle classes who insulted these values.   Does
present a picture of educational attempts to modernize begun
with government control of schools in 1920.   Yet, Koranic
schools remained teaching little but memorization.   Describes a
major attempt at education with the "Army of Knowledge" in 1961
including concern for women and women recruits to this army.
This drive and other demonstration projects raised literacy to
two thirds of men and half of women in the cities and to one

third of men and less than 10 percent of women in rural areas.
Does look inside school, to describe patterns of strong
authority and emphasis on strict discipline (preferences which
showed up in a common marriage pattern of middle-class girls
wedding their professors). For the middle-class woman teaching
became acceptable as an occupation, (the only other choice was
nursing which husbands--who had to approve work outside the
home--frowned upon). The revolution has strengthened
traditional values and would seem to have negative effects in
terms of women's education, but little firm evidence is given to
demonstrate this conclusion.

202. Soffan, Linda Usra. **The Women of the United Arab Emirates.**
London: Croom Helm, 1980. 127 pp.

Focuses on factors affecting women's status in the United Arab
Emirates (UAE) and argues that while Islamic law provides women
with status equal to men's, tribal custom combined with some
religious scholars' interpretations of Islamic law have combined
to keep women subservient. The book begins by examining Islamic
views of women, and the traditional position of women in UAE
society. It then turns to marriage and the family, including
child and arranged marriages, the role of education in improving
women's status, women in the laborforce and public services
designed to aid women.

Articles

203. Cosar, Fatima Mansur. "Women in Turkish Society." **Women in the
Muslim World.** Edited by Lois Beck and Nikki Keddie. Cambridge:
Harvard University Press, 1978, pp. 124-140.

Examines the extent to which the position of women has changed
in Turkey as a result of republican laws, changes in social
attitudes and changes in the structure of society. Finds that
many girls do not attend school because parents do not value
girls' education, but this attitude disappears with middle and
upper-class parents. Believes that education is the key in the
long run to women's emancipation in Turkey because it will serve
to change attitudes.

204. Fischer, Michael M.J. "On Changing the Concept and Position of
Persian Women." **Women in the Muslim World.** Edited by Lois Beck
and Nikki Keddie. Cambridge: Harvard University Press, 1978,
pp. 189-215.

Examines the changes in the position of Persian women and
discusses the reasons and consequences for them. Uses
ethnographic data from the author's field work in Yazd (1970-71)

and in Orum (1975), two Iranian towns. Headings include
"Indexes of Change: Erosion of an Ideology", "Marriage and
Inheritance", "Community Religion" and "Honor, Dignity,
Liberation, and Emancipation." Talks about women's education,
which is a very minor part of this essay, under "Indexes of
Change." Points out that though the admission of women to
education and public employment is dramatic, the statistics
demonstrate that only a beginning has been made. The government
claims to be and is among the major forces promoting change.
There has been increasing public education for girls since the
1920s. In 1940, the University of Tehran became coeducational.
Today there is an impressive increase of women university
students, although getting equal degrees does not yet mean
obtaining equally good jobs. Argues that change is occurring
even in the most conservative circles--the religious schools.

205. Hayani, I. "The Changing Role of Arab Women." Convergence 13
     (nos. 1-2, 1980): 136-141.

     Outlines the status and roles of women in the Syrian Arab
     Republic. Points out that educated women are but a small
     proportion of women. Seventy-five percent of all Syrian women
     are illiterate as opposed to 50 percent of all men. Educated
     women have entered nontraditional fields such as animal
     husbandry and industry. Concludes that in most Arab countries
     women's inferior status in the society and their lack of
     education is due to social values and not to any constraints
     imposed by Islam. Believes that programs aimed at modernizing
     Arab countries will provide women with equality, especially as
     women become educated.

206. Jaynes, G. "Iranian Women: Looking Beyond the Chador." New
     York Times Magazine 22 (April 1979): 36-38, 94.

     Explores women's attitudes under the Islamic Republic of Iran.
     Points out that three quarters of women in Iran are illiterate
     and that they are uninterested in obtaining equality with men.
     Most educated women, who form a very small minority, insist on
     equality and have formed a group urging the extension of
     education to women.

207. Maher, Vanessa. "Women and Social Change in Morocco." Women in
     the Muslim World. Edited by Lois Beck and Nikki Keddie.
     Cambridge: Harvard University Press, 1978, pp. 100-123.

     Examines the relationship between women and social economic
     changes in Morocco. Suggests that in Morocco, women have been
     forced to represent a traditional model of social reality.
     Discusses issues concerning women in the town and country, the
     relation of women to property and women in the market, French

colonialism, women in contemporary Morocco, attitudes about fertility, contradictions between ideology and reality and education of women. Finds that in the province where the research was undertaken, 8 percent of girls of primary school age are at school. The proportion of girls to boys in the first year of secondary school is one to five, there is a sharp fall in the number of girls attending college after the first year relative to boys and only a negligible proportion carry on after the fourth year. On the whole, about 50 percent of town girls and 10 percent of rural ones are at school. Concludes that the underrepresentation of girls schooled is because the Arabs and Berbers both view education as a waste for girls and is proper only if it does not disturb traditional relationships.

208. Minces, Juliette. "Women in Algeria." Women in the Muslim World. Edited by Lois Beck and Nikki Keddie. Cambridge: Harvard University Press, 1978, pp. 159-171.

Focuses on women in Algeria in traditional society, during the resistance and since independence. Points out that in colonial Algeria Algerians were denied educational opportunity and were forced by the French to choose between educating their sons and daughters. After independence there has been rapid expansion of the schools, but despite this women are still a minority at all levels and their social status remains inferior to men's.

209. Molyneux, Maxine. "Women and Revolution in the People's Democratic Republic of Yemen." Feminist Review 1 (1979): 5-20.

Describes the changes in women's rights in and after the 1967 revolution in Yemen. Shows that since independence and the socialist revolution, women have received access to schools. Key to changes in women's roles has been the Women's Union, which is discussed in some detail.

210. Pakizegi, Behuaz. "Legal and Social Position of Iranian Women." Women in the Muslim World. Edited by Lois Beck and Nikki Keddie. Cambridge: Harvard University Press, 1978, pp. 216-226.

Examines women's status as defined through Iranian law. Points out that while elementary education is compulsory, parents do not often send their girls to school. Argues, however, that legal change is a precursor to other changes--in education and in daily life.

211. Qayyum, Shah Abdul. "Women in the Muslim World--A Case Study of Egypt." Women of the World: Illusion and Reality. Edited by Urmila Phadnis and Indira Malani. New Delhi: Vikas, 1978, pp. 150-174.

Argues that since the 1952 Revolution, women's social status has improved and women have gained the right to divorce, polygamy has been abolished and women have had expanded access to education and to political and executive positions in society.

212. Tessler, Mark A. et al. "Women's Emancipation in Tunisia." Women in the Muslim World. Edited by Lois Beck and Nikki Keddie. Cambridge: Harvard University Press, 1978, pp. 141–158.

Examines and discusses women's emancipation in Tunisia in the 1950s, 1960s and 1970s. Shows a change of attitudes toward women's emancipation at different time periods by using both literature and interview studies conducted in 1967 and in 1973. During the first decade of independence, Tunisia had a particularly coherent and explicit program of planned social transformation. Points out that the greatest stimulus for change was education. In the decade following independence, literacy climbed from 15 percent to over 30 percent, the proportion of children attending primary school grew from 25 percent to 70–80 percent, the proportion of students completing high school increased from 3 percent to almost 30 percent. Women were 31 percent of the school population in 1958 and they were 39 percent in 1968. The expansion of education introduced new patterns of thought and behavior and added to the pressure for women's emancipation. Finds that the government today places less emphasis on education than in the past. Concludes that the future for women's education and liberation is not encouraging. Tunisia is no longer the radical and daring innovator it once was.

We have included in this part of the bibliography histories of women's education and historical studies that focus either on biography of educated women in the past, on institutional histories or intellectual histories about women's schooling.

1. Africa

Books and Monographs

213. Cutrufelli, Maria Rosa. **Women of Africa: Roots of Oppression.** London: Zed Books, 1983. 186 pp.

Focuses on the conditions of women in Africa and argues that the slave trade, colonialism and ensuing poverty led to the depopulation of much of Africa.   These trends led to greater emphasis on "maternity" and the reproductive functions of women than was the case in pre-colonial Africa.   At the same time, because of the impoverishment that colonialism brought, women's work in production became more critical.   The sexual division of labor in Africa was not between production and reproduction as was the case in much of the West; it was based on women as productive laborers in the subsistence sector of the economy while men worked in the modern, industrial sector earning wages. Such a sex role division of labor further impoverished women. Chapter 5 focuses on women's education and on women's organizations.   Reviews women's initiation rites in traditional society which focus on fecundity.   Points out that male initiation had no such emphasis. Formal education introduced by the West discriminated against women from the start. It tended to provide women with training in sewing.   In the present glaring inequalities exist in women's access to education relative to men.

214. Strobel, Margaret. **Muslim Women in Mombasa, 1890-1975.** New Haven and London: Yale University Press, 1979. 258 pp.

Studies the changes in women's status under colonialism in Mombasa, Kenya, from 1890 to 1975. This was a time of the transformation of patriarchy.   As wage labor was extended to men, women's status relative to men declined and in World War I, men had even taken over women's wage labor as domestic servants. Not only did colonialism undermine women's economic life, it also changed the ideology of sex roles. Under colonialism the British introduced new sex roles and ideologies via the schools and the cinema. Muslim elders introduced limited female education (discussed in some detail in chapter 4) to prevent the colonial administration from establishing more objectionable schools. The education introduced helped women enter the modern workforce initially in occupations which served women—medicine and teaching—and increasingly in secretarial work (described in chapter 5). Schooling did broaden women's experiences and educated women did go on to form a number of women's organizations such as the Muslim Women's Institute and the Muslim Women's Cultural Association.

Articles

215. Adams, Lois. "Women in Zaire: Disparate Status and Roles." Comparative Perspectives of Third World Women. Edited by Beverly Lindsay. New York: Praeger, 1980, pp. 55-57.

Shows that women have been disadvantaged in educational attainment both under colonialism and under the post-independence government in Zaire. During the colonial period, Congolese women had few opportunities to gain a western education. Women's education was inferior and often limited to training in homemaking skills. Higher education was not open to women until well after independence. Even after independence, women's access to education was limited. Girls are often directed to home economics programs despite their real aspirations. Their education suffers from inferior facilities, inadequate instruction and society's negative attitudes toward girls' learning. Women's enrollment in secondary and higher education is still low. Argues that scarcity of educational statistics on women even today indicates the relative neglect of women in academic life.

216. Barthel, Diane. "Women's Educational Experience Under Colonialism: Toward a Diachronical Model." Signs. 11 (1985): 137-154.

Builds a historical model of colonial educational opportunities for women. Evidence is from Senegal, West Africa. The model demonstrates that women's education has been determined by a generational progression, a process in which women have been actors rather than simply subjects. Suggests also that development of women's education in Africa followed a three-step progression from an early effort to educate men, to a later attempt to educate a few women pioneers for "modern" female roles, to a final plan for extending educational opportunity for more women.

217. Campbell, Penelope. "Presybterian West African Missions: Women as Converts and Agents of Social Change." **Journal of Presbyterian History** 56 (1978): 121-132.

Traces the evangelical and educational efforts of American Presbyterian missionaries in West Africa in the 19th Century and examines the role of women in establishing African churches as well as the missionary impact on women's position in African society. By educating girls, the missionaries tried to create a supply of potential Christian brides who would found Christian homes. However, female education suffered from the reluctance of African villagers to send their daughters to school as well as from practical problems such as a dearth of volunteers. Concludes that the Presbyterian impact on the position of women in West Africa seems to have been scant, but that female African converts were the backbone and sustaining power in the African mission churches.

218. de Carvalho, Abilio. "Intrução e Educação da Mulher Africana." **Portugal em Africaa** 13 (March-April, 1950): 65-75.

Traces educational activity of Jesuits and Dominicans back to the 1500s but this included little female education. Notes first female education in the 1890s especially aftter the arrival of the Sisters of St. Joseph de Cluny. A major expansion took place in the 1920s from 90 to 225 schools and 6,600 (one tenth female) to 24,000 (one fifth female) pupils. By 1940 there were 56,000 children in school of whom 16,500 were female. Although statistics for all Mozambique were not available, those from one geographic area showed continued expansion into the 1950s. In 1944 in this district there were 99,000 pupils of whom 44,000 were girls.

219. Lamba, Isaac C. "African Women's Education in Malawi, 1875-1952." **Journal of Educational Administration and History** 14 (1982): 46-54.

Traces the development of women's education in Malawi since 1875 when the first mission arrived in the country. For fifty years after 1875 education in Malawi operated solely as a missionary enterprise. Points out that missionary education placed an emphasis on spiritual training for evangelism rather than on academic and professional training. Women's education was neglected because of the scarcity of teachers and European views of Africans and women as inferior. Argues that the depressing element in both missionary and colonial educational policies was the intent to ensure the perpetuation of white dominance and

African docility, and that the trend of neglecting women's
education continued until an African government could reassess
their education from their own perspective.

220. Morrow, S. "No Girl Leave School Unmarried: Mable Shaw and the
Education of Girls at Mbereshi, Northern Rhodesia, 1915-1940."
The International Journal of African Historical Studies 19
(1986): 601-635.

Describes Mabel Shaw, the assertive black principal of Mbereshi
Girls' Boarding School in Northern Rhodesia and examines the
school's attempt to inculcate a form of Christian indoctrination
whereby students were educated above all for Christian marriage.
Describes the life of Mabel Shaw, her ideals and goals to have
African women living for God, not just for men, the pupils and
their backgrounds, the aim of the school and its organization,
the finding of suitable husbands for the students, the setting
up of the maternity training and Infant Welfare Center, the
concepts of education, and the conflicts resulting from Shaw's
ideas and the secular education authorities--the changes she
made and what followed her tutelage.

221. Whitehead, Clive. "The Education of Women and Girls: An Aspect
of   British   Colonial   Policy."   Journal   of   Educational
Administration and History 16 (1984):   24-34.

Examines British policy toward the education of women and girls
in British Africa during the period since the First World War.
Concludes that the low enrollments of girls in colonial schools
at the time should not be interpreted as evidence of any
official lack of interest or concern for female education by the
Colonial Office or the territorial governments but should be
regarded as the influence of financial constraints and the
philosophy of indirect rule which provided the basis for
colonial policy.

222. Yates, Barbara. "Church, State and Education in Belgian Africa:
Implications for Contemporary Third World Women." Women's
Education in the Third World: Comparative Perspectives. Edited
by Gail P. Kelly and Carolyn M. Elliott. Albany: SUNY Press,
1982, pp. 127-151.

Traces the transference of Belgian attitudes towards women to
Zaire via the colonial education system. Points out that
Belgians offered very little education to women and the
education which they provided girls was confined to domestic
sciences and the development of female virtues. These values
were transmitted through the Catholic Church. Points out that
the legacy today is that women in contemporary Zaire have lost

status, sex role divisions of labor in society have become
distorted and women remain undereducated.

223. Yates, Barbara.   "Colonialism, Education and Work: Sex
Differentiation in Colonial Zaire."   **Women and Work in Africa.**
Edited by Edna Bay.   Boulder, Colorado: Westview Press, 1982,
pp. 127-152.

Traces the development of education from 1908 to 1960 in the
Belgian Congo and provides evidence from curriculum and
legislation to show how schools were used as agents for
socializing Africans into conservative western views
particularly those of family life and occupation.   The schools
prepared males to be religious assistants for evangelism and
subalterns for the administration and females to be Christian
wives and mothers.   Presents educational outcomes and
occupational consequences of such education which left women
economically disadvantaged.   Concludes colonialism created a gap
between male and female participation in education and the
modern economy because of deliberate and continuous efforts to
provide differential education by gender, which continues to
affect the lives of women in Zaire.

la.   **Nigeria**

Books and Monographs

224. Callaway, Helen.   Gender, Culture and Empire: European Women
in Colonial Nigeria.   London: The Macmillan Press, Ltd., 1987.
278 pp.

Studies women who came to Nigeria either in the British colonial
service or as wives to British administrators.   Points out that
there were few women in the colonial service; those who were
tended to be nurses and teachers.   They initially came to
Nigeria to serve the British community, but by the interwar
years were instrumental in opening schools for Nigerian girls
and in extending health care services as nurses.   These women
were, despite their British nationality, discriminated against
by the colonial bureaucracy.   Argues that without them education
for girls would have been more seriously retarded than it was
when independence came.

Articles

225. Johnson, Cheryl. "Class and Gender: A Consideration of Yoruba Women During the Colonial Period." Women and Class in Africa. Edited by Claire Robertson and Iris Berger. New York: Africana Publishing Co., 1986, pp. 237-254.

Examines how colonialism changed the status of Yoruba women of southwestern Nigeria. Discusses women's anticolonial activity and three organizations; The Lagos Market Women's Association, The Nigerian Women's Party and the Abeokuta Women's Union and their accomplishments for girls' education, literacy for adult women, employment and economic and political rights for women.

226. Mann, Kristin. "The Dangers of Dependence: Christian Marriage among Elite Women in Lagos Colony, 1880-1915." Journal of African History 24 (1983): 37-56.

Examines the African Christian elite women's acceptance of Christian marriage and the impact of Christianity, European education and colonial legal and economic changes on elite women's roles and opportunities.

Odoyoye, Mercy Amba. "Standing on Both Feet; Education and Leadership Training of Women in the Methodist Church, Nigeria." The Ecumenical Review 33 (1981): 60-71.

See item #415.

227. Okonkwo, Rina. "Adelaide Casely Hayford Cultural Nationalist and Feminist." Phylon 42 (1981): 45-51.

Provides a brief biography of Adelaide Casely Hayford (1868-1960), wife of the Gold Coast nationalist Joseph Ephriam Casely Hayford.

228. Tibenderana, Peter Kazenga. "The Beginning of Girls' Education in the Native Administration School in Northern Nigeria, 1930-1945." Journal of African History 26 (1985): 93-109.

Argues that although opposition to female education existed among Muslims during the colonial era, it was not the main factor which retarded the advancement of girls' education between 1930 and 1945. Suggests that the British educational policy, which placed much emphasis on coeducation, instead of building girls' schools, coupled with the parsimony with which the British administration spent money on girls' education, were mainly responsible for hindering the devlopment of female education in Northern Nigeria during the colonial era. The introduction of coeducation made western education for girls unappealing to many Muslim parents who otherwise would have sent

their daughters to school if girls' schools had existed in
sufficient numbers.

229. Yeld, Rachel. "Education Amongst Women and Girls in the Kebbi
Emirate of Northern Nigeria." Education and Politics in
Nigeria. Edited by Hans N. Weiler. Freiburg: Verlag Rombach,
1964, pp. 65-79.

Traces and describes the development of women's education in the
Moslem Hausa society of Northern Nigeria. Attempts to introduce
girls' education in the Northern Region were started over two
decades after boys' education was introduced at the beginning of
this century. Argues that because of the relation of school
education of girls to subsequent marriage to men of high status
who practice purdah, the education of girls has not improved
women's inferior position within the household or in religious,
social and political life. Points out that educational efforts
in the region have had a limited impact on social change because
there are no overall social or economic advantages to be
achieved through education, and because certain aspects of the
formal education conflict with the customary roles of
individuals in the society or with religious doctrine.

2.   Asia

Articles

230. Bryson, Hugh. "The Education of Girls in the Nineteenth
Century." Malaysia (November 1970): 11-14.

Gives an overview of education of girls in Malay Peninsula in
the 19th Century. Argues that the education for girls in the
beginning was merely a means for the missionaries to preach the
Gospel and to convert people to Christianity, and that it was
not until the latter half of the century that schools gained
official financial support.

231. Bocquet-Siek, Margaret. "The Peranankan Chinese Woman at a
Crossroad." Women's Work and Women's Roles: Economics and
Everyday Life in Indonesia, Malaysia and Singapore. Edited by
Lenore Manderson. Canberra: The Australian National
University, Development Studies Center, 1983, pp. 31-53.
(Monograph no. 32)

Explores the social and educational changes for Peranankan
Chinese women in Indonesia in the 1920s and 1930s. These women
were educated in Chinese/English and to a lesser extent Dutch

colonial schools. Points out that education in the 1920s and 1930s did not result in new careers or occupations for these girls. Yet, educated girls did begin to change marriage patterns and were involved in intergenerational struggles with parents over the right to choose their marriage partners.

232. Langmore, D. "A Neglected Force: White Women Missionaries in Papua 1874-1914." Journal of Pacific History 17 (1982): 138-157.

Describes the works and the lives of the women who accounted for more than one-third of the missionaries who served in Papua New Guinea during the forty years before 1914. Besides teaching, nursing and welfare work, they contributed to the improvement of the status of the women on the island. Despite the great contribution, they were not given the same exalted status that male missionaries enjoyed.

Manderson, Lenore. "Bottle Feeding and Ideology in Colonial Malaya: The Production of Change." International Journal of Health Services 12 (1982): 597-616.

See item #1044

233. Manderson, Lenore. "The Development and Direction of Female Education in Peninsular Malaysia." Journal of the Malaysian Branch of the Royal Asiatic Society 51 (1978): 100-122.

Reviews the history of female education in Malaysia. Points out that from early in the 19th Century to Independence female enrollments were lower than those of males. After independence school enrollments increased dramatically for children of all races and sex differences in school attendance declined. The vocational bias of female education has persisted in curriculum. Parental and societal attitudes that allocate women to roles as mothers and wives still prevent women from attaining full educational equality.

234. Soriano, Liceria Brillantes. "Women and Education." Philippine Law Journal 50 (1975): 88-102.

Provides a short history of women's education in the Philippines since the first schools for females were opened in the 17th Century. Argues that the American occupation provided coeducational schooling and extended access to schooling. Women have attained the same educational levels as have men. The major problem today is educating rural women so they can contribute to national development.

2a.   China

Books and Monographs

235. Martin-Liao, Tienchi.   Frauenerziehung im Alten China: Eine
Analyse der Frauenbucher.   Bochum: Herausgeber Chinathemen,
1984.   145 pp.

Analyzes textbooks for women in use in China from 200 B.C.
through 1911.   The texts covered subjects like sexual behavior,
women's secondary place in society, acceptable social roles for
women and work expectations.   About half of the book contains
translation excerpts from the textbooks.

236. Yao, Esther S. Lee.   Chinese Women: Past and Present.
Mesquite, Texas: Ide House, 1983.   260 pp.

Provides a history of women's changing status in China from
before 208 B.C. to the present.   Argues that women's status
deteriorated greatly under the Ch'ing dynasty.   The women's
movement which arose in the late 19th Century focused on
footbinding and access to education.   Points out in chapter 5
that the earliest educational initiatives for women were made by
missionaries.   Education for women became a cause of the
self-strengthening movement as it was seen as a means for
modernizing China and throwing off imperialism.   Chapter 6 looks
at women in the People's Republic of China, and the advances
they have made in legal status and in the workforce.

Articles

237. Chan, Itty.   "Women of China: From the Three Obediences to Half
the Sky."   Journal of Research and Development in Education 10
(no. 4, 1977):   38-52.

Describes women's education and virtual enslavement in pre-20th
Century China.   Women were educated to be obedient to their
fathers, husbands and sons.   Despite this, there were a number
of significant women poets and political figures who came from
elite families.   After the Kuomintang Revolution in 1912, new
educational opportunities opened to women.   These have been
expanded under the Communist government which has promised full
equality.   Major gains have been made for women in all areas,
including education, despite the fact that equality between men
and women has not yet been attained.

238. Bradshaw, Sue.   "Catholic Sisters in China. An Effort to Raise
the Status of Women."   Women in China: Current Directions in

Historical Scholarship. Edited by Richard W. Guisso and Stanley Johannesen. Youngstown, NY: Philo Press, 1981, pp. 201-214.

Reviews the work of the American Catholic sisters in China from the middle of the 19th Century to the early 1950s. Appraises the contribution that they made to improving the status of women in China. Describes how they provided the women in China with a basic education along with handicrafts to enable them to improve their earning abilities and how they introduced improved health care services and health habits.

239. Liu, Mei Ching. "Women and the Media in China: An Historical Perspective" Journalism Quarterly 62 (1985): 45-52.

Reviews the history of the first decade of the 20th Century, in which Chinese women began their fight for emancipation with the help of a few male reformists and the first women journalists. Describes the important part that educated women played in this period.

240. Spade, Beatrice. "The Education of Women in China During the Southern Dynasty." Journal of Asian History 13 (1979): 15-41.

Focuses on the role of the women scholars during the period of the Southern Dynasties (A.D. 400-500). This was a period of disorder in China and, as a result of factional warfare, the educational system fell into dissolution. Despite this, the Southern Dynasties competed with each other and with the North in areas of erudition and civilization. In this context a group of intelligent, highly educated women from bureaucratic and court families became prominent in family instruction. These women often entered Buddhist monastaries as scholars and later became prominent as scholars and teachers in Taoist sects.

2b.   India

Books and Monographs

241. Ahmad, Karuna The Social Context of Women's Education in India, 1921-1981: Tentative Formulations. New Delhi: Nehru Memorial Museum and Library, 1982.

Discusses women's education in India during the period 1921-1981. Focuses on certain key issues that have emerged on the subject such as growth and expansion of women's education, regional variation, religious variation, co-education and curricular changes. Attributes these issues to socio-cultural factors like the practice of Purdah. sex segregation, the framework of role socialization and early marriage among certain communities and parts of India.

242. Agnew, Vijay. **Elite Women in Indian Politics.** New Delhi, Vikas Publishing House, 1979. 163 pp.

Describes the history of women's involvement in the anticolonial struggles in the late 19th and early 20th Centuries. Women from wealthy and liberal families, for example the Nehru family, actively participated in the nationalist movement with support of their male family members. These women were educated by private tutors or by missionaries and later at universities in Britain and Europe. The mass participation in the 1930 Satyagraha led by Mahatma Gandhi gave women opportunities for political training and enabled them to gain social recognition. Social reform movements also promoted education among widows of the upper middle class in order to make them teachers for girls' schools. However women politicians and leaders of women's organizations, such as the Women's Indian Association, accepted the conventional ideal of Hindu womanhood and women's role in the separate domestic sphere. They also accepted male authority and leadership and never asserted women's cause. Concludes that the right of women to seek fulfillment outside the home or to strive for power and prestige was never recognized in the past women's political movement in India.

243. Borthwick, Meredith. **The Changing Role of Women in Bengal, 1849-1905.** Princeton: Princeton University Press, 1984. 402 pp.

Chronicles the changes in the lives of Bengali Brahim (Bhadramahila) women between the years 1849 and 1905. Argues that education was one of the major change agents for women—it broadened women's knowledge of their own society and the world around them. Chapter 3 of the book focuses specifically on changing views of women's education and the development of women's education through the period. Women's education was seen as making women better wives and mothers. The introduction of women's education meant that women used literacy to lessen the hardships of life within the family and to express themselves within a larger circle than the family. In addition, education brought women new values of cleanliness, orderliness, responsibility, intelligence and knowledge of the public world of men. While these women remained within the traditional sphere of the family and never challenged women's role, they transformed the role of wives and mothers. Education also had the unintended effect of a rise in the marriage age, a decline in women's familiarity with traditional household skills and the beginning of white-collar female employment.

244. Devendra, Kiran. **Status and Position of Women in India.** New Delhi: Vikas Publishing, 1985. 186 pp.

    Presents a history of women's legal status in India since independence.   Includes provisions for education.   Looks at changes in education and attitudes toward women.   Education has increased the use of dowry (which is illegal) in some areas, otherwise it is viewed as the most positive change along with changing social behavior.   Religion, employment and other factors seem to change only slowly.

245. Gulati, Saroj. **Women and Society: Northern India in 11th and 12th Centuries.** Delhi: Chanakya Publications, 1985.   282 pp.

    Discusses the position of women and examines the influence of the different social institutions and customs on the position of women in Northern India in the 11th and 12th Centuries.   The first chapter deals with family relationships and the status of women.   Different roles and experiences of a woman as a daughter, wife, daughter-in-law and mother are discussed.   The next chapter focuses on rituals performed at different stages of women's lives and the degree to which they reflect the status of a person in the family as well as in society.   The chapter on the Status of the Widow describes three aspects concerning a widow; niyoga (appointment of a wife or a widow to procreate a son for an appointed male), widow remarriage and the custom of suttee (self-immolation of a widow at her husband's death).   The chapter on The Legal Status of Women discusses why women were not given the right to inherit their husbands' property.   The fifth chapter talks about the status of women in social institutions such as prostitution, seclusion, slavery, the education of women and women as rulers. The education of women was sharply distinguished from that of men. Women of the higher castes were mostly educated by tutors at home.

246. Maskiell, Michelle. **Women Between Cultures: The Lives of Kinnaird College Alumnae in British India.** Syracuse: Maxwell School of Citizenship and Public Affairs, Foreign and Comparative Studies, Syracuse University, 1984. 202 pp. (South Asia Series no. 9)

    Provides a history of Kinnaird College in the Punjab. Kinnaird was a British missionary school for women founded in 1913 in British India (it is now located in Pakistan).   The book provides a history of gender-segregated education, the attitudes toward the education of girls in the 19th Century and British policies and the development of an ethos of liberal education for girls which would be the same as males. Part Two presents a collective biography of the graduates as daughters and their life styles.   Points out that the college gave women greater

options, many pursued careers but most remained wives and
mothers in traditional modes. These women did assume social
roles 20 years earlier than Wellesley and Bryn Mawr women
graduates who stayed home because the economic opportunities for
women were too limited and there were too many social norms
which functioned to keep women out of the workforce.

247. Mathur, Y.B. Women's Education in India 1813-1966. Bombay:
Asia Publishing House, 1973. 208 pp.

Provides a historical survey of women's education in India. The
focus is on women's education from British colonial occupation
of India to 1966. Points out that traditionally there had been
a prohibition against educating women among Hindus. Before 1854
there was virtually no education given to girls. As late as
1884 only 2697 girls' schools existed serving about 127,000
students. In the 1880s the British paid more attention to the
problems of girls' education. Women's access to schooling
accelerated in the first two decades of the 20th Century, but it
was not until independence that women made major gains in
education. Ends with a history of the development of women's
higher education.

Mehta, Sushila. Revolution and the Status of Women in India.
New Delhi: Metropolitan, 1982. 278 pp.

See item #165

248. Misra, Lakshmi. Education of Women in India, 1921-1966.
Bombay: MacMillan, 1966.

Focuses exclusively on formal education initiated under
colonialism. The work is organized chronologically beginning
with the period 1700-1921, which represents missionary endeavors
and colonial education policy; it then turns to the 1921-1937
interwar years, the period immediately prior to independence,
independence through the first Five-Year Plan and subsequent
educational plans through 1965. The work is based on government
and missionary sources.

249. Saxena, Rajendra K. Education and Social Amelioration of Women:
A Study of Rajasthan. Jaipur: Snaghi Prakashan, 1978. 231 pp.

Provides a historical account of education in Rajasthan
beginning in 1818 and ending in 1935. Traces missionary efforts
to start girls' schools which over time served but a fraction of
the female population. By 1932, for example, less than 1
percent of all girls were in school. Most of these girls were
Christians and Hindus. Points out that the government did
nothing to provide education for girls; without the missions

girls would have remained ignorant. One-third of the book is on
the history of girls' education; the remainder looks at suttee,
widow remarriage and infant and child marriage.

250. Sharma, Radha Krishna. Nationalism, Social Reform and Indian
Women. Patna: Janaki Prakashan, 1981. 311 pp.

Discusses the impact of the nationalist and reform movements on
Indian women from 1921 to 1937. Covers the situation of Indian
women under Hindu tradition, including a tendency to value
illiteracy in women. Contains a chapter on the organization of
women's education in the 1920s and 1930s with detailed lists of
secondary and collegiate level schools, descriptions of the
founding of Women's University and the beginning of
coeducation.

Articles

251. Bhandari, R.K. "Development of Women's Education." New
Frontiers in Education 12 (1982): 32-38.

Traces the development of women's education in India after
independence. Despite the progress, nearly two-thirds of the
total nonenrolled population of the age group 6-14 are girls.
Suggests several measures to increase the enrollment and
retention of girls, such as free education for girls up to the
secondary stage, provision of schools nearer to their residence,
increase of women teachers, establishment of child-care centers,
common curricula for both girls and boys, development of
nonformal education, etc.

252. Borthwick, Meredith. "The Bhadramahila and Changing Conjugal
Relations in Bengal 1850-1900." Women in India and Nepal.
Edited by Michael Allen and S.N. Mukherjee. Canberra:
Australian National University, South Asia History Section,
1982, pp. 105-135. (Monographs on South Asia, no. 8)

Traces the changes in conjugal relations in Bengal in the latter
half of the 19th Century, when for the first time there was a
group of literate and articulate women who left records of their
lives. Argues that although, with the growth of female
education, the rising age of marriage, etc., the relationship
between wives and husbands changed, it was at a personal level
and therefore did not change the power relationship between the
couple nor women's position in the economic structure.

253. Forbes, Geraldine H. "In Search of the 'Pure Heathen':
Missionary Women in Nineteenth Century India." Economic and
Political Weekly 21 (April 26, 1986): WS 2-8.

Examines the motives of the British missionary women, their careers in India and the impact of their work on Indian and British women. Uses sources from personal letters, record books, associational records and other documents preserved in the archives of the Society for the Propagation of the Gospel in Foreign Parts. Concludes that the missionary women had great difficulty simply existing in the Indian environment. Even when they survived, they had difficulty accomplishing their goals.

254. Ghosh, Srabashi. "Birds in a Cage: Changes in Bengali Social Life as Recorded in Autobiographies by Women." Economic and Political Weekly, 21 (October 25, 1986): WS 88-96.

Traces the changes in Bengali social life as experienced by women and recorded in their autobiographies. Focuses on women's lives in their families, marriage, education and women's changing aspirations as well as the psychological tensions that women experienced in the face of patriarchy. Of special interest is the ways in which the spread of English education acted as a positive force to change women's lives for the better. Traces how missionaries established girls' schools in rural areas and the opposition to women's education from men and older women. Points out that educated women were often caught between two worlds.

255. Hironaka, Kazuhiko. "Education for Girls and Women in India: Progress and Problems." Research Bulletin of the National Institute for Educational Research (Tokyo) 13 (1975): 53-60.

Gives a historical overview of women's education in India from early 19th Century to independence on such topics as traditional education, social attitude towards women's education and colonial policies for women's education. Traditional India denied formal education to girls. Colonial administration first supported education for women in 1854, but the spread of education was limited until independence. The improvements in the status of women were promoted by various social movements as well as by women's organizations.

256. Jahan, Mehraj. "Women's Education in a Man's World: A Comparison Between Japan and Bengal in the 19th Century." Women, Development, Devotionalism and Nationalism: Bengal Studies, 1985. Edited by John Thorp. East Lansing: Michigan State University, 1985, pp. 13-20. (South Asia Series, Occasional Paper no. 34)

Discusses the historical background of the growth and spread of women's education in Japan after the Meiji Restoration in 1868 in comparison with what happened in Bengal. Argues that a similar orientation of Japanese local elites to that of the

foreign missionaries promoted women's education in Japan, while
conflicts and resistance that Bengalese elites held against the
modernizing influences of the missionaries hindered not only the
development of women's education but also the socioeconomic
modernization of India as a whole.

257. Karlekar, Malavika.   "Kadambini and the Bhadralok: Early
Debates Over Women's Education in Bengal."   Economic and
Political Weekly 21 (April 26, 1986): WS 25-31.

Reviews the debates over women's education in Bengal in the
1860s.   Utilizes data from the existing literature and uses
Kadambini, one of the first women graduates of Calcutta
University, as an example. Shows that from the third quarter of
the 19th Century onwards, education became an important status
symbol necessary for familial mobility.   Controlled learning for
girls had an increasingly significant role to play in the
evolution of modern Bengali society.   At the same time, by
creating the stereotype of the well-educated yet unquestioning
and docile girl, modernizing educators minimized the purportedly
liberational potential of learning for women. Finds that rather
than fostering equality, the education system brought about a
new difference in access to knowledge.   Points out that in
present day India arguments on women's roles and their
relationship to education have not changed much from the days of
those who initiated the early debates.

258. Kishwar, Madhu.   "Arya Samaj and Women's Education: Kanya
Mahavidyalaya, Jalandhar." Economic and Political Weekly 21
(April 26, 1986): WS 9-24.

Provides a history of the Kanya Mahavidyalaya, Jalandhar, which
was one of the first girls' schools established in the Punjab.
The school was founded in the 1890s and developed into a college
which served as a model for women's colleges in India.   Points
out that women's education was advocated primarily as a means to
bridge the mental gap between husbands and wives and mothers and
sons.   The education offered in Kanya Mahavidyalaya, Jalandhar
brought an English Victorian education to Indian girls.
Concludes that the Arya Samaj movement sought to reform women
rather than to reform the social conditions which oppressed
women.

259. Maskiell, Michelle.   "Social Change and Social Control:
College-Educated Punjab Women: 1913 to 1960." Modern Asian
Studies 19 (1985): 55-83.

Probes the impact of higher education on the lives of South
Asian women. Uses a collective biography of college-educated
women spanning a half century as well as the records of Kinnaird

College for Women, Lahore, Pakistan, as a starting point. The
lives of 600 of the 3019 women listed in the admissions register
from 1913 to 1960 are studied. Finds that Kinnaird College was
a rare early 20th Century institution that promoted female
intellectual   equality   and   encouraged   women   to   consider
professional careers after graduation. The value of service to
society was stressed continuously in the college rhetoric. But
the College was also instrumental in the continuation of social
structures built on the family control of women. That is why
women's   colleges   which   had   opportunities   to   perform   true
rolechanging functions in South Asia often did not do so.

260. Molla, M.K.U.   "Women's Education in Early Twentieth Century
     Eastern Bengal."   **Women, Development, Devotionalism and
     Nationalism: Bengal Studies 1985.** Edited by John Thorp. East
     Lansing: Michigan State University, 1985, pp. 41-48. (South
     Asia Series, Occational Paper no. 36)

     Provides an overview of women's education in early 20th Century
     Eastern Bengal. Before Eastern Bengal became a new province,
     little schooling was given to girls. Significant progress made
     in the early 20th Century generated an educational awakening
     among women and provided opportunities to participate in the
     governmental   decision   making   process   and   nation-building
     activities for women with university degrees.

261. Mukherjee, S.N.   "Raja Rammohun Roy and the Status of Women in
     Bengal in the Nineteenth Century."   **Women in India and Nepal.**
     Edited   by   Michael   Allen   and   S.N.   Mukherjee.   Canberra:
     Australian   National   University,   South   Asia   History   Section,
     1982, pp. 155-178. (Monographs on South Asia, no. 8)

     Examines   the   views   on   women   expressed   by   social   reformer
     Rammohun Roy (1772-1833) against the social and political
     background of his time. Roy advocated equal rights for women
     and argued such issues as child marriage, female rights to
     property, polygamy and female education. Claims that despite
     the limitation of the liberal reformist views, Roy deserves to
     be called one of the male feminist thinkers of the 19th Century.

262. Pearson, Gail.   "The Female Intelligentsia in Segregated
     Society--Bombay, A Case Study."   **Women in India and Nepal.**
     Edited   by   Michael   Allen   and   S.N.   Mukherjee.   Canberra:
     Australian   National   University,   South   Asia   History   Section,
     1982, pp. 136-154. (Monographs on South Asia, no. 8)

     Surveys the role the female intelligentsia in Bombay has played
     since   the   late   19th   Century.   Argues   that   the   female
     intelligentsia mediated between the female world and the male
     world, and that their participation in the male world of affairs

did not challenge the Hindu patriarchial social order and remained subject to a social structure of male control. Points out that segregation gives elite status to a few women as mediators in a patriarchial world, but desegregation diminishes their status.

263. Phadke, Sindhu. "Special Problems of the Education of Women." Papers in the Sociology of Education in India. Edited by M.S. Gore et al. Delhi: NCERT, 1967, pp. 173-200.

Surveys historic changes in the position of Indian women as they affect women's education, discusss problems of women's education in contemporary India and examines the interaction between education and social institutions. Argues tht problems such as gender and regional disparities, wastage and inadequate educational facilities are linked with multiple factors and that a complex interaction operates between women's education and family relationships, marriage, social roles and values.

264. Pratima, Asthana. "Progress in Education." Women's Moot In India. Delhi: Vikas Publishing House, 1974, pp. 130-145.

Describes the historical development of women's education under colonial rule. During the first half of the 19th Century, education for women was limited to only a small minority of aristocratic families who demanded education for their daughters so that they could help the management of their huge estates. Since Indian private efforts were almost exclusively devoted to boys, most private schools for girls were run by missionaries or British philanthropists. In the early 19th century, because of the rise of age of marriage among the upper classes in urban areas, women's education considerably advanced. In 1916 the Indian Women's University was established in Bombay. The wave of interest in science subjects almost submerged the old domination of literacy subjects. As the political struggle for independence progressed, the demand for women's education emerged. Throughout the colonial period, the government remained almost aloof and did not give financial asistance to any project for educational progress. Therefore, women's education was largely limited to the upper class in urban areas.

Southard, Barbara. "Bengal Women's Education League: Pressure Group and Professional Association." Modern Asian Studies 18 (1984): 55-88.

See item #1196

265. "Women and Co-education." Education in India (1781-1985): Policies, Planning and Implementation. New Delhi: Centre for Research in Rural and Industrial Development, 1985, pp. 234-270.

Gives a historical overview of women's education and the development of coeducation in India. The official effort for women's education did not start until 1870 when special primary and secondary schools for girls began to be established. After independence, all boys' institutions started to open to girls. At present, coeducation is the prevalent practice especially at the primary and college levels; more than 50 percent of the girls study in coeducational schools and there are no girls' primary schools. However, despite efforts in the six five-year plans during 1951-1985, women's education still lags behind that of men.

2c.   Indonesia

Articles

266. Awanohara, Susumu. "Secularism Does Little to Fray those Old-School Ties with Islam." Far East Economic Review 124 (June 1984): 76-77.

Illustrates the daily life of the Diniyah Putri, the oldest and easily the most celebrated modernist Muslim girls' boarding school in Indonesia. Despite their devotion to Islam and strict school regulations, girls are strong and self-confident based on the traditional matrilineal system. The purpose of the schools is to nurture women who are animated by Islam and are capable and active educators with a sense of responsibility to their country and for the general welfare of the people. Despite significant impact of Islamic reform movement, total enrollment in Islamic schools declined because parents increasingly shifted their daughters to modernist (secular) day schools.

267. Beekman, E.M. "Kartini: Letters from a Javanese Feminist, 1899-1902." Massachusetts Review 25 (1984): 579-616.

Provides a short biographical sketch of Raden Adjeng Kartini, the second oldest daughter of a Javanese aristocrat, who received Dutch primary education, was forced into a traditional marriage and purdah and died in childbirth when she was but 25 years old. Kartini is remembered as one of the first advocates of women's rights in Indonesia. She also was a mediator between European and Javanese culture. Translates several letters that Kartini wrote to her Dutch feminist friends, Stella Zeehandelaar, Mrs. Ovink-Soer, and Mrs. Abendanon. These letters express Katrini's commitment to feminism, to educating women and to Indonesian nationalism.

268. Penders, L.M.   "Kartini: Indonesian Patriot and Reformer."
     Indonesian Women: Some Past and Current Perspectives.   Edited
     by B.B. Herring.   Brussels: Centre d'Etude du Sud-Est Asiatique
     et de l'Extreme Orient, 1976, pp. 20-48.

     Focuses on Kartini, an Indonesian feminist and social reformer
     who lived at the turn of the century.   The author discusses
     Kartini's views on the liberation of women from the strictures
     of Islamic law and Javanese tradition and her attempts to
     formulate a modern education for women.   Advocates that
     Kartini's views be acted upon today.   Calls for making secondary
     and higher education accessible to women and to the working
     classes in order to modernize Indonesia.

269. Taylor, Jean.   "Education, Colonialism and Feminism: An
     Indonesian Case Study."   Education and the Colonial Experience.
     Edited by P.G. Altbach and G.P. Kelly.   Rutgers, N.J.
     Transaction Books, 1984, pp. 137-154.

     Provides biographies of Pangeran Aria Achmad Djajadiningrat
     (1877-1943) and Raden Ajen Kartini (1879-1904).   Both were from
     aristocratic families in Java who were colonial administrators
     for the Dutch.   Kartini was the first woman of the aristocracy
     to go to a Dutch school; Djajadiningrat was one of the first
     Javanese men to complete western secondary school.

3.   Latin America

Books and Monographs

270. Borges, Wanda Rose.   A Profissionalizaçào Feminia: Una
     Experiência no Ensino Publico.   São Paulo: Ediçoes Loyola,
     1980.   149 pp.

     Traces the history of a major school for girls in Sao Paulo from
     its origins to the early 19th century.   The school began as an
     orphanage.   By 1850 it came to serve as a private school for
     daughters of the wealthy.   From 1870 to 1935 the school was
     transformed into a normal institution with a middle and lower
     middle class clientele.   Today the school is a technical school.
     The book contains a detailed discussion of school curricula,
     education law and school administration.

271. Foz y Foz, Pilar.   La Revolución Pedagógica en Nueva España:
     1754-1820.   Madrid: Instituto "Gonzalo Fernandes de Oviedo,"
     1981.   2 volumes.   779 pp.

Presents in Volume I a detailed history of the founding of
women's education by the Sisters of Mary led by Maria Ignacia de
Azlory Echeverez, a descendent of conquistadors and powerful
figures of New Spain (Mexico). The order brought a pedagogy
that balanced the logic and humanism of Montaigne with the
Catholic reformation thinker Juana de Lestonnac. The order was
run centrally and created four schools open to the public, one
of which worked with native girls. Numbers served were under
1500--the largest school served about 350, some were boarding
pupils others external (the former got far more attention). The
order rarely numbered more than 100 sisters. Included are
architectural layouts of the schools and financial reports.
Volume II is a compilation of documents and photos of the
baroque style of the churches and schools used by this order.

272. Martin, Luis. Daughters of the Conquistadores: Women of the
     Viceroyalty of Peru. Albuquerque: University of New Mexico
     Press, 1983. 354 pp.

Explores the role of women in colonial Peru. Focuses on the
system of women's education, colonial marriages, daily life of
women in the cities and their impact on colonial society.
Points out that women were caught in three cultural factors:
Don Juanism, Marianism, and courtly life. Women in Peru thus
either lived confined to the household upholding moral virtues,
in convents in a world of women, or as prostitutes and/or street
people. Chapter 4 focuses on women's education. Points out
that by the mid-16th Century an educational system staffed by
professional educators emerged. The Church forbade coeducation
and a system of female schools emerged. Two types of schools
were available: convent schools which served the wealthy and
charged stiff fees and lay schools which were supported by
benefactors and served poor Spanish and mestizo girls. None of
the schools provided professional education; rather they were
devoted to developing the spirit and the intellect and strove to
socialize girls around the cult of Mary. Subsequent chapters
are on marriage, concubinage, convents and daily life.

273. Susa de Newton, Lily. Las Argentinas de Ayer y de Hoy. Buenos
     Aires: Ediciones Zanetti, 1967.

Explores the history of women's subordination in Argentina and
the factors which contributed to women's undereducation. Points
out that the Catholic church and the patriarchial family delayed
the development of schooling for women. After 1900 women were
allowed greater access to education and entered the workforce in
education as teachers, in medicine, in literature and in social
work. By 1947 women gained the vote and while they entered
higher education in increasing numbers, they remained
concentrated in philosophy and pharmacy, and underrepresented in

law and social sciences, medicine, architecture, economics, agriculture and engineering.

274. Susto, Juan Antonio. **La Educación de la Mujer Panameña el Siglo XIX.** Panama: Imprenta Nacional, Ministerio de Educación, 1966. 63 pp.

Provides a history of women's education in Panama, tracing it from the opening of Catholic schools in the period 1821 to 1847. Points out that it was not until 1860 that the government began to provide for female elementary education. Surveys the differentiated curricula offered girls and the development of teaching as a career for women in the late 19th Century.

Articles

275. Cole, Joyce. "Official Ideology and the Education of Women in the English-Speaking Caribbean, 1835-1945, with Special Reference to Barbados." **Women and Education. Women in the Caribbean Project Vol. 5.** Edited by Joycelin Massiah. Cave Hill: Institute of Social and Economic Research, University of the West Indies, 1982, pp. 1-34.

Analyzes the ideology underlying educational provision for girls in Barbados between 1835 and 1945. Points out that while girls had access to schooling, as in Britain, education prepared girls for future roles as mothers and wives. Girls thus were given education inferior to boys and remained at a disadvantage in entering the labor market. As the schools became more differentiated and specialized in the 20th Century, sexual stratification in the schools grew.

276. Correas, E. "Sarmiento's Daughters: Sixty-Five Who Dared (19th Century Educator)." **Americas** 32 (Jan. 1980): 49-54.

Traces the life history of Domingo Sarmiento, an Argentine educator who recruited 65 women teachers from the United States to teach in his country in the late 19th Century. These teachers organized and taught in 18 teacher training schools in Argentina. The author argues that these women, through example, changed public perceptions of women's roles and helped to liberate women "from the cloistered existence and prejudices" extant in Argentinian society at that time. The article also discusses Sarmiento's meeting in 1847 with Horace Mann.

277. DeGallo, Maria Gowland. "Amanda Labarca: Chilean Educator." **Americas** 27 (no. 8, 1976): 12-16.

Portrays an extraordinary Chilean woman, Amanda Labarca
Hubertson, as an educator, a feminist and an individual. She
dedicated her whole life to social and political causes. She
also directed many educational establishments in her country and
abroad. Her main efforts in her eighty-eight years of life were
devoted to Chilean education and the improvement of the status
of women both in Chile and throughout Latin America. This brief
biography is a translation from Spanish.

278. Drayton, K.B. "The Education of Girls in Barbados: The Past."
Report of the Barbados National Commission on the Status of
Women. Vol. 2. Edited by Norma Forde. Bridgetown: Government
Printery, 1978, pp. 81-99.

Presents a history of women's education in Barbados from
missionary times through emancipation to the present. Provides
data on enrollment patterns and expenditures as well as specific
institutional histories.

279. Gálvez Berrera, Ana M. "Historical Status of Women in Peru."
Impact of Science on Society 30 (1980): 7-9.

Traces the process by which Peruvian women, who were once near
equal with men, became subordinate to them. Education is only
one means by which this occurred.

280. Hahner, June E. "Feminism, Women's Rights, and the Suffrage
Movement in Brazil, 1850-1932." Latin American Research Review
15 (1980): 65-111.

Traces the women's movement in Brazil from the 19th Century to
the 1930s when the suffrage movement won a victory. A small
group of 19th Century feminist pioneers, through their
newspapers, had laid part of the groundwork for changes in the
status of some women. Institutions of higher education were
opened to women in 1879 and more middle-class women found
employment outside the home, especially in schools, government
offices and commercial establishments. The professional women
who led the suffrage movement in the 20th Century were only a
small segment of the nation's female population, and they
regarded the right to vote as a means to enhance the role of
women as mothers. The vote proved useful only to some women and
most women remained in auxiliary positions in a male-dominated
society.

281. Hernández de Alba, Guillermo. "Homenaje a la Compaña de María y
al Colegio de la Enseñanza con ocasión del Segundo Centenario de
su Fundación." Boletin de Historia y Antigüedades 70
(April-June 1983): 539-546.

Chronicles the founding of the first teacher's college in Bogota in 1783 by the militant counter-reformation order of sisters, the Company of Mary. Stresses the strong Catholic nature of the education offered both in the past and the present.

282. Herrmann, Eleanor Krohn.   "Belizean Nursing Education in the 19th Century."   Belizean Studies 7 (1979):   16-24.

Traces how nursing training was started in Belize as early as 1894, when it was still one of the British Colonies. The decision to establish a training course for nurses in Belize was made by the then governer in 1892. The first instructor arrived from England in 1894.   Unlike those in England, students in Belize started their training by working in the hospital immediately. Supported by the colonial government, the training was without a religious affiliation and offered women in the colony an opportunity for a secular career.

283. Little, Cynthia Jeffress.   "Education, Philanthropy, and Feminism: Components of Argentine Womanhood, 1860-1926." Latin American Women: Historical Perspective.   Edited by Asuncion Lavrin.   Westport, Conn.:   Greenwood Press, 1978, pp. 235-253.

Explores ways in which education, philanthropy and feminism allowed some groups of Argentine women to break away from the Spanish tradition of sheltered womanhood and to emerge as participants, albeit secondclass, in the nation's growth during 1860-1926, when rapid urbanization, high foreign immigration, and drastic economic changes combined to alter many aspects of Argentine life. Reviews the contributions made by 19th Century Argentina's most outstanding educational reformer Domingo F. Sarmiento to secular public education and to women's educational opportunities.

284. Lobo, Francisco Bruno. "Duas Pionieras - (Madame Durocher - Rita Lobata)."   Revista do Instituto Histórico e Geográfico Brasileiro 328 (July-September, 1980):   53-56.

Describes the struggles of the first woman to enter the law faculty at the university in Rio de Janiero in the 1830s and the first woman to enter the medical faculty in the 1870s.

285. Nizza da Silva, Maria Beatriz.   "Educação Feminina e Educação Masculina no Brasil colonial."   Revisita de História 55 (no. 109): 149-154.

Focuses on the legal constraints to educating women and girls in colonial Brazil and discusses educational provision in Church schools.

286. Perez-Venero, Mirna M.   "The Education of Women on the Isthmus of Panama."   **Journal of the West** 12 (1973): 325-334.

Sheds some perspectives on the education of women on the Isthmus of Panama in the 19th Century. This is the first study on this topic and consists of a historical account of the establishment of girls' schools. Reveals that from the early 1800s, the government made special efforts to enhance women's education. Finds that during the last century in Panama, education for women was encouraged because there were no particular anti-feminist attitudes among the ruling classes with regard to education. It was the dismal economic movements and political upheavals that were to blame for retarding the intellectual growth of Isthmian women as well.

287. Russel-Wood, A.J.R.   "Women and Society in Colonial Brazil." **Journal of Latin American Studies** 9 (May 1977): 1-34.

Demonstrates that white women played a significantly more central role in the social, economic and ideological development of Portuguese American colonies than had been formerly realized. Women were the stabilizing element in colonial society. Women managed estates and properties as well as played a major role in ensuring the maintenance of the Portuguese language and culture. Women also were mothers and wives and raised and educated children.

288. Vaughan, Mary K.   "Women, Class and Education in Mexico, 1880-1928."   **Latin American Perspectives** 4 (nos. 1/2, 1977): 135-152.

Reviews the political and social factors which have served to maintain women in a subordinate domestic role in Mexican society. Sees education as both an ideological institution as well as an institution which has allocated women into home and marginal sectors of the economy. Focuses on education only as an institution which contributes to women's subordination. Argues that women's role in the family replicates patriarchial relations in the society which intensify with capitalist development.   Traces the drastic decline of women's participation in Mexican industry which has resulted from the trend toward more capital intensive industry.

289. Vazques, Josefina Zoraida.   "The Education of Women in Mexico during XVIII and XIX Centuries."   Dialogo (Mexico) 17 (March-April 1981): 10-16.

Describes the importance of women's education during the colonial as well as the republican historical times. Highlights the ideas, values and purposes which forwarded the establishment of the new public instructional system after 1867. Argues the progressive movement became a failure in Mexico because its pioneers denied the importance of women in the social movement of the whole country.

290. Yeager, Gertrude M. "Women's Roles in Nineteenth Century Chile: Public Education Records, 1843-1883." Latin American Research Review 18 (1983): 149-155.

Reviews the roles of women in 19th Century Chile through the documentary and analytical window that education provides. Points out that education was part of an ambitious strategy to revamp and modernize every aspect of Chilean society. Finds that women have been consistent victims of the law of documentary elitism because they have not occupied positions of recognized importance.

4.   The Middle East

Books and Monographs

291. Davis, Fanny. The Ottoman Lady: A Social History from 1718 to 1918. Westport, Conn. Greenwood Press, 1986. 321 pp.

Focuses on the life of upper-class Ottoman women in Turkey from 1718 to 1918, during which time period their status changed appreciably. Turkey went to a relative backwater from a major Islamic empire and in the late 19th and early 20th Centuries underwent far-reaching reforms designed to make Turkey modern. Davis stuctures the book around the palace and the harem, childbirth, education, marriage, the female slave, divorce, social life within and outside the household, costume, intrigue, house and furnishings, architecture and the arts, religion and finally illness and old age. Chapter 3, which is on education, traces the history of women's schooling to the first decades of the 20th Century.

292. Galal, Salma. Emanzipationsversuche der ägyptischen Frau. München: Verlag frauenpolitik, 1977. 131 pp.

Presents a historical survey of women's schooling including foreign and missionary schools and 19th Century Egyptian reform attempts. Shows that by 1920 24 percent of primary school enrollment was female (rising to 38 percent by 1970) in real terms from 21,000 to 1.4 million. Traces a small segment of segregated vocational education from 1920 to 1970. Secondary enrollment for women went from 28 in 1920 to 95,000 in 1970 (32 percent of the total) while university enrollment rose from 16 in 1929 to 60,000 in 1970 (21 percent of the total). The university enrollment had typical differentiation between the social sciences and humanities as female fields with the hard sciences and engineering more male fields--although women were 7.5 percent of the latter field in 1965.

293. Kader, Soha Abdel. Egyptian Women in a Changing Society, 1899-1987. Boulder and London: Lynne Rienner Publishers, 1987. 163 pp.

Provides a history of the women's movement in Egypt from mid-1800s to the present. Argues that the women's movement arose from two sources: Egyptian nationalism and anti-colonialism and western education. Both educated women and men agitated for women's emancipation via extended schooling. Women were active in the Egyptian nationalist movement which was at its height in the 1920s. The nationalist movement became a disappointment to women and in the 1930s a feminist movement arose which agitated for women's rights and the extension of schooling. Many of the intellectual women were concerned about the relation of their feminism to Arab culture. In the 1950s under Nasser many of women's demands became law, but in the 1970s many of the promises of Egyptian socialism were retracted in the face of economic recession and Islamic fundamentalism.

294. Knauss, Peter R. The Persistence of Patriarchy: Class, Gender and Ideology in Twentieth Century Algeria. New York: Praeger, 1987. 176 pp.

Argues that despite women's participation in the anti-colonial and revolutionary movement in Algeria, patriarchical relations have been reaffirmed in post-independence Algeria. Attributes the persistence of patriarchy to the fact that French colonialism made a wholesale assault on Algerian institutions--the family, Koranic schools and religion--and Algerian anti-colonialism took the form of reasserting traditional Islamic sex role divisions of labor. Points out that western educated girls particularly were active in the anti-colonial movement and initially saw a return to Islamic practices of sex seclusion and veiling as nationalism rather than a reimposition of patriarchy.

295. Richter-Dridi, Irmhild. Frauenbefreiung im einem islamischen Land--ein wilderpruch? Das Beispiel Tunesien. Frankfurt am Main: Fischer Taschenbuch Verlag, 1981. 252 pp.

Decribes the patriarchial tradition of Tunisia and the beginnings of female emancipation under French colonialism. "Beginnings" needs to be stressed since the greatest change came

after the 1950s. Describes the female literacy campaigns of the
post-colonial government. Denotes the rise in primary school
enrollment from 25 percent in 1955 to 39 percent in 1976 and
almost as great a rise in secondary school enrollments.
However, over 60 percent of women were still illiterate in 1966.
Relates education to occupation and compares modern vs.
traditional women.

296. Sabri, Marie Aziz.   Pioneering Profiles: Beirut College for
Women. Beirut: Khayat Book and Publishing, 1967. 314 pp.

Presents biographies of ten outstanding women graduates or
teachers of the Beirut College as a means of indicating the
importance of its history.   Includes a brief history of the
school from its 19th Century missionary origins. A statistical
appendix shows a total of three thousand graduates.   Some of
their achievements are listed in a survey of graduates in the
text.

297. Timm, K. and Schahnus Aalami.   Die muslimische Frau zwischen
Tradition und Fortschritt: Frauenfrage und Familienentwicklung
in Ägypten und Iran. Berlin: Akademie Verlag, 1976. 322 pp.

Focuses on the history of women's education in Egypt and the
transition from traditional to modern roles.   Points out that
women entered the workforce in the 1920s and by the 1952
revolution, women's status was greatly enhanced.   Urban women
have obtained more education and have entered the professions.
Women account for 40 percent of primary, 30 percent of secondary
and 25 percent of the student enrollment in higher education.
Points out that rural women have not fared as well, most of
female illiteracy is in the countryside.   The section on Iran
presents a biography of Parwin E'tesami, a 20th Century Iranian
poet who advocated women's liberation.

Articles

298. Attir, Mustafa O.   "Ideology, Value Changes and Women's Social
Position in Libyan Society." Women and the Family in the Middle
East. Edited by Elizabeth Warnock Fernea. Austin: University
of Texas Press, 1985, pp. 121-133.

Describes the attempts to change traditional roles of women in
Libya from independence in 1952 to the 1980s. In the 1950s and
1960s, despite the government's efforts to make elementary
education compulsory for all children, parents resisted sending
their daughters to school. Thus, female education lagged behind
that of males. In the 1970s real changes occurred in women's
enrollment patterns. Despite these increases, women's social

position did not change. In the 1980s the government introduced policies designed to provide greater equality outside of the school system.

299. Mujahid, Ghazy. "Education for Girls in Saudi Arabia." **Muslim Education Quarterly** 4 (1987): 45-71.

Gives an overview of girls' education in Saudi Arabia. Section I gives a historical account of education in the Arabian Peninsula. Section II describes the introduction and development of female education in quantitative terms since 1960, when formal schools for girls were first established. Contends that the strict segregation of sexes in education was the most important key to the rapid progress of women's education in the country and that adherence to tradition can prove an indispensable aid for progress.

V. WOMEN'S ENROLLMENT IN SCHOOLS

The books and articles included here focus specifically on two clusters of interrelated issues: women's educational enrollment pattern and the factors that affect that pattern. Sometimes scholars write about the two simultaneously. We have attempted here to distinguish betwen them, but this has not always been successful.

The materials grouped under women's educational enrollment pattern are limited to studies which describe women's participation in the school system as a whole. (Works which confine themselves to enrollment in Higher Education are listed in Part VIII of this bibliography.) Statistical compedia which chart school attendance are included here as well.

There is a smaller literature than we would have expected on the factors affecting women's access to schools. Given the way in which the literature has evolved, we have subdivided the literature on factors affecting access into three parts: general studies of a number of factors (like social class, distance to school, birth order); parental attitudes towards female education; and religion. It should be noted that most of the literature on the factors relating access to education with religion focuses on Islam in general and the Middle East in particular.

A.   Women's Participation in the Schools

1.   General

Books and Monographs

300. Deblé, Isabelle.   The   School   Education   of   Girls: An International Comparative Study on School Wastage and Girls and Boys at the First and Second Levels of Education.   Paris: UNESCO, 1980. 180 pp.

Presents statistical data on girls' versus boys' enrollment patterns and dropout rates in 62 countries, including third world nations of Latin America, Asia and Africa. Shows that inequality in education between the sexes persists despite the growth in female enrollment. In school systems where there is universal primary education, sex differentiation appears in secondary and in higher education. Argues that one of the greatest barriers to gender parity in education is the lack of government concern about women's underenrollment and dropout rates.

301. McGrath, Patricia L.   The Unfinished Assignment: Equal Education for Women. Washington: Worldwatch Institute, 1976. 47 pp.

Provides an overview of women's educational enrollments worldwide, including women's access to primary, secondary and higher education as well as to technical and vocational training.

302. UNESCO. Division on Statistics on Education. Comparative Analysis of Male and Female Enrollment on Illiteracy. Paris: UNESCO, 1980. 165 pp.

Compiles UNESCO statistics, selfreported from countries, to present a basic statistical picture of most countries of the world. Basic raw number data are given, but most comparisons between age groups, levels of education, and geographic region are presented in graph form. Generally shows progress in women's enrollment and reduction of illiteracy.

Articles

03. Bowman, Mary Jean and C.A. Anderson.   "The Participation of Women in Education in the Third World." Comparative Education Review 24 (1980): S13-S32. (Also in Women's Education in the Third World: Comparative Perspectives. Edited by Gail P. Kelly and Carolyn M. Elliott. Albany: SUNY Press, 1982, pp. 11-30.)

Surveys the fragmentary data on women's enrollment patterns in third world nations. The authors try to explain variance in educational inequality between males and females. Their data indicate that level of economic development and cultural/religious traditions have little to do with explaining gender-based educational inequality. They argue that within nation variance in female versus male enrollment ratios are as great as those between nations. They point out that girls who attend school are from higher social class backgrounds than are their male peers, and that girls usually receive less education than do boys. They conclude that explanations of variance in sex based inequalities among nations should consider the relation of education to the economic and social roles of each relation of education to the economic and social roles of each sex.

304. Eliou, Marie. "Equality of the Sexes in Education: And Now What?" **Comparative Education** 23 (1987): 59-67.

Provides an international overview of women's educational enrollments based on UNESCO statistics. Points out that in all countries female enrollments lag behind those of males. In developing nations, the majority of primary school enrollments are males; 60 percent of illiterates in the world are female. Girls are underrepresented in secondary and higher education, especially in scientific and technical fields. Educational inequality leads to women's pattern of workforce participation.

305. Elliott, Carolyn M. and Gail P. Kelly. "Perspectives on the Education of Women in Third World Nations." **Comparative Education Review** 25 (1980): S1-S12.

Reviews the research on women's educational attainment and achievement in third world countries and the relation of education to women's participation in productive labor. Argues that female education is not a function of culture or the level of a nation's economic development. Women's education, rather, is a function of educational policies that seek to provide educational and employment opportunities to women.

306. Finn, J.D., Loretta Dulberg and Janet Reis. "Sex Differences in Educational Attainment: A Cross-National Perspective." **Harvard Educational Review** 49 (1979): 477-503.

Reviews the literature on women's educational attainment in countries throughout the world. Points out that the data is at best fragmentary, especially when it come to third world nations in Africa, Asia and Latin America. Nonetheless, women's educational attainment lags behind that of men. Argues that, as a result, women's educational achievement also is below that of men. This lower educational outcome is also due to lack of academic support for women who go to school, the lack of role models for women and sex role stereotyping in the curriculum.

307. Friderich, Nicole. "Access to Education at All Levels." **Annals of the American Academy of Political and Social Science** 375 (January 1968): 133-144.

Surveys world education in the early 1960s. Shows broad improvement in all regions, but demonstrates problems of urban-rural difference, poor schooling that extends illiteracy and segmentation of training with women dominating the teacher training.

308. Kelly, Gail. "Education and Women: Equality is Still Elusive."
Decade for Women. Edited by Aisla Thomson. Toronto: Canadian
Congress for Learning Opportunities for Women, 1986, pp. 57-62.

Asks if the unparalleled school expansion of the past years has
benefitted women and if it helped remove the genderbased
educational inequality throughout the world. Finds that gender
continues to predict strongly whether a child will go to school
and how much and what type of schooling she or he will receive.

309. Kotwal, Marilyn. "Inequalities in the Distribution of Education
between Countries, Sexes, Generations and Individuals."
Education, Inequality and Life Chances. Vol. 1. Edited by
Organization for Economic Cooperation and Development. Paris:
OECD, 1975, pp. 31-108.

Explores the distribution of education in 19 OECD countries by
sex and by age cohort between 1950 and 1970. Finds that the
range in educational enrollment distributions between OECD
countries varies but there are some trends toward convergence.
Finds also that sex differences in educational access diminish
over time and that over the past few years, with the rapid
increases in education, the generation gap in educational
attainment levels has grown.

310. Sutherland, Margaret B. "Sex Differences in Education: An
Overview." Comparative Education 23 (1987): 5-9.

Provides an overview of worldwide trends in the education of
women. Points out that in developing countries on the primary
level, male and female enrollments have equalized, but this has
not occurred in secondary or higher education despite increased
female enrollments.

311. Vander Voet, Susan McCrae. "The United Nations Decade for
Women: The Search for Women's Equality in Education and
Employment." The Decade for Women. Edited by Aisla Thomson.
Toronto: Canadian Congress for Learning Opportunities for
Women, 1986, pp. 75-90.

Surveys the changes in women's enrollment patterns during the
span of the United Nations Decade for Women. Finds that the
differences between male and female enrollments are declining
gradually, although regional differences are enormous. Looks at
the workforce outcomes of education as well.

2.   Africa

Books and Monographs

312. Abeille, Barbara. A Study of Female Life in Mauritania.
Washington, D.C.:   U.S. Agency for International Development,
Office of Women in Development, 1979. 51 pp.

Decribes the status of women's education in Mauritania and
interviews 15 women from differing socioeconomic, ethnic and
educational backgrounds to understand the factors affecting
women's access to education.

313. Adams, Milton N. and Susan E. Kruppenbach. Some Issues of
Access and Equity in the Education of African Females: Progress
and Prospects. East Lansing: Michigan State University, Women
in International Development, 1986. 30 pp. (Working Paper no.
16)

Examines women's educational enrollments in Africa in the
mid-1980s and finds that although women's enrollments grew
markedly in the 1960s and 1970s, they have stagnated in the
1980s. The pattern in Africa appears to be that once education
becomes universal for males, females are then brought into the
system. While the gains for women are at the primary level,
women still are underrepresented in secondary school and there
have been fewer gains in higher education than at other levels.

314. Bruchhaus, Eva-Maria. Frauen in Obervolta; Situationsanalyse
und   entwicklungspolitiche   Ansatzpunkte   unter   besonderer
Berucksichtingung nicht-staatlicher Organisationen. Frieburg im
Breisgau: Arnold-Bergstrasser Institut, 1979. 148 pp.

Presents school enrollment statistics in Upper Volta from the
mid-1970s and underscores the fact that only 14 percent of males
and 11 percent of females of school age attend. Describes
nonformal and higher education as well.

315. Women in the SDR.   An Appraisal of Progress of the
Implementation of the World Plan of Action of the United Nations
Decade for Women - 1975-1985. Mogadishu: Somali Women's
Democratic Organization, 1985. 67 pp.

Provides an overview of women's progress toward equity in
Somalia between 1975 and 1985. Claims that progress is real,
but figures presented for higher education in 1983-84 show women
as a small minority. They are 9.9 percent of students enrolled
in the sciences. Chapter 3 is on education and provides
enrollment statistics for primary and secondary school between
1973/74 and 1983/84. Girls are 35.7 percent of all students in
primary school in 1983/84 and 34.3 percent of secondary
students. The chapter also provides detailed statistics of

women in technical secondary school and higher education as well as women in the teaching profession and administrative posts.

Articles

316. Adams, Milton and Susan Kruppenbach. "Gender and Access in the African School." International Review of Education 33 (1987): 437-453.

Compares female access patterns to formal education in Botswana, Liberia, Niger and Somalia. Finds out that enrollment levels are linked with general economic development. Analyzes the comparatively high rate of female access to primary level education on one hand and a very low rate of post-primary enrollment on the other.

317. Comhaire-Sylvain, S. "L'Instruction des Filles a Lomé" Problèmes Sociaux Congolais 82 (September 1968): 93-122.

Provides an overview of girls' school attendance in Lome, Togo, in the 1960s. Less than 60 percent of girls 8-14 were in school versus 90 percent of the boys. The quality of education is low and less than 15 percent of the girls sitting for the primary certificate examination pass. The problems in female education are problems for males as well. In the primary schools there is chronic overcrowding, unqualified staff and poor facilities and equipment. Girls are a smaller minority of post-primary students; they tend to concentrate in short-cycle non-baccalaureat programs in both public and private schools. Very few girls go on to higher education. Attributes gender disparities in education to attitudes concerning women's schooling. Men prefer less educated wives and many families find it acceptable to train their daughters at home rather than pay fees to send them to school.

318. Cooksey, Brian. "Education and Sexual Inequality in Cameroun." Journal of Modern African Studies 20 (1982): 167-177.

Provides statistics on female enrollment, dropout and repetition rates in the Camerounian schools. Notes wide regional variations in the extent of gender based inequalities. Females are usually older when they enter school than males. Finds also that girls in rural areas are least represented in the school system.

319. Eliou, Marie. "The Education and Advancement of women in Africa (Ivory Coast, Upper Volta, Senegal)." International Review of Education 19 (1973): 30-46.

Provides an overview of education for girls in the Ivory Coast, Upper Volta and Senegal. Points out that girls were undereducated relative to boys (neither received much education). Under colonialism girls were denied school places as the French tried to maintain Islamic traditions which favored male education. Girls' education still lags behind boys' despite government policies to expand education.

320. Mbilinyi, Marjorie J. "The Problem of Unequal Access to Primary Education in Tanzania." Rural Africana: Current Research in the Social Sciences. No. 25. Access to Education in East Africa. East Lansing: African Studies Center, Michigan State University, 1974, pp. 5-28.

Focuses on access to primary eduction in two districts of Tanzania: Mwanza rural district and Tango. Finds that different determinants of educational access exist for differing social strata, although gender appears to be a determinant which transcends class lines. Parents have lower educational expectations for girls than for boys. School fees appear to be the greatest obstacle to universal enrollments and girls' work in the household is an obstacle to school attendance only in the poorest subsistence families.

321. Robertson, Claire L. "The Nature and Effects of Differential Access to Education in Ga Society." Africa 47 (no. 2, 1977): 208-219.

Examines the effects of differential access between males and females to education in Ghana. Points out that denial of educational access to women has created a class structure where women have become less socially mobile than men and have not always assumed their husbands' social status.

322. Robertson, Claire. "Women's Education and Class Formation in Africa, 1950-1980," Women and Class in Africa. Edited by Claire Robertson and Iris Berger. New York: Africana Publishing Company, 1986, pp. 92-113.

Documents the growth of primary schooling in Africa and uses UNESCO statistics to analyze patterns of gender based inequalities in educational access.

323. Weis, Lois. "Women and Education in Ghana: Some Problems of Assessing Change." International Journal of Women's Studies 3 (1980): 431-453.

Asks whether the democraticization of educational opportunity in Ghana has equalized male/female educational attainment and outcomes. Finds that while democratization of access for girls in secondary school is evident between 1961 and 1974, girls are disproportionately represented in low status secondary schools and have greater problems than do boys in obtaining employment upon graduation.

3.   Asia

Books and Monographs

324. Bangladesh, Ministry of Education. **Development of Education in Bangladesh, 1975-1977: A Country Report.** Dacca: Ministry of Education, 1977. 28 pp.

Presents an overview of education since 1975, describing nonformal education as well as the formal system. Special emphasis is placed on efforts made toward improving women's education and on literacy programs for women. Includes a number of statistical tables.

325. Cheng, Soik Hwa. **Women in Singapore—Legal, Educational and Economic Aspects.** Singapore: Institute of Humanities and Social Sciences, College of Graduate Studies, Nanyang University, 1976. 32 pp.

Provides an overview of women's educational enrollment in Singapore. Points out that female illiteracy rates and the gap between male and female enrollments in primary, secondary and pre-university classes have significantly improved. A growing number of women are enrolled in nontraditional disciplines in higher education such as Law, Medicine, Social and Natural Sciences, Commerce, Civil Engineering, Electrical Engineering. Women outnumber men in treacher training colleges. Points out that women's enrollment in higher degree courses is relatively low because of lack of opportunities for women in employment in government, business and the professions and because of traditional attitudes that militate against women's education.

326. Endagama, Malani. **Impact of the UN Decade for Women in Sri Lanka.** Columbo: Women's Bureau of Sri Lanka, 1985. 109 pp.

Surveys education enrollments and finds equality of access to primary level and more women than men enrolled at the secondary level. This pattern existed before the UN decade. Does find improvement in technical schools, but limited to commerce not craft or industrial skills. Few women were in engineering courses at the university.

327. Islam, Shamima.   Women's Education in Bangladesh: Needs and
Issues.   Dacca: The Foundation for Research on Educational
Planning and Development, 1977.   146 pp.

Provides an excellent overview of women's educational pattern in
Bangladesh, with complete statistics for literacy rates of males
versus females, primary, secondary and higher education
enrollment patterns, and dropout rates.   Argues that while there
has been an absolute increase in educational opportunity for
women in Bangladesh since independence, women's literacy and
enrollment rates still lag behind those of men and the gap
between males and females is growing, rather than narrowing.
Argues that Universal Primary Education, as envisioned by the
Bangladeshi government, which provides for 8 years of primary
education, will widen, rather than close male/female
differential patterns of educational enrollments.   Girls attend
school less often than boys for economic reasons and the older
the girl, especially in rural areas, the more likely the family
will withdraw her from school to help rear younger children and
help with the household economy.   Believes that greater emphasis
on non-formal education rather than UPE will be key to closing
the gap between male and female literacy and educational
attainment levels.

328. Khawaja, Sarfraz.   Promotion of Girls Education in the Context
of Universalization of Primary Education.   Islamabad: Academy
of Educational Planning and Management, 1985.   65 pp.

Examines women's educational enrollment in primary education in
Pakistan and focuses on rural/urban disparities.   Investigates
as well educational provision and how that affects female
enrollment patterns.

329. Kumerloeve, Arnd D.   Bildungs-und Berufsnachfrage in der Dritten
Welt.   Eine Fallstudie in Thailand aus geschlectsspezifischer
Sicht. Tübingen: Horst Erdmann Verlag, 1982.   406 pp.

Describes women's access to education in Thailand, using a sample
of over 1000 secondary school students.   Finds that women's
enrollment in upper secondary school is higher than males.
Girls' fathers come from white collar families and tend to have
higher class status than boys.   In the schools girls tend to
study foreign languages, Thai culture and tradition while boys
concentrate on science.   Girls aspire to study medicine and
pharmacy or prepare for teaching while males plan to take up
careers in natural science and engineering.

330. Nepal.   Siksha Anusandhan, Pravartana, tatha Vikasa Kendra.
Equal Access of Women to Education Program in Nepal.   Kathmandu:

Center for Educational Research, Innovation and Development, 1978. 50 pp.

Evaluates the effectiveness of the Nepalese Ministry of Education's project of "Equal Access to Women of Education" (GAWEP). Surveys 10 school districts served by the program and interviews school teachers and education officers. Finds girls have a slightly better retention rate than boys and that the hiring of female teachers has served to increase girls' enrollment.

331. **Report on National Workshop on Female Literacy.**   Islamabad: Government of Pakistan, Literacy and Mass Education Commission, 1983. 74 pp.

Reports the first National Workshop on Female Literacy held in 1983 in conjunction with UNESCO Regional Office for Education in Asia and the Pacific. The workshop sought to identify the low level of female literacy in rural areas and the barriers to enhancing women's literacy.

332. **Towards Equality of Educational Opportunity: Inter-country Exchange of Experiences. Report of the Visits of the Regional Panel on the Education of Girls, 27 May - 10 June 1985.** Bangkok: UNESCO Regional Office for Education in Asia and the Pacific, 1985. 47 pp.

Describes proposed programs to enhance female enrollment in Bangladesh, India, Nepal and Pakistan where less than half primary school age girls are in school. Presents an overview of enrollment patterns by country as well as government programs designed to increase girls' enrollments.

Articles

333. Daro, B. "The Papua New Guinea Women in Education: Today and Tomorrow." **Education in Melanesia.** Edited by J. Brammall and Ronald J. May.   Canberra and Port Moresby: Research School of Pacific Studies, The Australian National University and University of Papua New Guinea, 1975, pp. 323-327.

Examines progress made in women's education and the factors affecting the pace of progress. Presents enrollment statistics at all levels for 1961-1972. They indicate that while there are more women in school at all levels than ever before, the increases in male educational enrollment are greater.

334. Don, Fatimah Hamid.   "Educational Opportunities for Girls in Malaysian Secondary Schools." **World Yearbook of Education.**

1984. **Women and Education.** Edited by Sandra Acker et al.
London: Kogan Page, 1984, pp. 110-122.

Provides an overview of women's access to education in Malaysia
and identifies the barriers to equality in educational
opportunity. Points out that at the secondary level, girls'
enrollment is slightly lower than that of boys. Girls' access
to vocational education is still limited and girls' vocational
preferences are still restricted to traditional female subjects.
Girls' enrollment is higher in sex segregated schools. At the
university level, half as many girls attend as do boys.
Believes that inequality in education is in large part an
outgrowth of government policies which discriminate against
women, low parental education and income levels, traditional
views of parents regarding women's education, early marriage and
female socialization.

335. Flores, Pura. "The Education of Women in Asia with Emphasis on
the Philippines." The Educational Dilemma of Women in Asia.
Edited by Alma de Jesus-Viardu. Manila: Philippine Women's
University, 1969, pp. 55-70.

Surveys changes in the pattern of female enrollment in the
Philippines. Shows that the proportion of women enrolled in
higher education has risen rapidly and that women have entered a
number of traditionally male dominated fields. In addition,
women have taken on leadership roles in the school system.

336. Hirschman, C. "Political Independence and Educational
Opportunity in Peninsular Malaysia." Sociology of Education 52
(1979): 67-83.

Focuses on the educational attainment levels of Malays by sex,
ethnicity and region using a sample drawn from the 1960 Malay
census. Finds that educational inequalities have diminished
since Malay independence. In the case of women, inequalities
with men still remain. Ten percent less women than men go on
for secondary education. Argues that the major factor
inhibiting women's educational equality with men is lack of
school places. Malay education is sex segregated and there are
fewer schools for girls than for boys, especially in rural
areas.

337. Jusuf, Naftuchah "The Education of Women in Developing
Countries: Focus on Indonesia." The Educational Dilemma of
Women in Asia. Edited by Alma de Jesus-Viardu. Manila:
Philippines Women's University Press, 1969, pp. 401-423.

Surveys enrollment patterns of women in Indonesian schools and considers the role of nonformal education in filling in the gaps between male and female literacy.

338. Kamikamica, Esiteri. "Problems of Women's Education in Fiji." Women in Development in the South Pacific. Barriers and Opportunities. Papers Presented at a Conference Held in Vanuatu from 11 to 14 August 1984. Canberra: Development Studies Centre, The Australian National University, 1985, pp. 71-87.

Provides a statistical overview of educational provision for women in Fiji in 1981-82. Points out gender disparities still remain. Women are concentrated in commercial and secretarial studies while men dominate science and technology. Inequalities in enrollment in higher education remain despite the lifting of formal barriers against women in the university.

339. Siriwardena, Subadra. "The Education of Girls and Women in Ceylon." International Review of Education 19 (1973): 115-120.

Provides an overview of women's access to education in Ceylon (Sri Lanka). Points out the educational system has expanded during the last few decades and more girls are enrolled in schools, but there is no provision for adult education to make illiterate and semi-literate women better housewives and mothers. Contends that women could contribute to the country's economic progress by entering agriculture and industry if they were given enough opportunities.

340. Smith, Peter C. and Paul P.L. Cheung. "Social Origins and Sex Differential Schooling in the Philippines." Women's Education in the Third World: Comparative Perspectives. Edited by Gail P. Kelly and Carolyn M. Elliott. Albany: SUNY Press, 1982, pp. 51-67.

Relates the distribution of education in the Philippines to social class and gender based on the May 1968 and May 1973 national demographic surveys. Finds that sex differentials in access to education as well as urban/rural differentials have lessened in time. In addition, the data demonstrated that father's schooling and occupation persist as determinants of educational attainment despite changes in the economy leading to greater industrialization and government policies aimed at opening access to education.

3a.   India

Books and Monographs

341. Bhandari, R.K. Educational Development of Women in India. New Delhi: Ministry of Education and Culture, Government of India, 1983. 109 pp.

Presents an overview of women's education in India. Points out that the gap between male and female literacy has grown rather than narrowed over time, despite government policies that have sought to encourage female education. Women's workforce participation rates have remained stagnant and women's life expectancy is lower than men's and is declining. Presents very detailed statistics on women's enrollment, women as teachers and women's literacy rates. Concludes that the following are major problems that should be addressed to improve women's education: 1) quantitative development of schools so that women can be accommodated; 2) provision of single sex institutions; 3) increase the number of women teachers; 4) provide girls with the same curricula as boys; 5) increase security for female students; 6) provide child care; 7) experiment with flexible hours.

342. Desai, Chirtakum. Girls' School Education and Social Change. Bombay: A.R. Sheth and Co. Educational Publishers, 1976. 293 pp.

Focuses on girls' educational access in Gujarat State. Finds that girls' access to education only began its upward trends after British colonialism. European literature and science, humanities and liberal thought, particularly in the 20th Century, helped stimulate women's education. Suggests that a separate infrastructure for the planning and administration of women's education with its own budgetary allocation is necessary to solve the problems of female illiteracy and undereducation.

343. Naik, J.P. Equality, Quality and Quantity: The Elusive Triangle in Indian Education. Bombay: Allied Publishers, 1975. 172 pp.

Provides a broad survey of Indian education and asks whether educational expansion and decolonizaton have contributed toward equalizing educational opportunity and class, caste and gender based inequalities in Indian society. Presents statistics on women's educational enrollment patterns from 1855 to 1974. Advocates the extension of nonformal education in tandem with the expansion of formal schooling to provide greater educational opportunities for women, the rural poor and the unscheduled castes.

344. Patel, Tara. Development of Education Among Tribal Women. Delhi: Mittal Publications, 1984. 198 pp.

Studies education among tribal women in Gujarat and compares their educational levels, wastage rates and workforce participation patterns with that of Harijan women and men. Points out that the education of tribal women is even lower than that of the scheduled castes and that there has been little change since 1960. There are variations in educational attainments of tribal women due to urban versus rural residence and social class. Also Dhodia and Chaudhari women have higher educational levels than women of other tribes. Explains the low educational levels in terms of traditional norms for women's education, poverty, poor communication between teachers (who are not from tribes) and families, parents' low educational levels which mean that parents are unable to help daughters with their school work, lack of boarding facilities for girls and lack of local school facilities.

Articles

345. Bhansali, Kamalini. "Education of Women in Modern India: Some Achievements and Problems." Education Quarterly   21 (1969): 36-43.

    Discusses problems in providing equal access to education for women in India despite the fact that the Indian Constitution guarantees equality of the sexes. Women's educational levels still lag far behind men's and girls tend to drop out of school at a higher rate than boys. Points out that women's dual role as a worker and homemaker prevents women from effectively using their education in public life.

346. Bhasin, Kamala. "Role of Educated Young Women in Changing India." The Crisis of Changing India. Edited by V.D. Sudhir. Delhi: National, 1974, pp. 214-223.

    Criticizes the wastage in education of Indian educated women. Argues that women who receive vocational, college or higher education do not use their education adequately to contribute to the development of Indian society.

347. Gould, Ketayun. "Sex Inequalities in the Dual System of Education: The Parsis of Gujarat." Economic and Political Weekly 18 (September 24, 1983): 1668-1676.

    Uses a sample of 551 Parsi households to look at female education across rural/urban differences, language of teaching and family characteristics. Finds equal access to education except among girls 16 to 26 years of age living in rural areas attending schools in the Gujarati language. After 4 to 7 years of educaton 27 percent of this group had dropped out of education (vs. 8 percent of the male population). Parents' and mother's language ability predicted whether girls would go to English or Gujarati language schools. This relatively uneducated group attacks the stereotype of the Parsi woman as being overeducated.

348. Kamat, A.R. "Women's Education and Social Change in India." Social Scientists 59 (no. 1, 1976): 3-27.

Describes the development of women's education in post-independence India and then explores the effects of education on the employment opportunities for women. Shows that the situation of women's education is far from satisfactory, despite the expansion of educational provisions. In 1973-74, one out of three girls of the primary school age group was still not in school. Dropout and repetition rates were significantly higher among girls than among boys. In higher education, the enrollment of women was only 1.3 percent of the age group of 17-23. Points out the shortage of adequate female teachers and separate girls' schools inhibits female enrollment as does accommodation and transportation for female teachers in rural areas. Other factors inhibiting access include child marriage, heavy household responsibility, conservative social and parental attitudes to women's education.

349. Shah, Madhuri R. "Status and Education of Women in India." Journal of Duyarat Research Society 38-39 (October 1976-January 1977): 15-24.

Reviews the development of education for women since India's independence. Notes that the growth rate is slow, and that most of the women enrolled in higher education are in female dominated fields like the arts, education, medicine and pure sciences. Discusses women's utilization of education. Those who have liberal arts or pure science degrees find it difficult to get jobs. Women are to be mostly found in the traditionally female fields of employment which are poorly paid and less prestigious and involve routine work.

4.   Latin America and the Carribean

Books and Monographs

350. Jerez Alvarado, Rafael. La Educación de la Mujer en Honduras. Tegucigalpa: Publicaciones del Ministerio de Educación Publica de la Republica de Honduras, C.A., 1957. 250 pp.

Provides an overview of women's education in Honduras, beginning with preschool socialization in the family and the role of the Catholic Church. Traces the evolution of schooling in the country and the development of school provision for women. Schooling for women initially consisted of a curriculum quite different from that of males. This differentiation exists today and is evident in the sex segregation of higher education; women go into education and into the arts and letters. Ends the book with a discussion of the outcomes of women's education in the workforce, in arts and letters and in the family. Contends that marriage is the major female aspiration and explains women's educational pattern.

351. Melo Cardona, Ligia A. **Participación de la Mujer en la Educación Sistimátic en La Republico Dominicana.** Santo Domingo: UASD, 1977. 15 pp. (Colección UASD Critica no. 19, vol. 238.)

Briefly reports education statistics for women from the early 1970s which show women dominate upper portions of primary, are more than half of secondary and nearly two thirds of higher education. Denotes there are major problems in rural areas.

352. Rosemberg, Fulvia, et al. **A Educação da Mulher no Brasil.** São Paulo: Global Editora, 1982.

Surveys literacy and educational enrollment statistics for Brazil, presenting urban/rural, male/female differentials. Finds that in some areas like the northeast females outnumber males in the school because there are fewer job opportunities for females in that region. Also looks at the relation of education to work. Finds that women in the workforce are better educated than their male peers, but they are not paid as well. Women with higher education tend to work in teaching or health care.

Articles

353. Bonilla de Ramos, Elssy. "Women, Family and the Educational System of Colombia." **Two Thirds** 1, no. 3 (Winter 1978-79): 19-23.

Examines women's enrollments in primary through university education in Colombia. Finds the school system discriminates against children of the poor as well as children from urban areas. Gender also is a determinant of whether a child will attend school and how long that child will be retained in school. Argues that class is as significant as gender in the pattern of schooling.

354. Collazo-Collazo, Jenaro. "Participación de la Mujer en la Fase
Educativa de la Vida Puertoriquena." Educación 22 (1969):
41-53.

Analyses female enrollment in Puerto Rican schools. Finds that
while girls outnumber boys in preschool through secondary
school, in higher education women become a minority.

355. Eichelbaum de Babini, Ana M. "La Desiqualdad Educacional en
Argentina." Argentina Conflictiva. Edited by J.F. Marsal.
Buenos Aires: Editorial Paides, 1972, pp. 19-59.

Looks at inequalities in education with one third the article
devoted to gender questions. Traces illiteracy, showing the
historical limits of women's education. Compares late 1940s
statistics with those of the 1960s to show an emergent female
domination of the middle level of education. Compares social
class attitudes towards education of boys and girls showing the
lower class has greater expectations for women's education than
does the upper class.

356. Hamilton, Marlene and Else Leo-Rhynie. "Sex Roles and Secondary
Education in Jamaica." Women and Education. World Yearbook of
Education, 1984. Edited by Sandra Acker et al. London: Kogan
Page, 1984, pp. 123-138.

Focuses on sex differences in educational enrollment patterns in
secondary education in Jamaica. Points out that girls are
enrolled in the arts and language courses while boys specialize
in science and mathematics. Argues that the socialization
process accounts for these differences in courses of study.
Concludes that inequality in women's educational processes and
outcomes will not be addressed simply by providing women with
greater access to education; rather social expectations and the
socialization processes need to be changed.

357. Lynch, Enid. "The Education of Women in Barbados." Report of
the Barbados National Commission on the Status of Women. Vol.
2. Edited by Norma Forde. Bridgetown: Government Printery,
1978, pp. 67-80.

Provides a background on the origins of sex differential
education in Barbados. Shows that female education was slow to
be organized and was inferior to men's. Few girls' schools had
laboratory facilities or taught mathematics. Their staffs were
unqualified until the University of the West Indies opened its
College of Arts and Sciences in 1948. Recent trends to
coeducation have benefitted males more than females, since they
have meant more educational facilities were opened, taking in
boys who had previously not gone to school faster than they took

in girls. Finds also that in Barbados sex differentiation in curriculum occurs only for students who are low achievers. High achieving girls tend to be exposed to the same course of study as high achieving boys.

358. McKenzie, Hermione. "The Educational Experiences of Caribbean Women." Social and Economic Studies 35 (no. 3, 1986): 65-105.

Surveys the education of women in St. Vincents, Antigua and Barbados, presenting comparative data on ages at entering and leaving primary school, post-secondary education and university education. Looks also at women's educational aspirations and finds that they are high and center on obtaining technical and vocationally oriented schooling as well as traditional university studies.

359. Meyer, V.I. "Women in Mexican Society." Current History 72 (March 1977): 122-123; 130-131.

Describes persistence of inequality between men and women in Mexico despite constitutional reforms which have legislated the end of discrimination based on gender. Women's education is constrained by attitudes which associate education with a threat to women's virtue. Despite this, there has been a gradual increase of women in higher education: in 1972, 26 percent of university enrollments were female; by 1976, 30 percent were female.

360. Mohammed, Patricia. "Educational Attainment of Women in Trinidad-Tobago 1946-1980." Women and Education. Women in the Caribbean. Vol. 5. Edited by Joycelin Massiah. Cave Hill, Barbados: Institute of Social and Economic Research, University of the West Indies, 1982, pp. 35-77.

Surveys educational pattern and performance of women from 1946 to the present. Shows that school attendance of females 5 to 19 years of age outstrips that of males. However, in higher education, women remain a minority. Finds a relation between women's education and their laborforce participation.

361. Ochoa Nuñez, Hernado. "La Mujer en el Sistema Educativo." La Mujer y el Desarrollo en Colombia. Edited by Magdalene Leon de Leal. Bogota: Asociación Colombiana para de Estudio de la Población, 1977, pp. 71-122.

Provides a statistical survey of the education system, making comparisons between the late 1930s and the mid 1970s (occasionally only mid1960s data were available). Shows education more than doubled at all levels and women greatly increased their share of the system to half of all primary enrollment, almost half of secondary enrollment and one quarter of university enrollment. Presents statistics on rural vs urban education and the influence of parents' education on the education of daughters. Both of these relationships are in the expected directions.

362. Rosemberg, Fulvia.   "A Escola e as Diferenças Sexuais." Cadernos de Pesquisa 15 (Dezembro 1975):   78-85.

Studies the educational status of women in Brazil. The data are derived from a Brazilian census reporting educational statistics for the country as a whole and for the state of Sao Paulo on literacy rates, school enrollment patterns, achievement patterns, examination pass/fail ratios and drop out rates. Points to the following patterns: 1) women's literacy lags behind that of men's as does women's educational enrollment at all levels; 2) the differences in literacy and educational enrollment ratios between males and females have lessened over time; 3) women's dropout rates relative to men's over time have declined and their graduation rates have increased.

363. Schiefelbein, Ernesto.   "La Mujer en la Educación Primaria y Media."   Chile: Mujer y Sociedad. Edited by Paz Covarrubias and Rolando Franco.   Santiago: Alfebta Impr., 1978, pp. 693-713.

Analyzes changes in women's educational enrollment patterns between 1930 and 1973. Finds that women's enrollment in 1973 in primary education was about the same as in 1930. During most of the period women outnumbered men in secondary education, although they tended not to go to technical schools. In Chile girls repeat grades less often than boys and tend to achieve better than them.

5.   Middle East

Books and Monograph

364. Oman.   Ministry of Education and Youth Affairs.   The Internal Efficiency of the Omani Educational System: A Study of the Phenomenon of Wastage.   Oman: Ministry, 1984.   302 pp.

Provides statistics, broken down by gender, of school enrollments in Oman for the years 1973-74 through 1980-81 for primary and preparatory (secondary) levels. These statistics also focus on dropout rates of males versus females and the productivity and efficiency rates by gender in primary and secondary education.

Articles

365. Abu-Laban, Baha and Sharon McIrvin Abu-Laban. "Education and Development in the Arab World." **Journal of Developing Areas** 10 (April 1976): 285-304.

Provides statistics on school enrollment in Middle Eastern countries. Compares 1950 to 1971 statistics for three levels of education. In 1971 women in primary education ranged from 10 percent to 45 percent of enrollment and all countries had improved this percentage by 5 percent or more. In general secondary enrollment in 1971 women were from 20 percent to 43 percent of those in school; most had improved but Algerian female enrollment had dropped. In higher education the percentage of female enrollment ranged from 49 percent to 12 percent. In all categories Kuwait was the leader and Lybia, Saudi Arabia, and Yemen among the least advanced.

366. Al-Sanabary, Nagat. "Continuity and Change in Women's Education in the Arab States." **Women and the Family in the Middle East.** Edited by Elizabeth Warnock Fernea. Austin: University of Texas Press, 1985, pp. 93-110.

Examines women's participation in education in the Arab states using data obtained from the UNESCO Statistical Yearbook for 1976 and 1977. Finds that the number of girls enrolled in schooling has increased at all levels, although primary education enrolls about two-thirds of all girls in school in the Arab world. Access to secondary education remains limited and girls tend to cluster in teacher preparation programs when they do go to secondary schools.

367. Barazangi, Ni'mat Hafez. "The Position of Women in the Contemporary Muslim World." **Al-Ittahad** 13 (April 1976): 18-25.

Argues that educational inequality persists in the Middle East despite advancement in women's enrollment in higher education and their entry into the professions. Shows that 83 percent of women in Muslim countries are illiterate and points out that those literacy rates will not be changed unless the government provides large numbers of girls' schools. Advocates increasing women's educational opportunities so that women can assume roles that will be acceptable to Islamic conceptions of women's separate spheres.

368. Harfoush, Samira.   "Nontraditional Training for Women in the Arab World." **Africa Report** 26 (1981): 51-55.

Describes women's educational enrollments in the Arab states of the Middle East and points out that women are denied access to vocational and technical training.

369. Jones, Marie T.   "Education of Girls in Tunisia: Policy Implications   of   the   Drive   for   Universal   Enrollment." **Comparative Education Review** 24 (1980): S106-S123.   (Also in **Women's Education in the Third World: Comparative Perspectives.** Edited by Gail P. Kelly and Carolyn M. Elliott. Albany: SUNY Press, 1982, pp. 31-50).

Describes the Tunisian government's commitment to universal primary education for girls.   Points out that the growth in female enrollments has generated major problems in educational expenditure and in finding employment for girls.   Male/female gaps remain and are not likely to be resolved easily.   Female demand for education has slackened in part because of the nature of schooling offered them and in part because employment opportunities for girls has declined as the number of educated males and females has risen.

370. Moorman, P. "The Golden Age of Islamic Education." **Change** 10 (1978): 13-14, 16-17.

Focuses on educational expansion in Saudi Arabia where one quarter of all government monies are allocated to education. While the government has modernized the school system and attempted to use education as a means of providing skilled personnel when oil revenues run out, girls' education has scarcely modernized.   Female education is kept strictly segregated from that of males and educated women are restricted to occupations in nursing and teaching other females.

371. Mustaffa-Kedah, O. "The Education of Women in the Arab States." **Literacy Discussion**, 6 (Winter 1975/76): 119-139.

Surveys the literacy rates in the Arab states and finds that out of the 75,000,000 females aged 15 and above, in 1970 86 percent were illiterate. This rate is 26 percent higher than that found in most of the third world. The major obstacles toward women's education   identified   are   traditions,   customs   and   social attitudes.   It is hypothesized that improvement in living conditions, smaller families and domestic laborsaving devices will give women more opportunity to become educated.

372. O'Shaughnessey, T.J.   "Growth of Educational Opportunity for Muslim Women, 1950 to 1973." **Anthropos** 73 (1978): 887-901.

Argues, using statistics provided by the United Nations and the United States Agency for International Development, that women's educational expansion has been as great in the Middle East as it has been in other developing nations. In 1950, women were 9.3 percent of all students enrolled in higher education; by 1973 women constituted 21.7 percent of the student population at this level as compared to 24.5 percent in African and 28.4 percent in Asian countries. Despite these gains, in the Middle East the proportion of females enrolled in primary and secondary level school lags behind female enrollments in other developing nations. There is some variation among Middle Eastern nations. Those countries with oil wealth or who have undergone a socialist revolution tend to have extended greater opportunities for women to attend school.

373. Taamallah, Lemouria. "La Scolarisation et la Formation Professionnelle des Femmes en Tunisie." **Revue Tunisienne de Sciences Sociales** 19, (no. 68/69m 1982): 107-128.

Presents statistics from the mid1970s on women's education in Tunisia including literacy rates, the educational levels of the population by age group and urban/rural residence and enrollments in apprenticeship and administrative training programs.

B. Factors Affecting Women's Access to Education--General

1.   General Studies

Books and Monographs

374. Smock, Audrey Chapman. **Women's Education in Developing Countries: Opportunities and Outcomes.** New York: Praeger, 1981. 292 pp.

Investigates the factors affecting women's opportunities for formal education in Mexico, Ghana, Kenya, Pakistan and the Philippines and relates changes in enrollment patterns to women's workforce participation outside of agriculture, fertility and marriage and family patterns.

Articles

375. Anderson, G.M. "Women and Literacy in Developing Nations." **America** 141 (July 28, 1979): 27-29.

Outlines a number of obstacles to literacy development, among which are religion, culturally conditioned attitudes, the sex role division of labor and the general lack of support for literacy campaigns by some governments. Successful literacy campaigns in the socialist nations of China, Cuba, Vietnam and the USSR are delineated as are UNESCO programs designed to increase educational opportunities for women.

376. Barber, Elinor G. "Some International Perspectives on Sex Differences in Education." Signs 4 (1979): 584-592.

Reviews the literature on sex differences in education internationally and suggests some of the factors affecting women's educational access, attainment and outcomes. Maintains that obstacles to women's access to education are not easily identifiable because they are constrained by cultural context. There is wide variance in the sex differences in educational attainment as well. Urges further scholarship that goes beyond the reanalysis of fragmentary data and speculations based on that reanalysis so that a stronger base of knowledge can be developed which would be relevant to social policy formation.

377. Kelly, Gail P. "Women's Access to Education in the Third World: Myths and Realities." Women and Education. World Yearbook of Education, 1984. Edited by Sandra Acker et al. London: Kogan Page, 1984, pp. 81-89.

Analyzes factors affecting women's access to education in the third world. With existing evidence from Africa, Asia, Latin America and the Middle East points out that women's educational enrollment has been depressed in spite of massive educational expansion. Class, ethnicity, religion and national development fail to adequately explain women's underrepresentation in schools. The availability and accessibility of schools and the relation between content of schooling and employment seem more highly related to women's educational enrollment.

378. Kelly, Gail P. "Setting State Policy on Women's Education in the Third World: Perspectives from Comparative Research." Comparative Education 23 (1987): 95-102.

Points out that the causes of women's undereducation are not necessarily the same as those of men's and urges that the following special policies be implemented to ensure women attend and remain in school: 1) Flexible scheduling and part-time schooling should be implemented. Points out that research has shown that rigid age and time-specific aspects of schooling prevent women from attending school; 2) Women should be provided with the material conditions that will enable them to attend schools. This should include the introduction of laborsaving technologies, the provision of transportation, and the development of child-care facilities; 3) Women's education should be linked to workforce opportunities.

2.   Africa

Books and Monographs

379. Scudder, Thayer and Elizabeth Colson. **Secondary Education and the Formation of an Elite.** New York: Academic Press, 1980.

Studies a sample of 500 secondary school leavers, only 12 percent of whom were women. Contains a good short survey on why so few women appear in the schools. Reasons include polygamy and pregnancy, puberty isolation, etc.

Articles:

380. Glazer, Daphne. "Problems of the Education of Girls in Nigeria." **Aspects of Education** 19 (1977): 33-42.

Underscores the regional differences in Nigeria in girls' access to education. Argues that access is affected by ethnicity and religion. Yuroba and Ibo girls have more education than do Hausa girls. Part of the differential access is religious as well. Muslim Hausas are reluctant to send their daughters to school. Finds also that there is more education in southern than northern Nigeria and where there are more schools and education becomes universal for boys, more girls go to school as well.

381. Mbilinyi, Marjorie J. "Education, Stratification and Sexism in Tanzania: Policy Implications." **African Review** 3 (no. 2, 1973): 327-340.

Investigates the factors affecting women's access to schools in Mwanza, Tango, Morogoro and Iringa districts in Tanzania. Finds that parental social class, parents' attitudes towards girls' education, sex role divisions of labor in the family, as well as government policy affect whether or not females will attend schools.

Tardits, Claude. "Reflexions sur le Problème de la Scolarisation des Filles au Dahomey." **Cahiers des Études Africaines** 3 (1962): 266-281.

see item #1041

382. Wallace, Tina. "Educational Opportunities and the Role of
Family Background Factors in Rural Buganda." **Rural Africana:
Current Research in the Social Sciences, No. 25. Access to
Education in East Africa.** East Lansing: Michigan State
University African Studies Center, 1974, pp. 29-46.

Studies factors affecting access to education in a rural village
in Uganda 15 miles outside of Kampala in 1969-1972. Finds that
the most noticeable individual factor in a child's chance to
attend and stay in school is sex which is more important a
determinant of educational access than   religion and
ethnicity. Father's educational level has an important impact
on the education of sons, but not necessarily that of daughters,
but mother's education has an even stronger impact.

3.   Asia

Articles

383. Doeriat, F. "Overpopulation, Population Growth and the Status
of Indonesian Women." **Indonesian Women: Some Past and Current
Perspectives.** Edited by B.B. Herring. Brussels: Centre
d'Etudes du Sud-Est Asiatique et de l'Extreme Orient, 1976,
pp. 151-155.

Argues that population growth is undermining women's status in
the family and public domain. With the growth of population,
women are less well nourished and receive less than sufficient
medical and sanitary services. In addition, educational gains
made by women erode. In Indonesia because of population growth,
women's access to education has not improved appreciably.

384. Hermalin, Albert I., Judith A. Seltzer and Ching-Hsiang Lin.
"Transitions in the Effects of Family Size on Female Educational
Attainment: The Case of Taiwan." **Comparative Education Review**
26 (1982): 254-285.

Analyzes the effect of family size on female educational
enrollment and attainment in Taiwan. The study is based on a
survey of 20 to 39 year old women conducted in 1973. Shows that
while number of children in the family affects whether a girl
will go to school, other factors are as important. Claims, as
the country has become richer, education has become important
for social mobility for both girls and boys and parents have
become more willing to invest in their daughter's schooling.

385. Jayaweera, Swarna. "Gender and Access to Education in Asia."
International Review of Education 33 (1987): 455-466.

Argues that equal access of women to education, even at the
primary level is illusory in Afghanistan, Bangladesh, Bhutan,
India, Nepal and Pakistan because of patriarchical social
structures which have operated to keep women out of school.

386. Shrestha, Gajendra Man et al.   "Determinants of Educational
Participation in Rural Nepal." Comparative Education Review 30
(1986): 508-522.

Studies gender among other variables predicting access to
schooling. Finds that household and school factors combine with
gender to keep girls from obtaining an education. Among the
school   factors   identified   are   teacher   ethnicity   and
qualification. Believes that more adult education projects are
necessary to change parents' attitudes toward their daughters'
education if educational access for girls is to be widened.

387. Wang, Bee-lan Chan. "Sex and Ethnic Differences in Educational
Investment in Malaysia: The Effect of Reward Structures."
Comparative Education Review 24 (1980): S140-S159.   (Also in
Women's Education in the Third World: Comparative Perspectives.
Edited by Gail P. Kelly and Carolyn M. Elliott. Albany: SUNY
Press, 1982, pp. 68-87.)

Examines the effects of increased occupational mobility and
university attendance on women's decisions to attend and remain
in school in Malaysia. Argues that the expectation of greater
benefits from post-secondary education overrides the effects of
class, poor academic performance and ethnicity in women's
educational attainment.

3a.   India

Articles

388. Ghosh, Ratna. "Sexism in Indian Education." The Dalhousie
Review 65 (1985): 437-455.

Relates women's access to schooling to sex role divisions of
labor in the family, attitudes toward women and their education,
the stage of economic development and the type of educational
provision. Points out that in India the gap between male and
female education is wide and that women when they do go to

school still remain in female fields and do not receive
technical and engineering training.

389. Ghosh Ratna. "Women's Education in the Land of the Goddess
Saraswati." Canadian and International Education 15 (1986):
25-44.

Examines the factors that hinder women in India from achieving
equal participation in education and equality of status and
opportunity. Although women's sociocultural and political
status has been remarkably improved after independence,
socioeconomic and religious structures and cultural norms
continue to act as barriers to the equality of educational
opportunity in terms of access, participation, results and
educational effects on life chances.

390. Naidu, Usha S. "Child Labour and Education in India--A
Perspective." Education and the Process of Change. Edited by
Ratna Ghosh and Mathew Zachariah. New Delhi: Sage
Publications, 1987, pp. 178-197.

Describes the situations of working children of the ages 5 to 14
in India and various programs to improve their status. Most of
the working boys and girls both in urban and rural areas are
illiterate and only 10 percent of the working boys and 5 percent
of the working girls have primary education. Educational
programs for working children are mostly limited to parts of a
few cities and are not adequate enough to motivate the children
for school education. Contends that the strategies for
educating working children be directed by short term and long
term measures with the different content from what children in
regular schools learn.

391. Pimpley, P.N. and B.L. Kappoor. "Educational Problems of Female
Scheduled Caste Students in Punjab." Interdiscipline 12 (no. 2,
1975): 85-100.

Finds that parental education and occupation affect female's
education more than men's through a survey study of 254 school
students and 233 college students. Females tend to be better
students than males. Their social adjustment is also better.
Despite this, parents favor educating males rather than females.
Believes female enrollments can be stimulated in the educational
field by engaging in extension work among the parents and by
providing extra incentives like a larger amount of scholarship
aid.

392. Sharma, M.L. "Girl Dropout in Rural Haryana: A Socio-Economic
Analysis." Indian Educational Review 20 (1985): 109-116.

Looks at the relation between the availability of educational facilities and girls' dropout rates in rural India. Uses the data collected from 100 girls in a village with a girls' school and 15 girls in the village without a girls' school. Finds out that despite various government efforts to promote women's education high dropout rates remain. Attributes this to the negative attitude towards women's education and girls' special household responsibilities. Argues that the situation can be improved by expanding educational facilities for girls, educating parents, providing employment opportunities and promoting income generation.

4.   Latin America and the Caribbean

Articles

393.   Cross, Malcolm and Allan M. Schwartzbaum. "Social Mobility and Secondary School Selection in Trinidad and Tobago." Social and Economic Studies 18 (1969): 189-207.

Studies social selection in secondary schools in Trinidad and Tobago. Among a sample of 1415 school children (24 percent were from private schools and 57 percent were female) finds there are more girls than boys in secondary schools and that the schools favor those who come from urban areas. Paternal occupation is one of the predictors of who goes to secondary school. Ethnic groups are not represented equally in secondary schools. Black males are represented in selective secondary schools to a considerably greater degree than Indian males and Black girls.

C.   Factors Affecting Women's Access to Education--
Attitudes Toward Educating Females

1.   Africa

Books and Monographs

394. Mbilinyi, Marjorie J. Attitudes, Expectations and the Decision to Educate in Rural Tanzania. Dar Es Salaam: Bureau of Resource Assessment and Land Use Planning, University of Dar Es Salaam, 1973. 50 pp.

Examines attitudes and expectations of peasants about girls'
education in Tanzania in the context of the educational system
as it developed before and after independence. Data were
collected in a survey of peasant households in 9 districts of
Tanzania in 1969, in which 382 school girls, 349 nonschool girls
and their respective household heads were interviewed. Finds
that a household head weighs probable costs and benefits of his
investment in education, especially forgone labor of a child in
the family, in deciding whether or not to send the child to
school. Contends that this decision reflects the complexity of
the nature of production relations and the mode of the
production in the household economy which should be given more
attention. Suggests that the most crucial investment in
education be primary education rather than secondary and higher
education in order for formal education to contribute to
increased productivity and social transformation.

395. Mbilinyi, Marjorie J. The Education of Girls in Tanzania. Dar
Es Salaam: Institute of Education, University College, 1969.
82 pp.

Examines the attitudinal and socioeconomic factors affecting
girls' access to schools in Tanzania by interviewing 288 school
attending and non-attending girls and their parents in four
rural and urban areas in 1968. Finds that fathers' SES, school
costs, the demand for girls' labor in the household, and general
ignorance of the value of educating females affects girls'
access to the schools.

396. Republique Rwandaise. Ministère des Affaires Sociales et du
Mouvement Cooperatif. Recherche sur les Conditions de Vie des
Femmes Rwandaises. Kigali: The Ministry, 1975. 115 pp.

Presents a public opinion survey of about two thousand men,
women and children of both sexes. Areas covered include: work,
employment, law, education, equality, health and development.
Responses are given by gender. The section on education shows
strong support for education that trains for traditional roles
and some negative attitudes towards women with secondary and
higher education.

2.   Asia

Books and Monographs

397. Hassan, Iftikhar N., et al.   The Attitude of Rural Population Toward Female Education.   Islamabad: National Institute of Psychology, 1980.   203 pp.

Reports a survey of over 700 households in rural villages in Pakistan to ascertain their attitudes towards educating girls. Finds that the rural population has very positive view of girls' education and does not believe that education will make girls irreligious or unmarriageable. Villagers sampled wanted their daughters to receive primary education, but did not desire secondary schooling (attributes this to the lack of secondary schools in most villages). Parents approved outside teachers for their daughters, but most did not want their daughters to work outside the household for an income. Finds that women are more willing to have daughters work outside the home for money than are men; more highly educated parents tend to want their daughters to go beyond primary school. Few differences in attitudes toward daughters' education exist between extended and nuclear families or by occupation. There were variations by region--some provinces had more negative views of girls' education than others. Concludes that the major barrier to girls' education in Pakistan lies in the provision of schooling.

398. Greenhalgh, Susan.   Sexual Stratification: The Other Side of 'Growth with Equity' in East Asia.   New York: The Population Council, 1985.   90 pp.   (Center for Policy Studies Working Papers no. 111)

Focuses on the ways patriarchical institutions are perpetuated in Taiwan through family socialization. Begins with a description of traditional family institutions which have been key to mediating change in women's status since World War II. Turns to a discussion of economic changes which exacerbated family context of sex stratification and traces trends in inequality between sons and daughters in access to education, occupation, income and property as well as in residence and control of income. Argues that greater sexual stratification occurred as a result of family decision making not the state or multinationals. Education and the workplace had little discrimination. Parents simply take from their daughters to give to sons but they did see daughters' education as an investment from which they could get repayment. Data show that girls go to work to pay for brothers' schooling.

Articles

399. Ashby, A. Jacqueline.   "Equity and Discrimination among Children: Schooling Decisions in Rural Nepal."   Comparative Education Review 29 (1985): 68-79.

Examines farming households' decision making by interviewing 302 households in Kahvre Palanchowk District in Nepal. Finds that a rapid extension of formal education contributes to sex inequalities. Poor households are more likely to send sons than daughters to school because of the structure of nonfarm employment opportunities, sex role divisions of labor in agriculture which require routine female labor, and women's roles in marriage and the family.

400. Bhatty, Zarina. "Muslim Women in Uttar Pradesh: Social Mobility and Directions of Change." Women in Contemporary India and South Asia. Edited by Alfred D'Souza. New Delhi: Manohar Publications, 1980, pp. 199-211.

Finds that attitudes toward educating women have changed in the Muslim community in Uttar Pradesh. These changes have resulted from economic betterment and the value of education in obtaining a suitable mate.

401. Kurian, George and Mariam John. "Attitudes of Women Towards Certain Selected Cultural Practices in Kerala State, India." Women in the Family and Economy: An International Comparative Survey. Edited by George Kurian and Ratna Ghosh. Westport, Connecticut: Greenwood Press, 1981, pp. 131-142.

Studies the attitudes of rural women in India towards four areas of cultural practices, marriage ceremony, dowry system, aspiration towards children's education and profession and children's decisionmaking, and their relationships with the educational and occupational levels of the women. Sixty Christians, 60 Hindus and 30 Muslims from younger and older generations in equal numbers were selected. Finds that the more educated the women, the more progressive the attitude, that generation significantly affects the progressive attitudes and that although the influence of occupation is not significant, all occupational levels showed a high aspiration for children's education and profession. Points out that the practice of dowry is still dominant across the different communities.

3. Latin America and the Caribbean

Articles

402. Malta Campos, Maria M. "Relação entre Sexo da Crianca e Aspirações Educacionais e Ocupacionais das Mães." Cadernos de Pesquisa 15 (Dec. 1975): 37-46.

Studies mothers' educational and occupational aspirations for their children in Brazil.   Compares middle class women in Sao Paulo to working class women from that city and Brazilia. Finds that all the women held higher aspirations for their sons' than their daughters' education and careers.

403. Preston, Rosemary.   "Gender, Ideology and Education: Implications at the Ecuadorian Periphery."   Compare 15 (1985): 29-40.

Talks about gender relations, the transmission of gender ideology and education and gender in Ecuador, especially in rural areas. Although exposure to education and to other modern institutions and processes has increased consciousness of women about their position in rural society and participation in some action groups, this has not contributed to the modification of the prevailing gender ideology in Ecuadorian society.   In order to overcome this, there has to be a change in power relations between women and men in society as a whole.

4.   The Middle East

Articles

404. Shafii, Forough et al.   "Formal Education in a Tribal Society, Iran."   Sociologia Rurales 1 (no. 1-2, 1977): 151-157.

Examines the relationship between the family income and the educational aspirations of parents for their children.   Deals with the Qashghaii tribal population in Fars province of Iran in 1973 using an interview survey of 2930 households (half the total nomadic population of the area).   Finds that the literacy rate is 20 percent, within which the rate of males is seven times greater than that of females.   The data indicate that the higher the income of the family, the greater is the desire for their daughter's education.   Regardless of the household income, parents express a desire for their sons' formal schooling.

D.   Factors Affecting Women's Access to Education--Religion

1.   General

Books and Monographs

405. Al-Hatimy, Said Abdullah Seif. **Women in Islam**. Pakistan: Islamic Publications LTD., 1979. 155 pp.

Describes women's status and positions in Islamic society as well as in other parts of the world. Chapter 1 gives an overview of women's status in various societies and religions, such as India, ancient Greece, Rome, Scandinavia, China, Judaism, Christianity, etc. Chapter 2 talks about women in Islamic society in terms of religion, family relationships and social and political spheres. Argues that health and education are the two best fields for women to have jobs in, because a woman's role in Islamic society is regarded as that of a mother and wife. Chapters 3, 4 and 5 talk about polygamy in various societies and religions in the world as well as in Islamic society. Argues that polygamy is reasonable and natural for both men and women. Chapter 6 deals with sexuality and argues that there should be no coeducation in Muslim society.

Articles

406. Bam, Brigalia H. "God's Purpose for Women and Men in a Third World Perspective." **New Perspectives for Third World Women**. Madras: Christian Literature Society, 1976, pp. 1-26.

Discusses the role of women according to Christianity and Christian conceptions of women's place in the economy, the political system and the family. Christianity believes women and men should stand with each other in a relationship of companionship and complementarity and that women's education is important in this regard.

407. King, Ursula. "Women and Religion: The Status and Image of Women in Some Major Religious Traditions." **Women in Contemporary India and South Asia**. Edited by Alfred D'Souza. New Delhi: Manohar Publications, 1980, pp. 179-197.

Examines women's roles and positions in the world's major religions. Points out that with the gradual development of the higher religions, a more definite institutionalization of religious roles occurred and the sacred authority became male. The exercise of religious functions, including teaching, became a male perogative.

408. King, Ursula. "World Religions, Women and Education." **Comparative Education** 23 (1987): 35-49.

Provides an overview of women's access to religious knowledge. Points out that until the rise of feminist scholarship, gender specific research on religious education was neglected.

Reviews gender specific knowledge in Indian religions, especially Hinduism and Buddhism, Judaism, Islam and Christianity. Points out that women have always had some access to religious knowledge through informal training, but were generally excluded from formal education in religion. Women received religious education in the home.

409. Smith, Jane I. "Women in Islam: Equity, Equality and the Search for the Natural Order." American Academy of Religion Journal 47 (1979): 517-537.

Focuses on the Koran's interpretations of the roles of women and argues that custom in many Islamic countries has gone beyond religious prescriptions. While the Koran considers women intellectually inferior to men, there is no prohibition to women's education. Points out that the Koran's advocacy of purdah and the separation of the sexes does place major limitations on women's access to education and to employment.

410. White, Elizabeth H. "Legal Reforms as an Indicator of Women's Status in Muslim Nations." Women in the Muslim World. Edited by Lois Beck and Nikki Keddie. Cambridge: Harvard University Press, 1978, pp. 52-68.

Looks at the impact of Islam on women's roles and surveys Muslim nations and ranks them as to the legal restrictions they impose on women and the impact of those legal restrictions on women's educational enrollments. Finds that countries which have the most restrictions have the lowest female school enrollment ratios and the highest female rates of illiteracy. Points out that there is a strong relation between legal reform and women's education--countries which are more liberal in their interpretation of Islam have higher rates of female school enrollment.

2.   Africa--Nigeria

Articles

411. Callaway, Barbara J. "Ambiguous Consequences of the Socialization and Seclusion of Hausa Women." Journal of Modern African Studies 22 (no. 3, 1984): 429-450.

Looks at how Islam and female seclusion affect women's life in Kano, Nigeria. Details women's socialization and their religious seclusion which renders them a "muted group." States that the slowly rising level of education for girls may lead

Hausa women to begin to challenge their role and place in society.

412. Callaway, Barbara J. and Enid Schildkrout. "Law, Education, and Social Change: Implications for Hausa Muslim Women in Nigeria." Women in the World, 1975-1985: The Women's Decade (sec. rev. ed.) Edited by Lynne Iglitzen and Ruth Ross. Santa Barbara: ABC-CLIO, 1986, pp. 181-206.

Discusses the situation of Hausa Muslim women in Nigeria and the interaction among Hausa culture, Islamic beliefs and modern secular law as they affect women's status. Studies women in Kano, Nigeria from 1976 through 1983. Points out that Nigerian constitutional rights for women are in conflict with the Islamic law. Predicts that educational leglislation will affect women more than legislation directly bearing on women's status because schooling will change women's attitudes about struggle against the strictures of Islam.

413. Csapo, Marg. "Religious, Social and Economic Factors Hindering the Education of Girls in Northern Nigeria." Comparative Education 17 (1981): 311-319.

Looks at the religious, social and economic reasons why UPE in Nigeria did not affect female school enrollment in the Muslim north. Points out that Hausa Muslims are antagonistic toward western education in general and to the education of girls in particular. Marriage customs and the seclusion of women as well as general attitudes that education lowers a women's morality function to keep girls out of school.

414. Galadanci, Alhasi S.A. "Education of Women in Islam with Reference to Nigeria." Nigerian Journal of Islam 1 (1971): 5-10.

Argues that Islam has no strictures against women's education and cites from the Koran and Hadith to show that Islam obliges women to seek knowledge. Discusses the Muslim communities' views on educating girls in Nigeria and points out that there is a tradition of learned women in Kano and Zaria.

415. Oduyoye, Mercy Ambo. "Standing on Both Feet: Education and Leadership Training of Women in the Methodist Church, Nigeria." The Ecumenical Review 33 (1981): 60-71.

Reviews the Methodist church's views on the training of women for religious leadership. Points out that the church did differentiate between males and females and through missionary schools provided women with a curriculum which was substantially changed from that offered males. Women were trained to play roles secondary to those of males and kept out of the Ministry.

3.   Asia

Books and Monographs

416. Education and Veil. Karachi: Peermahomed Ebrahim Trust, 1975.
     164 pp.

     Summarizes Islam's views on education in general and on the
     necessity of providing different educational forms and contents
     for women than for men. Warns against the "unbridled pursuit"
     of education by women in Pakistan and outlines a religious
     education deemed appropriate to women according to this very
     conservative interpretation of Islam.

417. Knabe, Erika. Frauenemanzipation in Afghanistan. Meisenheim am
     Glan: Verlag Anton Hain, 1977.   471 pp.

     Looks at religion, family sturcture, women's roles and the
     struggle for some emancipation in Afghanistan. Does contain a
     brief section (thirteen pages) which gives a summary history of
     women's education from the 1920s forward and presents a survey
     of enrollment over time (from 1933 to 1974). General enrollment
     has risen to over 800,000, but women's share at any level (and
     they are present at all levels) was at most 15 percent in 1974.

418. Maskiell, Michele. The Impact of Islamization Policies on
     Pakistani Women's Lives.   East Lansing, Michigan: Michigan
     State University, 1984. 23 pp. (Working Paper no. 69)

     Examines the effects of Zia's Islamization program since 1977 on
     civil law, educational institutions and employment, stressing
     the concrete and symbolic consequences for Pakistani women.
     Reviews Muslim family law and women's legal access in the recent
     past and points out that education was the main factor
     contributing to women's increased awareness of the law.   The
     concrete impact of the government's Islamization program has
     directly affected only a minority of women, largely articulate
     urban women.   Islamization policy in education has great
     potential to increase female literacy but has not yet much
     affected adult literacy programs.   In employment, the
     Islamization policies toward working women have not changed
     traditional employment patterns characterized by
     gender segregation. Reviews the reactions of educated women to
     the government Islamization program.

419. Weis, Anita. **Women in Pakistan: Implications of the Current Program of Islamization.** East Lansing, Michigan: Michigan State University, 1985. 23 pp. (Working Paper no. 78)

Explores the implications of the new Islamic laws for women's position in Pakistan as of 1984. Looks at government reforms in the economy, the judicial system, the penal code and in education which are designed to bring Islamic law to the country. Looks also at the impact of the reforms and points out that they had minimal effect on women's employment since most women were never employed in the cash economy. In education the changes involved courses and textbooks and also resulted in the opening of a women's university. Finds that Islamization also opened employment opportunities for women since sex segregation meant that more women were needed to teach and to practice medicine for women.

Articles

420. Ahmad, Shadbano. "Education and Purdah Nuances: A Note on Muslim Women in Aligarh." **Social Action** 27 (1977): 45-52.

Examines the relationship between education and variations in the observance of purdah among middle class Muslim women in Aligarh city, North India. Based on the data from interviews with 212 married Muslim women, finds that the practice of purdah is inversely related to the amount of education received and that despite this inverse relationship, the practice of purdah has not been discarded. Suggests that while Muslim women value secular education for the social status and the advantage in the marriage market, they may maintain their allegiance to certain traditional values.

421. Hyder, Qurratulain. "Muslim Women of India." **India Women.** Edited by Devaki Jain. New Delhi: Publication Division, Ministry of Information and Broadcasting, 1975, pp. 187-202.

Traces the Muslim women's position in different times in India. Analyzes a number of changes in Muslim society during the last few decades, pointing out that women's emancipation is limited to the upper class. The rural and urban poor continue to live their traditional lives.

422. Menon, M. Indu. "Education of Muslim Women: Tradition Versus Modernity." **Women and the Family and the Economy: An International Comparative Survey.** Edited by George Kurian and Ratna Ghosh. West Port, Conn.: Greenwood Press, 1981, pp. 107-115.

Discusses four major factors which hinder the educational progress of Muslim women of Kerala State in India (despite government programs for the improvement of the status of women): their religious education, early marriage, seclusion and the absence of socially defined occupational roles for Muslim women. Concludes that Muslim girls enter school late because of their religious education and leave the system after the 3rd or 4th standard because of their practice of seclusion. Education for occupational roles is devalued because Muslim women are not expected to work after marriage (most marry before age 15) but are to remain at home.

423. Nelson, Cynthia. "Islamic Tradition and Women's Education in Egypt." **Women and Education.** World Yearbook of Education. 1984. Edited by Sandra Acker et al. London: Kogan Page, 1984, pp. 211-226.

Focuses on the dynamic encounter between traditional Islamic and Western secular ideologies and the resulting influence on the structure and process of women's education in Egypt. Describes the Islamic tradition and the concept of complementarity between the sexes that supports female seclusion. Asks how secular education for women challenged traditional Islamic women's status and changed their roles in Egyptian society. By the mid-20th Century, Egyptian women obtained new rights and status in the public domain through secular education. However, recent political and economic crises after the defeat by Israel in 1967 have reinforced a reexamination of secular moral values among educated women and an alternative Islam is emerging.

424. Siann, Gerda and Ruhi Khalid. "Muslim Traditions and Attitudes to Female Education." **Journal of Adolescence** 7 (1984): 191-200.

Inquires as to whether Muslim women in Asia see girls' education as less important than boys'. Interviews 26 Muslim women in Pakistan and finds that they equally valued sons' and daughters' education.

425. Woodcroft-Lee, Carlien Patricia. "Separate but Equal: Indonesian Muslim Perceptions of the Roles of Women." **Women's Work and Women's Roles: Economics and Everyday Life in Indonesia, Malaysia and Singapore.** Edited by Lenore Manderson. Canberra: The Australian National University, Development Studies Centre, 1983, pp. 173-192. (Monograph no. 32)

Studies women's roles presented in two Indonesian Muslim journals, **Kiblat** and **Panji Masyarakat.** The ideal woman, despite Islamic revivalism, is the educated, career woman who dresses modestly and takes care of the children. Argues that the ideal woman is confined, despite her education, to a separate and unequal sphere.

4.   Latin America and the Caribbean

Books and Monographs

426. Confederación Interamericana de Educación Católica.   Formación de la Mujer en el Mundo Actual.   Bogotá: Secretaria General de la CIEC, 1976.   124 pp.

Focuses on women's roles in Latin America from the perspective of the Roman Catholic church.   Postulates that women's primary role is in the family and while admitting that women are discriminated against in employment, in education and in the culture, argues that women's liberation might be harmful to the family and make women a slave of the state.   Also cautions against confusing women's liberation with sexual liberation. Chapter 4 is on education.   Points out that there have been increases in women's education but that women are still undereducated in Latin America and that education still reinforces negative images of women.   Ends with a discussion of the Church's role in female education.   There are three appendices: appendix one is on women in the Catholic church; appendix two is on women in Venezuela and presents workforce and educational statistics for 1971; appendix three is on women in Columbia and the influence of education driving women into the workforce.

427. Ziogas, Marylin Godoy: Olga Caballero Aquino and Manuelita Escobar de Pena.   Pintadas por se Inismas: Historia de Diez Vidas.   Asunción, Paraquay: El Grafico S.R.I., 1986.   291 pp.

Takes an anthropological look at women in a small rural community by examining the lives of ten individual women of various ages and stations of life.   Generally finds strong traditional values, supported by education and more significantly religion, that keep and maintain women in male dominated modes of life.

5.   The Middle East

Books and Monographs

428. Lemsine, Aicha. Ordalie Des Voix. Les Femmes Arabes Parlent.
     Paris: Nouvelle Societe des Editions Encre, 1983. 369 pp.

     Provides a series of interviews relating to changing perceptions
     of the status of women in Islamic countries of the Middle East.
     The countries covered here include Saudi Arabia, the United Arab
     Emirates,   Syria,   Jordan,   Egypt,   Kuwait   and   Yemen.   The
     interviews relate to sex segregation, to women's roles in the
     family and in society, and whether women perceive female
     subordination to men has changed.   There are some interviews
     with professional women and in some of the countries a
     discussion of changes in women's educational pattern.

429. Minai, Naila. Women in Islam: Tradition and Transition in the
     Middle East. New York: Seaview Books, 1981. 283 pp.

     Focuses on changes in women's roles and status in Islamic
     societies of the Middle East.   Part I presents a history of
     women in the Middle East; Part II looks at childhood, growing up
     in a traditional as well as transitional society, love, sex and
     marriage, motherhood, divorce, polygamy, sponsors and divorcees.
     In part two education is discussed.   Points out that females
     have been denied access to education because of poverty and the
     need for female labor in the household.   In the region less than
     half the girls attend primary schools; while 2/3 of the boys
     attend.   Girls are withdrawn from secondary schools in part
     because of poverty and in part because of traditional beliefs
     about female virtue.   The underenrollment of girls is further
     reinforced by the insistence on single sex schools and the lack
     of school places on the secondary level for girls.   The greatest
     gains have been made for women in access to higher education.
     In some countries women outnumber men in universities.   Argues
     that the harem mentality has remained in society at large but
     that women who attend universities have increasingly challenged
     it.   The book ends with a discussion of women in the workforce
     and the Islamic revivalist movement.

Articles

430. Al-Hariri, Rafeda. "Islam's Points of View on Women's Education
     in Saudi Arabia." Comparative Eduction 23 (1987): 51-57.

     Looks at how Islam has shaped women's education in Saudi Arabia.
     Points out that rigid sex segregation has led to inequálities
     and that female education has suffered because there is a
     shortage of women teachers.   Argues that if educational
     opportunity is to be provided to all women, the Saudi government
     should open up a number of women's colleges to train women
     teachers.

431. Dodd, Peter C. "The Effect of Religious Affiliation on Women's Roles in Middle Eastern Arab Society. **Women in the Family and Economy: An International Comparative Survey.** Edited by George Kurian and Ratna Ghosh. Westport, Conn.: Greenwood Press, 1981, pp. 117-129.

Examines sex role expectations held by males and females of differing religions--Christian and Muslim--in Lebanon. Finds that religion made no difference but that there were differences between males and females on role expectations.

VI. EDUCATIONAL PROCESSES

Despite research linking educational processes with the persistence of gender based inequalities in the public sphere of the workforce and the political system and the domestic sphere of the household and family, little research has centered on the schools--the socialization patterns, texts and curricula, interaction between teachers and students and the like. Most of the studies of women's education in third world settings consist of educational outcome literature. Nowhere is this more obvious than in this section of the bibliography which is noteworthy for its brevity.

We have divided the sparse literature on educational processes in the third world into five parts: sex role socialization, curriculum and texts, classroom studies, achievement patterns and the attitudes and expectations of precollegiate students.

A. Sex Role Socialization in Schools and Society (General)

Books and Monographs

432. Arosemena de Tejeira, Otilia. La Jaula Invisibles: La Mujer en América Latina. México: Coleccion de Escritores Hispano-Americanos, 1977. 142 pp.

Discusses the sex role division of labor in Latin America and how it is maintained through socialization, mass media and the schools.

Articles

433. Al-Sa'Dawi, Nawal. "Growing Up Female in Egypt." Women and the Family in the Middle East. Edited by Elizabeth Warnock Fernea. Austin: University of Texas Press, 1985. pp. 111-120.

Describes the life history of a female physician growing up, in school and in her profession. The chapter is an excerpt of a novel published in Arabic in 1965. Discusses schooling's role in the struggle this woman experienced in her quest to become a doctor.

434. Barroso, Carmen L.M. et al. "Percepção de Controle e Inovação de Papéis Sexuais." Cadernos de Pesquisa no. 25 (1978): 53-94.

Describes sex role socialization processes in Brazil and urges changes in education to provide women with greater role options.

435. Chung, Sei-wha. "Socialization and Women in Korea from the Perspective of the Family, School and Social Education." Challenges for Women: Women's Studies in Korea. Edited by Chung Sei-wha. Seoul: Ewha Woman's University Press, 1986, 173-191.

Focuses on the process of socialization of Korean women in family, schools and society. Posits that if the notions of discrimination based on sex are eliminated in all phases of the socialization process, women can fully realize their potential.

436. Graciano, Marilia. "Acquisição de Papéis Sexuais na Infância." Cadernos de Pesquisa no. 25 (1978): 29-44.

Focuses on sex role socialization in Brazil. Reviews evidence showing that parents have stereotypic notions of sex appropriate behaviors of children from birth and documents the differential socialization of boys and girls in home and school. Reviews major theories about sex role learning.

437. Kakar, Sudhir. "Childhood in India: Traditional Ideals and Contemporary Reality." International Social Science Journal 31 (1979): 444-456.

Describes the traditional Indian ideas on the nature of the child and its influence on the ways adults have behaved with their children at home and at school. Hindu tradition has considered the child to be a valuable and welcome being who should receive the fullest protection and affection from adults. It has also put a much greater value on the son than the daughter.

438. Namo de Mello, Guiomar. "Os Esterotipos Sexuais na Escola." Cadernos de Pesquisa no. 15 (1975): 141-144.

Describes the ways in which Brazilian schools transmit and reinforce sex role stereotypes. Looks at texts, classroom interaction patterns and differentiated curriculum.

439. Saunders, Fay E.   "Sex Stereotypes in the Classroom."   UNESCO
     Courier 33 (April 1980):   33-37.

     Investigates the ways in which schools reproduce sex roles.
     Points out that despite the fact that in many countries barriers
     to schools have been removed, schools, through the curriculum,
     texts and teachers' attitudes, will not change basic systems of
     sexual stratification.

440. Shalinsky, Audrey C.   "Learning Sexual Identity: Parents and
     Children in Northern Afghanistan."   **Anthropology and Education
     Quarterly** 11 (1980):   254-265.

     Studies sex role socialization in northeast Afghanistan through
     life histories obtained in 1976-77.   Discusses birth customs,
     infancy, childhood socialization, formal and informal education,
     adolescence and marriage.

441. Ward, Colleen.   "Sex Trait Stereotypes in Malaysian Children."
     Sex Roles 12 (1985):   35-45.

     Examines the development of sex role stereotypes in Malaysian
     children by testing forty five year old and forty eight year old
     children including Malays, Chinese and Indians.   Finds that sex
     stereotype knowledge increases with age, that children identify
     the male stereotype more correctly than the female stereotype
     and that, though both boys and girls are more familiar with the
     male stereotype, the trend is more pronounced in boys.

                    B.   Curriculum and Texts

     Books and Monographs

442. Dupont, Beatrice.   **Unequal Education.   A Study of Sex
     Differences in Secondary School Curricula.**   Paris: UNESCO,
     1981.   88 pp.

     Investigates sex differences in access to secondary school
     academic, vocational and technical education in Afghanistan,
     Jamaica, Jordon, Madagascar, Mongolia, Portugal and Turkey.
     Finds that women are underrepresented in secondary school and
     that this underrepresentation deepens in high quality academic
     and technical programs.   In sex segregated school systems, girls
     have a narrower range of preparatory programs to select from and
     are usually taught by less qualified teachers than is the case
     in coeducational secondary schools.   Points out that there are
     differences in the patterns of inequality in access to different

types of secondary school curricula by country. A greater
proportion of girls are enrolled in technical and vocational
programs in Mongolia and Jamaica than in Portugal, Jordon or
Turkey. However, there is a great deal of sex segregation
within different kinds of secondary curricula. For example, in
Jordan and Afghanistan girls in vocational programs are barred
from agricultural education and segregated into handicrafts
training; in academic programs they cluster in the arts and
humanities. Inequality in the quality and type of secondary
education women receive persists in part because of lack of
government policies focusing on gender based inequalities in
school and society and because schools still transmit
traditional feminine stereotypes.

443. Kalia. N.N. Sexism in Indian Education: The Lies We Tell Our
Children. New Delhi: Vikas, 1979.

Presents a content analysis of Indian textbooks. Shows that 93
percent of all jobs males are portrayed in are highly
prestigious, while 87 percent of the jobs women are portrayed in
are of low prestige. Points out that women are excluded from
most of the occupations depicted in the texts.

444. Kalia, Narendra Nath. From Sexism to Equality: A Handbook on
How to Eliminate Sexist Bias from Our Textbooks and Other
Writings. New Delhi: New India Publications, 1986. 199 pp.

Investigates the extent of sexism in textbooks in use in Indian
schools. Conducts a computer-aided content analysis of 21
English and 20 Hindi language texts prescribed yearly for
students in Haryana, Punjab, Rajasthan, Uttar Pradesh and Delhi.
Finds the prevalent use of sexist language, stereotypical role
assignment to male and female characters, negative images of
women, and the like. Stresses the necessity of generating
nonsexist textbooks to encourage children of both sexes to
consider a range of options for their future. Recommends that
male and female characters be presented doing a wide range of
activities and that both sexes be portrayed at work and in the
family. Provides a number of recommendations to eliminate
sexism from the textbooks.

445. National Commission on the Role of Filipino Women. Optimizing
the Potential of the Filipino Woman as Man's Complement in
Development and Progress. (MEC-UNICEF Seminar Workshop in
Instructional Materials Writing on the Role of the Filipino
Woman). Manila: National Commission on the Role of Filipino
Women. 1980. 12 vols.

Consists of a series of instructional modules on women designed
in conjunction with UNICEF to integrate the study of women into

the social science curriculum.   The modules are on topics like human personal worth and dignity; optimizing women's intellectual potential; women and sports; women's quest for better status; rights and responsibilities of women; the Filipino woman as professional and worker, etc.

Ssenkoloto, G.M.   Toward Realistic Curricula for African Women in the Process of Development: What Realistic Contributions can Pan African Institute for Development Offer?   Cameroon: International Association for Pan African Institute for Development, November 1980.   20 pp.

see item #724

Articles

446. Alrabaa, Sami.   "Sex Division of Labour in Syrian School Textbooks."   International Review of Education 31 (1985): 335-348.

Analyzes 28 Syrian school textbooks for the proportion of male versus female characters, the extent to which females were leading figures and the images by which women are portrayed. Finds that the texts depict men in decision making roles while women are portrayed in the domestic sphere in the family. Argues that the texts do not present women accurately and criticizes the Syrian government for not producing textbooks conducive to sex equality.

447. Beran, Janice Ann.   "Growth and Development of Physical Education for Women in the Philippines."Silliman Journal 15 (1968):   427-438.

Examines the evolution of physical education for women in the Philippines.   Describes current physical education programs and finds there is an increasing awareness of the importance of this subject in the school program.

448. Chaui, Marilene, Maria Rita Kehl and Maria Jose Werebe. "Educação Sexual: Instrumento de Democratização ou de Mais Repressão?"   Cadernos de Pesquisa no. 36 (1981):   99-110.

Criticizes sex education as given in the Brazilian schools and argues that it tends to perpetuate the oppression of women.

449. Kalia, N.N.   "Images of Men and Women in Indian Textbooks." Comparative Education Review 24 (1980): S209-S223.   (Also in The Education of Women in the Third World: Comparative

Perspectives. Edited by Gail P. Kelly and Carolyn M. Elliott Albany: SUNY Press, 1982, pp. 173-187.)

Analyzes texts in use in Indian schools to show how they differentiate male from female roles and characteristics. Points out that the texts praise women for passivity and dependence while they portray men as active agents and achievers.

450. Lodgesdon, Martha. "Gender Roles in Elementary School Texts in Indonesia." Women in Asia and the Pacific. Edited by Madeleine Goodman. Honolulu: Women's Studies Program, University of Hawaii, 1985, pp. 243-263.

Notes that texts do not reach all school children but that the Indonesian government attempts to use texts to foster change. Demonstrates there is considerable gender distinction in the texts--mothers and fathers with distinct roles, girls appearing far less than boys and the only work role for women that is depicted is teaching. Language is not sexist. All of this denies the matrifocal nature of society and the strong economic role of market women.

Martin-Liao, Tienchi. Frauenerziehung im Alten China: Eine Analyse der Frauenbucher. Bochum: Herausgeber Chinathemen, 1984. 145 pp.

see item #235

451. Nischol, K. "The Invisible Woman: Images of Women and Girls in School Textbooks." Social Action 26 (1976): 267-281.

Examines the images of women and girls in English language textbooks used in schools in India. Finds that women are "invisible" in the texts--they have no names and are assigned few roles. Females are mentioned much less frequently than are boys and are portrayed as passive and helpless.

452. Rivero, Enedia B. "Educacion Sexual en Puerto Rico." Revista de Ciencias Sociales 19 (1975): 167-191.

Focuses on attitudes toward sex education in Puerto Rico. Samples 953 people and finds that 63 percent favored sex education in coeducational settings, 57 percent favored sex education integrated into school courses and 47 percent favored sex education only in the middle and high schools. There was little difference in opinions between male and female respondents.

453. Verma, Margaret.   "Building Young Children's Self-Concepts through a Non-Sexist Approach to Early Childhood Education Curriculum Materials."   Indian Educational Review 20 (1985): 20-33.

Analyzes sex role stereotyping in early childhood curricular materials in India and advocates a nonsexist approach to early childhood education.

454. Williamson, Kay M. et al.   "Female Sports Participation in Nigeria." Canadian Association for Health, Physical Education and Recreation Journal 5 (Sept. - Oct. 1985): 58-61.

Reviews the factors influencing female sports participation in Nigeria with particular emphasis on Borno.   Examines the geographical, political and economic factors hindering the development of sports in general and the impact of the educational system as well as social and religious factors inhibiting women's participation in sports.   Identifies the following factors limiting women's entry into sports: 1) attitudes toward women's roles; 2) concepts of femininity antithetical to sports for women; 3) underenrollment in schools; 4) lack of physical education programs in the secondary schools.

455. Zouadi, Mustafa.   "Physical Education and Sport in Tunisia." International Review of Sport Sociology 10 (no. 3-4, 1975): 109-114.

Surveys physical education programs in Tunisia. Points out that the number of women participating in sports competition is growing yearly. Provides statistics on male versus female participation in sports and in sports competitions.

C. Classroom Studies

Books and Monographs

456. Biraimah, Karen.   Unequal Knowledge Distribution: The School Experience in a Togolese Secondary School. Buffalo: SUNY at Buffalo, Comparative Education Center, 1982.   55 pp. (Occasional Paper no. 9)

Studies an urban secondary school with a broad social representation of society in Togo. While school has equal access and uniform curriculum, discerns a negative "hidden curriculum" limiting women's roles. Argues that girls ignore this hidden curriculum because it does not correspond to roles played in the real world--roles open through graduation from secondary school.

457. Biraimah, Karen C. Educational Opportunities and Life Chances: Gender Differentiation within a Nigerian Elementary School. East Lansing, Michigan: Michigan State University, Women in International Development, 1987. 19 pp. (Working Paper no. 150)

Studies classroom interaction patterns in an elementary school in Nigeria and shows they vary by student gender, level of education and teacher gender. Argues that the gender biased classroom environment affects girls' achievements and career and educational aspirations.

Articles

458. Biraimah, Karen "Different Knowledge for Different Folks: Knowledge Distribution in a Togolese Secondary School." Comparative Education. Edited by Philip G. Altbach et al. New York: Macmillan, 1982, pp. 161-175.

Examines the transmission of knowledge at school through hidden curricula, such as teachers' perceptions and the pattern of gender differentiation within classroom interactions as well as formal curricula. Analyzes the values and expectations internalized by the students themselves. Observations and interviews were conducted in a secondary school in Togo. Finds that teachers' perceptions of the students tend to minimize female students' abilities and potentials and maximize male students' strengths, and that teachers are transmitting these negative and limited perceptions. However, the study also finds that female students are resisting the limited expectations and role allocations embedded within the knowledge transmitted at school. Concludes that students do not necessarily learn what is taught and that factors outside the school may curtail the internalization of messages transmitted at school.

459. Biraimah, Karen C. "The Impact of Western Schools on Girls' Expectations: A Togolese Case." Comparative Education Review 24 (1980): S196-S208. (Also in The Education of Women in the Third World: Comparative Perspectives. Edited by Gail P. Kelly and Carolyn M. Elliott. Albany: SUNY Press, 1982, pp. 188-202)

Studies the hidden curriculum of a coeducational secondary school in Togo. Suggests that the schools reproduce western sex role stereotypes through the authority structure of the schools, the staffing patterns and classroom interactions between students and teachers. Interviews conducted with teachers indicate teachers held stereotypical notions of girls' achievement, irregardless of girls' actual achievement. Female students did not accept the schools' hidden curriculum. They openly resisted the teachers' and schools' low academic and occupational expectations for them. Suggests that the girls' occupational and academic aspirations can be attributed to the actual role of women in Togolese society rather than to the messages of the schools.

460. Masemann, Vandra. "The Hidden Curriculum of a West African Girls' Boarding School." Canadian Journal of African Studies 8 (1974): 479-494.

Studies the interaction of teachers and students at a Ghanaian girls' boarding school. Shows how classroom interaction patterns, the formal and informal curriculum and teacher attitudes foster sex role divisions of labor similar to those found in western patriarchial society but which are not fully entrenched in Ghana.

D. Achievement Patterns

Books and Monographs

461. Passow, A.H. et al. The National Case Study: An Empirical Comparative Study of Twenty-One Educational Systems. Stockholm: Almqvist and Wiksell, 1976. 379 pp.

Identifies factors accounting for national variation in educational achievement in science and reading comprehension. These include sex differences in achievement.

Articles

462. Boothbody, Roger A. and David W. Chapman. "Gender Differences and Achievement in Liberian Primary School Children." International Journal of Educational Development 7 (1987): 99-105.

Examines gender differences in English and mathematics achievement in grade 1, 2 and 3 across three instructional approaches used in Liberia. Finds, on the average, across the three grades, students in the programmed teaching approach significantly outperformed students in comparison groups on the mathematics and English achievement tests; that males generally outperformed females in English and mathematics; and that the greatest differences in achievement occurred among students in the programmed teaching approach.

463. Engle, Patricia L. et al. "Sex Differences in the Effects of Nutrition and Social Environment on Mental Development in Rural Guatemala." Women and Poverty in the Third World. Edited by Mayra Buvinic, et al. Baltimore: Johns Hopkins University Press, 1983. pp. 198-215.

Examines sex differences in the effects of nutritional intervention on mental test performance of girls and boys in four traditional villages in rural Guatemala. The study was conducted fromm 1969 to 1977 and data on children's health, home environment, food consumption and cognitive development were collected. The results show that supplementary ingestion had a positive effect on mental test scores of boys in both fresco (calorie supplement) and atole (protein calorie supplement) villages, but little impact on the scores of girls in atole villages. Girls' scores, however, were higher at the end of the project than at the beginning. Some social changes in the villages over time are also mentioned as factors related to the increase in girls' scores.

Finn, J.D., Loretta Dulberg and Janet Reis. "Sex Differences in Educational Attainment: A Cross National Perspective." Harvard Educational Review 49 (1979): 477-503.

see item #306

464. Finn, J.D., Janet Reis and Loretta Dulberg. "Sex Differences in Educational Attainment: The Process." Comparative Education Review 24 (1980): S33-S52. (Also in Women's Education in the Third World: Comparative Perspectives. Edited by Gail P. Kelly and Carolyn M. Elliott. Albany: SUNY Press, 1982, pp. 107-126.)

Reviews the research literature cross nationally on the role of school processes in maintaining sex differences in educational achievement. Discusses three processes which affect women's educational achievement negatively: 1) personal and academic support given to women versus men, 2) role modeling and socialization implicit in staffing patterns of schools and in curricular materials, 3) opportunity to learn specific school subjects.

465. Hamilton, Marlene A. "Performance Levels in Science and Other Subjects for Jamaican Adolescents Attending Single-Sex and Co-Educational High Schools." Science Education 69 (1985): 535-547.

Explores the academic achievement of high school students who attend single sex versus coeducational schools in Jamaica. Using data collected from 529 boys and 617 girls attending three boys', five girls' and seven coeducational schools, finds that girls achieve better in single sex schools. Argues the lower achievement in coeducational institutions is attributable to peer pressures encountered when competing with numbers of the opposite sex in school.

466. Hamilton, Marlene A. "Sex Differences in the Qualitative Performance of Jamaican Adolescents on the Circles Test of Creativity." **Caribbean Journal of Education** 9 (1982): 124-134.

Studies Jamaican adolescents' performance on a test measuring creativity. Subjects were 70 boys and 177 girls attending secondary school in St. Andrew's Parish. Finds that there are no significant differences by sex on the level of creativity, but there are qualitative variations which can be explained by sex role socialization in school and society.

467. Harlen, Wynne. "Girls and Primary-School Science Education: Sexism, Stereotypes and Remedies." **Prospects** 15 (1985): 541-552.

Studies sex differences in science achievement and asks what kinds of science teaching and curricula in the primary grades are likely to enhance female performance. Analyzes social pressures affecting girls' achievement in science and recommends intervention programs warranted by current research.

468. Harnisch, Delwyn L., et al. "Cross-National Differences in Mathematics Attitude and Achievement among Seventeen-Year-Olds." **International Journal Educational Development** 6 (1986): 233-244.

Analyzes the cross national data on 13,056 students in ten countries, gathered in 1964 by the International Association for the Evaluation of Educational Achievement, in order to determine the direction and magnitude of gender differences in mathematics attitude and achievement and to illuminate factors contributing to the differences. Gender differences were found in 17 year old students, and although the differences were small, they were pervasive across cultures and in most cases favored males. However, the data suggest that the differences are not immutable and nonbiological factors play a role in determining the magnitude of gender differences.

469. Katiyar, P.C. and Gurpal Singh Jarial. "The Role of Sex in the Enhancement of Creativity among Adolescents through a Process-Oriented Training Programme." **Indian Educational Review** 18 (1983): 40-47.

Studies the effectiveness of a training program on developing fluency, flexibility, originality and overall creativity on 40 male and 40 female students in the 9th grade of two urban schools in India. Finds no sex differences in any measures used.

470. Keeves, John. "Differences Between the Sexes in Mathematics and Science, Courses." International Review of Education 19 (1973): 47-63.

Explores sex differences in mathematics and science achievement using data collected from 10 countries through the IEA Mathematics and Sciences Projects. Finds there are sex differences in opportunity to learn these school subjects in both the last year of secondary school and the first year of university. Boys have an advantage in learning mathematics and science and this accounts for their superior achievement.

471. Kelly, Alison. "Women in Science: A Bibliographic Review." Durham Research Review 7 (1976): 1092-1108.

Surveys the research on females' access to science instruction. Points out that women do not study science because science is labeled a masculine subject; females have little conception of what a career in science involves; girls self select not to enter science courses when given a choice by the schools and they are not encouraged to enter science.

472. Kutner, Nancy G. and D. Grogan. "Sources of Sex Discrimination in Educational Systems: A Conceptual Model." Psychology of Women Quarterly 1 (1976): 50-69.

Presents a model that relates two sets of independent variables--cognitive structures of students and the school system--to sex differences in educational attainment. Argues that sex role orientation, sex difference stereotypes, ego strength, self-concept and educational and occupational expectations are strongly associated with sex differences in educational outcomes.

473. Oleksy-Ojikutu, A.E. "Culture as an Influence on Sex-Typed Response Patterns in Creativity." Perspectives in Education 2 (1986): 47-51.

Examines sex typed patterns of responding creatively within the Nigerian context. A sample of 180 (90 males and 90 females) Nigerian primary school pupils through grade six were tested on the Torrance Tests of Creative Thinking, Figural Form B. Finds that males score significantly higher than females in four of the five creativity subjects: fluency, originality, elaboration and total creativity. No sex differences were found in the subjects on flexibility.

474. Reddly, A. Venkata Rami and Balakrishna Reddy. "Creativity of Adolescent Boys and Girls in Relation to Some Variables." Indian Educational Review 19 (1984): 60-72.

Examines the effect of locality of residence, class (grade) and sex on creativity. Uses the data collected from 540 students distributed equally between the sexes, three localities (urban, semi-urban and rural) and the three classes (VIII, IX, and X). Finds out there is a significant difference between the creativity of urban, semi-urban and rural children in favor of urban children. There is a significant difference between the creativity of Class X children and that of those in Class VIII or IX.

475. Shelley, Nancy. "An Approach to Innumeracy in Our Society and the Place of Women vis a vis Mathematics." Literacy Discussion 7 (1976): 17-31.

Focuses on the cultural barriers affecting women's achievement in mathematics. Emphasizes mechanical teaching approaches to instruction in mathematics as contributing to women's learning problems. Believes that special techniques for teaching mathematics to women will change women's achievement patterns in this subject area.

476. Simmons, J. and L. Alexander. "The Determinants of School Achievement in Developing Countries: A Review of Research." Economic Development and Cultural Change 26 (January 1978): 341-357.

Reviews studies on school variables which influence students' cognitive achievement. The research is based on reanalysis of IEA data. Gender and social class background of students predict academic achievement. Concludes that increasing the quality and quantity of educational inputs such as the number of years a teacher is trained or expenditures per student is not likely to improve student achievement or mitigate the effect of gender and class on it. However, the research does suggest that increased instructional time is likely to effect student achievement outcomes of schooling.

E. Attitudes and Expectations of Pre-Collegiate Students

The studies here are limited to students in primary and secondary schools (the attitudes and expectations of students in higher education are listed in Part VIII of this bibliography which focuses on higher education). Listed here are studies of student motivation, career and educational aspirations, attitudinal change (in some cases whether education makes for more modern attitudes toward society and women's roles) and attitudes toward school.

1.   General

Articles

477. Seward, Georgene H. and Robert C. Williamson. "A Cross-National Study of Adolescent Professional Goals." **Human Development** 12 (1969): 248-254.

Compares the professional goals of adolescents from the United States, the two Germanies, Chile, Poland and Turkey. Finds that there are significant differences between the sexes in career aspirations, with boys consistently having higher aspirations than girls. Finds also that German adolescents had higher career aspirations than their peers in the other countries studied.

2.   Africa

Books and Monographs

Biraimah, Karen. **Unequal Knowledge Distribution: The School Experience in a Togolese Secondary School.**   Buffalo: SUNY at Buffalo, Comparative Education Center, 1982.   55 pp. (Occasional Paper no. 9)

see item #456

478. Evans, David R. and Gordon L. Schimmel. **The Impact of a Diversified Educational Program on Career Goals: Tororo Girls' School in the Context of Girls' Education in Uganda.** Amherst: Center for International Education, University of Massachusetts, 1970.   375 pp.

Evaluates Tororo Girls' School in Uganda.   Focuses on the SES background of students in this school, which opened in the mid-1960s and which offers commercial and home economics courses as well as academic tracks, and the girls' career and educational aspirations and expectations.   Compares the Tororo

girls with girls in high and middle status traditional schools
for girls in Uganda and finds: 1) the higher the schools'
status, the higher the SES background characteristics of girls.
Girls in high status schools have parents who work in the modern
sector, speak English and have higher educational levels than
girls in lower status schools; 2) girls at higher status schools
tend to aspire to professional work, with technical occupations
as a close second choice. Girls at lower status schools like
Tororo aspire to clerical occupations; 3) the school does mold
students' aspirations. Students in commercial and home
economics tracks have lower occupational and educational
aspirations than students in academic tracks.

Articles

479. Akande, Bolanle E. "Rural-Urban Comparison of Female
Educational Aspirations in Southwestern Nigeria." Comparative
Education 23 (1987): 75-83.

Studies the educational aspirations of 400 rural and urban
female students enrolled in 15 high schools in Oyo State.
Finds a significant relation between urban/rural residence and
female educational aspirations. Urban students aspired to
university education while rural students sought vocational
training in nursing and teaching.

Biraimah, Karen C. "The Impact of Western Schools on Girls'
Expectations: A Togolese Case." Comparative Education Review
24 (1980): S196-S208. (Also in The Education of Women in the
Third World: Comparative Perspectives. Edited by Gail P. Kelly
and Carolyn M. Elliott. Albany: SUNY Press, 1982, pp. 188-202)

see item #459

480. Evans, David R. "Images and Reality: Career Goals of Educated
Ugandian Women." Canadian Journal of African Studies 6 (no. 2,
1972): 113-132.

Looks at various levels of schools, questioning women about
career aspirations. Finds realistic careers are teaching,
nursing and secretarial work—each will absorb a large number of
trained girls. However, more girls are trained at lower
educational levels (who plan to continue their education) than
there are positions at further training institutions. At least
40 percent of these girls will be frustrated. Those who succeed
in training for nursing and secretarial work will get jobs.
This is less certain in teaching and other professional,
technical areas. A small percentage aim for significant roles
of status and power, but most will be frustrated since there are

very few opportunities. All girls discount the attraction and push toward marriage.

481. Jahoda, Gustav. "Boys' Images of Marrriage Partners and Girls' Self-Images in Ghana." Sociologus 8 (1958): 155-169.

Surveys 60 girls and 60 boys in primary and middle school in Accra as to their expectations of an ideal marriage partner. Finds that young boys see an educated women as the ideal wife, but as they grow older they perceive women in traditional roles as traders and housekeepers as more important. Girls perceive themselves as emancipated but expect to assume traditional domestic roles.

482. Lindsay, Beverly. "Career Aspirations of Kenyan Women." Journal of Negro Education 49 (1980): 423-440.

Asks how socioeconomic status and ethnicity affect women's upper secondary and university enrollment patterns. Studies 228 Kenyan students. Enrollment patterns are explained by students' status as well as ethnicity. However, SES and ethnicity do not predict educational and career aspirations completely. The students follow individually generated aspirations rather than parental desires. Women in the sample believed that their brothers had received only limited preference over themselves in education. This bias was slightly higher among nonprofessional urban families.

483. Lindsay, Beverly. "An Examination of Education, Social Change and National Development Policy: The Case of Kenyan Women." Studies in Third World Societies 16 (1981): 29-48.

Examines the attitudes of female secondary students toward their fields of study and future careers. While students perceived better ability to study in subject areas in which they had specialized, they also showed a strong "professional" orientation that represented status goals rather than direct concern for their specific chosen profession.

484. Onibokun, Yemi. "Achievement Motivation: Disparity between Boys and Girls in a Nigerian Setting." West African Journal of Education 11 (1980): 108-112.

Explores sex differences in achievement motivation among a sample of 117 males and females enrolled in two single sex secondary schools in Ibadan, Nigeria. Finds that boys have higher achievement motivation than girls through an analysis of their dreams.

3.   Asia

Articles

485. Appleton, Sheldon.   "Sex Values and Change on Taiwan."   Value
     Change in Chinese Society.   Edited by Richard W. Wilson et al.
     New York: Praeger Publishers, 1979, pp. 185-203.

     Asks if there are differences between the sexes and in values
     among Taiwanese students. Finds that the expressed values of
     males and females are similar. Marginal differences appear
     between the sexes as women give higher priority to home and
     family while men give greater value to friends, community, the
     nation and the world.

486. Hariani, Kamala.   "Educational and Vocational Aspirations and
     Planning by High School Girls."   Journal of Education and
     Psychology 28 (1970): 122-128.

     Studies the vocational aspirations of 99 girls in the fourth
     year of higher secondary school. Finds that girls' aspirations
     are closely linked to the social prestige of prospective jobs,
     peer group pressure, parental advice and school teachers'
     influence.

487. Khan, M.W. "Educational and Vocational Aspirations of Hindu and
     Muslim School Students: A Comparative Study."   Indian
     Educational Review 20 (1985): 66-77.

     Studies the educational and occupational aspirations of 55 Hindu
     boys, 59 Hindu girls, 66 Muslim boys and 53 Muslim girls
     attending secondary school in India. Finds that there are
     religious as well as sex differences: Hindu boys and girls had
     higher educational aspirations than their Muslim peers--and
     girls had lower occupational aspirations than boys.

488. Ngean, Ng See. "The Effect of Race, Sex, Age and SES on School
     Anxiety and Coping Style." Malaysian Journal of Education 12
     (1975): 1-7.

     Studies race, sex, age and SES differences in school anxiety and
     coping styles. Finds that while there are no differences by
     ethnicity in Malaysia, there are sex and age differences.

489. Olsen, Nancy J. "Changing Family Attitudes of Taiwanese Youth."
     Value Change in Chinese Society. Edited by Richard W. Wilson et
     al. New York: Praeger Publishers, 1979, pp. 171-184.

Studies family attitudes and mate choice among Taiwanese eighth and ninth graders. Finds that urban boys are more likely than rural boys to prefer free choice in marriage and have egalitarian attitudes concerning the role of women. Urban girls, however, are less egalitarian in their attitudes towards sex roles than rural girls. Urban girls from highly educated parents expressed a preference for living in a nuclear rather than extended family setting.

490. Raina, M.K. and Arunima Vats. "An Exploratory Study of Quality of School Life: Relationship with Sex, Socio-Economic Status and the Type of School." **Perspectives in Education** 2 (1986): 161-169.

Explores how quality of school life in different types of schools influences students' attitudes in terms of their satisfaction with school life, commitment to classwork and reaction to their teachers. Students from five cities of India were used as samples for the study. Finds that types of school, sex and socioeconomic status are important factors which influence the students' perception of the quality of their school life, and that quality of school life has a profound influence on the students' learning activities.

491. Watkins, D. and E. Astilla. "Field Dependence and Self Esteem in Filipino Girls." **Psychological Reports** 44 (1979): 574.

Reports a study of 243 seventh grade girls in the urban Philippines. Finds that the ability to think about an environment in abstract terms (field dependence/independence) was related to personal esteem.

4.   Latin American and the Caribbean

Articles

492. Biaggio, Angela Maria. "Achievement Motivation of Brazilian Students." **International Journal of Intercultural Relations** 2 (Summer 1978): 186-196.

Studies the impact of an experimental program designed to increase the achievement motivation of 178 male and 276 female high school students in Brazil. Finds the 10th grade girls had significantly higher achievement motivation than did the boys and that the experimental program served to increase that motivation.

493. Miller, Errol L.   "Self-Evaluation among Jamaican High School Girls."   Social and Economic Studies 22 (1973): 407-426.

Studies self esteem of Jamaican girls and finds that class and race effects students' self evaluations and their manifest anxiety scores.

494. Powell, Dorian L.   "Occupational Choice and Role Conceptions of Nursing Students."   Social and Economic Studies 21 (1972): 284-312.

Studies nursing school life in Jamaica and asks about questions of who enters nursing, what the motivations are for the students' occupational choice and what self images emerge in the diverse relationships the student experiences.   Data were collected through interviews with students and nurses, observation, and examination of student records at two nursing schools in Kingston, Jamaica.   Finds that the majority of students are from rural areas and have minimum educational qualifications required for entry into nursing school, that most of the students were self motivated by humanitarian and altruistic reasons and that there was a tendency for students to see themselves in a lower status as students.

495. Sackey, J.A. and T.E. Sackey.   "Secondary School Students' Employment Aspirations and Expectations and the Barbados Labor Market."   Social and Economic Studies 34 (no. 3, 1985): 211-257.

Surveys students in 31 secondary schools in Barbados and finds that most students sex stereotyped jobs.   The girls overall had lower occupational aspirations than boys and wished to enter predominantly female fields.

5.   The Middle East

Books and Monographs

496. Razik, Taher A. and Howard R. Kight.   Student Occupational Preferences and Their Implications for Education, Vocational Training Planning, and Manpower Development in Oman: A Preliminary Study.   Buffalo: SUNY/Buffalo, 1985.   198 pp.

Surveys the vocational interest of secondary school students in Oman.   The sample consisted of 740 students, 72 percent of whom were male.   Finds there are sex differences in vocational interests, with girls having much lower aspirations than boys and with girls having stereotypical vocational interests.

Articles

497. Dodd, Peter C. "Youth and Women's Emancipation in the United
    Arab Republic." **Middle East Journal** 22 (1968): 62-87.

    Studies the attitudes of secondary school boys to women's
    emancipation in Egypt. Finds that mother's educational level,
    type of community from which the boy comes, and family SES
    predicts boys' attitudes toward women's roles. The higher the
    mother's educational level, the less opposed to women's rights
    the students are.

498. Klineberg, Stephen L.   "Intergenerational Change: Some
    Psychological Consequences of Modernization."   Change in
    Tunisia. Edited by Russell Stone and J. Simmons. Albany: SUNY
    Press, 1976, pp. 289-310.

    Finds major orientation of both sexes and both generations
    toward being moderns, but little change in actual activity or
    experience. Schooling was more significant for girls than boys
    because it allowed them contact with girls outside the family
    and the girls assigned it far more influence in their lives.
    Often schooling created the same attitudes in both genders but
    each gender thought those attitudes peculiar to itself.

499. Mehryar, A.H. and G.A. Tashakkor. "Sex and Parental Education
    as Determinants of Marital Aspirations and Attitudes of a Group
    of Iranian Youth." Journal of **Marriage and the Family** 40
    (1978): 629-637.

    Surveys 544 boys and 473 secondary school students (aged 16 to
    19) in urban Iran. Finds that all subjects tended to favor
    modern attitudes such as the safeguarding of young people's
    rights and freedom of choice in selecting a marriage partner,
    but only within the context of Iran's established traditions.
    Girls and boys whose parents were better educated had stronger
    tendencies to have modern attitudes.

500. Salili, Farideh. "Determinants of Achievement Motivation for
    Women in Developing Countries." **Journal of Vocational Behavior**
    14 (1979): 297-305.

    Administers a questionnaire to equal numbers of male and female
    Iranian students aged 9 to 18. The questionnaire focused on
    vocational aspirations and sex role perceptions and identities.
    Socioeconomic status, rather than gender, predicted vocational
    aspirations. Iranian females attributed success or failure in
    school and in work to external causes more often than did males.
    Girls who scored higher on measures of masculinity were more
    willing than girls who scored lower to take risks. Concludes

that the psychological profile of Iranian females is similar to
that of western women, however, the Iranian social milieu
affects their behavior.

VII. WOMEN AS TEACHERS AND ADMINISTRATORS IN PRIMARY AND SECONDARY SCHOOLS

The studies here focus on women as teachers in primary and secondary schools--their behaviors, attitudes and roles in the school system. There are a number of studies which have not been included here which do impinge on women as teachers--many studies, for example, of women in the workforce mention in passing that women form the core of the teaching profession. But these studies do not focus on women's behaviors, attitudes and roles as teachers, they merely mention that women are teachers. For that reason, such studies have been listed under women and the workforce or women in the professions. In addition, there are some studies that mention that women are enrolled in teacher training courses. Unless those studies look at the content of teacher preparation and how that relates to women's performance in the profession of teaching, we have not included those studies here. Finally, studies of women academics in higher education are included in Section VIII of this bibliography which focuses exclusively on higher education.

Books and Monographs

Agrawal, Manita. Education and Modernization: A Study of Hindu and Muslim Women. New Delhi: Eduresearch Publications, 1986. 136 pp.

see item #761

Callaway, Helen. Gender, Culture and Empire: European Women in Colonial Nigeria. London: The Macmillan Press, Ltd., 1987. 278 pp.

see item #224

Menta, Vimla. Attitudes of Educated Women toward Social Issues. New Delhi: National Publishing House, 1979. 127 pp.

see item #544

501. Miller, Linda. Female Educators, Development and Human Capital: A Brazilian Case. East Lansing, Michigan: Michigan State University, 1983. 16 pp. (Working Papers on Women in International Development, no. 35)

Studies women educators in the Brazilian Amazon community of Itaituba to study the effect of development programs. Argues that as the government invests in education to increase labor productivity and promote economic development, the middle class benefits and the poor do not. Middle class women benefit from such programs, since they involve educational expansion and greater opportunities for women as teachers (women make up the vast majority of primary and secondary school teachers in Brazil; teaching is an acceptable profession for middle class women who need to work to maintain middle class lifestyles for their families). Concludes that the benefits of development projects are tied more to class than to gender. Argues that middle class women educators contribute to sustaining class inequalities by promoting middle class cultural and communal norms and by spreading socialization to bureaucracy.

502. Perez Pelaez, Liria et al. La Educacadora de Primaria: Autopercepción de sus Roles como Maestra y Mujer. Medellin: Universidad de Antioquia, Facultad de Educación, 1984.

Reports an interview study of 412 school teachers in Colombia conducted in the early 1980s. Of the 412 interviewed 306 worked in government schools and 106 in private elementary schools. The study probed teachers' perceptions of their roles as women and as school teachers. Finds that most of the teachers found no role conflict between their work and household duties.

Articles

503. "Actitudes y Opiniones de Alumnos y Profesores Frente a la Sexualidad." Educación Hoy 8 (Sept.-Dec. 1978): 83-144.

Studies the attitudes of Colombian high school and college teachers toward women and a number of women's issues: abortion, rape, marriage, contraception, and sexuality. Finds that high school teachers are more conservative than college teachers in their attitudes.

504. Briones, Jose M. "Female Teachers: Where Do You Belong?" Philippine Journal of Education 54 (1975): 59-61.

Describes the personal traits of female teachers in the Philippines from an anti-women perspective.

Correas, E.   "Sarmiento's Daughters: Sixty-Five Who   Dared
(19th Century Educator)." **Américas** 32 (Jan. 1980): 49-54.

see item #276

505. Davies, Lynn.   "Women, Educational Management and the Third
World: A Comparative Framework for Analysis."   International
Journal of Educational Development 6 (1986): 61-75.

Focuses on women's roles in the school system, predominantly as
teachers rather than managers in the third world.   Calls for
research that would explain women's subordination in the school
system   along   individual,   institutional   and   relational
dimensions.

Davies, Lynn.   "Research Dilemmas Concerning Gender and the
Management of Education in Third World Countries." **Comparative
Education** 23 (1987): 85-94.

see item #64

506. Ejiogu, Aloy M.   "Sex Differences in the Leader Behavior of
Nigerian   College   Principals."   Journal   of   Educational
Administration and History 14 (1982): 55-61.

Surveys the status of women as principals in Nigerian schools.
Finds that despite a large proportion of women in the teaching
profession, only a negligible number of teachers are in
headships.   Those employed are found in low status girls'
schools.   In 1976-1977 of the 280 colleges in Nigeria, only 40
had female principals.   Describes the leadership behavior of
female principals and compares it with that of male principals.
Based on the principals of 55 colleges in Imo and Anambra
States, finds that there is little difference between males and
females in school headships.   Finds that women were scored
higher by their subordinates on the "consideration dimensions"
of leadership behaviors.

Langmore, D.   "A Neglected Force: White Women Missionaries in
Papua 1874-1914."   **Journal of Pacific History** 17 (1982):
138-157.

see item #232

507. Miller, Linda.   "Patrons, Politics, and Schools: An Arena for
Brazilian Women." **Studies in Third World Societies** 15 (1981):
67-89.

Describes women principals in Brazil and how they use political
power.   These principals, who vary in their political influence,

use schools to gain political power by mediating between
different power groups through providing gathering occasions;
through influencing community opinion on issues related to
education, children and families; by retaining a powerful
position within their own families due to steady government
salaries; and by virtue of administering one of the three
largest bureaucracies in the country.

508. Ruiz, Macario. "The Philippine Experience: Study Group for
Visayas." The Educational Dilemma of Women in Asia. Edited by
Alma de Jesus-Viardu. Manila: Philippine Women's University,
1966, pp. 261-305.

Surveys teachers in three public high schools and two private
schools in Iloilo. Finds that male and female teachers share a
stereotypical view of women's roles as wives, mothers and
homemakers. Both males and females believe that women had
equal rights.

509. Schurubsole, A.C. "Some Problems of Teacher Education in a
Rapidly Changing African Society." Women Today 4 (1965): 97-99.

Reports on a debate among women students who had been trained to
become teachers at Machakos Training College in Kenya. The
women believed that the biggest problem facing them as teachers
was learning to take an active role in public affairs.

510. Tan-Willman, C. "Prospective Teachers' Attitudes toward the
Rights and Roles of Contemporary Women in Two Cultures."
Psychological Reports 45 (1979): 741-742.

Compares the attitudes of prospective teachers in Canada and
the Philippines on the rights and roles of contemporary women.
Subjects were 193 Canadians and 246 Filipinos. Canadians had
more liberal attitudes towards women's roles than did the
Filipinos, but Filipino women had more liberal views than did
Filipino men.

511. Van Esterik, John. "Women Meditation Teachers in Thailand."
Women of Southeast Asia. Edited by Penny Van Esterik. DeKalb,
Illinois: Northern Illinois University Center for Southeast
Asian Studies, 1982, pp. 42-54.

Discusses two women in Bangkok who lead major lay Buddhist
meditation societies. Analyzes the doctrinal, political and
ideological background which supports the emergence of these
female leaders of meditation societies. Describes the
activities of these teachers.

512. Verma, Lokesh and Sumedha Sharma. "Anxiety Differences among Married and Unmarried Women Teachers." Indian Educational Review 20 (1985): 92-102.

Studies anxiety among 100 married and 100 unmarried female teachers working in government and private schools in Jammu City, India. Finds that teachers from low SES backgrounds have higher anxiety scores than teachers from high SES backgrounds. Undergraduate female teachers have higher anxiety scores than graduate female teachers.

513. Za'rour, George and Rwadah Z. Nashif. "Attitudes Towards the Language of Science Teaching at the Secondary Level in Jordan." International Journal of the Sociology of Language 14 (1977): 109-118.

Focuses on the debate between teaching secondary school science courses in Arabic or a Western language. Uses a preference questionnaire and samples of 330 secondary students, 130 university students and 30 secondary science teachers. Studies show a slight majority favor Arabic but this is less the case for women and those in private schools. The higher class status of the women in the samples explains their greater readiness to use Western language.

VIII. WOMEN AND HIGHER EDUCATION

The studies we have included here look at women and higher
education—women as students in universities and graduate
institutions, women as professors and academics, and the attitudes of
women students (as well as male students toward women). Like other
sections of this bibliography, there are a number of studies of women
and the workforce and women and the professions which study women who
have obtained higher education. We have not listed them here unless
they study women when they are students in higher education or focus
directly on the higher education of women (versus studies of women's
educational backgrounds). However, most of the studies of
professional women are studies of women who have received higher
education and the reader should look carefully at the studies included
in that section of the bibliography.

1. **General**

Articles

514. DeBopp, Marianne O. "La Mujer en la Universidad." Filosofía y
     Letras 30 (nos. 60-62, 1956): 147-163.

     Surveys the socioeconomic background of university students in
     England, Scandanavian countries, Germany, France, Spain, the
     Soviet Union, India, Japan and the United States. Looks at the
     history of women's participation in higher education and relates
     that history to the status of women in the workforce and the
     contemporary movements for women's rights.

515. Selowsky, Marcelo. "Women's Access to Schooling and the Value
     Added of the Educational System: An Application to Higher
     Education." Women and Poverty in the Third World. Edited by
     Myra Buvinic, et al. Baltimore: The Johns Hopkins University
     Press, 1983, pp. 177-197.

     Asks whether equalizing women's access to higher education
     enhances the value added effect of education in the third

world. Finds that it does in those countries which have a high ratio of female to male graduates in secondary schools. However, the value added effect of higher education is marginal in those countries where there are low female secondary school enrollments.

516. Smith, D.R. "Women Still Denied Access: Can You Help?" Journal of the National Association of Women Deans, Administrators and Counselors 41 (1978): 162-164.

Inquires as to how women in the U.S. can assist women foreign students, whether higher education in the U.S. helps female foreign students attain elite status at home and the impact of U.S. foreign student policies on women from developing countries.

Woodhall, Maureen. "The Economic Returns to Investment in Women's Education." Higher Education 2 (1973): 275-299.

See item #844

2.   Africa

Books and Monographs:

Asayehgn, Desta. The Role of Women in Tanzania: Their Access to Higher Education and Participation in the Labor Force. Paris: International Institute for Educational Planning, 1979. 31 pp.

See item #846

517. Fapohunda, Eleanor R. Male and Female Career Ladders in Nigerian Academia. East Lansing, Michigan: Michigan State University, 1983. 19 pp. (Working Paper no. 17)

Investigates wage differentials among male and female academics at the University of Lagos and argues they are not a result of discrimination but of academic rank differences and differences in productivity. The sample studied included all 36 female staff members and 1/3 of the male staff (82). Interviews 15 of the 36 women and finds that family structures and demands by relatives adversely affect women's productivity.

518. Wessels, Dinah M. Career Orientation and Work Commitment of University-Educated Women. Pretoria: Human Sciences Research Council, 1981. 52 pp. (Report MM-85)

Explores the career orientations of university trained white women in South Africa and their degree of work commitment.

Administers a mail questionnaire to a sample of 6123 university educated women obtained from the National Register for Natural and Social Sciences. About half were Afrikaaner; the other half were English. Most were betwen the ages of 25 and 50. Finds that women plan to combine home and career but expect to withdraw from the work force when they have small children and reenter once their children are grown. Many married women with children prefer part time employment or jobs that can be combined with family obligations. Women in nontraditional fields tend to have higher work commitment than do women in traditionally female fields like teaching, social work, library sciences. The lowest work commitments were among women who were underemployed in clerical jobs. Concludes that women do not leave jobs for lack of commitment but rather because of situations in home and the workforce and difficulty in combining the two.

Articles

Agheyisi, Rachel Uwa. "The Labor Market Implications of the Access of Women to Higher Education in Nigeria." **Women in Nigeria Today**. Edited by the Editorial Committee, Women in Nigeria. London: Zed Books, 1985, pp. 143-157.

See item #850

519. Beckett, Paul A. and James O'Connell. "Education and the Situation of Women: Background and Attitudes of Christian and Muslim Female Students at a Nigerian University." **Culture et Developpement** 8 (1976): 242-265.

Surveys 195 female students attending the main campus of Ahmadu Bello University. The focus is on the social origins of students. Points out that Christian girls from upper SES families are more likely to attend university than Muslim girls and that girls' SES backgrounds are higher than those of their male classmates.

520. Biraimah, Karen C. "Class, Gender, and Life Chances: A Nigerian University Case Study." **Comparative Education Review** 31 (1987): 570-582.

Asks how class and gender affect educational aspirations and career goals among undergraduate students in a Nigerian university. The data collected during 1983 and 1984 show that female students represent an elite segment of Nigerian society but hold equal or lower educational and career expectations than do the more socially and economically diverse male student sample. Points out that this example suggests that for many women, high SES may be necessary for university access, though this high status is not always reflected in equally high educational or career expectations.

521. Garmon, Martha. "Egerton College, Njoro Diploma in Agriculture and Home Economics." The Participation of Women in Kenya Society. Edited by Achola Pala, et al. Nairobi: Kenya Literature Bureau, 1978, pp. 179-186.

Describes the home economics department at Egerton College in Kenya. The college was founded in 1969 for women. It offers a three year diploma. Sixty percent of the students are in the agricultural program; 40 percent are in home economics.

Lindsay, Beverly. "Career Aspirations of Kenyan Women." Journal of Negro Education 49 (1980): 423-440.

See item #481

522. Mbilinyi, Marjorie. "Where Do We Come From, Where Are We Now and Where Do We Go from Here?" The Participation of Women in Kenya Society. Edited by Achola Pala, et al. Nairobi: Kenya Literature Bureau, 1978, pp. 187-200.

Traces inequality in education to inequality in the workforce. Much of the discussion is focused on higher education and the pattern of female enrollment at the University of Dar-Es-Salaam in Tanzania. Points out that women are segregated into a limited number of fields--education, liberal arts and the bachelors in science program in agriculture. This pattern of higher education articulates clearly with the sex segregation of the workforce.

523. Rousseau-Mukenge, Ida. "Conceptualizations of African Women's Role in Development: A Search for New Directions." Journal of International Affairs 30 (1976-1977): 261-268.

Questions how African women students studying in colleges and universities in America perceive themselves as participants in the development of their countries. Reports a pilot study of 36 undergraduate African women studying social, natural and applied sciences and the humanities and technology who were from Nigeria, Ethiopia, Liberia, South Africa, Ghana, Zambia, Tanzania, and Zimbabwe. States that the self selection of women out of some academic areas and into others such as arts, humanities and social sciences places women at a disadvantage and is one of the reasons women are excluded from full participation. Concludes that because of colonialism women became economically deficient and lost their former status.

African women must have opportunities opened to them as well as opportunities to overcome the barrier of underdevelopment.

3.   Asia

Books and Monographs

524. Ahmad, Anis and Muslim Sajjad. **Muslim Women and Higher Education.** Islamabad: Institute of Policy Studies, 1982. 107 pp.

Argues for the creation of a women's university in Pakistan. Part I focuses on coeducation in the West and its record in China and Pakistan. Concludes that the demise of women's colleges has and negative effects on women's occupational opportunities and women students' development. The cases are drawn from Israel, China and the United States as well as Pakistan. Part II presents a plan for the development of a women's university in Pakistan.

525. Still, Kathy and J. Shea. **Something's Got to Be Done So We Can Survive in this Place: The Problems of Women Students at UPNG.** Port Moresby, Papua New Guinea: Educational Research Unit, University of Papua New Guinea, 1976. 89 pp.

Studies 143 women and 729 men students admitted to the University of Papua New Guinea between 1971 and 1975. While there were no signficant differences between the sexes in academic performance, women did identify a number of problems they experienced in higher education specific to women. These included threats of physical violence against women, pregnancy and male drunkeness. Makes a number of suggestions on how to make the university more hospitable to females.

526. Tomeh, Aida K. **Familial Sex Role Attitudes Among College Students in Korea.** East Lansing: Office of Women in International Development, Michigan State University, 1982. 23 pp. (Working paper no. 12)

Examines family sex role attitudes among college students in Korea on three dimensions: the wife-mother role, the husband-father role and problematic husband-wife alterations role. Compares the findings with those of the same study in the United States. Two hundred and sixty-six university students in Seoul answered the questionnaires given in 1980. Finds that female students are more nontraditional than men only in their suppport for sex role equality in seeking positions of authority. However, this egalitarianism is supported only when it does not disturb the traditional family structure. Finds also that socioeconomic status of parents is of greater consequence to the formation of familial sex role attitudes among Koreans than Americans.

Articles

527. Benitez, Helena. "Innovation in Higher Education for Asian Women." The Role of Women in Development. Seminar Papers and Statements. Edited by Leonardo Z. Legaspi. Manila: University of Santo Tomas Press, 1976, pp. 117-124.

Analyzes innovations in higher education for women in Asia and increasing women's enrollments in universities and colleges.

528. Bonnell, Susanne. "Women at Vudal Agricultural College." Administration for Development 5 (1975): 26-31.

Describes the experiences of 30 young women who were the first to attend the all male Vudal Agricultural College in Papua, New Guinea.

529. Clemente, Ursula Uichanco. "Trends of Enrollment of U.P. Students." Educational Quarterly 5 (1955): 242-253.

Looks at the growth of women's enrollments at the University of Philippines from 1946/47 to 1956/57. During this period women increasingly entered engineering, agriculture, forestry and veterinary sciences. Points out that the female attrition rate has been high: of the 100 women who enrolled in the first semester of 1946, only 53 managed to graduate.

530. Crocombe, Marjorie Tuainekore. "Women at the University of the South Pacific." Pacific Perspective 11 (no. 2, 1983): 25-28.

Looks at the contribution of the University of the South Pacific in opening women's access to higher education. Focuses on special programs for women students including women's studies programs, extension services and preschool programs. Points out that women have little power and authority in the university and are absent among the administrators of the institution.

Diamond, Norma. "The Middle Class Family Model in Taiwan: Women's Place Is in the Home." Asian Survey 13 (1973): 853-872.

See item #1063

531. Fisher, Marguerite J.   "Higher Education of Women and National Development in Asia." **Asian Survey** 8 (1968): 263-269.

Argues, based on United Nations' documents and the discussions at the Manila seminar organized by the United Nations in 1966, that although the number of women participating in higher education has increased in most Asian countries, the increase is still modest. Women tend to concentrate in specific fields such as education, literature, and fine arts. More women than men come from the upper middle and upper classes. Since equal participation of women in the cultural and intellectual milieu is essential to national development, educated Asian elites should play an active role in diminishing the stranglehold of tradition and prejudice and in promoting change in social patterns.

532. Garfield, Richard. "Nursing Education in China." **Nursing Outlook** 26 (May 1978): 312-315.

Describes nursing education in China during the Cultural Revolution. Describes a two year program with emphasis on practice and limited courses of study (eight weeks on disease, for example). The program emphasizes group advancement and group learning and criticism. All nurses were trained for the same position with no specialization.

533. Kim, Okgill. "The Place of Women's Colleges: The Korean Experience, Ewha University." **New Frontiers in Education** 8 (1978); 47-56.

Presents a case study of a historically female university, Ewha University, which was one of the first public university opened for women in the Republic of Korea. Assesses its current program and describes the women's studies course in detail.

Korson, J. Henry. "Career Constraints among Women Gradute Students in a Developing Society: West Pakistan." **Women in Family and Economy: An International Comparative Survey.** Edited by George Kurian and Ratna Ghosh. Westport, Conn.: Greenwood Press, 1981, pp. 393-411.

See item #913

534. Lee, Hie-sung. "A Case Study on Achievement Motivation of Women Professors in a Women's University in Korea." Challenges for Women: Women's Studies in Korea. Edited by Chung Sei-wha. Seoul: Ewha Woman's University Press, 1986, pp. 192-229.

Studies the achievement motivation of professional women in Korea. Twelve married professors with children were interviewed and asked questions about their acheivement motivation, the process of growing up and their present family environment. Finds that the basic motivation is an individual's drive to pursue her goal by realizing her abilities to the maximum, and that this was facilitated by the support of parents and spouse. A serious role conflict among the respondents, between mother and worker, was not found.

Marsh, Robert and Albert O'Hara. "Attitudes Toward Marriage and the Family in Taiwan." **American Journal of Sociology** 67 (1961): 1-8.

See item #1065.

535. Mitchell, Edna M. "Women Leaders in Nepal: A Generation Gap." **Delta Kappa Gamma Bulletin** 44 (1977): 40-51.

Interviews 45 women--15 from each of three generations of university graduates in Nepal. Generation 1 was educated in the 1930s; generation 2 in the 1950s. These two generations went to universities outside of Nepal and reported difficulties in struggling against women's traditional roles. Generation 3, which was educated in the late 1960s, experienced less struggles in becoming professionals upon their graduation from university.

Navawongs, Tippan. **Career Plans and Fertility Expectations of College Women in Bangkok, Thailand.** Singapore: Southeast Asia Population Research Awards Program, Institute of Southeast Asian Studies, 1980. 96 pp. (Research Report no. 71)

See item #1145.

536. O'Brien, Leslie N. "Sex, Ethnicity and the Professions in West Malaysia: Some Preliminary Considerations." **Akademica** 14 (1979): 31-42.

Finds that there are gender as well as ethnic and class differences in access to higher education as well as in options and opportunities to use higher education.

Oey, Mayling. "Rising Expectations but Limited Opportunities for Women in Indonesia." **Women and Development: Perspectives from South and Southeast Asia.** Edited by Rounag Jahan and Hanna Papanek. Dacca: The Bangladesh Institute of Law and International Affairs, 1979, pp. 233-252.

See item #875.

O'Hara, Albert R.   "Changing Attitudes toward Marriage and the Family in Free China." Journal of the China Society 2 (1962): 57-67.

See item #1066

537. Palmier, Leslie.   "Degree and Gender Distinctions among Indonesian Graduate Officials." Higher Education 15 (1986): 459-473.

Looks at the extent to which differences between those with bachelor's degree (Bachelors) and those with Master's or higher degrees (Highers) and between the sexes, emerge in education, occupation and employment among graduate officials in Indonesia. Data were collected in 1982 from the files of about 1000 graduate officials of whom 56 percent were Bachelors and 44 percent Highers. Bachelors were distinguished from Highers in the distribution of subjects they had studied, occupation and the government departments in which they were employed. Women, at both levels of degrees, were found more in teaching and in the departments of education and religion except for the tertiary educational institutions.

538. Peralta, Maria Cid. "Problems of Higher Education for Women." Philippine Educational Forum 8 (March 1959): 52-55; 9 (July 1959): 53-59.

Surveys the problems of women in higher education in the Philippines, focusing particularly on curricular differentiation, discrimination against women in higher education, women dropouts, and the use of higher education in the workforce and the family.

539. "Systems Analysis of Higher Education for Women in Southeast Asia: Focus on its Relevance to their Present and Expected Roles." The Role of Women in Development: Seminar Papers and Statements. Edited by Leonard Z. Legaspi. Manila: University of Santo Tomas Press, 1976, pp. 162-180.

Describes women's enrollment in education in Southeast Asia, focusing mainly on higher education. Looks also at how women have used higher education in the family and in the workforce.

Thein, Mya Mya. "Women Scientists and Engineers in Burma." Impact of Science on Society 30 (1980): 15-22.

See item #806

540. Yossundara, Chintana. "Viable Programs in Higher Education for Women in Development in Southeast Asia." The Role of Women in

Development: Seminar Papers and Statements. Edited by Leonardo
Z. Legaspi. Manila: Univesity of Santo Tomas Press, 1976,
pp. 182-186.

Discusses the university's responsibility in preparing women
graduates to take an active role in society and outlines a
course in women's studies that would be a step in that
direction.

3a.   India

Books and Monographs

541. Goldstein, Rhoda L.   Indian Women in Transition: A Bangalore
Case Study. Metuchen: Scarecrow Press, 1972. 172 pp.

Presents a questionnaire study of 97 young college educated
middle class women in Bangalore. Questionnaire focuses on
family and marriage relationship and work possibilities of the
educated. Concludes that education and work have both entered
the marriage system--at first subordinate to it, but then
shaping it. Education is an acceptable alternative while
looking for a suitable marriage, but makes suitable marriage
more difficult (the male is presumed to require more education).
Work has a similar relationship. The economic value of both
education and work are recognized in the marriage equation.

542. Gorwaney, Naintara. Self-Image and Social Change: A Study of
Female Students. New Delhi: Sterling Publishers, 1977. 271 pp.

Studies self image of 300 girls enrolled at the University of
Rajasthan (Jaipur, India) in 1969/70. Administers a
standardized personality test and a questionnaire and analyzes
autobiographies written by the 300 respondents. Finds that 1)
girls' self esteem depends on others' images of them; 2)
structural features such as family composition, family size and
birth order do not have an important effect on self esteem, but
relations with parents do; 3) high self esteem relates to active
role performance; 4) high self esteem relates to attitudinal
modernization among girls.

Maskiell, Michelle. Women Between Cultures: The Lives of
Kinnaird Collee Alumnae in British India. Syracuse: Maxwell
School of Citizenship and Public Affairs, Foreign and
Comparative Studies, Syracuse University, 1984. 202 pp. (South
Asia Series, no. 9)

See item #246

543. Mehta, Rama. The Western Educated Hindu Women. Bombay: Asia
Publishing House, 1970.

Studies 50 women who were educated in convent schools and Indian
universities. The focus is on women's attitudes toward Hindu
traditions and to education, marriage and the workforce. Finds
that these women are not committed to Hindu traditions.

544. Mehta, Vimla. Attitude of Educated Women Towards Social Issues.
New Delhi: National Publishing House, 1979. 127 pp.

Reports a survey of 900 women teachers and university students
in Uttar Pradesh, India. Finds that younger women have more
progressive attitudes about women's position in the family,
religion, culture, education, marriage, women's professional
life and women's participation in politics than do older women.
SES, family education, religion and marital status had nothing
to do with women's attitudes. However, finds that women who
come from progressive minded families have more liberal views
about women's roles than do women who come from traditional
families.

545. Sharma, Savitri.   Women Students in India: Status and
Personality. New Delhi: Concept Publishing Company, 1979.
171 pp.

Administers   Standard   Progressive   Matrices,   and   the
Guilford-Zimmerman Temperament Test to 300 women students at
Magadh Malula College in Bihar (India) to see if there is a
relation between SES and personality characteristics. The
sample consisted of students distributed through the four years
of college. Finds that SES affects personality of these women
and that their personality characteristics do not change as they
progress through college.

Articles

546. Agarwal, Bina.   "Exploitative Utilization of Educated
Womanpower." Journal of Higher Education 2 (Autumn 1976):
186-195.

Quantifies the extent to which there is ineffective utilization
of women's potential among the university graduates in India.
Finds that 27 percent of women with Ph.D. degrees, 50 percent of
those with a master's and 65 percent of those with a bachelor's
degree are unemployed because of two major factors: the type of
educational qualifications and the attitudes of the women
themselves and their families. Women who decide to work have to
wait much longer than men for jobs. Women who have obtained a

job face discrimination in remuneration given. Argues that in order to utilize better the potential of the educated women, a reorientation of traditional role relationships and of the attitudes of women as well as their families and employers and a clear cut public policy in villages and urban areas are necessary.

547. Ahmad, Karuna. "Equity and Women's Higher Education." Journal of Higher Education 5 (no. 1, 1979): 33-49.

Focuses on women as students as teachers and students in higher education. Contains 11 tables on enrollment statistics, fields in which women are studying, types of higher education institutions they attend and other data for the years 1950-1979.

548. Bhargava, Gura. "Intra-Professional Marriage: Mate Choices of Medical Students in India." Social Science and Medicine 17 (1983): 413-417.

Interviews 270 students (125 female and 145 males) in 1973 and 1975 enrolled in the S.M.S. Medical College, Jaipur, India. The interviews focused on the process of professional socialization among female and male students. Finds that the females inclined to intra professional marriage significantly more strongly than did males. Women were more likely to allow their parents to arrange such marriages for them than were males. Gives the following reasons: 1)status congruency--since the higher status guaranteed to women by a medical education can best be maintained through intra professional marriage; 2) women marrying doctors gives them a better chance of pursuing a medical career since fellow doctors understand the nature of the woman's profession; 3) female students are socialized to prefer their parents arrange their marriage for them.

549. Bhargava, Gura. "Sex Stereotyping and Sex-Congruency: Components in the Sex Role Definition of Medical Specialities in India." Social Science and Medicine 17 (no. 15, 1983): 1017-1026.

Examines the sex role stereotyping of medical specialities in India by studying 270 students and 20 faculty members at S.M.S. Medical College in Jaipur, India.

550. Bhatt, R.V., I.M. Soni and N.F. Patel. "Performance of Women Medical Graduates from Medical College, Baroda, 1949-1974." Medical Education 10 (1976): 293-296.

Finds that at Baroda Medical College in India, female performance is consistently better than men's although the dropout rate for females is greater than for males. Women continue to specialize in obstetrics and gynecology. Finds that while in other countries, women's admission to medical college is increasing, at Baroda women's enrollments declined by 13 percent in the years 1969-1974.

551. Desai, Neera. "The Pattern of Higher Education of Women and Role of a Women's University." Journal of Higher Education 3 (1977): 5-19.

Discusses higher education of women in India in terms of enrollment, goals and objectives, social composition of students, utilization of education and the purposes of women's university. Despite significant progress, only 4.4 percent of women of the age group 17-23 years are enrolled in higher education and they tend to concentrate in fields such as arts and science. While students view education from intellectual and financial points, parents still seem to educate their daughters to prepare for a traditional role. Women with higher educational qualifications and training pursue a career. However, female arts and science graduates find it difficult to get jobs. Considering that more and more women are likely to seek employment, argues that the educational system will have to provide some job training as well as academic courses and that the economy should be developed so that more job opportunities will be created.

552. Jhabvala, Renana and Pratima Sinba. "Between School and Marriage--A Delhi Sample." Indian Women. Edited by Devabe Jain. New Delhi: Publications Division, Ministry of Information and Broadcasting, Government of India, 1975. pp. 283-287.

Surveys female students enrolled in Delhi University to ascertain their views of women's roles. Finds that most female university students drift and see college as a way of biding time until they get married. However, finds also that the years women spend at college make then open to new attitudes and roles and less satisfied with traditional women's roles in the family.

Krishnaraj, Maithreyi. "Employment Pattern of University Educated Women and Its Implications." Journal of Higher Education 2 (1977): 317-327.

See item #898

Maskiell, Michelle. "Social Change and Social Control: College-Educated Punjab Women: 1913 to 1960." Modern Asian Studies (1985): 55-83.

See item #259.

553. Mazumdar, Vina. "Higher Education of Women in India." **Journal of Higher Education** 1 (Autumn 1975): 155-165.

Describes women's advance in higher education in India based on data from the Census of 1971. While most states have made rapid progress, the rate of progress has been uneven, not only between states but between different levels of education within the same state. Argues that three issues affect the progress of women's education in India: the controversies over coeducation, differentiation of curricula for girls and boys and the social purpose of women's education.

Prasad, M.B. et al.   "Perception of Parental Expectations and Need Achievements."   **Journal of Social Psychology** 109 (1979): 301-302.

See item #1057

554. Rao, Amba U. "A Sociological Study of Occupational Choices of Under-Graduate Girl-Students." **Indian Journal of Social Work** 37 (1976): 1-11.

Studies the attitudes of female undergraduate students toward employment of women, their occupational choice and the impact of their social background such as caste/community, parents' occupation and educational levels in Gulbarga city, India. One hundred and sixteen female undergraduate students from four major caste groups, Brahmin, Lingayat, Muslim and Christian, were interviewed in 1974-75 academic year. The data show that students have positive attitudes toward employment of women and prefer occupations by personal interests; no association was found between occupational choice and caste or fathers' educational level.

555. Raza, Moonis and Aggarwal, Yash. "Higher Education: Regional Dimension." **Journal of Higher Education** 11 (Monsoon-Autumn 1985-86): 1-39.

Examines the regional disparities of different social groups in the development of higher education in India. Based on the data obtained from the University Grants Commission and others, analyzes the five aspects of regional variation: spatial spread of higher education, faculty wise enrollments, stage wise enrollments, enrollment of the scheduled castes and male female differentials in enrollment. Regional disparities are not only in the quantity, but particularly in the type of education. Male female disparities are still significant, especially when considered in the contexts of male female disparities among regions and castes.

Srivastava, Vinita.   "Professional Education and Attitudes to Female Employment: A Study of Married Working Women in Chandigarh."   Social Action 27 (1977): 19-30.

See item #902

556. Talesra,Hem Lata.   "Higher Education among Women: An Analysis of the Situation in a District of India."   Perspectives in Education 2 (1986): 121-124.

Looks at the social background characteristics of females enrolled in higher education in Udaipur, Rajasthan.   Finds that upper caste and upper class women have benefited the most from the expansion of higher education.

4.   Latin America

Books and Monographs

557. Labadie, Gastón J.   La Mujer Universitaria Urguaya.   Montevideo: Universidad de la Republica Oriental del Urguay, Instituto de Estudios   Sociales,   División   de   Publicaciones,   1980. (Investigación no. 5)

Looks at the pattern of women's enrollment in higher education in Uruguay and points that women are underenrolled because they have fewer opportunities to go to secondary school, they prefer short term to long term postsecondary courses of study and they tend to drop out of university when they get married or about age 25.

Articles

558. Aragonés, Maria.   "La Mujer y los Estudios Universitarios en Chile: 1957-1974."   Chile Mujer y Sociedad.   Edited by Paz Covarrubias and Rolando Franco.   Santiago: Alfebeta Imp., 1978, pp. 715-52.

Analyzes the growth and development of women's higher education in   Chile.   Focuses   on   enrollment   patterns   by   field   of specialization between 1957 and 1970.   Points out that women are a minority in higher education in Chile despite the fact that they form the majority of secondary school students.   Over time women's enrollment in national universities has increased while it has decreased in regional institutions and at the technical university.   Points out that women enter higher education in

Chile in increasing numbers and fields of study have come to be sex segregated.

559. Brown, M. and M. Amoroso. "Attitudes toward Homosexuality among West Indian Male and Female College Students." Journal of Social Psychology 97 (December 1975): 163-168.

Surveys the attitudes of 69 male and 51 female West Indian students toward homosexuality and compares them with attitudes of comparable samples drawn from Canada and Brazil. Women in the West Indies sample were less hostile to homosexuality than were males. West Indian males were significantly more hostile to homosexuality than were Canadian males but less hostile than were Brazilian males.

560. Fernández Berdaguer, Maria Leticia. "Educación Universitaria y Desempeño Profesional: El Caso de las Mujeres Estudiantes de Ciencias Económicas de la Universidad de Buenos Aires." Revista Paraguaya de Sociologia 20 (1983): 75-97.

Studies the female graduates of the Economics Department of the University of Buenos Aires and looks at their workforce and professional lives.

4a.   Brazil

Books and Monographs

561. Abramovich, Fanny. Quem Educa Quem? São Paulo: Summus, 1985. 141 pp.

Consists of polemic against the practice of education or differentiation by institution, teaching method or foreign degrees. Accuses men of using educational prestige--male professors who become professors because of who they are, an ex-minister, for example--while female professors are responding to real classroom needs and teaching the actual subject content.

Articles

"Actititudes y Opioniones de Alumnos y Profesores Frente a la Sexualidad." Educación Hoy 8 (Sept.-Dec. 1978): 83-144.

See item #503

Antrobus, Peggy.   "Reaching   Beyond   University   Walls."
Development (no. 4, 1984): 45-49.

See item #773

562. Barrosoa, Carmen Lucia de Maleo and G. Namu de Mello.   "O
     Accesso da Mulher au Ensino Superior Brasileior."   **Cadernos de**
     Pesquisa, no. 15 (Decembro 1975):   47-77.

     Focuses on women's access to higher education in Brazil.
     Analyzes women's enrollment patterns in higher education by
     field of study and relates this to career choices students
     articulate when they take university entrance examinations.
     Suggests research strategies to explore more deeply the
     occupational choices and achievement of female university
     students.

563. Ferretti, C.J. "A Mulher e a Escolha Vocacional."   **Cadernos de**
     Pesquisa 16 (1976): 20-40.

     Administers a questionnaire to students sitting for university
     entrance examinations in biology and related fields. Finds that
     careers   in   biology   were   sex   stereotyped   and   that   these
     stereotypes relate both to feminization of the careers and to
     attitudes toward the professional roles of women.

564. Gama, Elizabeth Maria Pinheiro.   "Achievement Motivation of
     Women: Effects   of   Achievement   and   Affiliation   Arousal."
     Psychology of Women Quarterly 9 (1985): 89-103.

     Studies   achievement   motivation   among   139   female   Brazilian
     university students.

565. Levine, R.L. and L. West. "Attitudes toward Women in the United
     States and Brazil."   **Journal of Social Psychology** 108 (1979):
     265-266.

     Compares the attitudes of 129 U.S. and 150 Brazilian high school
     and college students toward women's roles. Shows that females
     have more liberal attitudes than males; the more education an
     individual has the more liberal his or her attitudes and that
     Brazilian college students had more liberal attitudes than did
     their American peers.

4b.   Mexico

Articles

566. Beachy, Debra.   "Bias against University Women Is Decreasing
Slowly in Mexico."   Chronicle of Higher Education 21 (September
8, 1980): 15-16.

Outlines the discrimination against women in Mexican higher
education.   Points out that women generally obtain low paying
secretarial positions in higher education.   However, over the
past three years four women have been named deans of faculties
at the National Autonomous University of Mexico.   Women now head
departments in nontraditional fields such as medicine, law,
science, accounting and business.   Despite women's advancement
in higher education, the proportion of women students in higher
education has declined dramatically.   This is due to the
economic crisis in Mexico which has strained family resources.

567. Camp, Roderic A.   "Women and Political Leadership in Mexico: A
Comparative Study of Female and Male Political Elites."   Journal
of Politics 41 (1979): 417-441.

Studies the relationship between women's higher education and
entry into the Mexican political elite.   Finds that women
politicial elites come from background similar to those of men.
However, they do have lower educational and professional levels
of training than do males but come from higher socioeconomic
backgrounds.   Argues that as more Mexican women enter higher
education and receive professional degrees, they will have
greater access to political elite.

568. Lavalle Urbina, Maria.   "La Mujer, su Situación Legal y de Facto
me Daban el Asiento Pero no el Lugar."   Los Universitarios 29
(no. 15, 1974): 8-16.

Focuses on the legal status of women in Mexico and explores how
leading Mexican feminists have used higher education to advance
the legal rights of women.

569. Llano Cifuentes, Carlos.   "La Educación Superior Feminina como
Tarcia Específica."   Editora de Revistas 58 (Sept.-Oct. 1968):
24-28, 30-35.

Looks at women's underenrollment in Mexican higher education and
argues that the pattern is caused by discrimination against
women (university requirements are higher for women than for
men).   Points out that women are enrolled in low quality
programs that prepare them for traditionally female professions.

5.   Middle East

Books and Monographs

Abu Nasr, Julinda et al.   Women, Employment and Development in the Arab World.   Berlin: Mouton, 1985.   143 pp.

See item #971

Articles

570. Al-Bassam, Ibtissam A.   "Institutions of Higher Education for Women in Saudi Arabia."   International Journal of Educational Development 4 (1984): 255-258.

Describes colleges of higher education for women in Saudi Arabia--their organization, objectives and teaching staff. Points out that much has been achieved in providing women with higher education and urges that further expansion be postponed until such time as the needs of existing colleges are met and the quality of education in them assured.

571. Al-Nouri, Q.N.   "Modern Professionalism in Libya: Attitudes of University Students."   International Social Science Journal 27 (1975): 691-702.

Reports a field study carried out at the University of Tripoli. 24 percent of the students' fathers and 60 percent of their mothers were illiterate.   For females there was greater illiteracy rates among the parents.   Most students expected jobs upon graduation with the government: 57 percent of the females and 44 percent of the males expected jobs in teaching.   Students were disappointed with such job prospects.   Most men wanted a position in business or the professions.   Women expressed a strong preference for employment outside the arts.   Women had stronger attitudes supporting women's work outside the home. However, only 80 percent approved of women working alongside of men.   Almost 50 percent of males supported women working outside the home.   Of these only 34 percent supported women being employed in mixed sex settings.

572. Baali, Fuad.   "Educational Aspiration among College Girls in Iraq."   Sociology and Social Research 51 (July 1967): 485-493.

Surveys 470 college girls and shows a positive relation between aspiration for graduate study and fathers' socioeconomic status, educational level and willingness to participate in a more democratic home life.

573. El Guindi, Fadwa.   'Veiled Activism: Egyptian Women in the Contemporary Islamic Movement."   **Mediterranean Peoples** 22-23 (1983):   79-89.

Discusses women's progress in higher education in Egypt in connection with the increasing number of veiled women in public. In the last two decades, the ratio of male to female students in Egyptian universities has steadily decreased and women have made a great advancement especially in the previously male dominated fields such as medicine and engineering. Argues that the contemporary veiling, unlike the secular and discriminating character of the traditional veil dress, is egalitarian in character and that, although it separates women from men, it has helped women to participate more in society.

574. Meleis, Afaf Ibrahim, and Soad Hussein Hassan.   "Oil Rich, Nurse Poor: The Nursing Crisis in the Persian Gulf."   **Nursing Outlook** 28 (April 1980): 238-243.

Describes education projects to overcome a severe nursing crisis in the Gulf States—nurse patient ratios run from 1 to 150 to 1 to 3000 (U.S. is 1 to 150). Ministries of health and physician control have stressed quantity not quality. Argues for education in the hands of nurse educators and lauds matching programs with U.S. nursing schools. Advocates continued control by nurses and more reform.

575. Torki, Mostafa A.   "Achievement Motivation in College Women in an Arab Culture."   **Psychological Reports** 56 (1985): 267-271.

Studies achievement motivation and fear of success among female college students in Kuwait, Lebanon, Quatar and Iraq.   Finds there are no differences in achievement motivation between Arab men and women nor is there a correlation between feminity and fear of success.   Finds that Kuwaiti women showed less fear of success than has been found in studies of American women.

5a.   Lebanon

Books and Monographs

Sabri, Marie Aziz.   Pioneering Profiles: Beriut College for **Women.**   Beriut: Khayat Book and Publishing, 1967.   314 pp.

See item #294

Articles

576. Abu-Laban, Baha.   "Sources of College Aspirations of Lebanese Youth."   Journal of Developing Areas 2 (1968): 225-240.

    Studies the college plans of 2466 Lebanese youth. Finds that sex differences in aspirations for higher eduction are very slight in comparison with those found by McDill and Coleman for a similarly drawn American sample.

577. Tomeh, Aida K.   "Birth Order, Club Membership and Mass Media Exposure."   Journal of Marriage and the Family 38 (February 1976): 151-162.

    Studies 434 college women, aged 18 to 23 years old, and their receptivity to mass media. Finds that women who were the last born child were more interested and receptive to mass media and active in campus life than women who were first born. Girls who had both elder and younger siblings evidenced no clearcut pattern of interest in and receptivity to mass media. Since the entire sample consisted of women from upper socioeconomic strata of society, SES effect on attitude formation could not be tested.

578. Tomeh, Aida K.   "Birth Order and Alienation among College Women in Lebanon."   Women in Family and Economy: An International Comparative Survey.   Edited by George Kurian and Ratna Ghosh. Westport, Conn.: Greenwood Press, 1981, pp. 81-106.

    Studies 523 women college students in Lebanon to determine whether alienation depends on birth order. Finds no significant differences in alienation between first and last born females.

IX. ADULT AND NONFORMAL EDUCATION

Nonformal education broadly includes programs delivering eductional services outside of the age-specific, graded school system of primary through university level institutions. It covers extension services, radio and television instruction, short-term courses as well as literacy campaigns. The research on nonformal education and women in the third world has centered, for the most part, on bringing women into the development process. The argument which is made is that since the formal school system has neglected women, nonformal education can provide alternative paths to acquisition of skills and knowledge necessary to maximize women's contribution to the development process and/or to bring women the benefits of development. Provision of basic literacy to women is not the exclusive goal of nonformal education in much of this literature. Nonformal education is often expected to provide women with income-generating skills and with skills to perform better presumed roles as wives and mothers. Many of the studies focus on fertility control programs and on nutrition and health care. There is a debate in the literature here about whether such programs oppress or liberate women, for so many of the programs, as some of the critiques listed here point out, are designed to convince women of the primacy of the domestic sphere in their lives.

The articles and books listed here are not always discrete from studies that might be found in other parts of this bibliography. Many of them could be categorized under "women and development," "women and fertility" or "women and the family." While there is extensive cross-listing, here we have included those studies which discuss nonformal education in general, describe specific programs of delivery, critique nonformal education as it is applied to women and develop educational programs to empower women.

1.   General Works

Books and Monographs

579.   Ahmed, Manzoor and Philip H. Coombs.   Education for Rural Development: Case Studies for Planners.   New York: Preager, 1975.   661 pp.

Provides case studies of nonformal education programs in Indonesia, Cuba, Jamaica, Kenya, Mali, Thailand, Sri Lanka and Upper Volta.   The focus is on nonformal education and some of the chapters contain statistics on women participants in the programs.

Ali, Mohamed Adham.   Education, Fertility and Development: An Overview.   Khartom, Sudan: Economic and Social Research Council, National Council for Research, 1984.   36 pp.   (Bulletin no. 11)

See item #1079

Charlton, Sue Ellen M.   Women in Third World Development. Boulder and London: Westview Press, 1984.   240 pp.

See item #681

Clark, Noreen.   Education for Development and the Rural Women. Vol. 1.   A Review of Principles with Emphasis on Kenya and the Philippines.   New York: World Education, 1979.   66 pp.

See item #682

Derryck, Vivian L.   The Comparative Functionality of Formal and Non-Formal Education for Women: Final Report.   Washington: Women in Development, 1979.   196 pp.

see item #684

Droegkamp, Janis and F. Munger.   Women Centered Training: Responding to Issues and Ideas for Women in Development. Amherst, Mass.:   University of Massachusetts Center for International Educaltion, 1979.   51 pp.

see item #685

580.   Paolucci, Beatrice, et al.   Women, Families and Non-Formal Learning Programs.   East Lansing: Institute for International Studies in Education, Michigan State University, Program of

Studies in Non-Formal Education, 1976.   102 pp.   (Supplementary Paper no. 6)

Examines the connection between informal education, nonformal education, lifelong education and school systems and women's roles in the family.   Argues that women's education is key to improving human resource development.

Rogers, Barbara. The Domestication of Women: Discrimination in Developing Societies. London: Tavistock, 1981. 200 pp.

See item #809

Wichterich, Christa. Frauen in der dritten Welt. Bonn: Deutsche Stiftung fur internationale Entwicklung, 1984. 83 pp.

See item #694

Articles

581. Belloncle, Guy.   "A la Recherche de Nouvelles Formules Éducatives pour le Tiers-Monde."   Archives de Sciences Sociales de la Cooperatives et Communautaire 44 (1978): 77-96.

Calls for new educational approaches that involve community needs to teach less direct goals such as literacy. Sees needs for women in terms of sex education. Also advocates women's literacy schools built around teaching family and child health care needs.

582. Bernard, Anne K. and Margaret Gayfer. "Women Hold Up More Than Half the Sky: Report of the ICAE Women's Project." Convergence 14 (1981): 59-71.

Reports a study on women and adult education conducted by the International Council for Adult Education (ICAE). The project was carried out by coordinators in seven third world regions to find out more about quality and extent of the participation of women in adult and nonformal education, about the women working in this field and what still needs to be done. Points out that nonformal educational programs still reinforce female-assigned roles and skills and urges governments to formulate more effective policies to foster women's inclusion in development.

Callaway, Helen. "The Voices and Silences of Women." Literacy Discussion 4 (Winter 1975-1976): 17-34.

see item #698

583. Gayfer, Margaret. "Women Speaking and Learning for Ourselves."
Convergence 13 (1980): 1-12.

Focuses on the limited roles that women play in the planning,
implementation and evaluation of adult and nonformal education.
Argues that women's aspirations should be taken into account in
developing adult education programs and such programs should
support women's advancement and participation. Discusses the
International Council for Adult Education (ICAE) which
emphasizes women's participation in the planning and assessment
of adult education. ICAE emphasizes the need for women to
network with one another to share experiences and information on
adult education programs.   Comments on the scarcity of
opportunities for women to network at adult education workshops
because of limited financial resources made available to them.

584. Jenkins, Janet. "Non-Formal Education for Women: What Use is
It?" Educational Broadcasting International 12 (1979): 158-161.

Criticizes nonformal educational programs for women in the third
world for failing to improve women's status and provide them
with skills necessary for entry into the modern economy.

585. Mair, Lucille. "Adult Learning, Women and Development."
Prospects 8 (1977): 238-243.

Criticizes the development strategies of third world nations
which have been based on free enterprise models that emphasize
market economies and rapid industrialization to the detriment of
agricultural development.   Emphasizes, in contrast, human
resource development via education and argues that in order to
develop most third world countries need to emphasize
self-reliance.   Education of women is seen as key to
development, since female labor is critical in the agricultural
economies of the third orld.

586. Mair, Lucille. "Meaning and Implication of the Expanded
Concepts of Development for Action." Literacy Discussion 7
(1976-77): 85-96.

Argues that nonformal and lifelong education are more effective
than traditional, teacher centered schooling in educating women.
Criticizes traditional school systems for their elitism and
tendancy to perserve neocolonialism and dependency.

587. Oglesby, K.L. et al. "Adult Education for Women."
International Encyclopedia of Education. Vol. 1. Edited by
Torsten Husen and T. Neville Postlethwaite. Oxford: Pergamon
Press, 1985, pp. 125-136.

Discusses adult and nonformal education of women in developed as well as developing countries. Points out that in the case of developed countries, most of these programs are lifelong learning programs designed for leisure as well as programs designed to upgrade women's skills in jobs they already hold. In the developing countries nonformal and adult education focuses predominatly on health care, agricultural extension programs, vocational education, literacy programs and the like. Presents a critique of some of the nonformal education programs for contributing to women's subordination and discusses the potential of nonformal education for empowering women.

Peters, Joan Allen. "Some Guidelines for Planning Appropriate Programs for Women." The Decade for Women. Edited by Aisla Thomson. Toronto: Canadian Congress for Learning Opportunities for Women, 1986, pp. 99-108.

See item #707

588. Whiting, B.B. "Rapid Social Change: Threat or Promise." Ekistics, 43 (February 1977): 64-68.

Argues for nonformal education for women making the transition from an urban to a rural setting. Points out that women are the major socializers of their children and women who move from rural to urban settings are unable to pass down urban skills necessary for survival to their children.

"Women, Literacy and Development." Literacy Discussions 6 (Winter 1975-1976): 172 pp.

See item #710

Zeindenstein, G.   "Including Women in Development Efforts." World Development 6 (1978): 971-978.

See item #712

2.   Africa

Books and Monographs

Belloncie, Guy. Femmes et Développement en Afrique Sahélienne. L'Experience Nigierienne d'Animation Feminine (1966-1976). Paris: Editions Ouvriénes, 1980. 212 pp.

See item #713

Bryson, C. Judy. **Women and Economic Development in Cameroon.**
Washington: U.S. Agency for International Development, 1979.
153 pp.

See item #714

589. CADU Evaluation Studies: **Women's Extension.**   Asella: Chilalo
Agricultural Unit, 1970.   14 pp.

Reports the development of an instrument to evaluate a women's
extension program in rural Ethiopia.   Through interviews with 43
married women who had never attended school and who were
illiterate, pilot evaluations were conducted.   The extension
program covered gardening, hygiene, food preparation and
nutrition, child care, clothing, milk hygiene and poultry as
well as home improvements.

German Foundation for Developing Countries.   **Women in Economic
and Social Development in Africa.**   Berlin: German Foundation
for Developing Countries, 1970.   2 vol.

See item #716.

590. Luguga, Lucy.   **Training and Employment Opportunities for
Out-of-School Girls in Dar-Es-Salaam.**   Addis Ababa: United
Nations Economic Commission for Africa, African Training and
Research Center for Women, 1984.   32 pp.

Describes training programs in Dar-Es-Salaam for unemployed
primary school leavers.   Centers established in that city teach
girls home economics and boys carpentry and masonry.   Most of
these programs were underenrolled.   Girls often refused to
attend because the courses offered them had no connection with
future employment.   After 1976 the courses offered women
expanded to include typing, poultry raising, tailoring, bag and
mat making, tie dying and vegetable gardening.   Much of the
monograph describes the tailoring and tie-dying programs which
were deemed a great success in terms of helping women gain
employment.

591. Mitchnik, D.A.   **Improving Ways of Skill Acquisition of Women for
Rural Employment in Some African Countries.**   Geneva:
International Labour Organizations, 1977.   76 pp.

Reviews educational programs in Zaire and Upper Volta aimed at
improving women's skills in rural settings.   Points out that
many training programs for women ignore local needs as well as
women's needs and argues that women's education is critical for
improving health, hygiene and nutrition in rural Africa.   Urges
research on women's education, particularly on the use of women

as extension workers and on the training of women for non-farm employment in rural areas.

Petit, J.J. Integrated Family Life Education Project: A Project of the Ethiopian Women's Association. Project Assessment. Washington, D.C.: World Education, 1977. 98 pp.

See item #1104

Séminaire Operationnel Régional d'Alphabétisation Fonctionnelle, Banfora, Haute-Volta, 1975. La Place et le Rôle de la Femme dans le Développement Economique et Social de l'Afrique. Dakar: Bureau Régionale de l'UNESCO pour l'Éducation en Afrique, 1976. 90 pp.

See item #720

Ssenkoloto, G.M. Toward Realistic Curricula for African Women in the Process of Development: What Realistic Contributions Can Pan African Institute for Development Offer? Cameroon: International Association for Pan African Institute for Development, November 1980. 20 pp.

See item #724

592. Youngman, Frank, ed. Women and Productive Activities--The Role of Adult Education. Gaborone, Botswana: Institute of Adult Education, University College of Botswana, 1980. 44 pp.

Reports four papers presented and discussed at the seminar entitled "Women and Productive Activities--The Role of Adult Education" held in Botswana in 1980. The four papers talk about the socioeconomic status of women in Botswana, women's access to government services under National Development Plan V, the problems of women's access to credit, and women and agricultural development, respectively. The first paper argues that, despite legally guaranteed equality, women still lag behind men in education and that the high dropout rate of girls is due to pregnancy coupled with the increase of female headed families resulting from male migration. Maintains that adult education has an important role in helping women to participate in development by providing skills to be self-employed and self-sufficient.

Articles

593. African Training and Research Centre for Women. "Tâches Excessives des Femmes et Accès aux Techniques." Assignment Children/Les Carnets de l'Enfance no. 36 (1976): 38-52.

Critiques nonformal education programs which teach women only cooking, embroidery and other household skills and ignore teaching women the skills related to women's work in food production. Describes the African Training and Research Center which trains women volunteers. These volunteers, in turn, help form women's cooperatives that assist women in modernizing their farming and trading activities.

594. Brown, Lalage. "Adult Education and Its Role in National and Sectoral Development." **Literary Work** 4 (July/Sept. 1974): 67-85.

Argues that agricultural development will not occur unless there is a greater effort made to extend nonformal education to rural farmers and proposes the establishment of a National Institute of Adult Education to provide Nigeria a nationally coordinated set of programs in this area. Is critical of some the pre-existing nonformal education programs for not emphasizing numeracy as well as literacy skills. Since women form the majority of farmers in Nigeria, insists that women be brought into adult education programs, particularly in agriculture and commercial programs.

595. Cole, Jane. "Providing Access to New Skills and Modern Techniques: The Ghana National Council on Women and Development." **Assignment Children/Les Carnets de l'Enfance** no. 38 (1977): 71-79.

Describes the Ghana ten year plan to extend information about development to women. Critiques the failure of past programs to reach women.

596. Dawit, T. "Media et Femmes Rurales en Afrique." **Assignment Children/Carnets de l'Enfance** no. 38 (1977): 64-70.

Argues that the mass media in Africa ignores women's issues. Reviews six African daily newspapers over a six month period and finds that only a few articles focus on women. Of these, most were on urban women while the newspapers neglected rural women. Points out that countries like Ethiopia, Somalia and Tanzania have initiated mass education programs and Benin, Niger and Senegal run rural radio forums in areas such as agriculture, health, hygiene and water conservation. Argues that more effort should be made to reach women through these programs. Radio programs should be scheduled around times when women can be free to listen to them.

597. Fonseca, Claudia. "Functional Literacy for Village Women: An Experiment in Upper Volta." **Prospects** 5 (1975): 380-386.

Describes the functional literacy program for village women in Upper Volta started in 1967. The program tried to give practical information and suggestions to help villagers improve their living conditions through classes in health and hygiene, nutrition, childcare and sewing. Despite some obstacles in the villages (traditional attitudes and conservatism linked with poverty), women played major roles in the program.

598. George Igoche, Martha H. "Integrating Conscientization into a Program for Illiterate Urban Women in Nigeria." **Convergence** 13 (1980): 110-116.

Studies attitude change among 32 illiterate and semi-literate women in the slums of Ajegunle in Lagos State, Nigeria. The women participated in a home economics project run by Catholic church workers. Data were collected before and after their participation in the project via observations, interviews and questionnaires. There were changes in women's attitudes toward social, civic and domestic roles. Through the course of the program women became less apathetic about their living conditions. This change was attributed to their better understanding about the world gained through the program as well as the skills they learned in it to help generate income. Many of the participants began to augment their household income by selling baked goods and handicrafts. Concludes that conscientization is necessary in adult education if it is to have an impact on women's lives.

599. Gordon, Joanna. "Communicating with Women: Classes or Other Means." **Community Development Journal** 1 (1966): 10-21.

Evaluates a community development project in Ghana which was intended to help women enter the workforce. Points out that the project placed too much emphasis on activities by teachers and failed to bridge class experiences and practice. Argues that Mass Education Assistants who have served as teachers in these nonformal education programs become more sentitive to women's lives by visiting their homes and observing their women students' daily activities.

600. Higgins, Kathleen Mansfield. "What Kind of Training for Women Farmers." **Convergence** (1982): 7-18.

Evaluates nonformal education programs provided by the Botswana Ministry of Agriculture for female farmers at the Ministry's rural training centers. Finds that the women are being provided education in domestic science rather than in agricultural skills. Recommends that for nonformal education to make women more productive the content needs to be changed and go beyond instruction in home economics.

601. Jiagge, Justice Annie.   "The   Role   of   Non-governmental
Organizations in the Education of Women in African States."
Convergence 2 (1969): 73-78.

Discusses the role of non-governmental organizations in women's
education in African countries.   Argues that non-governmental
organization programs should try to meet the urgent need for
education in the African context and that education of the
mother as the preschool teacher of the child is important.
Contends that the development of both leadership at the
grassroots level and the potentialities of women should be the
special concern of non-governmental organizations.

602. Junge, Barbara Jackson and D. Tegegne.   "The Effects of
Liberation from Illiteracy on the Lives of 31 Women: A Case
Study."   Journal of Reading 28 (1985): 606-13.

Describes Ethiopia's mass literacy campgaign which began in 1979
and studies its effect on women.   Interviews 14 rural women who
were housewives, farmers and traders in Gudo Buret and 17 urban
women residing in Debre Berhan who were housewives or worked in
factories or for the government.   Finds that all the women were
motivated by the literacy campaign and acquired from it a wider
vision of women's role.   Finds also that the learning retained
was that related to the immediate needs and interests of the
women.   These needs and interests were different in rural areas
than urban areas.

Luseno, D.   "Education and the Social Status of Women in
Africa."   Kenya Journal of Adult Education 2 (1972): 17-22.

See item #739

603. McSweeney, Brenda Gael.   "Time to Learn, Time for a Better Life:
The Women's Education Project in Upper Volta."   Assigment
Children 49/50 (1980): 109-126.

Looks at the impact of the "Project for Equal Access of Women
and Girls to Education" in Upper Volta which began in 1967.   The
project, which was designed to provide women with knowledge and
skills that would save their labor on household tasks, involved
water purification and food milling.   Finds that while the
projects did save women and girls time, they did not use the
time to enter nonformal education programs that would teach them
literacy and more income generating skills, but rather used the
time to farm and to engage in handicrafts and trade.

604. McSweeney, Brenda G. and Marion Freedman.   "Lack of Time as an
Obstacle to Women's Education: The Case of Upper Volta."
Comparative Education Review 24 (1980): S124-139.   (Also in

Women's Education in the Third World: Comparative Perspectives.
Edited by Gail P. Kelly and Carolyn M. Elliott. Albany: SUNY
Press, 1982, pp. 88-106.)

Describes a United Nations Development Project in Upper Volta
which focused on providing the enabling conditions for women to
attend nonformal education programs. There were two parts of
the project: 1) a time-budget study which asked how much time
women had available to attend educational programs (this study
found that women had half the time as men free to engage in
non-income producing, non-household tasks); 2) programs to free
women's time so that they could go to literacy classes. These
programs consisted of water carting and purification projects.
While these programs freed women's time, women did not use the
time to attend literacy classes. They used the additional time
made available to them to engage in new income generating tasks.
Women stated that they would attend nonformal education classes
only if they were related directly to generating more money.

605. Meghji, Zakia.   "Women   and   Cooperatives--Some   Realities
Affecting Development in Tanzania."   Community Development
Journal 20 (1985): 185-188.

Describes the International Cooperative Alliance (ICA) which is
a non-governmental organization, and describes techniques that
it uses to encourage women to participate in cooperatives.
Among these are using women to reach other women, use of study
tour methods and developing women's skills in several areas of
income generation.   Analyzes a 1982 ICA project conducted in
conjunction with the Food and Agricultural Organization of the
United Nations in Kenya, Tanzania, Zambia, Lesotho and Swaziland
which provided employment and training opportunities for women
and young girls.

Nelson, Nici. "Mobilizing Village Women: Some Organizational
and Management Considerations." Journal of Development Studies
17 (1981): 47-58.

See item #705.

606. Nxumalo, Simanga. "Income-Generating Project Develops Skills of
Swazi Women." Convergence 15 (1982): 48-55.

Describes the Integrated Women Development Project to develop
income-generating skills for women in Swaziland. Describes the
social background of the project, the design for skill training,
support resources and the progress the project has made.
Concludes that the project has made women aware of their talents
and the ways in which women can improve their lives. This, in
turn, enhances women's contributions to development.

607. Osborne, R.J.   "Out-of-School Education for Women in African Countries." Convergence 6 (1973): 7-19.

Surveys vocational training and literacy programs for women in Ghana, Nigeria, Botswana, Zambia, Kenya, Tanzania, Senegal and the Cameroons.

608. Robertson, Claire C.   "Formal and Non-formal Education? Entrepreneurial Women in Ghana." Comparative Education Review 28 (1984): 639-658.

Asks how formalized education affects Ghanaian market girls' access to nonformal training that they receive in trading. Studies 42 school girls engaged in trading and 42 girls out of school and engaged in trading and finds that girls who went to school had less knowledge about marketing. In the long run the fact that formal education adversely affects women's access to knowledge they can use to earn a living in the Ghanaian economy means that women's subordinate position will be reinforced by the extension of formal education.

3.   Asia

Books and Monographs

609. Crone, C. Research on Innovative Non-formal Education for Rural Adults: Implications for Literacy Motivation. New York: World Education, 1978. 8 pp.

Discusses why adults in rural areas attend nonformal education programs. Focuses particularly on content and program design of education for women learners and programs undertaken in the Philippines and in Kenya.

610. Crone, C. Research on Innovative Non-formal Education for Rural Women, Phase 1. New York: World Education, 1977. 29 pp.

Outlines a program design for innovation in women's nonformal education projects in the Philippines. Discusses needs assessment techniques, guidelines for developing instructional methods and curricular materials and means for evaluation of programs.

611. International Labour Organization. Human Resources Development in Rural Areas in Asia and Role of Rural Institutions. Geneva: International Labour Office, 1975. 155 pp.

Focuses on nonformal education and rural development in Asia and argues that women should receive greater access to both formal and nonformal education given that education relates to women's role in agricultural production and in family planning.

Meesook, Kanitta M. The Economic Role of Thai Women. Bangkok: Bank of Thailand Discussion Paper Series, 1980. 17 pp.

See item #867

Articles

612. Bangun, Masliana. "The Advantage of Functional Education and Credit Facilities for Javanese Rural Women." The Endless Day: Some Case Material on Asian Rural Women. Edited by T. Scarlett Epstein and Rosemary A. Watts. New York: Pergamon Press, 1981, pp. 128-154.

Examines two functional literacy programs for village women in Indonesia. Focusing on rural women in their roles as wives and mothers, argues that, although literacy is essential in order to introduce appropriate technologies to alleviate women's work load, it is meaningless in itself unless it is linked with some income-generating activities.

613. Hussain, Ghulam. "Pakistan: The role of the Agricultural University in Promoting Adult Literacy." Literacy Work 4 (1975): 69-82.

Describes the adult literacy programs for the rural areas with which the University of Agriculture in Lyallpur, Pakistan, has been experimenting. In addition to the teaching of the 3Rs, regular lectures and discussions focused on such subjects as agriculture, animal husbandry, cottage industry, citizenship and religion. The university established a rural women's center at the university for the training of women and girls from rural areas and provided the skills in reading, writing and maintaining simple accounts to manage their domestic affairs more effectively.

614. Junge, Barbara and Shashi M. Shresta. "Another Barrier Broken: Teaching Village Girls to Read in Nepal." The Reading Teacher 37 (1984): 846-852.

Describes a nonformal education project for out-of-school untouchable girls, aged 6 to 13, in rural Nepal. Unlike the traditional system in primary schools, where the teaching starts by the memorization of Nepali alphabet, the class introduced reading of the words familiar to the girls from the first day.

Although the class was successfully operated, the question remained as to the future of the girls who attended the class. Despite official policy, the resentment against the education of untouchables by high caste parents and pupils remained a barrier to further education of the girls in the local government school.

615. Kindervatter, Suzanne. "How Thai Village Women Became Adult Educators." Convergence 18 (1985): 116-119.

Presents a case study of a nonformal adult education program for village women in Northeast Thailand. Describes how minimally literate rural women were trained as adult educators to motivate and organize village women to develop their communities.

616. Mahmud, Satnam. "Thoughts on Non-Formal Education for Women." Women and Development: Perspectives from South and Southeast Asia. Edited by Rounaq Jahan and Hanna Papanek. Dacca: The Bangladesh Institute of Law and International Affairs, 1979, pp. 402-424.

Gives a historical essay on women's position in various parts of the world, and then describes the current nonformal adult literacy programs for women in Pakistan and their impact. Contends that acquiring literacy is crucial for women for participating in all social and economic activities. Suggests that a separate ministry for developing nonformal education for women be set up.

617. Sajogyo, P. "Les Centres de Réhabilitation Nutritionnelle en Indonésie." Assignment Children/les Carnets de l'Enfance no. 38 (1977): 57-63.

Describes a feeding and nutrition education program that was offered to food deficient households (defined as households in which 37 percent of the children were below normal weight and 16 percent suffered from moderate to severe protein calorie malnutrition). The program, carried out in 6 rural villages in Indonesia, trained mothers in food preparation using local resources. At the end of two months, positive results were obtained for close to 80 percent of the children.

618. Smith, Mary Ann. "An Adult Education Programme for the Igorot Women of Northern Philippines." Convergence 8 (1975): 16-24.

Describes the programs in adult education offered by a center for adult training in Baguio City, the Philippines. The center was formed to provide migrant Igorot women with skills necessary for personal development as well as for employment. Describes the program which included basic adult education, skills training, social development skills as well as courses in sewing, crocheting and knitting. Points out that attendance remains a problem and suggests that programs in farming techniques be added to the center.

Wang, Virginia Li. "Application of Social Science theories to Family Planning Health Education in the People's Republic of China." American Journal of Public Health 66 (1976): 440-445.

See item #1124

3a.   Bangladesh

Books and Monographs

619. Gerard, Renee, et al. Training for Women in Bangladesh. Dacca: UNICEF Women's Development Programme, 1977. 99 pp.

Describes the range of training programs offered to women in Bangladesh and examines successful ways to implement such programs so that they can be effective with poor women in Bangladesh and lists government agencies responsible for these programs.

Germain, Andrienne. Women's Roles in Bangladesh Development: A Program Assessment. Dacca: The Ford Foundation, 1976. 49 pp.

See item #756

620. Hoque, N. Non-formal Education for Women in Bangladesh with Emphasis on Agency and Organizational Programs Serving Economically Disadvantaged Women. East Lansing, Michigan: Michigan State University, Institute for International Studies in Education, Program of Studies in Non-formal Education, 1976. 63 pp. (Supplementary Paper no. 5.)

Studies nonformal education for women in Bangladesh in the wake of the 1971 civil war. Uses a case study approach to show how rehabilitation programs were extended to poor rural women and the role of women's organizations in making these programs successful. Points out that the limits of nonformal education for women involve the traditional content of such programs, their restriction to urban areas, lack of coordination, and low level of financing.

Mabud, Mohammed A. **Women's Development, Income and Fertility.** Dhaka: The External Evaluation Union, Planning Commission and Canadian International Development Agency, 1985.   180 pp.

See item #1125

Articles

621. Durno, Janet.   "Can You Blot the Sun Out with Your Hand?   A Visit to Banchte Shekha."   The Decade for Women.   Edited by Aisla Thomson.   Toronto: Canadian Congress for Learning Opportunities for Women, 1986, pp. 125-132.

Describes Banchte Shekha, a nongovernment organization in Bangladesh which provides education and training for divorced, widowed and abandoned women.

622. Islam, Shamima.   "Strengthening Non-formal Education for Women in Bangladesh."   **Women and Development: Perspectives from South and Southeast Asia.**   Edited by Rounaq Jahan and Hanna Papanek. Dacca: The Bangladesh Institute of Law and International Affairs, 1979, pp. 379-401.

Examines nonformal education programs for women in Bangladesh and identifies measures to strengthen them.   Criticizes the existing programs for being concentrated in urban and semi-urban areas, putting too much emphasis on family planning and neglecting the existing life situation of women toward whom the programs should be directed.   Contends that priority should be given to devising and implementing programs which will reach the vast majority of rural women with new knowledge and skills.

623. Haque, Rezaul.   "A Bangladesh Experience in Education and Primary Health Care."   **Convergence** 15 (1982): 84-87.

Describes the activities of the People's Health Centre in Bangladesh which is designed to provide adequate health service to the rural areas.   A major part of the program is to provide education to women which will increase their independence and bargaining power as well as strengthen their roles in health care provision for their families.

Khatun, Sharifa.   "Women's Education in a Rural Community in Bangladesh."   **Women and Development: Perspectives from South and Southeast Asia.**   Edited by Rounaq Jahan and Hanna Papanek. Dacca: Bangladesh Institute of Law and International Affairs, 1979, pp. 253-274.

See item #758

624. World Education, New York.   "Special Report on BRAC."   World Education Reports 13 (1976): 1-16.

Describes the Bangladesh Rural Advancement Committee (BRAC) programs for training village women to participate in rural development.

3b.   India

Books and Monogaphs

Doraiswami, S.S. Educational Advancement and Socioeconomic Participation of Women in India. New Delhi: Directorate of Non-formal (Adult) Education, Ministry of Education and Social Welfare, 1976. 34 pp.

See item #880

625. India.   Ministry of Education and Social Welfare.   Committee on Adult Education.   Adult Education Programmes for Women.   New Delhi: Ministry of Education and Social Welfare, 1978.   15 pp.

Contains figures from 1951, 1961 and 1971 showing continuing high (although lowered) rates of illiteracy. Over 80 percent of these illiterates are women (more than 90 percent of illiterates in the lower castes or tribal groups are women). Advocates programs and makes simple suggestions--including providing child care, and involving local women.

626. Jesudason, Victor, et al. Non-formal Education for Rural Women to Promote the Development of the Young Child. New Delhi: Allied Publishers, 1981. 419 pp.

Reports an action-research project conducted in India. The project was entitled "An Experimental Non-formal Education Project for Rural Women to Promote the Development of the Young Child" and was cosponsored by the Indian government, WHO, UNICEF, and CARE. Its goals were to integrate maternal and child health, nutrition, child care and family planning programs into functional literacy programs. Contains program evaluations as well as summaries of project activities.

627. Khan, Nighat Said, et al. Women's Skill Development and Income Generating Schemes and Projects in the Punjab: Phase 1, Listing and Preliminary Analysis: Final Report. Lahore, Pakistan: UNICEF Punjab, 1984. 64 pp.

Lists women's income generating projects in the Punjab and provides a preliminary analysis of their effectiveness. Includes information on 14 government and 28 nongovernment sponsored projects and makes recommendations for the development of further income generating schemes.

628. Tellis-Nayak, Jessie B.   Non-formal Education for Women: The Grihini Training Programme.   New Delhi: Indian Social Institute, 1980.   112 pp.

Describes the Grihini Training Program which is a nonformal education program designed for neglected girls and women in tribal, rural and slum areas of India.   Discusses four approaches used in the planning, implementing and evaluating of these programs: the Network, Center, Mini Mobil Team and Live-in Village approaches.   Discusses practical aids that will assist in the development of successful programs in terms of physical facilities, course content, resource persons and organization. Argues that the most important element for program success is the staff.

629. Tellis-Nayak, Jessie.   Education and Income Generation for Women: Non-formal Approaches.   New Delhi: Indian Social Institute, 1982.   80 pp.

Advocates an emphasis on nonformal education to solve the problems of women's undereducation in India and to assist women in earning income.   Describes the Grihini training programs in India which cater to women and girls who are illiterate and which are functional for women's lives in the village environment.   Many such programs stress handicraft skills and the care of domestic animals as well as kitchen gardening. Discusses the factors to be taken into account in establishing such programs and provides guidelines for organizing, recruiting participants and evaluating Grihini programs.

630. Trivedi, Sheela.   Non-formal Education for Women Officers (Education Department U.P.) Lucknow: Literacy House, 1976.

Presents a bilingual training program for female literacy officers in Uttar Pradesh.   Includes discussion questions, a description of the provisions of nonformal education in the 5th five year plan of India, the provisions for nonformal education in Uttar Pradesh, statistics on literacy rates by state for 1971 and seminar questions on the role of women in development.

Articles

631. Bhasin, Kamla. "Dialogue for Literacy--The Why and How of Literacy for Women: Some Thoughts in the Indian Context." **Convergence** 17 (1984): 37-43.

Criticizes the literacy campaign for women in India as irrelevant to reality. Argues that current literacy campaigns regard illiterate people as ignorant and unintelligent, perpetuate stereotypes of women and domesticate the poor rather than liberate them. Asserts that a literacy campaign must be based on scientific analysis of socioeconomic and political realities and talk about how becoming literate can actually help the oppressed, and that without a wider movement and struggle to wipe out poverty, exploitation and inequalities, illiteracy cannot be eradicated.

632. Chhabra, Rami. "Establishing Linkage between Women's Literacy Programmes, Status Issues and Access to Family Planning." **Indian Journal of Adult Education** 41 (no. 4, 1980): 6-9, 24.

Urges revision of women's literacy programs. In India 4 out of 5 women as compared to less than 1 out of every 2 men are illiterate. Suggests new approaches for strengthening the economic and productive role of women and linking it with educational efforts. Recommends that educational materials place a high priority on disseminating information on animal husbandry, agricultural practices, sericulture poultry and bee-keeping and grain storage and processing. These materials should be simplified and geared to women's interests since women do most of the work in these areas. Recommends also the preparation of materials for neoliterate women focusing on family planning.

Elliott, Carolyn M. "Women's Education and Development in India." **World Yearbook of Education, 1984. Women and Education.** London: Kogan Page, 1984, pp. 243-256.

See item #764

633. Haque, Adhila. "Understanding Rural School Going Girls--An Implication for Non-formal Education." **Indian Journal of Adult Education** 39 (no. 4, 1978): 27-31.

Argues that nonformal education should attempt to reach lower middle class and lower class girls who drop out of school. Believes that many of these girls, identified through a survey of 10 to 18 year old girls in the rural area adjacent to Delhi, can become workers in rural literacy campaigns.

634. Hague, Adhila. "Needs of Rural School Going Girls: Implications for Non-formal Education." Indian Journal of Adult Education 39 (no. 10, 1978): 9-13.

Surveys 150 school girls, aged 10 to 18, in the rural areas adjacent to Delhi as to their needs. Argues that most of these girls will drop out of school and that nonformal education needs to be designed with their needs in mind.

635. Mathur, Anita and Rajesh Tandon. "Participatory Training for Illiterate Women Trainees." Convergence 19 (1986): 20-33.

Describes the training program for illiterate tribal women in India to act as village animators and instructors for preschool children. The training was divided into three phases and focused on fostering social change through the gaining of actual skills rather than on adult education. The learning process kept the tribal women enthusiastic throughout, despite the fact that they had no previous experience. The program indicates the potential of participatory training and implies that illiteracy seems to be no great loss or impediment for people living in a nonliterate environment.

636. Naik, Chitra. "Educating Rural Girls: A Review of an Action Research Project." Review of Education 33 (1987): 495-501.

Describes a program offering primary education to working girls in Maharashtra State, India. Sees community mobilization, relevant curricula, teacher recruitment and training and development of new teaching and evaluation techniques as critical to the success of the program. Argues that the project has been successful in raising the working girls' self esteem and self affirmation.

637. Naik, Chitra. "An Action Research Project on Universal Primary Education: The Plan and the Process." Women's Education in the Third World: Comparative Perspectives. Edited by Gail P. Kelly and Carolyn M. Elliott. Albany: SUNY Press, 1982, pp. 152-172.

Describes a project aimed at providing education to rural working children in India. The project set up night schools in villages staffed by village members. These schools managed to serve a predominantly female population, since poverty, gender, and rural residence are the strongest predictors of whether an individual will attend school. Concludes that schools which offer flexible hours are effective in extending education to rural female students who are employed at an early age.

638. Pugazhenthi, G. "Match Industries Non-formal Education Scheme for Child Labourers." Perspectives in Education 2 (1986): 179-185.

Examines a nonformal education program for drop out and push out children in India. The children attending the program were 920 boys and girls who worked in match industries; three fourths of them were girls. The aim of the program was to prepare students for Standard VIII examinations which only seven percent of the learners managed to pass upon completion of the program. Discusses how such a narrow goal limited the potential impact of nonformal education on these working children and recommends that the program include vocational training as well as examination preparation.

639. Ravindran, Sundari. "Confronting Gender, Poverty and Powerlessness: An Orientation Programme for and by Rural Change Agents." Community Development Journal 20 (1985): 213-221.

Describes an attempt by untouchable rural women to start a women's organization of their own in South India. Ten women, previously involved in literacy programs in their respective villages, initiated Rural Women's Social Education Centre which has focused on the issues related to women and health to provide rural women with a sense of power and contol over their lives. Points out that nondirective, nondominating support is necessary to promote the emergence of women's own groups at the local level to improve women's status.

Vijayaraghavan, K.D., et al. "India Population Project, Karnataka: Evaluation of Nutritional Activities." Hygie: Revue International d'Education pour Santé 1 (1982, no. 3-4): 9-14.

See item #1058

640. Jayaweera, S. "Programmes of Non-formal Education for Women." Indian Journal of Adult Education 40 (no. 12, 1979): 33-45.

Looks at four types of nonformal education programs aimed at providing vocational training: part time training in formal schools, apprenticeship programs, on-the-job training and courses offered by public and private agencies. Urges that more vocational training programs be offered women and critiques existing programs for women for not allowing women to play a positive role and for lacking the flexibility to accommodate to women's roles in the family. Stresses the need to relate nonformal education designed for women to development.

641. Brey, Kathleen Healy. "The Missing Midwife: Why a Training Programme Failed." South Asian Review 5 (1971): 41-54.

Evaluates a Government of India program to train indigenous midwives with the assistance of UNICEF and USAID. Points out that the program failed because it assumed that indigenous midwives were around to train, materials used in the training program often were not available and there were no incentives for practicing midwives to participate in the program.

4.   Latin America

Books and Monographs

642. Escudero, Christina Maria et al. Material Didactico pore Ser Utilizado en Sistemas de Educación no Formal pore la Mujer Adulta. Washington: Organización de los Estados Americanos, 1983. 144 pp. (Comisión Interamericana de Mujers, Estudios no. 10).

Defines adult education as dealing with immediate necessities and priorities. Advocates study to determine needs and stresses evaluation of projects undertaken. Seventy pages of the work are interviews to illustrate various needs and fifty pages present examples of actual materials used in programs. Includes comments on preparing and evaluating such materials.

Turner, June H. ed. Latin American Woman: The Meek Speak Out. Silver Spring, Maryland: International Educational Development, Inc., 1980. 230 pp.

See item #770

643. Viezzer, Moema. A Methodology of Research Training of Women's Groups. Port au Prince: UNICEF, 1979. 30 pp.

Describes a project in the late 1970s in Santo Domingo which examined education programs for lower class women. Project reflected that most educational programs seem to lock women in traditional roles and that education systems often lead to exploitation of women. Project organized research on what women wanted but with an awareness that such questions were often intensely political and critical of the status quo.

Articles

Bender, Deborah. "Women as Promoters of Health in the Developing World." Women, Health and International Development. Edited by Margaret I. Aguwa. East Lansing: Office of Women in International Development and African Studies Center, Michigan State University, 1982, pp. 7-20.

See item #1070

Benglesdorf, Carollee and Alice Hageman. "Emerging from Underdevelopment: Women and Work in Cuba. **Race and Class** 19 (1978): 361-378.

See item #775.

644. Bird, Edris. "Adult Education and the Advancement of Women in the West Indies." **Convergence** 8 (no. 1, 1975): 57-64.

Reviews the evolution of adult education for women beginning in the 1940s in the West Indies and the roles of nongovernmental organizations, national and regional federations of women and the churchs in providing adult education.

645. Browner, C.H. "Gender Roles and Social Change: A Mexican Case Study." **Ethnology** 25 (April 1986): 89-106.

Contrasts the circumstances under which women will be receptive to programs that seek to promote social change and development. Shows how over a ten year period, a group of women in a small rural Mexican village persistently promoted a number of social change projects over the continuing objections of the all-male political leadership. The structure of the community's economic and social resources and its distribution of political power blocked most of the women from taking advantage of the programs.

646. Cebotarev, Eleonora A. "A Non-Oppressive Framework for Adult Education Programs for Rural Women in Latin America." **Convergence** 13 (no. 1-2, 1980): 34-48.

Provides a critical survey of the adult education programs conducted by the Latin American Association for Rural Development in 12 Latin American countries. Proposes a framework for reorienting these programs which focus on women's roles as mothers and wives so that they will not continue to oppress women. Argues that an alternative to such programs would provide income generating activities and opportunities for personal learning and development which would not serve to erode women's status further.

Corkery, Mary. "Subversion: Chilean Women Learning for Changes." The Decade for Women. Edited by Aisla Thomson. Toronto: Canadian Congress for Learning Opportunities for Women, 1986, pp. 133-140.

See item #1193

647. Ellis, Pat. "Women, Adult Education and Literacy: A Caribbean Perspective." Convergence 17 (no. 4, 1984): 44-53.

Examines the relation between education, economic development and adult education in 12 countries in the English speaking Caribbean.   Describes current government initiatives in adult education and explores the ways in which governments can extend new opportunities for women as well as change the orientation of some of the existing programs to reflect women's realities. Argues that adult and nonformal education has the potential to be a powerful tool to help women confront development and provide women with literacy and work skills.

648. Fiore, Kyle and Nan Elsasser. "Strangers No More: A Liberatory Literacy Curriculum." College English 44 (no. 2, 1982): 115-128.

Describes an advanced language skill course conducted in a community college, the College of the Bahamas, for adult women. The method used to teach was adopted from Lev Vygotsky and Paulo Friere and was designed to help students gain a critical understanding of the connection between their own lives and the society.   The goal of the program was to empower working women. Describes how the program raised students' consciousness of themselves as women and enhanced these women's writing skills.

649. Hunter, Carmen St. John. "Training Women Workers in Brazilian Favelas." Convergence 18 (1985): 129-132.

Describes staff training activities undertaken as part of a larger project carried out with groups of women in low income neighborhoods in and around Rio de Janeiro, Brazil. Finds that despite differences in experience and levels of prior education, these women were able to become effective group leaders and to enjoy what had previously been a burden.   Introduces the training model and training procedures.

650. Kelly, Maria Patricia Fernandez.   "Alternative Education for Maquiladora Workers: Centro de Orientación de la Mujer Obrera." Grassroots Development 6-7 (Winter 1982-Spring 1983):   41-46.

Describes the self education programs organized by the Centro de Orientación de la Mujer Obrera for working women.   Points out that the program is organized around a curriculum which is designed to raise women's consciousness of themselves as women and as workers while providing women with new vocational skills.

651. McCall, Cecelia. "Women and Literacy: The Cuban Experience." Journal of Reading 30 (1987): 318-324.

Examines the Cuban experience in women and literacy in the 25 years since the Cuban Literacy Campaign. Describes women's literacy and employment rates before the campaign, how the campaign was started, how women have benefited from it and how women's education is now guaranteed by the Constitution. Explains also the role of the Federation of Cuban Women (FMC) in preparing women to participate in adult education campaigns and in better employment.

652. Ruddle, Kenneth and Ray Chesterfield. "The Venezuelan 'Demostradora Del Hogar': An Example of Women in Nonformal Rural Education." Community Development Journal 9 (1974): 140-144.

Describes a nonformal education program in rural Venezuela which has taken into consideration the economic role of women in traditional society. Home demonstrators are recruited and educated in two schools in the country operated by the Ministry of Agriculture. They are sent to rural areas to diffuse agricultural and other knowledge and techniques to village women through formal and informal meetings and classes. Shows a successful example on an island and points out that future programs should consider the actual relationships within the communities with which they deal.

653. Thiret, Michele and Ann-Marie Coutrot. "L'éducation aux Isles: Parents et Enfants de Guadaloupé." L'École des Parents 7 (1976): 50-59.

Describes a training program in family education in the Caribbean aimed at sexual education but also issues in parenting. Program shows concern for the unmarried mother and her situation in the community, trying to orient her for the benefit of self and child while involving the community in the project to overcome prejudicial resistence.

654. Watson-Franke, Maria-Barbara. "The Role of Education in the Life of Guajiro Women, Tradition and Change." International Journal of Women's Studies 3 (1980): 338-344.

Describes women's education among the Guajiro Indians who live in Venezuela and Columbia. Points out that female education is aimed at training the whole person and preparing women for roles in the workforce as well as in the family. Although urbanization has altered traditional educational forms among the Guajiro, mothers continue to express strong interest in their daughters' schooling and continue to provide the nonformal education in traditional ways.

5.   The Middle East

Books and Monographs

655. Chemli, M. L'Éducation Permanente: L'Exemple Tunisien. Tunis: Institut national des Sciences de l'Éducation, 1978. 28 pp.

Describes lifelong education programs in Tunisia which have been operating since 1956. These programs have focused on providing access to education and have used learner-centered approaches and media and literacy campaigns. Describes specific organizations that were developed for vocational training, the mobilization of rural girls, family education and women's education.

656. Mustaffa-Kedah, O. Towards a Rational Education for Women in the Arab World. Tehran: Institute for Adult Literacy Methods, 1976. 37 pp.

Focuses on formal and nonformal education programs designed to prepare women for work and to eradicate literacy. Explains women's literacy in terms of traditional Muslim beliefs.

Articles

657. "Plan For Action in Rural Areas." Literacy Discussion 4 (Winter 1975-1976): 152-162.

Discusses the recommendations which are contained in the final report of an international seminar on The Design of Educational Programmes for the Promotion of Women, held in Tehran, Iran, April 19-24, 1975. (That report investigated the Experimental Functional Literacy Project, the Saveh Pilot Project, located 70 miles southeast of Tehran and considered to be representative of the rural regions of central Iran, sponsored by the Women's Organization of Iran.) Considers what the appropriate education for rural women is, how the institutional process can effect the objectives established for the education of rural women, how appropriate organizational structures can be created to mobilize resources and coordinate project activities and what strategy methods of evaluation are most appropriate for nonformal education programs such as the Saveh Project.

X. WOMEN, EDUCATION AND DEVELOPMENT

The terms "development" and "modernization" are used quite loosely in the research literature. In fact, many studies of education in the third world, be they on women or not, call themselves studies of modernization and/or development even if the study simply charts school enrollments over time, describes eductional structures or the social class background characteristics of students. Similarly, many studies of women's education in the third world have the word "development" or "modernization" in their titles. However, some of these studies are devoted exclusively to describing a nonformal education program or the pattern of women's workforce participation. Others focus on women in the political system or fertility control. In this bibliography we defined the terms "development" and "modernization" more narrowly and have included here those studies which focus on the development process as the development process and ask about the role of women in development, seek for ways to include women in that process and are concerned with women's reactions to that process. Studies exclusively focused on women in the workforce, fertility control, nonformal education, etc. are listed elsewhere in this bibliography. We have done extensive cross listing when studies of this sort look at how, for example, fertility control is related to development processes.

We have divided the literature here into three sections. The first, and by far the largest, is strictly on women's education (or lack of it) and development. The second focuses on women and access to science and technology, which is a relatively new part of the literature. The third is on the role of women in international agencies that promote development. While related to development, this literature looks at how decisions about women's roles in development are made and we thought it might be best to separate that literature from the more general body of scholarship on women and development.

A.   Women, Education and Development

1.   General Studies

Books and Monographs

Ahmed, Manzoor and Philip H. Coombs.   Education for Rural
Development: Case Studies for Planners.   New York: Praeger,
1975.   661 pp.

See item #579

Ali, Mohamed Adham.   Education, Fertility and Development: An
Overview.   Khartom, Sudan: Economic and Social Research
Council, National Council for Research, 1984.   36 pp.

See item #1057

658. Boserup, Ester.   Women's Role in Economic Development.   New
York: St. Martin's Press, 1969.

Argues that the process of development has eroded women's
position in the third world and part of that erosion is
attributable to the pattern of women's undereducation relative
to men.   Points out that women are active in most third world
economies, often providing much of the agricultural labor.   In
development, women's manual labor in agriculture and in crafts
is undermined as mechanization and industrialization occur.
Production, which once was in female hands, transfers to male
hands.   Part of the reason this occurs is that women lack access
to education and to training programs which would equip them to
work in modern sector jobs.

Buvenic, Mayra et al.   Women and Development: An Annotated
Bibliography. Washington: Overseas Development Council, 1976.
162 pp.

See item #3

659. Charlton, Sue Ellen M.   Women in Third World Development.
Boulder and London: Westview Press, 1984.   240 pp.

Focuses on the meaning of development for women and how
development policies can be implemented which will enhance,
rather than detract from women's status.   Points out that
development has often hurt women more than it has helped them.
Chapter 2 contains a critical summary of the women in
development literature.   Points out that most development

policies have hurt women by displacing women's labor in household industry and substituting women's labor with machines. In addition, the introduction of technology has reduced the demand for unskilled labor--and women, given the systematic denial of education over the past decades, constitute the bulk of the unskilled labor force. Part II of the book focuses on women in the food cycle--as producers, processors, and distributors of food in third world countries as well as on hunger as a women's issue. The chapters emphasize women's lack of access to technology and suggest ways in which women's labor in the food cycle can be enhanced through the dissemination of appropriate technologies, agricultural credit, nutrition, and birth control programs. Chapter 7 is devoted exclusively to education and training as means of both involving women in development and in having development enhance women's status. Advocates nonformal education as a means for increasing women's participation in development and points out that many nonformal programs have in the past hurt women by emphasizing their roles as wives and mothers rather than their roles in production, particularly in agriculture, or their potential roles in the modern, industrial workforce. Provides the example of the Nicauraguan literacy crusade and the RWDC Kufra Settlement Project in Libya to show how government policies can both provide greater educational opportunities for women and involve women in the devlopment process.

660. Clark, Noreen. Education for Development and the Rural Woman. Vol. 1. A Review of Theory and Principles with Emphasis on Kenya and the Philippines. New York: World Education, 1979. 66 pp.

Argues that women's education in developing countries should not focus exclusively on family planning, literacy and nutrition, but rather should prepare women to work for a wage in the modern sector or for income in traditional agriculture and handicrafts. Believes that coeducation enhances women's possibility of gaining economic equality with men. Maintains that pre-packaged educational programs are detrimental to development since each community has diverse educational needs.

661. Cutler, Virginia F. Woman Power, Social Imperatives and Home Science. Accra: Ghana Universities Press, 1969. 19 pp.

Presents a lecture given at the University of Ghana in 1969. Argues that home science education is key to increasing women's contribution to development since it can help reduce homemaker load and increase women's economic activity.

Danforth, Sandra C. Women and National Development. Monticello, Illinois: Vance Bibliographies, 1982. 35 pp.

(Public Administration Series, Bibliography #P 916).

See item #6

662. Derryck, Vivian L.   The Comparative Functionality of Formal and
Non-Formal Education for Women: Final Report.   Washington:
U.S. Agency for International Development, Office of Women in
Development, 1979.   196 pp.

Describes a five phase AID funded project to investigate the
relative roles of formal versus nonformal education in
integrating women into development.

663. Droegkamp, Janis and F. Munger.   Women Centered Training:
Responding to Issues and Ideas for Women in Development.
Amherst, Mass.:   University of Massachusetts, Center for
International Education, 1979.   51 pp.

Argues that women have been left out of many development
programs.   Maintains that women should be brought into
development and that development programs should be tailored to
women's needs.   Presents a manual designed to serve as a model
for creating training programs adapted to women's needs.

664. Huston, Perdita.   Third World Women Speak Out: Interviews in
Six Countries on Change, Development and Basic Needs.   New York:
Holt, Rinehart and Winston, 1979.   154 pp.

Describes women's experience in development and change in six
countries--Egypt, Kenya, Mexico, Sri Lanka, Sudan and Tunisia.
The study is based on interviews with 200 women.   Finds striking
similarities in social practices that limit women's roles, heavy
work burdens for women, low income and poverty and women's
desire to learn and work and educate their children.

665. ISIS Women's International Information and Communication
Service.   Women in Development: A Resource Guide for
Organization and Action.   Philadelphia, Pa.:   New Society
Publishers, 1984.   225 pp.

Combines feminist perspectives with those of women and
development.   The chapters in this book (see abstracts elsewhere
in this bibliography) focus on multi-nationalism, rural
development and food production, health, migration, tourism and
education and communications.   Each chapter provides an overview
of the topic and lists resources for further research and
community organizations.

666. Kindervatter, Suzanne. **Women Working Together for Personal, Economic and Community Development.** Washington: Overseas Education Fund, 1983. 103 pp.

Provides a handbook of activities for women's learning and action groups in the third world designed to integrate women into development. The handbook is intended for women organizing women along needs which women identify.

667. Leghorn, Lisa and Katherine Parker. **Woman's Worth: Sexual Economics and the World of Women.** Boston: Routledge and Kegan Paul, 1980. 356 pp.

Investigates how women's culture mediates the effects of patriarchial institutions on women's lives. Focuses first on sexual economics which allocate women to subordinate roles in society and shows how economic development further subordinates women. Argues that lack of access to education has been one instrument of women's oppression in the past; today the kind of education international agencies stress--which is limited to women as mothers and reproducers of the labor force--continues to oppress women. Points out, however, that women in most countries have developed women's cultures which mediate the impact of sexual economics and have helped women use institutions like the schools for their own purposes. The analysis is based on data collected from most of the third world, although much of it is derived from the African setting.

Nwanosike, Eugene. **Women and Development: A Select Bibliography.** Buea, Cameroon: Regional Pan African Institute for Development, 1980. 33 pp.

See item #12

668. Papanek, Hanna. **Women-in-Development and Women's Studies: Agenda for the Future.** East Lansing: Office of Women in International Development, Michigan State University, 1984. 18 pp. (Working Paper no. 55)

Critiques academic researchers and development assistance agencies for not having developed a research literature integrating feminist perspectives with development studies. Argues for the need to develop research strategies that make gender central to analyses of social change and for the need to rethink development issues from women's perspectives.

Rihani, M. **Development as if Women Mattered: An Annotated Bibliography with a Third World Focus.** Washington, D.C.: Overseas Development Council, 1978. 137 pp.

See item #14

Saulniers, Suzanne Smith and Cathy A. Rakowski. **Women in the Development Process: A Select Bibliography on Women in Sub-Saharan Africa and Latin America.** Austin: University of Texas Institute of Latin American Studies, 1977. 287 pp.

See item #15

669. Sethi, R.M. **Modernization of Working Women in Developing Societies.** New Delhi: National Publishing House, 1976. 168 pp.

Analyzes the impact of modernization on women in Turkey and India. Surveys a sample of 125 women from Candigarh, India, and 120 women from Ankara, Turkey, who work for the government in white collar jobs. Finds that traditional attitudes are giving way to more modern ones among women.

Tinker, Irene et al. ed. **Women and World Development with an Annotated Bibliography.** New York: Praeger, 1976. 382 pp.

See item #16

670. UNESCO. **Women, Education, Equality: A Decade of Experiments.** Paris: UNESCO, 1975. 109 pp.

Focuses on UNESCO's programs promoting women's education. Describes the following projects: 1) educating women for further rural development in Upper Volta; 2) primary teacher training programs for women in Nepal and 3) technical and vocational education in Chile.

Ware, Helen. **Women, Demography and Development.** Canberra: Australian National University, Development Studies Center, 1981. 242 pp. (Demography Teaching Notes no. 3)

See item #1063

671. Weekes-Vagliani, Winifred and Bernard Grossat. **Women in Development: At The Right Time for the Right Reasons.** Paris: Development Centre of the Organization for Economic Cooperation and Development, 1980. 330 pp.

Argues that if women are to contribute to development, they must be encouraged to marry at the right time for the right reasons. The purpose of the study is to determine if this is the case. Analyzes secondary data from ten ethnic groups in four countries. The data sets used include the Malaysian Life Survey of the Rand Corporation and the World Fertility Surveys of Fiji,

Sri Lanka and the Dominican Republic. Finds that ethnicity rather than education determines accepted occupations for women and that education does not automatically determine women's job or participation in the workforce. In addition, finds that age of marriage varies among ethnic groups but in some ethnic groups there is a relation between late marriage and higher levels of education. Urges that development and education policies aimed at incorporting women into development take into account regional and ethnic variations in the relation between education and occuption and education, marrige age, marriage pattern and fertility.

Wellesley Editorial Committee. **Women and National Development: The Complexities of Change.** Chicago: University of Chicago Press, 1977. 346 pp.

See item #81

Women and Development: Articles, Books and Research Papers Indexed in the Joint World Bank-International Monetary Fund Library, Washington, D.C. Boston: G.K. Hall & Co., 1987. 181 pp.

See item #17

Women, Population and Development. New York: United Nations Fund for Population Activities, 1977. 47 pp.

See item #1064

672. Wichterich, Christa. **Frauen in der dritten Welt.** Bonn: Deutsche Stiftung für internationale Entwicklung, 1984. 83 pp.

Surveys the problems of women in development. Points out that the Victorian morality and patriarchy prevalent in colonial education created the general lag of education for women in all third world areas. Comments on nonformal education, especially on family relations and on political socialization.

673. **Women and Industrialization in Developing Countries.** Vienna: United Nations Industrial Development Organization, 1981. 81 pp.

Reports on the papers and criticism presented at the Preparatory Meeting on the Role of Women in Industrialization in Developing Countries organized by the United Nations Industrial Development Organization in 1978. The purpose of the meeting was to discuss the full integration of women in developing countries into social and economic activities especially the industrialization process. Part one summarizes discussions and recommendations

for action at national and international levels. Part two
analyzes the papers presented and discusses constraints to
women's participation in industrialization such as rapid
population growth, obstructive social and cultural traditions,
lack of education and training, lack of respresention in the
policy-making areas of the occupational hierarchy, inadequate
legislation, lack of credit availability and lack of
unionization. Part three contains three papers presented at the
meeting which focus on women and industrial development, the
relationship of industrial employment to fertility and cultural
traditions affecting the status of women and lack of education
and employment of women in Morocco.

Youssef, Nadia Haggag. **Women and Work in Developing Societies.**
Berkeley: University of California Institute of International
Studies, 1974. 136 pp.

See item #805

Articles

674. Arnand, Anita. "Rethinking Women and Development." **Women in
Development:** A Resource Guide for Organization and Action.
Edited by ISIS Women's International Information and
Communication Service. Philadelphia: New Society Publishers,
1984, pp. 5-11.

Asks why women have been left out of the development process in
third world countries. Believes part of the reason lies in the
nature of education given women in developing countries which is
irrelevant to economic self-sufficiency. Argues that if
education is to have any value for women it must raise their
consciousness about the oppressive structures that keep them in
positions of powerlessness. Rejects the opinion that technical
innovations ease the burden of women's work and enable women to
have a more equal relationship with men. Points out that these
technical innovations are male-dominated and often involve
resources alien to the local environment. Suggests that change
in societal status of women be based on a new theory of
development which embraces feminism and that both reformist and
radical movements should share a common goal for change.

Blitz, Rudolph C. "An International Comparison of Women's
Participation in the Professions." **Journal of Developing Areas**
9 (1975): 499-510.

See item #973

675. Boulding, Elsie. "Integration into What? Reflections on Development Planning for Women." Convergence 13 (no. 1-2, 1980): 50-58.

Calls for a re-evaluation of development strategies in third world nations. Points out that with development women's status has declined and that increased women's access to education has led to a growth of women's participation in the paid labor force while the disparity between male and female income has grown.

Brown, Lalage. "Adult Education and Its Role in National and Sectoral Development." Literacy Work 4 (July/Sept. 1974): 67-85.

See item #593

676. Callaway, Helen. "The Voices and Silences of Women." Literary Discussion 4 (Winter 1975-1976): 17-34.

Explores alternative approaches for education to bring women into the development process. Suggests the concept of development means more than growth in the GNP; rather, it needs to be thought of in terms of alleviating poverty and improving the quality of life for all. Documents how women have been excluded from the same economic activity as men and how the widening differences between the productivity and earnings of men and women have occurred. Explains how the "inside model" and "observers' model" can be used to analyze the local society to provide information to design relevant and practical educational programs where women can be made active participants in their own education. By successfully surmounting their problems through education, women can individually and collectively cope with larger problems to improve the reality of their daily lives.

677. Clason, Carla. "Women and Development: Three Experimental Projects." Literacy Discussion 6 (1975-76): 77-88.

Describes three UNESCO projects which focused on increasing women's access to education and development. One project in Upper Volta focused on providing women basic literacy. The project resources were strained because the men were illiterate and gained access to the programs targeted women. The second project described was in Nepal. It sought to provide greater access of girls to school by increasing the number of female teachers thereby providing greater job opportunities (and therefore educational incentives) for women. Nepalese parents responded by sending more of their sons to schools. The third project was situated in Chile. It sought to increase women's access to the workforce by establishing technical institutes for women. Girls, however, did not attend such schools, identifying technical occupations as male.

Colclough, Christopher. "The Impact of Primary Schooling on Economic Development: A Review of the Evidence." World Development 10 (1982): 167-185.

See item #1068

Danforth, Sandra. "Women, Development and Public Policy: A Select Bibliography." Women in Developing Countries: A Policy Focus. New York: Haworth Press, 1983, pp. 107-124.

See item #18

Dixon, Ruth B. "Education and Employment: Keys to Smaller Families." Journal of Family Welfare 22 (December 1975): 38-49.

See item #1071

Ellis, Pat. "Methodologies for Doing Research on Women and Development." Women in Development: Perspectives from the Nairobi Conference. Ottawa: International Development Research Center, 1986, pp. 136-165.

See item #67

678. "Integration of Women in Rural Development." Convergence 12 (1979): 72-74.

Describes a program of action adopted by the World Conference on Agrarian Reform and Rural Development held in Rome in 1979 by the FAO. The program seeks to integrate women into rural development.

679. Jaquette, Jane S. "Women and Modernization Theory: A Decade of Feminist Criticism." World Politics 34 (1982): 267-284.

Examines the new feminist theories of development, based on the growing number of empirical studies of the impact of modernization on women. Compares conventional modernization theory with feminist critiques. Points out that standard liberal development theory sees only the positive effects of development on women. Feminist theory, however, points out that improved technology in farming and other aspects of modernization undermine women's roles. Examines Marxist views of the role of women. Argues for adopting the female sphere perspective which asserts there is a female culture that can provide the basis for restructuring the process of change. Asserts that female sphere theory has heuristic value in both challenging male centric perspectives on what is valued and how society can and should be structured and in explaining why women are often most resistant to the changes intended to "liberate" them.

680. Joyner, C.C. and Nancy D. Joyner. "Women, Development and the Challenge of Global Education." Journal of the National Association of Women Deans, Administrators and Counselors 41 (1978): 157-160.

Outlines the positive effects educated women have on economic and political development. Criticizes developing nations for neglecting women's education despite the importance of women's education for achieving national development goals. Urges that the United Nations Decade for Women, 1976-1985, define goals in terms of the popular acceptance of women in the school and the workforce rather than solely in terms of legislative, economic, and financial measures.

681. Kelly, Maria Patricia Fernández. "The Sexual Division of Labor, Development and Women's Status." Current Anthropology 22 (1981): 414-419.

Summarizes a conference held in Burg Wartenstein, under the auspices of the Wenner-Gren Foundation for Anthropological Research. The main themes of the conference dealt with the changing structure of the division of labor by gender and the impact of economic development on women's work and status. Other issues addressed by the conference include the effects of the passage from household to factory production on the sexual division of labor and women's status.

682. Leal, Maria Angela. "Educação e Desigualdade Economica." Educação e Desigualdade no Brasil. Edited by Henry Levin, et al. Petrópolis: Editora Vozes, 1984, pp. 173-255.

Focuses on capitalist development and the role of education. Finds education does not completely answer women's needs under a capitalist system. The labor market for women's agricultural and domestic service work is undercut. New jobs appear--especially in the clerical sector of the economy for which education is necessary but these are at the lowest levels. New industrial jobs are often inconvenient for married women with domestic responsibilities. Only a few upper class women have benefitted fully from their education under the capitalist order. These conclusions are based on national statistics and changes in the decade of the 1960s.

Mair, Lucille. "Adult Learning, Women and Development." Prospects 8 (1977): 238-243.

See item #584

683. Nelson, Nici. "Mobilizing Village Women: Some Organizational
and Management Considerations." Journal of Development Studies
17 (1981): 47-58.

Explores the ways in which to effectively involve women in
development projects and points out organizational difficulties
which might arise. Reports on extended case studies of
integrated rural development programs in Bangladesh and Nigeria.
Stresses the need to recruit women into decision making
positions at national and regional levels in development
programs. Because women have been denied education it is often
difficult to locate qualified individuals. Provision thus
should be made for on the job training. If a program is to
mobilize village women, the following should be considered:
distance from the village to training centers, scheduling
activities so they do not interfere with family
responsibilities, providing child care facilities and utilizing
already existing women's groups.

684. Palmer, Ingrid. "Rural Women and the Basic-Needs Approach to
Development." International Labour Review 115 (1977): 97-107.

Argues that modernization does not improve women's status and
that women do not reap the benefits of modernization.
Criticizes modernization theories on the grounds that they do
not take into account woman's historically subservient position.
The application of policies based on the assumptions of
modernization theory thus increases the gap between males and
females as the cash economy becomes men's preserve and women
become allocated to the subsistence economy and to marginalized
service roles. Notes the paradox: men are able to avail
themselves of consumer goods produced in the West, while infant
and maternal mortality rates rise and malnutrition is on the
upswing. Advocates that the basic needs approach to development
be adopted. This approach can compensate for women's historical
economic position and will redistribute cash resources between
men and women more equitably.

Pampel, Fred and Kazuko Tanaka. "Economic Development and
Female Labor Force Participation: A Reconsideration." Social
Forces 64 (1986): 599-619.

See item #815.

685. Peters, Joan Allen. "Some Guidelines for Planning Appropriate
Programs for Women." The Decade for Women. Edited by Aisla
Thomson. Toronto: Canadian Congress for Learning Opportunities
for Women, 1986, pp. 99-108.

Presents a number of suggestions to help increase the probability that a development project would serve the needs of women. Among these are the development of strategies to increase women's self-help and the integration of health, nutrition, family planning and income generating skills. Points out also that successful programs should recognize women's double loads in the household and in production and be designed not to interfere with them. Finally suggests means by which the poorest of poor women can be brought into development programs.

686. Roodkowsky, Mary. "Women and Development Literature, A Survey." Women in Development: A Resource Guide for Organization and Action. Edited by ISIS Women's International Information and Communication Service. Philadelphia: New Society Publishers, 1984, pp. 13-21.

Surveys the literature on women and development and criticizes it on the basis that development has failed to benefit women. Sees three types of studies in the women and development literature: 1) descriptions of the negative impact of development on women, 2) development agency documents and reports and 3) critical analyses and feminist approaches to the women in the development process.

687. Verghese, Valsa et al. "Education and Communication: An Overview." Women in Development: A Resource Guide for Organization and Action. Edited by ISIS Women's International Information and Communication Services. Philadelphia: New Society Publishers, 1984, pp. 175-202.

Examines the role of education and communication regarding women and development and describes how women have responded to discrimination in education and communication media by creating their own alternatives. Argues that education systems, religion and the media have helped to reinforce traditional social attitudes towards women and keep them in subordinate positions. In the field of education and communication, however, women's studies, women's art, literature, music, etc., are beginning to create women's culture and knowledge based on women's own experiences. Includes annotated resources on education and the media such as information on groups, organizations and bibliographies.

688. "Women, Literacy and Development." Literacy Discussion 6 (Winter 1975-1976): 172 pp.

Sums up the educational situation of women in developing countries and discusses measures taken to combat illiteracy. This is a special issue of the journal Literacy Discussion which was prepared by the International Institute for Adult Literacy methods. The articles focus on the effects of the international year on women, women's access to education, their participation in rural development and women's work.

689. Woodhall, Maureen. "Investment in Women: A Reappraisal of the Concept of Human Capital." International Review of Education 19 (1973): 9-27.

Analyses the rates of return on investment in women's education worldwide. Finds that for the individual education beyond the minimum school leaving age offers direct benefits in the form of increased earning power, access to more desirable and enjoyable jobs, greater possibilities of re-entering the labor market after a period of child care and the probability of steadily increasing earnings after an interrupted working career. At the same time, education brings a woman indirect benefits and many personal satisfactions. Points out that there are vast differences between the rate of return on investment in education for men and women. These differences depend on the extent of wage and occupational discrimination in a given country and how women's time spent in non-market activities are valued economically. Argues that the concept of "investment in women" is as valid as that of "investment in men" and that investment in women should become part of development policy.

690. Ziedenstein, G. "Including Women in Development Efforts." World Development 6 (1978): 971-978.

Reviews projects in Bangladesh, central Africa, and Upper Volta which have tried to bring women into the development process. These projects introduced women to food production techniques through participatory programs. Urges participatory planning be used in nutritional, health and birth control nonformal education programs.

2.   Africa

Books and Monographs

Atkiewicz, Susan and M. Shimwaayi Muntemba. **Women and Development in Zambia: An Annotated Bibliography.** Addis Ababa: United Nations Economic Commission for Africa, African Training and Research Center, 1983. 98 pp.

See item #22

691. Belloncie, Guy. **Femmes et Développement en Afrique Sahélienne. L'Experience Nigerienne d'Animation Feminine** (1966-1976). Paris: Editions Ouvriénes, 1980. 212 pp.

Describes a series of rural development projects directed at women in Niger which were funded initially by French foreign aid and later by the European Development Fund. The project consisted of training women as rural development workers and these women's subsequent work in three pilot projects in villages in Niger. The training phase consisted of recruiting women 18 years of age and older who had at least a primary education. These women, as part of their preparation, conducted action research on village needs including agriculture, water purification, wood carting and child nutrition. They also took correspondence courses with the University of Abidjan and attended seminars conducted by doctors and agricultural extension workers. The projects put in place were health projects related to child birth, malaria control and nutrition; production projects focusing on the raising of poultry and water and wood projects. While the health projects had demonstrable results, the other projects were less successful. Annexed to the project report are examples of materials used to train women development workers and a description of a similar project in Mali.

692. Bryson, C. Judy. **Women and Economic Development in Cameroon.** Washington: U.S. Agency for International Development, 1979. 153 pp.

Argues that development will occur only if women are brought into systems of education. Surveys inequalities in educational enrollments in the Cameroons and points out that in Muslim areas girls are even more under-represented in the schools than in the Christian and animist parts of the country. Argues that out of school education should be expanded considerably in order to bring women into the development process. Recommends that such programs include training in literacy, agricultural skills, vocational skills and skills related to women's roles as wives and mothers.

693. Fortmann, Louise. **Women and Tanzanian Agricultural Development.** Dar Es Salaam: University of Dar Es Salaam Economic Research Bureau, 1977. 24 pp. (Paper 77.4)

Argues that women play a major role in agriculture and finds through a survey of rural Tanzanian women that women do use new technologies efficiently, know as much about these technologies as do their husbands and are involved in making decisions about agriculture. However, points out that Ujamma communities have tended to exclude women from decision making and that this, in

turn, will retard development. Identifies the special problems
of women in rural development in terms of negative attitudes
about women and women's limited access to resources--namely,
land, labor, and information. Women rely too much on their
husbands for information about agricultural innovation. In part
this is due to the fact that most agricultural extension workers
are men and are likely to remain so since women have no access
to agricultural training institutes and colleges. Urges that
women be given access to agricultural colleges and that the
government encourage their attendance by setting up day care
centers at the colleges and nonresidential courses.

694. German Foundation for Developing Countries. **Women in Economic
and Social Development in Africa.** Berlin: German Foundation
for Developing Countries, 1970. 2 vol.

Contains recommendations from a conference in Berlin in 1970
(Volume 1). The recommendations stress the need for adult
education of women so they can fulfill their daily tasks as well
as obtain employment. Volume 2 contains short background papers
on vocational education, rural education programs in Niger,
general education and health education.

Hafkin, Nancy. **Women and Development in Africa.** Addis Ababa:
United Nations Economic Commission for Africa, 1977.   172 pp.
(Bibliography Series no. 1)

See item #24

695. Langley, Philip.   **A Preliminary Approach to Women and
Development:** Getting a Few Facts Right. Buea, Cameroon:
Regional Pan African Institute for Development, 1979. 42 pp.

Examines women in development in Africa. Provides demographic
data and discusses the economic, cultural and historical
backgrounds of women. Analyzes the causes of underdevelopment
and its specific effects on women. Argues that women are drawn
into a set of economic relationships that exploit the poorer
sections of society. This results in overall worsening of
living and environmental conditions and increased economic
stratification and social differentiation. Describes women and
development programs. Contends that development strategies have
failed in various sectors such as plantations, agriculture and
education.   Criticizes the current education for failing to
consider women as producers. Suggests that policies should be
radically changed.

Mascarenhas, Ophelia and Marjorie Mbilinyi.   **Women and
Development in Tanzania.** Uppsala: Scandanavian Institute of
African Studies, 1983. 256 pp.

See item #25

Mitchink, D.A. **Improving Ways of Skill Acquisition of Women for Rural Employment in Some African Countries.** Geneva: International Labour Organization, 1977. 76 pp.

See item #591

696. Pellow, Deborah. **Women in Accra: Options for Autonomy.** Algonac, Michigan: Reference Publications, 1977. 272 pp.

Analyzes roles and relationships of Ghanaian women living in the Adabraka neighborhood in Accra, Ghana. Argues that urbanization and modernization have not liberated women; rather the process has led to greater gender ascription and women have become more dependent on men. In part attributes this decline in women's autonomy to lack of educational opportunity and the heritage of colonialism. One chapter of the book focuses on Victorian conceptions of women's roles which the British transferred to Ghana. These sex role ideologies were transmitted through European style schools established in the 1890s. A second chapter entitled "Modern Constraints to Access to Options" is devoted in large part to education and traces the educational expansion of the 1960s in which women began to enter schooling. However, despite the fact that in Accra girls outnumbered boys in access to the primary school in the 1970s, by fifth form boys outnumbered girls 3 to 1. Attributes female drop out rates to expense, lack of school places and persistent attitudes that girls' education is more of a risk than is boys'. Interviews a number of women and finds they do not see a value to girls' education and accept sex roles for women which are predominantly domestic. While women expect to work, they work to support their domestic role as wife, mother and sister in the extended patriarchical family. Trading is the predominant occupation for both illiterate and primary school educated women. Later chapters of the book dwell on changes in roles in urban areas. Argues that women remain dependent on men and that they make few friends with women outside the family and tend to see other women as sexual competitors. Their primary relation with men is as mates. Concludes that new roles are slow to emerge and that, given current trends in women's employment and education, women are likely to become less rather than more autonomous.

Robertson, Claire C. **Sharing the Same Bowl: A Socioeconomic History of Women and Class in Accra, Ghana.** Bloomington: Indiana University Press, 1984. 299 pp.

See item #129.

697. Schuster, Ilsa. **Female White Collar Workers: A Case Study of Successful Development in Lusaka, Zambia.** East Lansing: Michigan State Univesity, 1983. 31 pp. (Working Papers on Women in International Development, no. 29)

Contends that it is not always the case that development policies leave women out. Points out that the growth in Zambia of vocational training programs for girls and the opening of educational access for women has served to bring women into the development process so that women benefit as much as do men. Studies female white collar workers who have graduated from secondary school and work in offices. Focuses on their social relationships, family support networks, leisure time and their goals.

Schuster, Ilsa M. Glazer. **New Women of Lusaka.** Palo-Alto, California: Mayfield Publishing Company, 1979. 209 pp.

See item #974

Selassie, Alesebu Gebre. **Women and Development in Ethiopia: An Annotated Bibliography.** Addis Ababa: United Nations Economic Commission for Africa, African Training and Research Centre for Women, 1981. 58 pp.

See item #26

698. Séminaire Opérationnel Régional d'Alphabétisation Fonctionnelle, Banfora, Haute-Volta, 1975. **La Place et le Rôle de la Femme dans le Développement Économique et Social de l'Afrique.** Dakar: Bureau Régionale de l'UNESCO pour l'Éducation en Afrique, 1976. 90 pp.

Presents the report on the 1976 regional seminar in Africa on functional literacy and the role of women in development. Participants included representative of 13 African countries. The second part of the report focuses on projects in rural Upper Volta which provide practical training for women and attempt to bring them into the development process.

699. Simmons, Emmy B. **Economic Research on Women in Rural Development in Northern Nigeria.** Overseas Liaison Committee, American Council on Eduction, September 1976. 34 pp. (OLC Paper no. 10)

Presents the findings of a micro-level research project among rural women in Zaria province, northern Nigeria, which focuses on women's participation in development. Focuses on women's businesses and production of foodstuffs for sale and argues that in order for women to participate more actively in development, they need to have access to technical training.

700. Tall, Penda Sidibe. **L'Effet de la Modernisation sur le Travail des Femmes Exerçant une Activité Independante au Mali, en Côte d'Ivoire et au Sénégal.** Addis Ababa: Nations-Unies Commission Économique pour l'Afrique, Center Africain de Recherche et de Formation pour la Femme, 1981. 116 pp.

Traces the workforce participation of women in Mali, Ivory Coast and Senegal. Points out that women tend to work in nonwage labor in agriculture and in the Ivory Coast particularly in crafts. Modernization programs in agriculture have not attempted to make women more productive; most have been aimed at men. In these countries women form only a small percent of the wage earning workforce. Traces this directly to limited educational opportunities for women and argues that enhancing women's education will facilitate their entry into the paid workforce and will heighten their productivity in rural areas.

701. United Nations Economic Commission for Africa. African Training and Research Centre for Women. **Séminaires d'Information sur les Mécanismes Nationaux d'Intégration des Femmes au Développement, Rurundi et Rwanda.** Addia Ababa: United Nations, 1980.

Reports on a seminar held in Burundi in 1980 on the integration of African women into development. Contains speeches by government officials as well as policy statements about the necessity of providing women with access to appropriate technologies in rural areas.

702. Ssenkoloto, G.M. **Toward Realistic Curricula for African Women in the Process of Development: What Realistic Contributions Can Pan African Institute for Development Offer?** Cameroon: International Association for Pan African Institute for Development, November 1980. 20 pp.

Stresses the need to develop new curricula for formal school and nonformal programs for women in Africa. Discusses the work of the Pan African Institute for Development to curriculum development so that women can be integrated into the modernization process.

703. United Nations, Economic Commission for Africa. **Séminaire sur les Mécanismes Nationaux en Faveur de l'Intégration des Femmes au Processus de Développement Tenu a Niamey du 3 au 6 Septembre 1979.** Addis Ababa, Ethiopia: Nations Uniés Commission Économique pour l'Afrique, 1981. 26 pp.

Reports on a seminar on integrating women into development held in Niamey, Niger in 1979. Describes the UN regional plan focusing on women in development which calls for literacy programs for women, programs to train women for employment and the development of appropriate instructional materials. The text also includes the role of the Niger Women's Association in promoting the integration of women into development, different models that African governments might adopt to develop means to serve women and a discussion of Nigeria's and Mali's seminars on integrating women into development (annexes).

Wadsworth, Gail M. **Women in Development: A Bibliography of Materials Available in the Library and Documentation Centre, Eastern and Southern African Management Institute. Supplement to the Second Edition.** Arusha, Tanzania: Eastern and Southern African Management Institute, 1982. 26 pp.

See item #27

Articles

704. Bardouille, Raj. "Integration of Zambian Women in National Development: Analysis of Constraints and Prospects." **Women in Development: Perspectives from the Nairbobi Conference.** Ottawa: International Development Research Center, 1985, pp. 53-92.

Argues that Zambian women are only marginally integrated into the national development process. Despite the government's avowed equality of opportunity, women's access to education, training, employment and factors of production--land, labor, capital, technologies, etc.--is far behind the access of men. Government and nongovernmental agencies have not offered programs to integrate women into development. Criticizes these agencies for their lack of clearly defined development policies and programs designed specifically for women.

705. Cardoso E. Silva, Maria Luisa. "Aspectos da Reeducação da Mulher Nativa Angolana." **Ultramar** 22 (1965): 37-49.

Looks at women's roles in traditional society in the family and the community. Argues that with urbanization and modernization women lose some of their traditional power and status. Urges the extension of education for women to promote national development and argues that the most effective forms would be in daily practical skills such as cooking, health, child care and community development skills.

706. Due, Jean M. and Rebecca Summary.   "Africana: Constraints to
Women and Development in Africa."   Journal of Modern African
Studies 20 (1982): 155-166.

Points out that although women produce more than 60 percent of
the food crops in many African countries, less than one woman in
five has found employment in wage earning occupations.   Argues
that the process of development has undermined women.   In part
this is due to lack of access to education and capital.
Surveys factors affecting women's access to formal and informal
education in East Africa, Tonga, Tanzania, Buganda, Uganda,
Senegal, Kenya and sees women's lack of education a result of
public policy.   Finds women are discriminated against in
obtaining credit in the formal sector and are thus relegated to
working in the informal sector where little capital investment
is required.

707. Lewis, Shelby F.   "Education, Women and Development in Africa."
Patriarchy, Party, Population and Pedagogy.   Edited by Edgar B.
Gumbert.   Atlanta: Georgia State University Center for
Cross-Cultural Education, 1986, pp. 9-34.

Assesses the role of women in the development process in African
societies.   Finds that African education systems limit
opportunities and advancement of women.   Makes eight
recommendations to integrate women into development.   These
include changing traditional sex roles, using incentives and
penalties to discourage discrimination against women, reviewing
development plans concerning women and conducting more research
on rural women and the role of education in the development
process.

708. Mbilinyi, Marjorie J.   "The 'New Woman' and Traditional Norms in
Tanzania."   Journal of Modern African Studies 10 (1972): 57-72.

Argues gender based inequality has increased as Tanzania seeks
to become a developed nation.   Presents statistics on sex
inequality in primary school enrollments.   Because women are
educationally disadvantaged and do not obtain technical and
vocational training, they cannot get wage earning jobs.   Argues
that women's present status of social, political and legal
inferiority could be overcome if women obtain wage employment.
Concludes that fundamental changes in the economy need to take
place for women to participate fully and equally in economic
development.

709. Mburu, F.M.   "The African Social Periphery."   Social Science and
Medicine 22 (no. 7 1986): 785-790.

Looks at the problem of women's education from the standpoint of future child care and food supply. African women raise 70 percent of the crops but are being shut out of new agricultural knowledge. Women need development education. As food shortages occur, women and children withdraw to the fields to scratch out a living and the cycle of poverty is continued and deepened.

710. Myin, Marie Antionettte.   The Involvement of Rural Women in Village in Tanzania." **Convergence** 16 (1983): 59-69.

Examines women's participation in development projects in eight villages in Morogoro district, Tanzania, in 1978-80. Finds that efforts to increase labor productivity are aimed at men, partly because of the sexist ideologies of most administrators and partly because of the sexual division of labor that is characteristic of traditional societies. Formal school education and vocational agricultural training are tor boys and men, women's access to information is limited. Women are less educated than men, their time is less flexible because of child bearing and child rearing duties and their daily workload does not allow much time for agricultural demonstrations and meetings. Concludes with seven suggestions as to what can be done to improve women's involvement in village development.

Nxumalo, Simanga. "Income-Generating Project Develops Skills of Swazi Women." **Convergence** 15 (1982): 48-55.

See item #606

Oppong, Christine. "Women's Roles and Conjugal Family Systems in Ghana." **The Changing Position of Women in Family and Society**. Edited by Eugen Lupri. Leiden: E.J. Brill, 1983, pp. 331-343.

See item #1017

711. Robertson, Claire C.   "Women in the Urban Economy." **African Women South of the Sahara**. Edited by Margaret Jean Hay and Sharon Stichter. New York: Longman, 1984, pp. 33-49.

Talks about the changes modernization has brought for urban African women, especially in the economic sphere, which are often detrimental to their well being. Because of discriminatory hiring policies and lack of training, women are often denied wage paid jobs and forced into self-employmnent in the informal sector. Lack of access to credit and capital, the introduction of intermediate technology and universal primary education, etc., deprive women of the means of acquiring capital.

Robertson, Claire.   "Women's Education and Class Formation in
Africa, 1950-1980."   **Women and Class in Africa.**   Edited by
Clarie   Robertson   and   Iris   Berger.   New   York: Africana
Publishing Company, 1986, pp. 92-113.

See item #322

Rousseau-Mukenge, Ida.   "Conceptualizations of African Women's
Role in Development: A Search for New Directions." **Journal of
International Affairs** 30 (1976-1977): 261-268.

See item #523

712. Sudarkasa, Niara.   "Sex Roles, Education, and Development in
Africa."   Anthropology   and   Education   Quarterly   13   (1982):
279-289.

Examines the question of sex role differentiation in education
and occupations in Africa.   Points out that the spread of the
market economy in Africa adversely affected the economic status
of women, turning sexual differentiation within the economic
sphere into sexual discrimination.   The spread of Western
education served to increase the economic gap between male and
female.   Suggests that nonformal and continuing education along
side basic education programs might improve women's occupational
status.

713. Tinker, Irene.   "Women in Africa: Policy Strategies for Women
in the 1980s."   **Africa Report** 26 (March-April 1981):   11-16.

Reviews   current   strategies   for   integrating   women   into
development.   One reason for the adverse impact of development
on women is due to the lack of women in decision making roles.
Discusses the problems which arise because women's projects are
separate from development planning (in Kenya, Upper Volta and
India).   Suggests taking women's issues into the male world and
insisting that these be made central to development plans.

714. United Nations   Economic Commission for Africa, African Training
and Research Center Women.   "Women and National Development in
African Countries: Some Profound Contradictions."   **African
Studies Review** 18 (1975): 47-70.

Examines the economic division of labor by sex in traditional
sectors of the society and attempts to contrast it with that in
modernizing and modernized sectors.   Presents results of studies
from many African countries locating the amount and type of work
done by women.   Finds women not well represented in modern
sectors even though they are fully employed in traditional
sectors.   Shows the effects of the introduction of innovations

can be negative for women, increasing their burdens and effort. Women lag seriously behind men educationally and in vocational and technical training as well. Undereducated market women and traders are in danger of being squeezed out of their economic activity by big commercial undertakings. Finds most educated women participate in the progressive specialization of work. Lists five persistant attitudes which hinder women's participation in wage labor. Describes some women's initiatives for self-help, their organizations and political participation. Lists and discusses four areas of strategies for change identified by the Economic Commission for Africa Women's Center intended to bring women into the mainstream of development.

Van Allen, Judith. "African Women, 'Modernization' and National Liberation." **Women in the World: A Comparative Study.** Edited by Lynne B. Iglitzin and Ruth Ross. Santa Barbara: American Bibliographic Center, CLIO Press, 1976, pp. 25-54.

See item #138

2.   Kenya

Books and Monographs

715. Likimani, Muthoni. **Women of Kenya: Fifteen Years of Independence.** Nairobi: Likimani, 1979. 76 pp.

Focuses on women and development programs which are run by the Kenyan Government, Division of Women. These consist mainly of projects designed to help women participate in the economy. Much of the volume provides portraits of Kenyan professional women.

Articles

716. Abbott, Susan. "Women's Importance to Kenyan Rural Development." **Community Development Journal** 10 (1975): 179-182.

Reports Kenya's continuing commitment to improve the productivity of its predominantly small scale farms through farmer education. Points out the need to recognize that women are farmers and play major roles in making decisions about the adaptation of new crops. Argues that if rural development is to occur, women should be included in development programs. Recommends employing and training more women as farm extension workers.

717. Lindsay, Beverly. "An Examination of Education, Social Change and National Development Policy: The Case of Kenyan Women." **Women and Politics in 20th Century Africa and Asia, Studies in Third World Societies** 16 (June 1981): 29-48.

     Looks at how national development policy affects women's aspirations and educational enrollments in Kenya. Studies the career perceptions and aspirations of 192 Kenyans enrolled in secondary and higher education. Finds that women aspired to stereotyped roles in the family and the economy and attributes these stereotypes to government development policies which ignore women.

718. Luseno. D. "Education and the Social Status of Women in Africa." **Kenya Journal of Adult Education** 2 (1972): 17-22.

     Identifies the attributes of educational programs which maximize women's contributions to economic development. Argues that such programs depend on female leadership and the involvement of women's organizations in the planning and implementation of development projects.

719. Mutua, Rosalind. "Women's Education and their Participation in the Changing Societies of East Africa." **The Participation of Women in Kenya Society.** Edited by Achola Pala, Thelma Awori, and Abigail Krystall. Nairobi: Kenya Literature Bureau, 1978, pp. 160-169.

     Provides figures on women's formal education for the years 1966 and 1972 in Kenya and relates formal education to women's income. Argues that urban educated women's position has worsened as women have become less economically indispensible than they were in pre-colonial times. When women are uneducated, they are completely dependent on their husbands.

720. Staudt, Kathleen A. "Women Farmers and Inequities in Agricultural Services." **Women and Work in Africa.** Edited by Edna G. Bay. Boulder, Colorado: Westview Press, 1982, pp. 207-224.

     Examines how agricultural services are provided to female and male farmers in Kenya. Data were collected in 1975 from 212 small scale farm households, divided in two types, female management and joint management. Finds that women managers experience a significant bias in the delivery of services, and that this bias intensifies as the value of the service increases. Contends that eradication of this discrimination is crucial for both women's productivity and economy as a whole.

3.   Asia

Books and Monographs

Andors, Phyllis. The Unfinished Liberation of Chinese Women, 1949-1980. Bloomington: Indiana University Press, 1983. 212 pp.

See item #157

721. Aziz, Nov Laily. **Malaysian Women in the 1980s.** Kuala Lumpur: Lembaga Perancang Kelarga Negara Jabatan Perdana Menteri, 1981. 9 pp. (Occasional Paper no. 4).

Focuses on women's role in development in Malaysia and their educational, occupational, health and legal status. The paper was prepared for the Women in Management Seminar held in Kuala Lumpur in 1980. Maintains that in order to successfully integrate women in the development process, women themselves must develop psychologically, sociologically and economically, and society must recognize women's contributions to the economy and improve their educational, employment, health and legal status.

Gallin, Rita S. The Impact of Development on Women's Work and Status: A Case Study from Taiwan. East Lansing: Michigan State University, Women and International Development, 1982. 24 pp. (Working Paper no. 9)

See item #843

Jahan, Rounaq and Hanna Papanek eds. **Women and Development: Perspectives from South and Southeast Asia.** Dacca: The Bangladesh Institute of Law and International Affairs, 1979. 439 pp.

See item #88

722. Macy, Joanna. **Dharma and Development: Religion as Resource in the Sarvodaya Self-Help Movement.** West Hartford, Conn. Kumarian Press, 1983. 102 pp.

Reports a field study of the Sarvodaya Shramadana movement in Sri Lanka. The movement is a Budhist self help organization devoted to rural development. The book is based on interviews with village organizers and peasants which took place in 1979. Chapter 7 is devoted to women in the Sarvodaya movement. Points out that women are grass roots organizers, but they are only 10 percent of national executive committee members and only 1 out of 28 district coordinators are female. Claims that women remain out of leadership in large part out of their own choice and their roles in the family.

723. Reejad, Pushkar Raj. **Integration of Women in Development.** Kathmandu: Tribhuvan Centre for Economic Development and Administration, 1981. 200 pp.

Analyzes the impact of Nepal's 1956-1980 development plan on women. The plan covered agricultural production but emphasized transportation and the development of a communications infrastructure. Chapter 4 focuses on education and demonstrates that the expansion of education under the plan at all levels benefitted women more than men. Claims that any inequalities that persist in education are attributable to parental attitudes rather than to state policy. Argues that there is no reason why Nepal has to make special plans for female populations because women have made substantial progress under plans developed for the population as a whole.

724. **The Role of Women in Development: The Indonesian Experience.** Jakarta: KOWANI (Indonesian Women's Congress), 1980. 35 pp.

Focuses on the role of Indonesian women in development and discusses the changes in women's education, employment, health, social welfare, religion and politics since independence. Points out that great gains have been made in girls' access to schools and literacy rates have increased to 49 percent for women and 71 percent for men. Women's organizations have played a major role in encouraging the spread of education and literacy.

Strange, Heather. **Rural Malay Women in Tradition and Transition.** New York: Praeger, 1981. 264 pp.

See item #145

Women and Development in Asia: A Selected Bibliography. Bangkok: Population Education Clearinghouse, UNESCO Regional Office for Education in Asia and Oceania, 1979. 25 pp.

See item #37

Articles

725. Chen, F. K. Y. "The Role of Women in Economic Development: An Analysis with Special Reference to Hong Kong." **The Role of**

Women in Development: Seminar Papers and Statements. Edited by
Leonardo Z. Legaspi. Manila: University of Santo Tomas Press,
1976, pp. 136-159.

Uses a neo-classical model to look at women's role in
development in Hong Kong. Analyzes the supply factors affecting
female labor participation and level of educational attainment.
Finds that educating the public in general and women in
particular plays an important part in promoting economic and
social development in the sense that it enables supply to adjust
smoothly to the demand for women workers. Concludes that female
labor participation depends very much on effective policies to
educate the female population as a whole.

Cho, Hyoung. "Labor Force Participation of Women in Korea."
Challenges for Women: Women's Studies in Korea. Edited by
Chung Sei-wha. Soeul: Ewha Woman's University Press, 1986,
pp. 150-172.

See item #848

726. Frances, Jeanne. "Women's Participation in Two Irrigation
Projects in the Philippines." Women in Development:
Perspectives from the Nairobi Conference. Ottawa:
International Development Research Center, 1986, pp. 186-244.

Describes female farmer involvement in two rural development
projects in the Philippines: the Aslong and the Buhi-Lalo
projects. The study is based on data collected from 1979 to
1982. Shows that when women were adequately informed about the
project and their interest sufficiently aroused, they became
involved and that when more than one person from each household
was active, participation further increased. The employment of
female organizers provided the farmers with role models of
active female participation in the project. Urges community
organizers to encourge female participation in development
projects and to open up the association membership to
households, with husband and wife as alternate representatives,
in order to enhance women's involvement in community
development.

727. Ghimire, Durga. "The Role of Women in Development in Nepal."
Women and Development: Perspectives from South and Southeast
Asia. Edited by Rounaq Jahan and Hanna Papanek. Dacca: The
Bangladesh Institute of Law and International Affairs, 1979,
pp. 95-114.

Describes the changes the legal and social status of women in
Nepal society. Argues that the position of women has been
making progress since the political change in 1951, but it is

still far from satisfactory.   Contends that, in order to bring
women in the process of nation building, they should be given
more opportunities to be educated and that the bearing and
rearing of children and domestic work should be regarded as
women's contribution to the nation which is equal to the work
done by men.

728. Green Justin J.   "The Filipina Elite: Her Social Backgrounds and
      their Relationships to Development."   **Philippine Educational
      Forum** 19 (1970):   5-40.

      Examines Filipino female elite and relates this elite group to
      the process of Philippine development.   The data, obtained by
      interviewing   123   women   leaders,   found   out   that   the
      characteristics of Filipino female elite fit within a ruling
      class   in   accessibility   and   within   a   strategic   elite   in
      educational level.   Concludes that, considering that the
      Philippines is a multiple society, the mixed characteristics of
      the elite make sense and that this hybrid elite is not likely to
      be   transformed   into   a   strategic   elite   who   might   lead   a
      traditional society toward a modern industrial society.

729. Hooper, Beverley.   "China's Modernization."   **Modern China** 10
      (1984): 317-343.

      Argues that higher education and employment are key to women's
      participation in development in China.   Points out that
      gender based disparities are being widened in China by the
      government's retreat from ideological commitment to equality.
      Under the "Four Modernizations," greater stress has been put on
      women's domestic role at the expense of their productive role.

730. Mahajani, Usha.   "Women's Status and Modernization in Southeast
      Asia: The Philippines Model."   **Women of the World: Illusion
      and Reality.**   Edited by Urmila Phadnis and Indira Malani.   New
      Delhi: Vikas Publishing House, Ltd., 1978, pp. 55-86.

      Provides a historical overview of the change in women's status
      in Southeast Asian countries and the Philippines in particular.
      Although women are making great progress in education and in the
      business field, unlike in ancient times, women's status has not
      gained ground.   As countries in Southeast Asia have come under
      right-wing dictatorship, women have been losing more power.

731. Muni, Anuradha and S.D. Muni.   "Tradition vs Modernity—Women in
      Nepal and Sri Lanka."   **Women of the World: Illusion and
      Reality.**   Edited by Urmila Phadnis and Indira Malani.   New
      Delhi: Vikas Publishing House, Ltd., 1978, pp. 30-54.

Describes the effect of development on women in Nepal and Sri Lanka and discusses their current roles and status in social, economic and political life. Argues that, although women in both societies enjoyed the same status in their respective traditional societies, women in contemporary Sri Lanka are better placed in education, politics and leadership, which have much to do with the process of social and political modernization initiated during the British rule.

732. Noor, Yetty R.   "Indonesian Women's Participation in Development."   Indonesian Women: Some Past and Current Perspectives. Edited by B.B. Herring. Brussels: Centre d'Etudes du Sud-est Asiatique et de l'Extreme Orient, 1976, pp.156-163.

Points out that while development is thought to benefit women, this has not occurred in Indonesia. The government has passed many laws guaranteeing women equality with men, but in practice in the newly independent nations of Southeast Asia, women are denied equality in employment and in education.

733. Tan, Nalla.   "The Impact of Modernization on Women." Modernization in Singapore: Impact on the Individual. Edited by Tham Seong Chee. Singapore: University Education Press, 1972, pp. 63-77.

Examines the impact of modernization on Singapore women in terms of three major factors: education, economic independence and political involvement. Argues that, although education should improve women's social and economic situation, the progress in women's education in Singapore is not fast enough to have significant effect on these areas, nor has modernization brought changes in women's political roles.

Zhang, Shiao-chun.   "The Role Played by Urban Housewives in Modern Society." The Institute of Technology Academia Sinica (Taipei) 37 (1974): 39-82.

See item #1045

3a.   Bangladesh

Books

734. Germain, Adrienne. Women's Roles in Bangladesh Development: A Program Assessment. Dacca: The Ford Foundation, 1976. 49 pp.

Describes key aspects of the lives and work of rural Bangladeshi women as well as special programs for women, and gives recommendations for future research and action programs. Points out that programs for women are relief programs rather than development programs and are not providing women with technologies and other inputs that would increase productivity without displacing labor, that programs lack female staff and leadership and that craft programs arre only a partial solution for a country like Bangladesh where there are severe production and marketing problems.

Mabud, Mohammed A. **Women's Development, Income and Fertility.** Dhaka: The External Evaluation Unit, Planning Commission and Canadian International Development Agency, 1985. 180 pp.

See item #1103

Articles

735. Islam, Mahmuda. "Impact of Male Migration on Rural Housewives." Women in Bangladesh: Some Socio-Economic Issues. Edited by Janara Huq et al. Dhaka: Women for Women, 1983, pp. 46-53.

Examines the effects of male migration to urban areas on female members of the family left in the villages. Data were collected from 95 families in Dhaka district of Bangladesh. Findings show that although male migration has some positive impact on women and other family members, such as better economic situation, attainment of respect and allegiance, higher literacy rate especially among primary age children, etc., it did not change the traditional sex role divisions of labor or subordination of women. Points out that the existing power structure of the villages made marginal changes that male migration brought about.

736. Khatun, Sharifa. "Women's Education in a Rural Community in Bangladesh." **Women and Development: Perspectives from South and Southeast Asia.** Edited by Rounaq Jahan and Hanna Papanek. Dacca: The Bangladesh Institute of Law and International Affairs, 1979, pp. 253-274.

Critiques rural programs for being unrelated to the needs of women and girls in development. Through a study of decision making in education among 5 to 15 year old girls out of school in rural Bangladesh, shows that girls do not attend rural development programs in or out of school because they are irrelevant to income generation.

737. Qadir, Sayeda Rowshan. "Women's Income Earning Activities and
Family Welfare in Bangladesh." **Women in Bangladesh: Some
Socio-Economic Issues.** Edited by Janara Huq et al.   Dhaka:
Women for Women, 1983, pp. 36-45.

Examines income generation programs for women in Bangladesh
taken up by three types of organizations--national voluntary,
international voluntary and governmental--to assess the effect
of income earned by women on the welfare of their families.
Data were collected by interviewing 140 families in four
locations.   Points out that income generating activities for
women are important not only to meet the most basic needs of the
family but also to improve the quality of life beyond mere
survival. Suggests that women be organized in groups and that
more profitable economic activities be explored.

738. Westergaard, Kirsten. "Rural Pauperization: Its Impact on the
Economic Role and Status of Rural Women in Bangladesh." **Women
in Bangladesh: Some Socio-Economic Issues.** Edited by Janara
Huq et al. Dhaka: Women for Women, 1983, pp. 17-36.

Looks at the response to increasing pauperization in rural areas
among women of different economic groups in two villages in
rural Bangladesh. Finds that as landlessness and very small
holdings increase, more women are marginalized in the labor
process. This is accompanied by a systematic social devaluation
of women. Concludes that the traditional purdah norms have not
been outweighed either by a positive attitude toward female
education or by economic considerations in the face of
destitution.

3b.   India

Books and Monographs

739. Agarwal, Mamita. **Education and Modernization: A Study of Hindu
and Muslim Women.** New Delhi: Eduresearch Publications, 1986.
136 pp.

Surveys 150 Hindu and 150 Muslim women in Delhi. Of the 300,
100 were uneducated, 100 were college educated women between 17
and 25 years old and 100 were school teachers betwen 40 and 60
years old having secondary education or better. Finds Muslim
women are less modern than Hindu women and that age makes no
difference in terms of modern attitudes. Education does affect
attitudes toward marriage and educated women expect great
equality, although they do not reject arranged marriage.
Educated women have higher educational aspirations for their

children and are more conscious of their rights. Educated women also tend to regret the caste system.

740. Bam, Brigalia H. and Lotika Sarkar. **New Perspectives for Third World Women.** Madras: The Christian Literature Society, 1979. 43 pp.

Consists of two E.V. Mathews Memorial Lectures given in Bangalore under the auspices of the World Council of Churches. The first lecture by Brigalia Bam argues that women should be brought into development and that the World Council needs to make this a top priority. Maintains that education is key to women's participation in development, particularly nonformal education, since education articulates with women's participation in the workforce as well as in the political system. The second lecture focuses on women's legal status in India.

741. Heggade, Odeyar D. **Women and Economic Development.** Bangalore: Ramya Roopa Prakashana, 1984. 220 pp.

Analyses alternative methods to integrate women in India's economic development. Points out the male bias is prevalent in the development process world-wide and argues that this male bias, caused by sets of sociocultural and economic forces as well as moral and religious ideas, has brought an unequal relationship between women and men in the decision making process. Contends that the factors which prevent effective participation of women in the development process are the underestimation of women's labor, unequal distribution of education, the fact that most women do not possess any income generating assets, and social seclusion and segregation based on cultural and religious values. Believes that women's education can promote economic development of a nation as well as the participation of women in the development process. Suggests that the educational policy of the country should focus on making a woman's education more job-oriented and providing more nonformal education to illiterate women who belong to scheduled castes and tribes to improve their productivity.

Articles

Boserup, Ester. "Women in the Labour Market." **Indian Women.** Edited by Devaki Jain. New Delhi: Publication Division, Ministry of Information and Broadcasting, Government of India, 1975, pp. 99-111.

See item #873

742. Elliott, Carolyn M.   "Women's Education and Development in
     India."   World Yearbook of Education.   1984.   **Women and
     Education.**   London: Kogan page, (1984): 243-256.

     Focuses on the role of education in modernization in India.
     Points out that the development process has eroded women's
     status in India.   The number of adult women illiterates is over
     200,000,000 and is growing.   Formal education has failed to
     reach ˙poor rural girls and has been unable to keep apace of
     population growth.   Argues that adult and nonformal education
     run by women's group can successfully mobilize illiterate rural
     women for development.   Uses examples of the National Adult
     Education Programs, the Action for Welfare and Awakening in the
     Rural Environment (South India), the YWCA programs night classes
     to show how nonformal education run by women's groups can be
     effective in integrating women into the development process.

743. Jacobson, Doranne.   "Indian Women in the Process of
     Development." **Journal of International Affairs** 30 (1976-77):
     211-242.

     Provides educational statistics that show improvements in
     women's enrollment at all levels of schooling.   The drop out
     rates for girls are greatest in North and Central India where
     girls leave school at puberty.   Educational expansion has led to
     the emergence of urban, professional women who work as teachers,
     doctors and social workers.   Points out that the workforce in
     India is highly sex segregated.   Despite the gains in education
     and the emergence of urban professional women, schooling has yet
     to reach rural women.   Describes nonformal education programs
     developed by the Indian government and private foundations.
     Stresses the persistence of gender based inequalities in
     education and in the workforce.

     Jayaweera, S.   "Programmes of Non-formal Education for Women."
     Indian Journal of Adult Education 40 (no. 12, 1979):   33-45.

     See item #640

744. Mazumdar, Vina.   "Education, Development and Women's Liberation:
     Contemporary Debates in India."   **Education and the Process of
     Change.**   Edited by Ratna Ghosh and Mathew Zachariah.   New Delhi:
     Sage Publications, 1987, pp. 198-211.

     Discusses the debates about whether development coupled with
     educational expansion liberates women in India.   Focuses on how
     education has failed to eradicate gender inequalities and asks
     how educational policy can be changed to play a more active role
     in bringing about gender equality.   Points out that there has

been a shift in perception of the women's "problem" in education since 1985. Before 1985, the problem in India was perceived as one of discrimination against a deprived group. After 1985 the women's "problem" came to be seen as related to India's economic development.

745. Mazumdar, Vina. "Women, Development and Public Policy." Women and Development: Perspectives from South and Southeast Asia. Edited by Rounaq Jahan and Hanna Papanek. Dacca: The Bangladesh Institute of Law and International Affairs, 1979, pp. 39-54.

Describes the effects of the devlopment process and public policies on the position of women in India. Argues that the movement to improve the status of women was based on urban middle class biases, which created the illusion of rapid improvement in women's conditions and the achievement of equality. It has rendered invisible the widening gap between men and women of differing social classes. Points out that the development process and policies have emphasized education and welfare and displaced women from their traditional, socially guaranteed tasks.

4.   **Latin America**

Books and Monographs

746. Alvarez, Alberto Miguel Correa. The Role of Public Enterprises in the Advancement of Women in Mexico: A Case Study. Titova, Yugoslavia: International Center for Public Enterprises in Developing Countries, 1983. 87 pp.

Analyzes the position of women in Mexico, the role they play in the operation and functioning of public enterprises, the contribution of these enterprises to the improvement of the present situation and to the integration of women in the country's socioeconomic development.

Martorelli, Horacio. Mujer y Sociedad. Montevideo: Fundación de Cultural Universitaria, 1978.

See item #905.

Miller, Linda. Female Educators, Development and Human Capital: A Brazilian Case. East Lansing: Michigan State University,

1983.   16 pp.   (Working Papers on Women in International Development, no. 35)

See item #500

Nash, June and Helen I. Safa, eds.   Sex and Class in Latin America.   New York: Praeger, 1976.   330 pp.

See item #100

Recchini de Lattes, Zulina.   Dynamics of the Female Labor Force in Argentina.   Paris: UNESCO, 1983.   98 pp.

See item #909

Saffioti, Heleieth I.B.   The Impact of Industrialization on the Structure of Women's Employment.   East Lansing: Michigan State University, Office of Women in Development, 1983.   (Working Paper no. 15)

See item #938

747. Smucker, Jacqueline Nowak.   The Role of Rural Haitian Women in Development.   Port-au-Prince, Haiti: USAID Mission, 1981. 73 pp.

Studies the role of rural Haitian women in development.   The purpose of the research, which was undertaken under USAID in 1980, was to provide information to enhance the role of rural women in development while strengthening the family and alleviating poverty.   Interviews with rural women and men, with people active in development programs for women, and fieldwork observations were conducted.   The first two chapters illustrate women's lives and activities in the household and in commerce and agriculture, which are their primary roles.   The book also talks about other economic activities of women, including nonagricultural employment, education and development programs for women, community organization and credit.   Although parents are willing to send both girls and boys to school with the expectation of its economic reward, rural children rarely complete primary education, and projects to teach adults Creole literacy have had little success.   Suggests that a national commitment to universal literacy in the official language, namely French, be encouraged and development programs aim at improving women's economic circumstances.

748. Turner, June H. ed.   Latin American Women: The Meek Speak Out. Silver Spring, Maryland: International Educational Development Inc., 1980. 230 pp.

Presents the point of view of women working in development projects in Bolivia, Peru, Columbia, Ecuador, Costa Rica, Nicaraugua, Honduras and El Salvador. These women activitists include a nurse, a nun, a Ph.D. in education. Their essays describe nonformal education programs that try to serve women and increase their consciousness in rural communities. Some of these projects consist of forming women's organizations; others like the National Center for Integrated Learning (CENAFI) in Bolivia, focus on literacy skills and semi-vocational training.

749. UNESCO. Oficina Regional de Educación para América Latina y el Caribe. **Curso Regional de Formación para los Responsables de la Educación de la Mujer en Areas Rurales de América Latina y el Caribe.** Pátzcuaro, México 1980. Santiago: UNESCO, 1980. 200 pp.

Presents the proceedings of a congress on rural women and development organized around three themes: 1) the organization of the countryside by soil type, crop orientation and plantation, social movement to the city and rural--expert--visitation by the educated and professional; 2) how the first theme interacts with the situation, education, family, health and occupation of women (generally, education is only a part of making a life cycle--focused on reproduction and basic biological functions and acts--more reasonable), 3) development projects that attempt to change health, education and social development through informal education. Surveys the projects the general education levels of women in each of the 17 countries participating in the conference.

Articles

750. Antrobus, Peggy. "Women in Development: The Issues for the Caribbean. **Convergence** 13 (1980): 60-63.

Describes the many forms of discrimination against women in the Caribbean: while 62 percent of all women work, they occupy the lowest status, lowest paying jobs and produce approximately 70 percent of all foods consumed locally. Women have made real gains in education. Despite this, increased educational levels have not changed women's position in the workforce. Attributes this to sex role stereotyping in the curriculum.

751. Antrobus, Peggy. "Reaching Beyond University Walls." **Development** (no. 4, 1984): 45-49.

Describes the work of the Women and Development Unit of the Extra-Mural Department of the University of the West Indies established in 1978. The objectives of the unit are to build awareness of women in development issues in the region as well as the personal and institutional capacity for promoting change in the status of women through technical assistance, training and communications. These activities resulted in a body of knowledge and experience of the process related to the integration of women in development and the creation of the network of individuals, groups and agencies. Points out that the effectiveness of strategies for change depends on the extent to which contact with women is maintained at every level of the society.

Aranha Bruschini, Maria Cristina. "Sexualização das Ocupaçoes: O Caso Brasileiro." Cadernos da Pesquisa 28 (1979): 5-20.

See item #929

752. Barbin, Christina. "Neuvas Prioridades Para la Educación en América Latina." Folia Humanistica 18 (no. 205, 1980): 45-48.

Describes factors influencing the development of Latin American countries and argues that education should be a strong priority in development plans. Points out that the education of women lags behind that of men and recommends that it be strengthened as well. Contains a summary of Latin American Ministries of Education and Economic Planning meeting organized by UNESCO in Mexico in 1979.

753. Bengelsdorf, Carollee and Alice Hageman. "Emerging from Underdevlopment: Women and Work in Cuba." Race and Class 19 (1978): 361-378.

Describes the unprecendented gains in women's participation in the workforce made in post-revolutionary Cuba. Argues that these changes for the most part were made possible through nonformal education programs which targeted women. The key programs were the literacy campaign and special nonformal classes which imparted job training to former domestic workers. While optimistic about the changes in women's status that have arisen from the extension of both formal and nonformal education in Cuba, recognizes that not all of women's problems have been addressed: women are underrepresented in leadership roles and they still face the double burden of work in the labor force and in the household.

754. Channey, Elsa M. and Marianne Schmink. "Women and Modernization: Access to Tools." Sex and Class in Latin America. Edited by Jane Nash and Helen Ickes Safa. New York: Praeger, 1976, pp. 160-182.

Argues that modernization not only fails to confer equal benefits to both sexes, but that it worsens women's situation. Points out that women become relatively "unproductive" by virtue of their limited access to modern tools. In agriculture, most women remain in subsistence production while men participate in the wider cash economy. Most women are denied the opportunity to learn how to use machines and technologies. In industries, women mostly remain in the low paying, less skilled jobs. In politics, women in Latin America are only expected to take responsibilities concerning the "domestic" affairs of society. Concludes that in many ways women's position deteriorates as technological development proceeds and women's access to education, both formal and nonformal, stagnates.

755. Draper, Elaine. "Women's Work and Development in Latin America." **Studies in Comparative International Development** 20 (1985): 3-20.

Looks at the problem of women's employment patterns under capitalist development, and criticizes modernization theory by examining the two types of work (domestic service and informal work) in which most Latin American women are engaged. Contends that domestic service and informal jobs should be seen in relation to the other forms of labor and to total social production and that women's social status should be measured not only in reference to education, political participation, work and income, but also in terms of relative power and the social rewards of prestige associated with their activities.

Elizaga, Juan C. "The Participation of Women in the Labour Force of Latin America: Fertility and Other Factors." **International Labour Review** 109 (1974): 519-538.

See item #913

Ellis, Pat. "Women, Adult Education and Literacy: A Caribbean Perspective." **Convergence** 17 (no. 4, 1984): 44-53.

See item #646

Rosen, Bernard C. and Anita L. LaRaia. "Modernity in Women: An Index of Social Change in Brazil." **Journal of Marriage and the Family** 34 (1972): 353-360. see item #1050

756. Shaw, Kathryn. "Patterns for Change." **Américas** 32 (March 1980): 49-51.

Describes a project aimed at assisting women in Costa Rica in moving out of slum shanty towns to new modern communities. The project consisted of organizing a sewing cooperative and became a model for other projects launched by the Federation of Voluntary Organizations and the Overseas Education Fund.

757. Swain, Margaret B.   "Being Cuna and Female."   **Sex Roles and Social Change in Native Lower Central American Societies.** Edited by Christina Loveland and Franklin Loveland.   Urbana: University of Illinois Press, 1981, pp. 103-123.

Presents an anthropological view of a community which is breaking down through the intervention of health, education and economic institutions.   Education seems to reenforce helping roles for women but also seems to promote migration from the local area.

Tienda, Marta.   "Community Characteristics, Women's Education and Fertility in Peru."   Studies in Family Planning 15 (July-August 1984): 162-169.

See item #1141

Vasques de Miranda, Glaura.   "Women's Labor Force Participation in a Developing Society: The Case of Brazil." Signs: Journal of Women in Culture and Society 3 (1977): 261-274.

See item #933

Vaughan, Mary K.   "Women, Class and Education in Mexico, 1880-1928."   Latin American Perspectives 4 (nos. 1/2, 1977): 135-152.

See item #288

758. Watson-Franke, María-Barbara.   "The Urbanization and Liberation of Women:"   A Study of Urban Impact on Guajiro Women in Venezuela." Antropologica 51 (1979): 93-117.

Discusses the urban impact of Guajiro women, the largest ethnic minority in Venezuela, and asks how their cultural background leads to the particular problems they face in the city. Focusing on three areas, educational and occupational opportunities, kin group and other social networks and the marital relationship, argues that Guajiro women lose their traditional support systems without regaining new opportunities and resources in a male-dominated world of the urban cities. Suggests that supporting female solidarity and developing groups outside kinship relations would be a useful step for Guajiro women to become independent and self reliant.

759. Wilson, Flona. "Women and Agricultural Change in Latin America: Some Concepts Guiding Research." World Development 13 (1985): 1017-1035.

Explores the differential impact of agricultural development programs on women of different social classes and ethnicities in Latin America.

760. Zeidenstein, Sondra. "A Regional Approach to Women's Needs: The Women and Development Unit in the Caribbean." Assignment Children, (no. 49/50 1980): 155-171.

Describes the Women in Development Unit that resulted from a 1977 seminar for women in the Caribbean. The activities described include training programs, technical assistance projects, informational brochures and collaboration with local and international agencies to strengthen and coordinate programs for women.

5.   The Middle East

Books and Monographs

761. Al-Sabah, S.M. Development Planning in an Oil Economy and the Role of the Women: The Case of Kuwait. London: Eastlords Publishing Ltd., 1983. 380 pp.

Proposes a framework strategy for development planning in Kuwait which focuses on developing domestic production other than in oil, minimizes the non-Kuwaiti laborforce, and encourages Kuwaiti female participation in the labor force. In addition, studies the determinants of Kuwaiti women's "commitment to work." Administers a survey to 500 women. The sample was highly educated with about 51 percent attending universities in Kuwait. Finds that education of a woman and of her husband was greatest predictor of woman's "commitment to work" (a combination of attitudes to a career and maintenance within the workforce through marriage and childbearing and rearing.) Argues that education will therefore be important to development planning since it encourages women's entry into paid labor and can be used to replace expatriates in the Kuwaiti economy.

762. Myntti, C. Women and Development in Yemen Arab Republic. Eschborn, Germany: German Agency for Technical Cooperation, 1979. 169 pp.

Focuses on the status of women in Yemen Arab Republic and the
relation of that status to development. Points out that women
live in a patriarchial, patrilineal society in Yemen. In rural
areas women constitute the majority of labor in the subsistence
agricultural sector; in the urban, modern sector of the society,
few women work for a wage--less than 1 in 25 workers in
government employ are female. Part of the reason women are not
in the workforce can be attributed to low education levels.
Points out that women are 12.4 percent of primary school
enrollments and 10.8 percent of the secondary school students.
They are between 7 and 8 percent of students in higher
education, but are concentrated in the arts faculties. Argues
that women will not take part in development unless more
education, both formal and nonformal is extended to them. Also
argues that development projects currently do not include women,
especially in the rural areas. Reviews internationally funded
development projects in Yemen and also includes in an appendix
translations of the Yemen Arab Republic Labor Law of 1970 as
well as development agencies' policies regarding women and
development.

Articles

763. Abadan-Unat, Nermin. "The Modernization of Turkish Women."
Middle East Journal 32 (1978): 291-306.

Describes the modernization of women in Turkey through legal
emancipation, the transition to a multi-party system, the
extension of the franchise to all citizens including women over
21 and deep rooted structural changes such as rapid
urbanization, industrialization and mechanization of
agriculture. Increasing entry of women into higher education
and the pressure of rising standards of living within the middle
class helped to develop a group of women professionals who
achieved equality with men. Rural women have remained in
traditional society and roles.

764. Belhachmi, Zakia. "The Unfinished Assignment: Educating
Moroccan Women for Development." International Review of
Education 33 (1987): 485-494.

Analyses western theories of development and the resulting
strategies and planning which represent major structural
barriers to Moroccan women's liberation. Advocates a shift from
current anti-participatory strategies to a new people-oriented
approach, emphasizing the multiple roles of women within an
integrated strategy. Recommends that educational projects be
linked with other parts of the infrastructure.

Farooq, Ghazi M. and Baran Tuncer. "Fertility and Economic and Social Development in Turkey: A Cross-Sectional and Time Series Study." **Population Studies** 28 (1974): 263-276.

See item #1148

765. Fox, Greer Litton. "Some Determinants of Modernism among Women in Ankara, Turkey." **Journal of Marriage and the Family** 35 (August 1973): 520-529.

Measures Turkish women's attitudinal modernity. Data are taken from the Ankara family study conducted in 1965-66. Sample consists of 803 married Turkish women. Finds that modern education is a key factor in the process of change from constrained to emancipated behavior and from traditional to modern minds. Concludes that a woman's modernism or traditionalism is determined by a variety of factors among which amount of education is one of the most important.

766. Klineberg, Stephen L. "Parents, Schools and Modernity: An Exploratory Investigation of Sex Differences in the Attitudinal Development of Tunisian Adolescents." **International Journal of Comparative Sociology** 14 (1973): 221-244.

Examines the relative contribution of school experience and parental attitudes, as mediated by sex roles and school attendance, to the attitudinal modernity of Tunisian adolescents. Two hundred fifty four adults (122 fathers, 132 mothers) and 272 adolescents are surveyed. Finds that the social context in which schooling occurs, the sex role distinctions that pervade the lives of the adolescents and the social environment of the school itself are the important forces that appear to account for differences among the adolescents in modern attitudes. However, formal education itself does not appear to play a pre-eminent role in accounting for such differences.

Klineberg, Stephen L. "Intergenerational Change: Some Psychological Consequences of Modernization." **Change in Tunisia.** Edited by Russell Stone and J. Simmons. Albany: SUNY Press, 1976, pp. 289-310.

See item #497

Mehryar, A.H. and G.A. Tashakkor. "Sex and Parental Education as Determinants of Marital Aspirations and Attitudes of a Group of Iranian Youth." **Journal of Marriage and the Family** 40 (1978): 629-637.

See item #498

767. Wiesinger, Rita. "Economic Development and Functional Literacy for Women: A Pilot Project in Iran." International Review of Education 19 (1973): 96-120.

Describes a Work-Oriented Adult Literacy Pilot Project for women in Iran that commenced early in 1967. Points out that changes among Iranian women brought about by this project do not herald the transition from traditional to modern society but they do mean a change for the better in women's condition. Attributes the success of this project to the new methodologies used in providing functional literacy which include discussion, demonstration, practice and assimilation.

768. Youseff, Nadia H. "Education and Female Modernism in the Muslim World." Journal of International Affairs 30 (1976/77): 191-209.

Asks if the expansion of education in the Middle East has resulted in female modernism. Shows that education has resulted in later marriage and reduced fertility. Education also has some relation to workforce participation, 70 percent of university educated women in Syria and Turkey work. Argues that women's participation in the workforce will depend in the long run on the extension of vocational and nonformal education.

B.   Women and Science and Technology

Books and Monographs

769. African Training and Research Centre for Women. The Role of Women for the Utilization of Science and Technology for Development. Addis Ababa: United Nations Economic Commission for Africa, 1978. 62 pp.

Focuses on women's access to science and technology. Part I focuses on the history of women and industrialization in the U.S. Argues that the history of African development is quite different. In the U.S. industrialization has brought women into the workforce; in Africa, women's workforce participation in the industrial and paid sectors has actually declined from 29.5 percent in 1950 to 26.4 percent in the 1970s. In the African context, science and technology have served to displace female labor and, without renewed emphasis on education, women will not be able to participate in evolving industrial, urban economies. Argues that development will also occur at a faster rate if women are given access to science and technology.

770. D'Onofrio-Flores, Pamela M. and Sheila M. Pfafflin. Scientific Technological Change and the Role of Women in Development. Boulder, Colorado: Westview Press, 1982. 206 pp.

Contains six articles (which are abstracted individually in this bibliography) on the access of women to technology. The appendix reproduces the resolutions of United Nations Conference on Science and Technology for Development about women, science and technology as well as the resolutions of the caucus of women scientists at the UNCSTD Forum.

771. Jain, S.C. ed.   Women and Technology.   Jaipur: Rawat Publications, 1985. 200 pp.

Reports the discussions and papers presented at the Workshop on Women and Technology and a follow-up program of an Exhibition-cum-Demonstration of Technology for Women held in Gujarat, India in 1983. The purpose of the workshop was to bridge the gap between scientists, technicians, social scientists, social workers and women beneficiaries. The papers look at lack of access to education in scientific and technological fields, lack of adequate mechanical aids for carrying out economic activities and the tendency to provide new technology only for men. Other topics covered include women's effective use of technology, the provision of extension credit and entrepreneurial and marketing support services.

772. United Nations Economic Commission for Africa, African Training and Research Center for Women. The Role of Women in the Utilization of Science and Technology for Development: An ACA Contribution to the African Regional Meeting on United Nations Conference on Science and Technology for Development, Cairo 24-29 July 1978. Addis Ababa: United Nations Economic Commission for Africa, 1978. 62 pp.

Examines African women's access to science and technology and points out that women have not been able to use either because they have, by and large, remained undereducated. Even in African countries where women's educational enrollments have soared, women have been segregated into fields of study which are outside of science and technology like the humanities and education. Argues that if economic development is to occur in Africa, women must be provided with scientific and technological training, particularly in agriculture.

Articles

773. Ahooja-Patel, Krishna.   "Women, Technology and the Development Process." **Economic and Political Weekly** 14 (September 8, 1979): 1549-1554.

    Argues that although women's education level has greatly advanced they have been left out of technical and scientific education. Having been left out of technical education, there is virtually no room for women in a modern industrialized community. Sees major problems in this limitation, for example, some agricultural technology is being simplified for female use with negative economic consequences.

774. D'Onofrio-Flores, Pamela M.   "Technology, Economic Development, and the Division of Labor by Sex."   **Scientific-Technological Change and the Role of Women in Development.** Edited by Pamela M. D'Onofrio-Flores and Sheila M. Pfafflin. Boulder: Westview Press, 1982, pp. 13-28.

    Argues that contemporary technology, promoting a dependent type of development internationally as part of the culture and institutions of a classbound society, is likely to add to the continued oppression of women.   Contends that western technology, which was shaped and developed by dominant social classes in developed western countries, has been utilized by an international male elite class to reinforce its dominance as well as the division of labor between nations, classes and the sexes.

    Kelly, Alison.   "Women in Science: A Bibliographic Review." **Durham Research Review** 7 (1976): 1092-1108.

    See item #471

775. Kelly,   Alison.   "Girls   and   Science   and   Technology." **International Review of Education** 33 (1987): 501-503.

    Describes the Girls and Science and Technology (GASAT) Project. Shows that over time research has shifted from an emphasis on female underachievement in and avoidance of science and technology to developing intervention programs to encourage more girls and women to enter science and technology. The research literature has begun to emphasize compensatory education in technology for adult women.

776. Krishnaraj, Maithreyi.   "The Status of Women in Science in India." **Journal of Higher Education** 5 (Spring 1980): 381-393.

Shows, based on census and other data, how sex role stereotyping has created a secondary status for women in India through segregation in occupation, particularly in the scientific profession. Points out that formalization of scientific activity created a dichotomy between traditional women's knowledge (mass women) and advanced knowledge (elite women). Among the few highly educated women who are scientists, there exists not only female typing in selection of field but also a gender differentiated occupational pattern. Neither in their domestic role nor in their occupational role have women in India benefited from the dissemination of scientific knowledge.

777. Leet, Mildred Robbins. "The Power of Persistence: Consciousness Raising at International Fora--The Case of UNCSTD." Scientific-Technological Change and the Role of Women in Development. Edited by Pamela M. D'Onofrio-Flores and Sheila M. Pfafflin. Boulder: Westview Press, 1982, pp. 149-178.

Describes a year's effort to set up a committee for the 1979 United Nations Conference on Science and Technology for Development (UNCSTD) which would focus on women's access to science and technology. The Task Force on the Roles of Women in Science and Technology for Development, formed in 1978 held a number of meetings to prepare an item on women to add to the UNCSTD agenda. The resolution adopted at the 1979 UNCSTD included the decision to integrate women into the development process and to provide them with equal access to science and technology. Concludes that UNCSTD had a far reaching impact on the roles of women in science and technology for development.

778. Pfafflin, Sheila M. "Some Reflections on Women in Science and Technology after UNCSTD." Scientific-Technological Change and the Role of Women in Development. Edited by Pamela D'Onofrio-Flores and Sheila M. Pfafflin. Boulder: Westview Press, 1982, pp. 179-193.

Discusses the participation of women in science and technology and argues how important it is for women in terms of their potential role in science policy making. Maintains that the problem to be solved is the achievement of equal career opportunity for women in the science workforce rather than entries into science fields. Suggests that women, especially in developing countries, be provided with training appropriate to the advancing technologies.

779. Presvelou, Clio. "La Technologie et la Science, Sont-Elles au Service des Femmes Rurales?" Femmes et Multinationales. Edited by Andree Michele, et al. Paris: Editions Karthala, 1981, pp. 65-79.

Argues that the science and technology policies of third world governments and of international agencies ignore women. Sees this as a problem both for women and for development since women constitute the vast majority of the agricultural labor force. Failing to provide women with access to technology means that agriculture will remain underdeveloped. Points out that to date there has been a real regression in women's status as a result of devlopment policies: in 1960 women were 58 percent of the world's illiterates; in 1970 they were 60 percent. Importation of technology into most third world countries and evolving trade relations have driven women out of productive labor, as imported goods compete with women's produced goods. Trends to provide girls with technical education have not stopped the erosion of women's status. Girls who have obtained technical diplomas have remained unemployed mainly because multinationals who have a demand for technical labor demand women's labor only if it is manual labor or in textiles or handwork which the multinationals export.

780. Rajeswari, A.R.   "Employment Pattern of Women in R & D Organizations--A Statistical Analysis." Science and Technology for Women.   Edited by Malcolm S. Adiseshiah.   Madras: Affiliated East-West Press, 1985, pp. 6-28.

Estimates the number of women scientists active in India from the late 1970s. Finds 4000 women scientists. These are categorized by education level and educational area. Twelve of the 22 pages of this article are basic data.

781. Tadesse, Zenebeworke. "Women and Technology in Peripheral Countries: An Overview." Scientific-Technological Change and the Role of Women in Development.   Edited by Pamela M. D'Onofrio-Flores and Sheila M. Pfafflin.   Boulder: Westview Press, 1982, pp. 77-111.

Surveys the impact of technology on women in agriculture, trade and commerce, the formal labor market and education. Argues that in every sector of third world economies the introduciton of new technology has often led to displacement of women, reinforced sex segregation and increased inequality between the sexes in wealth, opportunity and employment, and that the educational system preselects women away from scientific and technological subjects and continues to reproduce the sexual division of labor and subordination of women. Concludes that positive changes in the status of women and the transformation of a country depend on the use of technology within a totally different socioeconomic framework, the focus on the special needs of women and the redress of the gap and inequality reproduced through the existing sexual division of labor.

782. "Some Ideas from Women Technicians in Small Countries." **Impact of Science on Society** 30 (January-March 1980): 3-66.

Surveys women technicians in 17 countries and reports on their educational backgrounds, the type of jobs in which they work, their domestic situation and their professional lives.

783. Srinivasan, Mangalam. "The Impact of Science and Technology and the Role of Women in Science in Mexico." **Scientific-Technological Change and the Role of Women in Development.** Edited by Pamela D'Onofrio-Flores and Sheila M. Pfafflin. Boulder: Westview Press, 1982, pp. 113-148.

Surveys the position of women in basic and applied science and women's participation in science policy making. Analyses the place of women in selected technologically based industries. Statistics indicate that both education and employment in science and technology remain the hardest fields for Mexican women to enter. Studies the textile industry (which employs 36 percent of all working women in Mexico), electronics, oil refining and related technologies in relation to their impact on women. The offshore assembly plants, which mainly employ unmarried young women, have had ill effects on the domestic service market and created many problems. Concludes that Mexican public policy towards technology is mostly concerned with technology investments, expenditures and employment, rather than on the impact of technology on people.

784. Thein, Mya Mya. "Women Scientists and Engineers in Burma." **Impact of Science on Society** 30 (1980): 15-22.

Describes women's position in Burmese society, especially in the fields of science and engineering in higher education and occupations. More males than females are enrolled in dentistry, engineering and veterinary science, but in zoology and botany women outnumber men. Women make up 42 percent of the teaching staff in the science departments of the Rangoon Arts and Science University, but most occupy the positions at the lower levels. Concludes that despite prejudices and notions of inferiority of women, women enjoy the rights of equality, which is due largely to the Budhist notion of the equality of sexes.

785. Ward, Barbara E. "Women and Technology in Developing Countries." **Impact of Science on Society** 20 (1970): 93-101.

Describes the effect of technological development on women in developing countries. Argues that modern transportation, new household devices, etc., have had a liberating influence, while the spread of education has resulted in widening gap between women and men. Contends that except for the field for health, especially birth control, technological development has emancipated some women and at the same time chained other women more tightly to their domestic duties.

C. Women and International Development Agencies

Books and Monographs

Belloncie, Guy. **Femmes et Développement en Afrique Sahélienne. L'Experience Nigerienne d'Animation Feminine** (1966-1976). Paris: Editions Ouvriénes, 1980. 212 pp.

See item #691

786. **Inter-American Specialized Conference on the Integral Education of Women.** August 21-25, 1972. Washington, D.C.: Organization of American States, 1972. 89 pp.

Contains the proceedings and resolutions of the 1972 Buenos Aires meeting of the InterAmerican Council for Education, Science and Culture and the Inter-American Council of Women. Presents the conference's recommendations for improving women's status in Latin America. These recommendations include programs for expanding women's educational opportunities and access to vocational training programs as well as provisions for child care and family services and improved opportunities for women in the workforce.

787. Rogers, Barbara. **The Domestication of Women. Discrimination in Developing Societies.** London: Tavistock, 1981. 200 pp.

Illustrates discrimination against women as practiced in development agencies and by development planners through an in-depth analysis of UNDP programs. Finds programs intended to raise the status of women more often decrease women's status in traditional society. Suggests three ways to overcome the discriminatory processes and provide resources that women would control in third world countries.

788. **Women in Africa and Development Asistance.** Uppsala: Scandinavian Institute of African Studies, 1978. 55 pp.

Summarizes a conference entitled "Women in Africa and Development Assistance," held in Sweden in 1978. The central issues addressed were the impact of foreign aid on women, the kinds of foreign aid and assistance necessary to improve women's status and the modes of developing and designing women's projects. Argues that the basic condition for creating useful projects for women is to involve female recipients of aid at all levels of project design and implementation.

Articles

789. Blumberg, Rae Lesser and Cora Hinderstein. "At the End of the Line: Women and United States Foreign Aid in Asia, 1978-1980." **Women in Developing Countries: A Policy Focus.** New York: Haworth Press, 1983, pp. 43-66.

   Describes recent United States development assistance projects to third world women. While the projects have provided direct benefits to the target groups, women tend to be "at the end of the line" at least as far as their economic wellbeing and integration into development is concerned. Suggests attention be paid to the resources available to women and that women should be considered at the beginning as well as the end of aid projects.

790. Buvinic, Mayra. "Projects for Women in the Third World: Explaining Their Misbehavior." World Development 14 (1986): 653-664.

   Analyses international aid projects for women in Third World countries and points out that over time they have evolved into welfare action projects rather than projects designed to increase women's long term productivity.

791. Chaten, Jeanne H. "The UNESCO Long-Range Program for the Advancement of Women." Annals of the American Academy of Political and Social Science 375 (January 1968): 145-153.

   Provides a laudatory description of contemporary UNESCO programs for women. These include extending education for both sexes, creating adult literacy programs primarily to reach women and trying to build scientific and technological knowledge among women. The programs are seen as fulfilling the UN Declaration of Human Rights.

792. Cohn, Steven et al. "U.S. Aid and Third World Women: The Impact of Peace Corps Programs." Economic Development and Cultural Change 29 (1981): 795-811.

   Explores the extent to which the inclusion or exclusion of women as participants in Peace Corps activities varies with the type of Peace Corps program, the sex of the volunteer and by country. Based on questionnaires administered by the Evaluation Division of ACTION's Office of Policy and Planning in 1978 to 4442 volunteers in 60 countries, finds that women are generally underrepresented in Peace Corps programs, particularly in those which involve the transfer of marketable skills. Also finds that Peace Corps assigned women volunteers to work with women. Concludes that aid programs may weaken the status of women in the third world relative to men by providing disproportionate shares of economic resources to men. Argues that involving women in aid programs is not enough--the issue is what type of programs are offered to women and the ways in which women are involved.

793. Deblé, Isabelle. "La Deuxième Strategie de l'UNESCO a l'Égard des Femmes." Tiers - Monde 26 (1985): 283-297.

Describes UNESCO's policies adopted for 1984-1989 on women. While UNESCO has gone on record for gender equality in education and against discrimination, most of the educational programs focus on universalization of primary education and are not directly targeted at women. The goal in the second plan is to integrate women's concerns into all aspects of UNESCO's programming. Criticizes UNESCO's policy documents for failing to deal directly with women's issues. They tend to be against discrimination on the basis of sex, but they do not deal with the poor condition of women in much of the world. Women are still excluded from most of UNESCO's professional and scientific staff.

794. Fasheh, Munir. "Talking About What to Cook for Dinner When Our House Is On Fire: The Poverty of Existing Forms of International Education." Harvard Educational Review 55 (1985): 121-126.

Criticizes the way programs in international education in U.S. universities avoid relevant issues and fail to learn from the experiences and perspectives of other cultures. Urges international education to go beyond "how to" types of questions and respond to the realities of third world women.

795. Flora, Cornelia Butler. "Incorporating Women into International Programs: The Political Phenomenology of a Private Foundation." Women in Developing Countries: A Policy Focus. New York: Haworth Press, 1983, pp. 89-106.

Analyses the Ford Foundation's development assistance programs for women. Believes the programs were successful because the foundation responded only to direct problems, had both U.S. and international divisions and hired women staff members. Ford also established a committee headed by a woman to oversee and demand accountability from field staff.

796. Herbert, Suzanne and Virginia Dichie. "Women in Decision-Making and Leadership Positions in International Development Agencies." The Decade for Women. Edited by Aisla Thomson. Toronto: Conadian Congress for Learning Opportunities for Women, 1986, pp. 109-116.

Examines how several international agencies treat women on their staff. The agencies studied included United Nations agencies, regional development banks and international non-governmental organizations. Finds that although the agencies claim they are commited to empowering women, women are absent from decision making bodies in the agencies.

797. Jiagge, Annie. "The Role of Non-governmental Organizations in the Education of Women in African States." Convergence 2 (no. 2, 1969): 73-78.

Discusses role played by nongovernmental organizations in providing vocational education, continuing education and workers, colleges for women.

798. Karl, Marilee. "Integrating Women into Multinational Development?" Women in Development: A Resource Guide for Organization and Action. Edited by ISIS. Women's International Information and Communication Services. Philadephia: New Society Publishers, 1984, pp. 25-57.

Surveys the impact of multinational corporations on women in developing countries in such businesses as electronics, textiles and agribusiness, and describes women organizing themselves to combat the negative effects of multinationals. Argues that multinationals not only exploit women as cheap labor but also have detrimental effects on women's culture.

799. "Le Droit de la Femme a l'Éducation." Literacy Work 5 (Winter 1976-1977): 27-32.

Summarizes 1975 conferences and seminars organized by the Women's International Democratic Federation in collaboration with UNESCO. Most of these focused on equal educational opportunities for women.

800. Rizika, Jill. "After the Decade: UN and Women." Africa Report 30 (September/October 1985): 75-81.

Describes problems encountered by nations which have established national plans for the advancement of women as a result of the UN Decade for Women (1976-1985). Among these problems are limited resources, cultural and social inertia and women's double burden of work in the household and in the laborforce.

Examines the programs put on paper by the governments of Ghana, Mozambique and Botswana.

Tabak, Fanny. "U.N. Decade and Women's Studies in Latin America." **Women's Studies: International Forum** 8 (no. 2, 1985): 103-106.

See item #1188

801. Thom, Betsy. "Women in International Organization: Room at the Top." **Access to Power: Cross National Studies of Women and Elites.** Edited by Cynthia F. Eptstein and Rose Laub Coser. London: George Allen and Unwin, 1981, pp. 169-184.

Analyses the barriers facing women who are employed in international organizations. Points out these barriers arise from the nature of the overall occupational structure and how it affects the opportunties afforded to women, for example, the cultural definition of male and female roles, appropriate behavior both within and outside the work situation and the interaction between family and work as well as between employees in the occupational hierarchy.

802. "United Nations Decade for Women, 1976-1985." **UN Chronicle** 22 (1985): i-xxiv.

Includes a report on the Nairobi Conference held from July 15 to 27, 1985 which reviewed the achievements of the United Nations Decade for Women. Describes the historical background of the Nairobi Conferences and analyses economic, social and political factors and trends expected to influence the advancement of women over the next 15 years.

XI. WOMEN, EDUCATION AND THE WORKFORCE

The relation between women's education and their participation in the workforce has received more attention than any other topic when it comes to the study of schooling and women in the third world. We have listed here studies on a range of topics related to women's education and the workforce: many ask whether education increases the rate of women's entry into the paid laborforce; some ask whether education changes the jobs women hold; others look at the remuneration women receive for their work; still others focus on the attitudes of working women and potential conflict between their roles in the work place and in the family. A handful of studies focus on problems related to studying women in the workforce.

Studies of women's laborforce participation in the third world are often labeled development studies. There is all too often little discretion between the two since some of the literature implicitly equates women working for a wage as development. There is also great overlap between the study of women's fertility and the workforce; sometimes studies link education with fertility reduction because of the presumed relation between women's educational levels and their participation in the workforce and partcipation in the workforce with fertility reduction.

This, which is the single largest section of the bibliography, is divided into two parts. The first, containing the vast majority of studies, is devoted to women's education and their workforce participation. The second part is on women working in the professions.

A. Women's Education and the Workforce

1.   General Studies

Books and Monographs

803. Curtin, Leslie B. Status of Women: A Comparative Analysis of Twenty Developing Countries. Washington, D.C.: Population Reference Bureau, Inc., 1982. 60 pp.

Analyses women's status in 20 developing countries (12 Asian/Pacific countries and 8 Latin/Caribbean countries), based on World Fertility Survey data. Examines and compares the distribution of women according to level of education, pattern of work and occupation among the 20 countries and analyses the interrelationship between educational attainment, residence and pattern of work. The results show that educational attainment for women has improved in most countries over the past 25 years, that an extreme gap still exists in illiteracy rates between women and men, that many more men than women have attained secondary or higher levels of education, that work patterns are more evenly distributed in the Latin/Caribbbean countries than Asian/Pacific countries and that in some South and East Asian countries, female labor force participation rates are very high, especially in agriculture.

Kohen, A.I. et al. **Women and the Economy: A Bibliography and Review of the Literature on Sex Differentiation in the Labour Market.** Columbus: Ohio State University, Center for Human Resource Research, 1975. 88 pp.

See item #11

Safilios-Rothschild, Constantina. The Status of Women and Fertility in the Third World in the 1970-80 Decade. New York: Center for Policy Studies, The Population Council, 1985. 49 pp. (Working Paper no. 118).

See item #1061

Smock, Audrey Chapman. **Women's Education in Developing Countries: Opportunities and Outcomes.** New York: Praeger, 1981. 292 pp.

See item #374

804. Standing, Guy and Glen Sheehan. **Labour Force Participation in Low Income Countries.** Geneva: International Labour Office, 1978. 338 pp.

Describes women's workforce participation in more than a dozen countries in all areas of the world, with an emphasis on Latin America. Education usually appears as one background variable along with income, fertility, marriage rate and age. Usually all or some of these statistics are included in a regression analysis. Countries covered include Colombia, Chile, Costa Rica, Ecuador, Venezuela, Mexico, San Salvador, Ghana, Nigeria, Afghanistan, Singapore, Sri Lanka, Papua New Guinea, Thailand, Melanesia, Philippines and Yugoslavia.

805. Youssef, Nadia Haggag. **Women and Work in Developing Societies.**
     Berkeley: University of California Institute of International
     Studies, 1974. 136 pp.

Studies the relation between economic development, education and
women's workforce participation in 13 Middle Eastern and Latin
American countries (Chile, Colombia, Costa Rica, Ecuador,
Mexico, Peru, Egypt, Iran, Libya, Morocco, Pakistan, Syria and
Turkey). Finds that economic development does not necessarily
draw women into paid nonagriculture work. In Latin America, and
the Middle East women's workforce participation rates remain
low despite economic development. In Latin America, however,
women's workforce pattern is different from the Middle East:
women in Latin America enter the service occupations and factory
work; in the Middle East women do not enter service or factory
work--increases in female employment occur solely in
professional work. Argues that education does make a difference
in workforce participation patterns as well as in the rate of
women's entry in the workforce. In the Middle East, where
Islamic traditions of sex segregation and purdah hold, middle
class women enter the professions via the schools, but only
those professions which serve other women. In Latin America
education articulates with workforce participation across all
social strata, but women tend not to enter professional work as
much as they enter clerical and domestic service.

Weekes, Vagliani, et al. **Women in Development: At the Right
Time for the Right Reasons.** Paris: Development Centre of the
Organization for Economic Cooperation and Development, 1980.
330 pp.

See item #671

Women and Industrialization in Developing Countries. Vienna:
United Nations Industrial Development Organization, 1981. 81
pp.

See item #673

Articles

806. Benería, Lourdes. "Conceptualizing the Labor Force: The
     Underestimation of Women's Economic Activities." Journal of
     Development Studies 17 (1981): 10-28.

Criticizes the conventional laborforce studies which
underestimate women's contribution to production. Argues that
available statistics must be used with caution and international
comparisons can be very misleading. Active labor should include

all workers engaged in use value as well as exchange value production which includes activities such as household production and all types of subsistence production.

807. Blau, Francine D. and Carol L. Jusenius. "Economic Approaches to Sex Segregation in the Labor Market: An Appraisal." Signs 1 (1976): 181-199.

Reviews and criticizes neoclassical approaches used to explain sex discrimination in the laborforce. Argues that approaches based on monetary theories fail to connect male-female differences in income directly to sex segmented and segregated laborforce. Maintains that internal labor market approaches which distinguish between the primary and secondary labor markets are more useful in studying women. Points out that women are working within the secondary labor markets which are characterized by multiple entry points and few if any opportunities for promotion and almost no job security. Argues that the internal labor market approach (sometimes called dual market analysis) explains women's status in the laborforce in terms of both supply and demand.

Boulding, Elsie. "Integration into What? Reflections on Development Planning for Women." Convergence 13 (nos. 1-2, 1980): 50-58.

See item #675

808. Cebotarov, E.A. "Women, Work and Employment: Some Attainments of the International Women's Decade." The Decade for Women. Edited by Aisla Thomson. Toronto: Canadian Congress for Learning Opportunities for Women, 1986, pp. 63-74.

Discusses issues related to women's unpaid and paid work, and the reasons for the "invisibility" and low appreciation for what women do. Examines world trends of women's participation in the laborforce. Finds women are overworked and underpaid, and they remain the largest group of unemployed throughout the world.

809. Finegan, T.A. "Participation of Married Women in the Labour Force." Sex Discrimination and the Division of Labour. Edited by Cynthia B. Lloyd et al. New York: Columbia University Press, 1975, pp. 27-60.

Summarizes data originally presented in Finegan's earlier book, The Economics of Labor Force Participation, which focuses on the workforce participation work of married women from 1945 to 1960. Analyses women's workforce participation by looking at family size, women's education and race, labor market conditions (unemployment and industrial mix) as well as wage structure and the cost of replacing women's work in the household with paid labor.

810. Jusenius, Carol L.   "The Influence of Work Experience, Skill Requirement and Occupational Segregtion on Women's Earnings." Journal of Economics and Business 29 (1977): 107-115.

Argues that because women have less work experience and work in female segregated jobs, women are paid less than are men. Argues that as long as women do not participate in the labor market continuously, their wages will remain lower than men's and women will remain in female segregated low skill occupations which offer little chance of occupational mobility.

811. MacDonald, John Stuart and Beatrice MacDonald.   "Women at Work in Britain and the Third World."   New Community 5 (Summer, 1976): 76-84.

Examines available statistics on women's economic activities in Britain and the developing countries.   Finds that women's activity rates vary dramatically from country to country as well as from one age bracket to the next.   This reflects not only the extent of real differences in sex and economic activity but also differing national definitions which undercount women's participation.   Shows that the developed countries have experienced large increases in the participation of women in the laborforce since the end of World War II and female laborforce will continue to grow more rapidly than the male laborforce in 1980s.   In many developing countries, laborforce participation rates of women in nonagricultural sectors have been very slow to expand and migration, urbanization and economic growth do not automatically open up more employment to women in the modern sectors; rather they often deprive women of their work without providing alternative opportunities.

812. Mincer, J. and S. Polacek.   "Women's Earnings Re-examined." Journal of Human Resources 13 (1978): 103-134.

Argues that sex based wage differentials are in large part caused by women's pattern of workforce participation rather than women's qualifications.   Women do not have a pattern of consistent workforce participation.   Rather they tend to enter, withdraw and reenter paid employment.   This pattern has a greater impact on wages as levels of women's education and skill rise.

813. Niemi, Albert W. Jr.   "Sexist Differences in Returns to Educational Investment."   Quarterly Review of Economics and Business 15 (1975): 17-26.

Discusses variation by sex in returns to schooling in 1960 and
1970 for three population groups (total, white and black) and
three completed levels of education (high school, college, and
graduate school). Finds that the expected rates of return on
female educational investment are sufficiently high to warrant
further spending; the high rates of return to female schooling
are not sufficient to lead to parity with male income levels,
and that the income of females relative to males has declined in
most age-education cells during the past decade.

814. O'Donnell, Carol. "The Relationship between Women's Education
and their Allocation to the Labour Market." Studies in Higher
Education 9 (no. 1, 1984): 59-72.

Investigates the relation between women's educational level and
type of education with their workforce allocation and discusses
in this context human capital and screening theories. Argues
that the relation between women's education and workforce
participation is not only an economic question, but also a
political one. Point out that in order to explain that relation
historical studies need to be made of labor struggles and the
roles of men and women in obtaining better working conditions
and employment.

815. Pampel, Fred and Kazuko Tanaka. "Economic Development and
Female Labour Force Participation: A Reconsideration." Social
Forces 64 (1986): 599-619.

Looks at the impact of economic development on female labor
force participation as well as the effect of family size, female
education, sex ratio in the adult population, economic
dependency and laborforce growth. Finds, using data collected
from 70 countries for 1965 and 1970, that there is a curvilinear
relation between economic development and women's laborforce
participation which influences the relative impact of family,
education and other social factors on women's employment.

816. Ram, Rati. "Sex Differences in the Labor Market Outcomes of
Education." Comparative Education Review 24 (1980): S53-S77.
(also in Women's Education in the Third World: Comparative
Perspectives. Edited by Gail P. Kelly and Carolyn M. Elliott.
Albany: SUNY Press, 1982, pp. 203-227.)

Describes three major aspects of sex differences in the labor
force outcomes of education: market activity rates; wages,
earning profiles and rates of return in investment in education;
and distribution in occupations. Reviews the literature and
points out that for women, as for men, schooling increases
female market activity rates although in several countries the
relation between women's education and laborforce participation

rates appears curvilinear. The gap between male and female earnings do not decline with increases in educational levels of women throughout the world, although this is the case in third world countries. The limited research base on the occupational distribution of males and females does indicate that education does not have the same effect on women's occupational distribution as it does on men's. Discusses discrimination and human capital or 'household production' models for explaining sex differences.

817. Shields, N.G. "Female Labor Force Participation and Education: Developing Countries." International Encyclopedia of Education vol. 4. Edited by N. Postlethewaite and Torsten Husen. London: Pergamon, 1985, pp. 1854-1861.

Argues that the economic growth in the developing countries has not benefited women because women have been disadvantaged in gaining access to education. Argues that the determinants of women's employment are social and economic demand factors (extent to which the economy demands female labor and the attitudes towards women in the paid workforce), and supply factors such as marriage and fertility and women's desire to work. Concludes that the relation between education and female employment is complicated. Women expect positive economic returns from education but unless the supply of cheap labor is available to take care of their families and their household, educated women may not find it profitable to work.

818. Silver, P. "Sex Equity in Educational Employment." International Encyclopedia of Education. Vol. 8 Edited by N. Postlethewaite and Torsten Husen. London: Pergamon, 1985, pp. 4550-4555.

Argues that inequality in employment still persists for women. This is due in part to inequalities in women's access to education, conservative social norms and sex role stereotyping. Women's income increases at a rate lower than does men's with equivalent educational levels. Women are employed in sex segregated occupations—in domestic service, low skill industrial and agricultural work, secretarial and clerical occupations and in nursing and primary school teaching. This pattern of sex segregation is common to most countries. Believes that employment opportunities for women will improve if there are changes in school curricular and instructional materials, changes in teachers' behaviors, affirmative action programs and the like.

819. Singh, K.P. "A Comparative Study of the Attitudes of Working and Non-Working Women towards Women's Education and Employment." Interdiscipline 11 (no. 3, 1974): 89-99.

Studies the attitudes of working and nonworking women toward education and women's occupations. Finds that working women have a tendency to value education for women more than nonworking women and support women entering a broader range of fields. Both working and nonworking women believed that women should take up employment before marriage and before they have children. These women did have reservations about whether women should work once they had children. Working women tended to believe that they had higher status than nonworking women because they had greater economic independence by virtue of their jobs.

820. Smock, Audrey Chapman. "Sex Differences in Educational Opportunities and Labor Force Participation in Six Countries." Comparative Education. Edited by Philip G. Altbach et al. New York: Macmillan, 1982, pp. 235-251.

Examines the relationship between sex differences in educational opportunities and in patterns of laborforce participation in six countries, Kenya, Ghana, Egypt, the Philippines, Mexico, and Pakistan. Argues that improvements in women's access to schooling have failed to have a significant impact in raising their levels of employment in the modern sector of the economy or in broadening their occupational roles. This is, in part, due to the limited changes in educational opportunities, persisting sex differences in enrollment patterns at the secondary or tertiary levels, lack of reforms in the curriculum, streaming or sex stereotyping in the educational system, as well as to the nature and the structure of the modern sector of the economy. Concludes that, unless there are substantial educational reforms and direct intervention into the labor market, major change in women's pattern and levels of participation in the modern sector is not likely to happen.

821. Standing, Guy. "Education and Female Participation in the Labour Force." International Labor Review 114 (November-December 1976): 281-297.

Argues that women's education has a weak relationship with workforce participation in most modernizing economies. This weak relationship is due to tradition in which women have not worked in manufacturing and in the modern industrial sector. Men, on the other hand, have worked in manufacturing and the modern service sector where education has a strong relation to income and employment. As a result, male demand for education is strong; female demand is weaker. The cycle is reinforced by the fact that women cannot get good jobs because they do not possess education. Poses two questions that should be answered to determine whether developing countries should invest in women's education: first, what is the relationship between female education and the productivity of the labor force? Second, what factors maximize such a relationship? Criticizes theories of opportunity cost, relative opportunities and aspiration effect which have been often applied to answer these questions. Presents an alternative hypothesis of sexual dualism. Sexual dualism appears when vocational/occupational training is distributed only to males, leaving women with skills that do not articulate with employment even when women have received some education.

Standing, Guy. "Women's Work Activity and Fertility." Determinants of Fertility in Developing Countries. Edited by Rodolfo A. Bulatao and Ronald D. Lee. New York: Academic Press, 1983, pp. 517-546.

See item #1077

Vander Voet, Susan McCrae. "The United Nations Decade for Women: The Search for Women's Equality in Education and Employment." The Decade for Women. Edited by Aisla Thomson. Toronto: Canadian Congress for Learning Opportunities for Women, 1986, pp. 75-90.

see item #312

822. Woodhall, Maureen. "The Economic Returns to Investment in Women's Education. Higher Education 2 (1973): 275-299.

Shows that the rates of return on investment to secondary and higher education (as measured by life-long income) are on an average, points lower than men's in nine countries. Education increases the earning capacity of women and the time women spend in the workforce. Women's wages, however, remain depressed because of discrimination in hiring, women's nonmarket work in the household and because of the nature of the occupations in which women work.

Woodhall, Maureen. "Investment in Women: A Reappraisal of the Concept of Human Capital." International Review of Education 19 (1973): 9-27.

See item #689

823. "Women: Their Access to Education and Employment." Literacy Discussion 6 (Winter 1975/1976): 35-40.

Studies the relation between education and employment of women in Argentina, the Ivory Coast, Lebanon, Sierra Leone and Sri Lanka. Argues that women's participation in the labor force is underestimated in most countries, especially in Sierra Leone and

Sri Lanka. Discrimination in employment, despite educational
levels women attain, is widespread. Women are underrepresented
in high status and highly paid work. Employment in the police,
army, public works, the navy and aereonautics are closed to
women. Believes that with increased educational levels women's
employment pattern can change.

2.   Africa

Books and Monographs

824. Asayehgn, Desta. The Role of Women in Tanzania: Their Access
to Higher Education and Participation in the Labour Force.
Paris: International Institute for Educational Planning, 1979.
31 pp.

Examines the relation between women's laborforce participation
in Tanzania and women's SES background, urban/ rural residence,
region of origin, field of study they pursued in higher
education, initial and current earnings and time elapsed before
ending school and obtaining a job. The study is based on IIEP
field study conducted in 1977. Finds that the sex disparities
in the laborforce are directly attributable to women's lack of
access to secondary and higher education and the fact that
within secondary and tertiary education women are segregated
into female fields of study. Women who obtain higher education
and thus enter the workforce are from high SES urban backgrounds
and they wait longer than their male peers for employment.

825. Butterfield, Cynthia. Women and the Modern Wage Sector: A
Study of Female Participation in Commercial Banks and Finance
Companies in Nairobi. Nairobi: Institute for Development
Studies, May 1977. 28 pp. (Discussion Paper no. 256)

Studies women's participation in commercial banks and finance
companies in Nairobi, Kenya. Finds that women were heavily
concentrated in secretarial, telephone operator and typist jobs
which had no job mobility. Identifies four barriers restricting
female mobility and employment: education, discrimination in
employment, paid maternity benefits which employers perceive as
too costly and socialization of women. Argues that increasing
educational opportunities may by itself not serve to increase
women's workforce mobility because of the role which
discrimination and costly benefits play in employer decisions
not to hire women.

826. May, Joan.   African Women in Urban Employment: Factors Influencing Their Employment in Zimbabwe. Gwelo: Mambo Press, 1979. 83 pp.

Interviews 132 working women in Harare as well as a number of employers to identify the motivational factors leading women into the workforce as well as the constraints to wage labor for women. Finds that women work because they need money--the majority of respondents were heads of household.   Women also send money back to relatives in rural areas. Constraints to working for a wage include lack of education on the part of women, shortages of unskilled work for which women qualify, employer discrimination against women, labor regulations protecting women, lack of vocational training programs to serve women. Urges that job training programs be established for women and the development of a women's bureau which would provide services for women.

827. Muchena, Olivia N. A Socio-Economic Overview: Zimbabwe Women. Addis Ababa: United Nations Economic Commission for Africa, 1982. 48 pp.

Provides an overview of women's status in Zimbabwe and some factual information concerning women's workforce participation and educational attainment levels.   Points out that most Zimbabwe women are uneducated and employed in the rural areas while males migrate to the cities for wage employment. Women constitute only 6.8 percent of the total number of Africans and Europeans working in the nonagricultural sector. Women work predominantly in teaching (23 percent) and nursing (48 percent). Points out that women's salaries are lower not only because of occupational segregation, but also because of discrimination (female teachers make one quarter less the salary than do men). Points out that there are prejudices against women in the modern occupation sector where women are considered temporary workers. Through letters of Zimbabwe women argues that the following are women's demands for transformation of their status: 1) better housing; 2) greater family stability (instability is caused by male migration in search of wages); 3) changes in marriage laws giving women more rights; 4) access to education and health care. Argues that nonformal education may be the most efficient means of fulfilling women's educational needs.

Shuster, Ilsa. Female White Collar Workers: A Case Study of Successful Development in Lusaka, Zambia.   East Lansing: Michigan State University, 1983. 31 pp. (Working Papers on Women in International Development no. 29)

See item #697.

Tall, Penda Sidibe. L'Effet de la Modernisation sur le Travail des Femmes Exerçant une Activité Indepdendante au Mali, en Côte-d'Ivoire et au Sénéga Addis Ababa: Nations Unies Commission Économique pour l'Afrique, Centre Africain de Recherche et de Formation pour la Femme, 1981. 116 pp.

See item #700

Wessels, Dinah. M. Career Orientation and Work Commitment of University-Educated Women. Pretoria: Human Sciences Research Council, 1981. 52 pp. (Report MM-85)

See item #518

Weinrich, A.K.H. Women and Racial Discrimination in Rhodesia. Paris: UNESCO, 1979. 143 pp.

See item #131

Articles

828. Agheyisi, Rachel Uwa. "The Labor Market Implications of the Access of Women to Higher Education in Nigeria." Women in Nigeria Today. Edited by Editorial Committee, Women in Nigeria. London: Zed Books, 1985, pp. 143-157.

Presents an overview of the Nigerian labor market and women's participation in it. Finds that women's participation in the modern sector is low, particularly working at skilled jobs, technical and scientific fields and as professionals. Most women are employed in the traditional agricultural and trade sectors of the economy. Argues that the low participation of women in modern professional and scientific work is a function of their lack of access to higher education and to technical/scientific fields in tertiary institutions.

829. Awosika, Keziah. "Women's Education and Participation in the Labour Force: The Case of Nigeria." Women, Power and Political Systems. Edited by Margherita Rendel with the assistance of Georgina Ashworth. London: Croome Helm, 1981, pp. 81-93.

Examines factors other than the level of economic development which determine women's participation in the modern paid labor force. Presents data on the educational levels of women, age-specific participation rates in the modern work force by educational level and ethnicity in Lagos city, and the occupational distribution of women within the laborforce. Finds that over 50 percent of the women in the modern labor force work in sales and that women are, given their educational levels, disproportionately clustered in lower paying service sector jobs.

830. Blaug, Mark.   "Employment and Unemployment in Ethiopia." International Labor Review 110 (August 1974): 117-143.

Summarizes a report of the Exploratory Employment Policy Mission, organized by the International Labor Organization, to the Ethiopian government in 1973. Contains information on the structure of employment in Ethiopia at this period, the employment of women in various sectors of the economy and educational levels broken down by gender, region and ethnicity. Argues that if economic development is to come to Ethiopia, women must be brought into the workforce and that this is best done through the extension of education to women.

831. Clignet, Remi. "Social Change and Sexual Differentiation in the Cameroon and the Ivory Coast." Signs: Journal of Women in Culture and Society 3 (1977): 244-260.

Advances two hypotheses to explain changes in the status of women as they apply to the Ivory Coast and the United Republic of the Cameroon: 1) the extent and form of sexual inequalities may depend on the complexity of indigenous social structures and hence upon the expansion of schools, cities and modern enterprises and 2) sexual inequalities are affected by past and present cultural modes and stereotypes of women's roles.

832. Greenstreet, Miranda.   "Employment of Women in Ghana." International Labor Review 103 (February 1971): 117-129.

Surveys the role of women in the Ghanaian workforce for the 1960s a and discusses the relation of female education and training opportunities to women's participation in the modern sector of the economy.

833. Hansen, Karen Tranberg. "Married Women and Work: Explorations From an Urban Case Study." African Social Research 20 (1975): 777-799.

Examines women's participation in the laborforce in Zambia. Interviews 160 women who are semi- or skilled workers in Lusaka whose incomes were not sufficient to maintain their families. These women are expected to work in order to contribute to the household. Presents overview of Zambian society including education opportunities and states that education is a prerequisite for job attainment throughout the economy. Presents personal data such as age, number of children, amount of education, management of family finances, husband's attitudes

toward wives working and number of years couple resided in city.
Finds that the number of women working in the paid laborforce is
small. Entrepreneurial activities (such as participating in the
illegal beer making trade) provide limited opportunities for
extra income because that market became institutionalized and
competitive. Concludes the lack of education is the greatest
obstacle to women's employment in urban area.

834. Harper, J. "Educated Women in Niugini." **Australian and New
Zealand Journal of Sociology** 10 (June 1974): 90-95.

Surveys 100 female high school graduates to gather data bout
their postschool employment. Finds that all the women worked at
jobs which employed an all female laborforce. Many reported
there were pressures once they were married against their
continued employument. Half reported gender rather than race as
the major barrier to their mobility in the workforce.

835. Karanja, Wambui Wa. "Women and Work: A Study of Female and
Male Attitudes in the Modern Sector of an African Metropolis.
Education and Modernization of the Family in West Africa.
Edited by Helen Ware. Canberra: Department of Demography,
Australian National University, 1981, pp. 42-66. (Changing
African Family Project Series Monograph no. 7)

Examines the female and male attitudes to women and work among
employees in the modern sector of the Lagos, Nigeria economy.
Interviews 150 males and 150 female civil service workers in
1978 and 1979. Finds that males and females have similar
attitudes toward women working. Finds also that working women
in Lagos have greater economic freedom than their western
sisters. They do not use their income for the household.
Despite women's economic position, the status of these working
women relative to men has weakened. In large part this is due
to the fact that women work in lower positions than do men,
which is in part due to their lower educational levels.

836. Kinyanjui,   Kabiru.   "Educational   and   Formal   Employment
Opportunities for Women in Kenya: Some Preliminary Data."
Kenya Education Review (December 1975): 6-25.

Provides some basic data regarding women's access to formal
education and examines how this affects their entry into formal
sector employment. Shows that women have unequal access to
primary education which, coupled with their high dropout rates,
results in fewer women than men having access to higher
education and training. Men dominate middle and high level
occupations and women must perform much better than men at
school to obtain equal rewards in the labor market. Contends
that in order for women to advance in education and employment,

not only increasing educational opportunities for girls but also serious commitments towards equality on the social, economic and political level are necessary.

837. Kinyanjui, Kabiru. "Educational and Formal Employment Opportunities for Women in Kenya: Some Preliminary Data." The Participation of Women in Kenya Society. Edited by Achola Pala et al. Nairobi: Kenya Literature Bureau, 1978, pp. 16-41.

Provides basic data on women's access to formal education and their participation in the waged workforce. Points out that women are clustered in a few occupations: 69 percent of all women in the workforce are nurses, midwives, teachers and clerical workers. Clerical work is the largest single occupation at which women work in Kenya. Sees women's occupational roles related directly to the educational opportunities offered them.

Keonig, Dolores B. "Education and Fertility among Cameroonian Working Women." Education and Modernization of the Family in West Africa. Edited by Helen Ware. Canberra: Department of Demography, Australian National University, 1981, pp. 134-153. (Changing African Family Project Series Monograph no. 7)

See item #1086

838. Kokuhirwa, Hilda. "Toward the Social and Economic Promotion of Rural Women in Tanzania." Literacy Discussion 6 (Winter 1975/76): 47-64.

Surveys changes in women's status in Tanzania over the past century. In precolonial Tanzania women were considered inferior to men and were farmers who worked with little or no remuneration. The status of women further deteriorated under British colonization as women were denied access to western education and entry to the modern paid workforce. The remainder of the article focuses on changes since Nyerere's Urusha Declaration in the 1960s. Argues that government policies, the programs of the Union of Women of Tanzania and UNESCO's literacy projects have improved women's condition.

Lewis, Barbara C. "Economic Activity and Marriage Among Ivorian Urban Women." Sexual Stratification: A Cross-Cultural View. Edited by Alice Schlegal et al. New York: Columbia University Press, 1977, pp. 161-191.

See item #1016

Lewis, Barbara C. "Fertility and Employment: An Assessment of Role Incompatibility among African Urban Women." Women and Work in Africa. Edited by Edna G. Bay. Boulder, Colorado: Westview Press, 1982, pp. 249-276.

See item #1087

839. Matsepe, Ivy. "Underdevelopment and African Women." **Journal of Southern African Affairs** 2 (April 1977): 135-143.

Argues that lack of education may not be the reason for poor income for African women. Uses the high education levels of girls in Botswana, Lesotho and Swaziland to suggest that job segregation into the service sector and isolation from the productive side of the economy is the real culprit.

Mbilinyi, Marjorie. "Where Do We Come From, Where Are We Now and Where Do We Go From Here?" **The Participation of Women in Kenya Society.** Edited by Achola Pala et al. Nairobi: Kenya Literature Bureau, 1978, pp. 187-200.

See item #522

Robertson, Claire C. "Women in the Urban Economy." **African Women South of the Sahara.** Edited by Margaret Jean Hay and Sharon Stichter. New York: Longman, 1984, pp. 33-49.

See item #711

840. Robertson, Claire C. "The Nature and Effects of Differential Access to Education in Ga Society." **Africa** 47 (1977): 208-219.

Examines the effect of the formal education on Central Accra Ga society in Ghana that denied women's access to it from the nineteenth century until after World War II. Argues that the differential educational opportunity for women and men has resulted in the separation of women and men into different spheres of activity and destroyed the earlier system of cooperation between the sexes in economic activities. Contends that the initial deprivation of girls' access to education has handicapped women permanently in terms of obtaining white collar jobs and totally with regard to blue collar jobs.

841. Stichter, Sharon. "Appendix: Some Selected Statistics on African Women." **African Women South of the Sahara.** Edited by Margaret Jean Hay and Sharon Stichter. New York: Longman, 1984, pp.188-194.

Provides statistical information regarding the laborforce participation and education of African women. Points out that the concept of economically active population when applied to women undervalues and under remunerates of the work of women. A major reason for the difficulties African women face in the labor market is their relative lack of access to education. Africa has one of the highest levels of illiteracy especially for women in the world and the dropout rates among women in secondary school is very high.

Sudarkasa, Niara. "Sex Roles, Education and Development in Africa." Anthropology and Education Quarterly 13 (1982): 279-289.

See item #712

United Nations, Economic Commission for Africa, African Training and Research Center for Women. "Women and National Development in African Countries: Some Profound Contradictions." African Studies Review 18 (1975): 47-70.

See item #714

3.   Asia

Books and Monographs

842. Chaudhry, Rafiqual Huda. Married Women in Urban Occupations of Bangladesh: Some Problems and Issues. Dacca: Bangladesh Institute of Development Studies, 1976, pp. 92 (Research Report Series, New Series no. 22)

Studies 582 working and 548 nonworking women in Dacca to determine factors other than education which affect women in the workforce. Finds that working women have fewer preschool children than nonworking women of the same educational levels. Family size and family type had no relation to whether women worked or not, although working women's husbands had lower educational, occupational and income levels than the husbands of nonworking women. Finds also that women work for economic reasons and most use maids to care for their children and do household work. Role incompatability was strongest among more highly educated women. The only adverse effect of work on the family the women noted was on children who were raised by maids. Working women were satisfied with their jobs, but the more highly educated women were less satisfied with work than less well educated women. Concludes that the major barrier to women's increased workforce participation are male's negative attitudes toward women working outside the home, lack of job opportunities for women when educated and preferential treatment of males on the job.

843. Gallin, Rita S. The Impact of Development on Women's Work and Status: A Case Study from Taiwan. East Lansing: Michigan State University, Women and International Development, 1982. 24 pp. (Working Paper no. 9)

Argues that despite the spread of education and increased participation of women in the workforce, women's status has not changed within the Taiwan social structure. Through a case study of the village of Hsin Hsing shows that the traditional family has prevented women from gaining autonomy and independence as they enter the paid workforce.

844. Lazo, Lucita. Work and Training Opportunities for Women in Asia and the Pacific. Islamabad: International Labour Office, Asian and Pacific Skill Development Programme, 1984. 256 pp. (Monograph no. 4)

Provides an overview of employment and training programs in Asia and the Pacific. Points out that, despite variations in the workforce participation rates, women are employed as unskilled labor in agriculture and service sectors of the economy. In most countries there are few vocational and technical training programs for women and women's workforce participation pattern reflects this lack of opportunity to receive vocational and technical training.

845. Meesook, Kanitta M. The Economic Role of Thai Women. Bangkok: Bank of Thailand Discussion Paper Series, 1980. 17 pp.

Examines the current economic role of Thai women, focusing on the problems of women of low income classes and specifically rural women who comprise 90 percent of the Thai female workforce. Raises three questions: What has been women's role? To what extent have women contributed to the economy through housework and tending to their families without receiving a financial reward? What efforts have been made to increase women's status? Using the data from the Labor Force Survey, shows that although the female role in the market place has been increasing, farming is still a dominant activity for women in rural areas. Rural women are often overburdened, underremunerated and less educated. Criticizes the various assistance programs for rural women as being limited to traditional roles and recommends that training aimed at raising women's income should emphasize improvement in agricultural productivity and be integrated into the mainstream of economic activities.

Shah, Nasra M. and Peter C. Smith. Nonfamilial Roles of Women and Fertility: Pakistan and the Philippines Compared.

Honolulu: East-West Center, 1981.   47 pp.   (Papers of the East-West Population Institute no. 73)

See item #1118

846. Shrestha, Neeru.   An Analysis of Women's Employment in Financial Institutions.   Kathmandu: Tribhuvan University, 1982.   112 pp.

Focuses on the current position and problems of women employed in Nepal's banks and financial institutions.   Provides data on the ratio of male to female employees, the employment opportunities for women, employer attitudes toward women and women's attitudes toward their work.   Administers a questionnaire to 242 employers and employees and finds that there are less opportunities for women that men and than employers would prefer to have male employees.

Articles

847. Blake, Myrna.   "Education, Research, Mobilization Needs of Women's Employment Trends in Asia" Convergence 13 (1980): 65-78.

Examines changes in women's employment brought about by the rapidly expansion of the electronics industry in Asia.   Reviews the electronics industry and its demand for female labor; the relations between multinational corporations and host countries, multinationals and feminist issues and the costs and benefits of women's entry into employment in electronics.

Chaudhury, R.H.   "Female Status and Fertility Behavior in a Metropolitan Urban Area of Bangladesh." Population Studies 32 (1978): 261-273.

See item #1105.

Chaudhury, R.H.   "The Influence of Female Education, Labor Force Participation and Age at Marriage on Fertility Behavior in Bangladesh." Social Biology 31 (1984): 59-74.

See item #1107

848. Cheng, Siok-Hwa.   "Singapore Women: Legal Status, Educational Attainment and Employment Patterns." Asian Survey 17 (1977): 358-374.

Points out that there has been a major revolution in women's status and roles in Singapore since World War II.   Women have received equal access to primary and secondary education, but not in higher education.   Women's income lags behind that of men and is attributable to their lower educational levels. Women have become leaders in education and in business, but not in politics, government and religion.

849. Cho, Hyoung. "Labor Force Participation of Women in Korea." Challenges for Women: Women's Studies in Korea. Edited by Chung Sei-wha. Seoul: Ewha Woman's University Press, 1986, pp. 150-172.

Examines the trends and the pattern of women's labor force participation in Korea, focusing on the mechanism of sex segregation in the labor market. Although women's labor force participation has increased with economic growth, the pattern of sexual division of labor has changed little and the wage gap between women and men has widened. Argues that the segmentation in the laborforce market developed throughout the industrialization process through the rules of exclusion and of selection. Points out the importance of the political decisions in making changes in women's laborforce participation.

850. Jones, Gavin. W. "Economic Growth and Changing Female Employment Structure in the Cities of Southeast and East Asia." Women in the Urban and Industrial Workforce: Southeast and East Asia. Edited by Gavin W. Jones. Canberra: The Australian National University, 1984, pp. 17-60. (Development Studies Centre Monograph no. 33)

Looks at female workforce participation rates in Taiwan, Hong Kong, Indonesia, Singapore, Korea, Thailand and Manila and finds that women's workforce participation has risen in the 1970s, but more so in urban areas than in rural areas. Women's workforce participation in all these countries has risen more rapidly than that of men (although their rates are lower in most instances than are men's). Argues that educational levels of women have risen during the same period but that the empirical evidence relating education and the workforce participation rates of women is mixed: weak positive or a nonliner relationships are found. In Southeast and East Asia trends in the economic structure favor employment of women with a high school education or above, but the less skilled part of the workforce have declined (cottage industry work for women). In the region laborforce participation rates are still not higher for more highly educated women because poverty exerts a strong influence on whether women will enter the workforce at all. The most common employment for women remains household service and trade. The workforce in Asia is still very sex segregated despite the increases in female education levels.

851. Kannagara, Imogen. "Women's Employment in Ceylon." International Labor Review 93 (1966): 117-126.

Describes women's employment pattern in Ceylon. Attributes the reduction of female workforce participation to historical factors, the nature of educational expansion, lower remuneration for women and protective legislation. Finds that the introduction of universal free education increased women's demand for schooling. As a result the percentage of women enrolled at every level of education is quite high. There are, despite the increases in female education, striking differences between the sexes in the use of education. Recommends legislation which will help encourge women's entry into the workforce.

852. Oey, Mayling. "Some Demographic Notes on Indonesian Women and their Achievements." **Prisma** (English Edition) 1 (1975): 74-80.

Examines Indonesian women's status and its progress in terms of literacy, education and laborforce participation, based on data from the two censuses in 1961 and 1971. More men than women have been consistently literate and enrolled in schools, but women have made greater progress than men. Although there was a significant increase in the size of the female labor force, female unemployment rates increase with higher levels of education, the average level of education of the female labor force is low and only very few women work as professionals. Concludes that despite progress, the status of Indonesian women is still far from being equal to that of men.

853. Oey, Mayling. "Rising Expectations but Limited Opportunities for Women in Indonesia." **Women and Development: Perspectives from South and Southest Asia.** Edited by Rounaq Jahan and Hanna Papanek. Dacca: The Bangladesh Institute of Law and International Affairs, 1979, pp. 233-252.

Examines the changes in educational opportunities for women and men and their laborforce participation in Indonesia, using the data from two population censuses in 1961 and 1971. Finds that, although the gap between levels of literacy, education and labor force participation is declining, this has not been reflected in the laborforce. It has remained more difficult for women than for men to find employment, especially for those women with higher education.

854. Raharjo, Yulfita and Valerie Hull. "Employment Patterns of Educated Women in Indonesian Cities." **Women in the Urban and Industrial Workforce: Southeast and East Asia.** Edited by Gavin W. Jones. Canberra: The Australian National University, Development Studies Centre, 1984, pp. 101-125. (Monograph no. 33)

Studies the relation between education and workforce participation in Indonesia and points out that the relationship is J-shaped—lower class women work out of economic necessity whether they have education or not, women with low and intermediate education levels are less likely to be economically active, and a small group of highly educated who have the highest laborforce participation rates and work in modern skilled occupations. Focuses on the employment pattern of the highly educated women, the work they perform and their demographic characteristics. Most had general education and were from urban areas. One third of the educated women worked as teachers; government administration is the second highest employer.

Wang, Virginia Li. "Application of Social Science Theories to Family Planning Health Education in the People's Republic of China." American Journal of Public Health 66 (May 1976): 440-445.

See item #1102

855. Wickramasinghe, Shanti and David Radcliffe. "Women and Education in South Asia." Canadian and International Education 8 (1979): 117-125.

Considers the status of women's education in Sri Lanka with reference to other South Asian nations. Points out that women's literacy rates have risen and more women get more education than every before. However, the increased qualification of women does not mean increased women's workforce participation and higher status for women within the workforce. Discusses the barriers to women in the workforce in Sri Lanka which hold in other Asian nations.

Wong, Aline. "Maternal Employment, Education and Changing Family Values in Singapore." Journal of Economic Development and Social Change 6 (1976): 23-40.

See item #1023.

3a.   India

Books and Monographs

Anant, Suchitra et al. Women at Work in India: A Bibliography. New Delhi: Sage Publications, 1986. 238 pp.

See item #39

856. Andiappan, P. **Women and Work: A Comparative Study of Sex Discrimination in Employment in India and the U.S.A.** Bombay, New Delhi: Somaiya Publication Pvt. Ltd., 1980.

Investigates sex discrimination in employment in the U.S. and India in the private and public sectors. As in the U.S., the laborforce participation of females in India varies depending upon the type of education. The participation rate of women with technical education (64 percent) is substantially higher than it is for women holding nontechnical degrees (38 percent). Finds that literacy and suitable employment do not correlate. The increased education of women is evident in the growing number of female job seekers (0.5 million in 1971; 0.9 million in 1974). Stresses the importance of the Indian government developing placement services for women as well as extending vocational training to females.

857. Devi, Lalitha U. **Status and Employment of Women in India.** Delhi: B.R. Publishing Corp., 1980. 186 pp.

Asks if white collar employment enhances women's status independent of educational levels. Hypothesizes that employment increases women's role in decision making in the family, provides women with greater freedom in spending family income and gives women greater household responsibility. Interviews random sample of 300 women employed in administrative jobs in Trivandrum City, Kerala and 100 randomly selected women who were not in the workforce. Finds that level of education does not enhance decisionmaking power in the family among working women (the women sampled were college graduates and post-graduates) but it does among women who are not in the workforce. Finds also that employed women have greater control over the family income than do unemployed women and have greater household supervisory responsibilities.

858. Doraiswami, S.S. **Educational Advancement and Socioeconomic Participation of Women in India.** New Delhi: Directorate of Nonformal (Adult) Education, Ministry of Education and Social Welfare, 1976. 34 pp.

Surveys changes women's educational levels in India in the period 1951 to 1971 and relates them to women's workforce participation. Argues that lack of education is the major barrier to workforce participation and stresses the need for nonformal programs for women in literacy training linked to employment. Recommends also nonformal education for girls 6 to 14 who are out of the formal school system.

859. Ferree, Myra Marx and Josef Gugler. **The Participation of Women in the Urban Labor Force and in Rural-Urban Migration in India.**

East Lansing: Office of Women in International Development, Michigan State University, 1984. 22 pp. (Working Paper no. 46)

Examines factors which contribute to greater female laborforce participation in urban areas of India and the role which opportunities for laborforce participation play in bringing women to the city. Uses data on 148 major cities from the 1971 Census of India. Among the factors, four measures of the status of women were included: literacy, infant mortality, fertility and age at marriage. Finds that where women enjoy higher status, in terms of these four variables, especially in the southern part of the country, they are more likely to be found in the urban laborforce and among rural-urban migrants. The higher the proportion of the total laborforce of a city employed in construction work or household industry, the higher the proportion of women employed in that city. Concludes that an increase in the participation of women in the urban labor force improves their status and provides a powerful incentive to redress the imbalance between the sexes in rural-urban migration.

860. Kapur, Promilla. The Changing Status of the Working Woman in India. Delhi: Vikas Publishing House, Ltd., 1974. 178 pp.

Focuses on changing attitudes of educated working women toward marriage and work, using data from the author's 1970 survey and research conducted by others since that time. Finds that educated women see marriage more in terms of personal fulfillment than was in the case earlier. Charts the changes in women's workforce participation. While there has been a dimunition in women's entry into paid labor, educated women have entered white collar work. Surveys women in clerical work and in "unusual" work in the professions (where women are a small minority). Finds that there is increasing unemployment of highly educated women and delineates the barriers to women's work in white collar jobs. Among these are women's attitudes toward their roles as wives and mothers, lack of opportunities for employment for highly educated women, employer prejudices, attitudes of the community and lack of support services for working women and mothers in terms of childcare and food preparation.

861. Lebra, Joyce et al. Women and Work in India: Continuity and Change. New Delhi: Promilla, 1984. 310 pp.

Focuses on women and changing patterns of work by interviewing women in Delhi, Bombay and Kerala from 1978 to 1979. Individual chapters present case studies of women from different class, caste and occupational backgrounds. In each women discuss their education, their worklives and the changes women perceive they have undergone as a result of changes in work patterns. Concludes pessimistically about the prospects of improvement in women's status. Argues that women's status in India has undergone significant deterioration as women have been pulled out of the workforce, displaced by "modern" technologies. Warns that unless more education is extended to women, this trend will continue.

Meis, Maria. Indian Women and Patriarchy: Conflicts and Dilemmas of Students and Working Women. Delhi: Concept Publishing, 1973. 266 pp.

See item #1027

862. Mitra, Asok et al. The Status of Women: Shifts in Occupational Participation 1961-1971. New Delhi: Abhinav Publications, 1980. 201 pp.

Focuses on the decline in female workforce participation in India from 1901 to 1961. The 1971 Census charts a steeper decline between 1961 and 1971. Describes where women are employed in the workforce and shows that nearly 20 percent were in nonagricultural occupations before 1961. This figure remained stable through 1971. Shows also that the real shift in female work has been into modern occupations: in 1961 but 6 percent were in these occupations, but by 1971 20 percent were so employed. Points out that in urban areas women tend to be employed in modern occupations while most rural women workers remain in traditional sector employment.

Patel, Tara. Development of Education Among Tribal Women. Delhi: Mittal Publications, 1984. 198 pp.

See item #345

863. Ramanamma, A. Graduate Employed Women in an Urban Setting. Poona: Dastane Ramchandra and Company, 1979. 159 pp.

Studies 505 secondary school graduates to ascertain their work force roles and their attitudes toward the family. Finds that most of the women were employed as teachers and worked for economic reasons. One fifth indicated that working enhanced their social status. Most of the graduates preferred living in a nuclear rather than extended family setting and over half desired to have but two children. One fifth of the women's marriages were arranged by parents. Surveys also these women's educational aspirations and finds that they put a high value on education and 55 percent had gone on to higher education.

864. Rani, Kala. Role Conflict in Working Women.   New Delhi:
     Chetana Publications, 1976. 242 pp.

     Interviews 150 working women in Patna, India to: 1) identify the
     causes of role conflict among working women, 2) understand the
     behaviors by which role conflict is manifested, 3) determine the
     relationships between income and occupation when such conflicts
     occur and 4) how such conflicts might be minimized. Compares
     her findings with those of similar studies conducted in France,
     Sweden, Great Britain and the United States. Argues that Indian
     traditions and the lower level of household labor saving devices
     limit the comparisons that can be drawn. Concludes that woman's
     perception of her roles has a relation to the amount of role
     conflict she experiences. Women who work because their income
     is needed for their families to survive are less likely to
     experience conflict than women who are not faced with similar
     financial constraints.

     Roy, Shibani. The Status of Muslim Women in North India.
     Delhi: B.R. Publishing, 1979. 241 pp.

     See item #1028

865. Seminar on the Status of Women. Status of Indian Women.
     Hyderabad: Mahila Adhuudaya Samstha, 1981.

     Presents a series of papers on women in the workforce in India
     (although one chapter is on personal law in India and a second
     is a general chapter on women and development). Several
     chapters focus on women in the workforce and relates the decline
     of women in paid work in India to changes in the labor market
     system, women's lack of education, and the difficulties women
     experience in combining wage labor with family obligations.
     Several chapters focus on specific occuptions, notably social
     work, women sanitary workers, women construction workers and
     women domestics.

866. Sethi, Rajmohini. Modernization of Working Women in Developing
     Societies. New Delhi: National Publishing House, 1976.
     168 pp.

     Studies the impact of modernization of attitudes of women in
     India and Turkey. The study is situated in Ankara (1965-1966)
     and Chandigarh (1968) and involves administering a questionnaire
     to 120 Turkish and 320 Indian working women with higher
     education. The questionnaire was an adapted version of the
     Inkeles and Smith OM Scale. Finds that modern women assert
     themselves against traditional male authority, participate in

mass media, have interests in extra-local affairs and are free from extended family obligations. They have high educational aspirations as well.

867. Srivastava, Vinita. **Employment of Educated Married Women in India: Its Causes and Consequences.** New Delhi: National Publishing House, 1978. 192 pp.

Compares nonworking married women with similarly educated married working women (150 in each group) in Chandigarh in the Punjab. Through a series of interviews, looks at the consistency between the occupational prestige of husbands and wives, the effect of working on fertility patterns, family composition and domestic work and social interactions on women's attitudes. Finds that the family situation and age of the last child have little effect on women's participation in work. Argues that the extent to which wife's occupational prestige is congruent with that of her husband's is a stronger predictor of whether women enter and remain in the workforce. Finds also that in families of working women there is greater cooperation and sharing of domestic tasks than in households where women do not work. Working women have a wider arena of social interaction than do nonworking women and working provides women with more independent and modern attitudes.

868. Talwa, Usha. **Social Profile of Working Women.** Jodhpur, India: Jain Brothers, 1984. 252 pp.

Interviews 400 working women and 400 nonworking women in Jodhpur City, northern India, focusing on the social characteristics of working women, why they work, the sex role division of labor in the family, leisure activities and attitudes. Finds that working women are from lower and scheduled castes and tribes and work mostly unskilled laborers. Most of the uppercaste working women were highly educated and worked in clerical, professional and semi-professional jobs. Finds that married working women have more power in family decisionmaking than nonworking married women.

869. Wadhera, Kiron. **The Bread Winners.** New Delhi: Vishwa Yuvak Kendra, 1976. 377 pp.

Studies the working lives of 1000 young women. Education is a background factor and over 70 percent of the sample graduated from secondary school. The educated women desired to stay on the job or in the profession through childbearing and child rearing. One of the major groups of workers followed are women in education establishments where working conditions and chances for advancement appear slightly better than for those in other fields.

870. **Women's Work and Employment:** Struggle for a Policy (Selections from Indian Documents). New Delhi: Centre for Women's Development Studies, 1983. 46 pp.

Reprints the following documents focusing on improving the status of women in India: Summary of the Recommendations of the Committee on the Status of Women in India (1974); Views of the Empowered Committee (Inter-Ministerial) of the Government of India on the Recommendations of the Committee on the Status of Women in India; Extracts from the Blue Print of Action Points and National Plan of Action for Women (1974); Recommendations of the ICSSR's Advisory Committee on Women's Studies (1976); Report of the Working Group on Employment of Women (1978); Extract from the Report of the National Conference on Women and Development May 19-21, 1979; Indian Women in the Eighties: Development Imperatives--1980; Extract from the Report of the National Conference on Women's Studies, April 20-24, 1981; Extracts from the Sixth Five Year Plan--Chapter on Women and Development. All these documents refer to the need to provide greater educational and training opportunities for women.

Articles

871. Agarwal, Bina. "Exploitative Utilization of Educated Woman Power." *Journal of Higher Education* 12 (1976): 185-195.

Studies the employment patterns of educated women. Finds that 27 percent of all female Ph.D. holders, 50 percent of the Master's degree holders and 65 percent of the B.A. recipients were unemployed because most held degrees in Arts and Humanities. Female gradutes of vocational training courses were concentrated in handicrafts and sewing. Believes that there will be greater employment for women if they obtain technical and vocational skills and receive a career oriented education.

872. Ahmad, Karuna. "Studies of Educated Working Women in India: Trends and Issues." *Economic and Political Weekly* 14 (1979): 1435-1440.

Surveys the dominant trends in the employment of working women in India and argues that what is called for is a new orientation of the research on the topic. The paper does not discuss the problem of employment itself, but indicates certain research areas and raises certain questions of approach which may help in understanding trends and processes in the employment of white collar women workers. Shows several broad trends in the employment of women in white collar occupations: women tend to cluster in a few occupations and receive lower salaries than men, etc. Although education and employment have propelled many women out of the domestic sphere, it has not brought radical changes in societal attitudes, particularly those of men.

873. Boserup, Ester. "Women in the Labour Market." **Indian Women.** Edited by Devaki Jain. New Delhi: Publication Division, Ministry of Information and Broadcasting, Government of India, 1975, pp. 99-111.

Analyses how sex role divisions of labor evolve and are maintained in the labor markets of industrializing India. Points out that because females have less education than males and lack vocational training, they are placed in subordinate jobs in the workforce.

D'Souza, A. "Women in India: Fertility and Occupational Patterns in a Sex-Segregated Less Developed Society." Social Action 26 (1976): 66-79.

See item #1111

874. D'Souza, Alfred. "Women in India and South Asia: An Introduction." **Women in Contemporary India and South Asia.** Edited by Alfred D'Souza. New Delhi: Manohar Publications, 1980, pp. 1-29.

Presents an overview of women's status in India, focusing on changes in workforce participation, women's education, marriage and the family and women's studies. Points out that the relation between education and workforce participation is nonlinear for women with high educational levels. Cultural and religious factors determine not only whether women will go to school, but indirectly employment opportunities and women's propensity to enter the workforce.

875. D'Souza, Victor S. "Family Status and Female Work Participation." **Women in Contemporary India and South Asia.** Edited by Alfred D'Souza. New Delhi: Manohar Publications, 1980, pp. 125-140.

Examines the relationships between family status, women's education and their workforce participation. Asks why some women work whereas others do not. Reexamines an earlier model which proposes that the wife is compelled to work when the husband's income is not adequate to support the family. Finds that while at the lower levels of education, with increasing education of women, the rate of female workforce participation declines; at higher educational levels, the rate goes on increasing. The two trends together represent a curvilinear relationship between the rate of female work participation and the education of women. Concludes that women's occupation is related to family status consistency and that the workforce participation of women in the U.S.A. and India follow similar broad patterns.

876. Krishnaraj, Maithreyi.   "Employment Pattern of University Educated Women and Its Implications."   **Journal** of **Higher Education** 2 (1977): 317-327.

Investigates the employment patterns of Indian university educated women based on the 1971 Census. Finds that the majority of women graduates are employed: 58 percent hold jobs in the public sector, 37 percent in the private sector and 5.1 percent are self employed. Most women are employed in teaching. In higher education they are concentrated as teachers in arts, science and education. A little less than half of all female degree holders and 70 percent of those possessing the arts degrees do not work. Concludes that the utilization of educated women is part of larger social issues.

877. Mahadevan, Meera.   "India's Mobile Creches: An Imaginative Experiment in Child Care."   **UNESCO Courier** 31 (May 1978): 24-26.

Describes how poor female construction laborers' needs are met through childcare centers situated at the work place. These centers have expanded to cover nursery and elementary education for children and adult education courses for women as well.

Rao, Kamala G. "Status of Women: Factors Affecting Status of Women in India." **Sub-regional Seminar on Status and Role of Women.** Bangkok: International Labour Organization, 1978, pp. 1-60.

See item #1115.

878. Rao, N.J. Usha.   "Disparities in Literacy and Work: Participation Rates of Women in Karnataka." **Women and Society: The Developmental Perspective.** Edited by Amit Kumar Gupta. New Delhi: Criterion Publications, 1986, pp. 224-251.

Looks at the relation between literacy rates and educational levels and women's active participation in the paid workforce. Demonstrates, using data from 1961 to 1981, that there is wide variation in the relation between literacy and workforce activity. The only consistent pattern found is high workforce participation among illiterate women, especially those from the lower castes.

879. Singhal, Sushila. "The Development of Educated Women in India: Reflections of a Social Psychologist." **Comparative Education** 20 (1984): 355-369.

Investigates the employment pattern of educated women in India and the emergent social and psychological issues relevant for studies of women's education. Finds that there are geographical, caste, religious and urban/rural disparities both in women's access to education and to the workforce. Families in which there are more than one female working tend to be more sympathetic to working women's problems than families in which but one woman works. Concludes that microlevel research is needed to understand the social psychology of working educated women.

880. Srivastava, Vinita. "Professional Education and Attitudes to Female Employment: A Study of Married Working Women in Chandigarh." Social Action 27 (1977): 19-30.

Examines the relationship between female professional education, women's attitudes to employment and job satisfaction in India. One hundred and fifty working women and as many housewives were interviewed in 1972. Finds that attitudinal changes in women are related more to the number of years of education, especially college education, and to actual work experience rather than to the type of education received.

881. Sundaram, K. "Working Life-Span in the Indian Labour Force: Sex and Level of Education." World Development 4 (1976): 111-120.

Examines the working lifespans of individuals within the Indian workforce by educational attainment levels, sex and place of residence. The data are derived from the Indian national census. Finds that women work on an average 24 to 41 years while men's work span averages range from 33 to 46 years. The number of years in the labor force is inversely proportional to the number of years of schooling an individual possesses. Men are more highly educated than are women. Rural dwellers spend a longer time in the workforce than do their similarly educated urban peers.

882. Visaria, Pravin. "Labour Force Participation by Age, Sex and Educational Level in India." Journal of the University of Bombay 40 (1971): 178-204.

Examines the relationship between laborforce participation and workers' age, sex and educational attainment in India based on the data from the 1961 Census and the National Sample Survey conducted between 1960-1967. Finds that in all age groups above 20, the female laborforce participation rates form a J- or U-shaped curve with respect to education, while those of males do not show substantial differences. Contends that the more intensive studies on the differentials in the female laborforce participation with different levels of educational attainment are needed, considering the rapid spread of women's education in urban India and the paucity of employment opportunties.

3b.   Malaysia

Books and Monographs

883. Canlas, Dante B. and Mohd Razak. **Education and the Labour Force Participation of Married Women: West Malaysia 1970.** Quezon City: Council for Asian Manpower Studies, University of the Philippines, 1980. 23 pp. (Discussion Paper Series no. 80-03)

Reports a crosssectional analysis of the effects of education on the laborforce participation of married women in West Malaysia. Finds that among very poor Malays, education has little effect on laborforce participation; however, with richer Malays, education does have some effects. These results are less clear among the nonMalays in the sample.

Harrison, David S. **The Effects of Education and Wages on Fertility: Some Evidence from Malaysia.** Clayton: Monash University, 1981.   50 pp.   (Department of Economics Seminar Paper no. 15/81)

See item #1090

Articles

884. Chapman, Bruce J. and J. Ross Harding.   "Sex Differences in Earnings: An Analysis of Malaysian Wage Data."   **Journal of Development Studies** 21 (1985): 362-376.

Analyses sex differences in average earnings and finds that less one third of the average monthly wage differences appear to be the result of females having lower productivity than males. Points out that the major reason for wage differentials in Malaysia derives from sex segregation of occupations.

885. Halim, Fatimah. "Workers' Resistance and Management Control: A Comparative Case Study of Male and Female Workers in West Malaysia." **Journal of Contemporary Asia** 13 (no. 2, 1983): 131-150.

Argues that employers seek out undereducated females--particularly school dropouts--to create a docile, lowpaid workforce. This group seems to have little ambition or long term goals in the labor market.

886. Hirschman, Charles and Akbar Aghajanian. "Women's Labour Force Participation and Socioeconomic Development: The Case of Peninsular Malaysia, 1957-1970." Journal of Southeast Asian Studies 11 (1980): 30-49.

Analyses, based on 1957 and 1970 census data, changes in labor force participation of women in both the agricultural and nonagricultural sectors in Malaysia. Examines patterns among the three major ethnic groups of Malays, Chinese and Indians. Finds that there were gradual increases in women's laborforce participation, especially among younger women, which resulted from a combination of a decline in agricultural employment and growth in nonagricultural employment. Suggests that the effect of education on modern sector employment is strong and that there are common trends across ethnic groups.

887. Nasir, Rohany. "Sex Role Attitudes of Malaysian Women: Implications for Career Development and Counseling." Sojourn 2 (1986): 172-182.

Studies the sex role attitudes of 630 women, 18 years of age and older, in Kuala Lumpur and Selangor. Finds that women working in careers which have not been traditionally open to women are more liberal in the attitudes toward women's roles than women working in traditionally female occupations.

888. Strange, Heather. "Education and Employment Patterns of Rural Malay women, 1965-1975." Journal of Asian and African Studies 12 (nos. 1-2, 1978): 50-64.

Compares the roles of Malay women who completed secondary school in two eras: 1965 and 1975. Finds that women educated in 1975 had a stronger secular orientation and held salaried jobs. Role conflict characterized women who worked and were married with small children.

3c.   Pakistan

Books and Monographs

889. Hafeez, Sabeeha. The Metropolitan Women in Pakistan: Studies. Karachi: Royal Book Company, 1981. 406 pp.

Studies working women in Pakistan including factory workers, highly educated female administrators and teachers as well as housewives, half of whom had secondary or better education, and college students. Looks primarily at work and how it affects family and marital relations.

890. Irfan, Mohammad. The Determinants of Female Labour Force
Participation in Pakistan. Islamabad: Pakistan Institute of
Development Economics, 1984. 48 pp. (Studies in Population,
Labour Force Migration Project Report no. 5)

Identifies the correlates and determinants of married women's
workforce participation. The survey was based on a two stage
stratified random sample covering the entire country of 10,500
households. Finds that high levels of education for women are
associated with paid workforce participation as an employee. In
rural areas when women tend to be self employed, high levels of
education appear to detract from women's entry into the
workforce.

Articles

891. Korson, J. Henry. "Career Constraints among Women Graduate
Students in a Developing Society: West Pakistan." Women in
Family and Economy: An International Comparative Survey.
Edited by George Kurian and Ratna Ghosh. Westport, Conn.:
Greenwood Press, 1981, pp. 393-411.

Examines the employment experience of female graduate students
with no Masters' degrees in Pakistan. Data were collected in
1968 by interviewing 142 female graduates from the University of
Karachi and 100 female graduates from the University of the
Punjab in Lahore, both from the class of 1966. Finds that 64
percent of the Karachi graduates and 33 percent of the Lahore
graduates are in the laborforce and about two thirds of the
employed group in both samples are engaged in teaching. They
are largely limited to the occupations where purdah conditions
of employment apply. Suggests that the greater the degree of
participation in the laborforce as wage earners, the greater the
degree of economic and social independence the female graduates
will achieve.

892. Papanek, Hanna. "Purdah in Pakistan: Seclusion and Modern
Occupations for Women." Separate World. Edited by Hanna
Papanek and Gail Minault. Delhi: Chanakya Publications,
1982, pp. 190-216.

Deals with the role of women in purdah in Pakistan. Analyses
the purdah system by explaining social forms and psychological
features, pointing that the purdah system is related to status,
the division of labor, interpersonal dependency, social distance
and maintenance of moral standards as specified by the society.
Describes the characteristics of women's work--women work with
other women in and around the home at one set of tasks and they
do not participate to any significant degree in the laborforce.

Traces the development process of women's education, pointing out despite the tremendous advance in women's education in the last few decades, it has continued to reflect the historical development of Muslim thought about the status and training of women. Explains the purdah system in recruitment for modern occupations, finding out the importance of occupations in which women have a recognized place as serving a female clientele. Concludes that the charactertistics of purdah are based on extremely complex infrastructures of values and attitudes which affect almost every relationship in the society.

Shah, Nasra M. "Fertility of Working vs. Non-Working Women in Pakistan, 1973." Women and Development: Perspectives from South and Southeast Asia. Edited by Rounaq Jahan and Hanna Papanek. Dacca: The Bangladesh Institute of Law and International Affairs, 1979, pp. 275-318.

See item #1142.

893. Shah, Nasra M. and Makhdoom A. Shah. "Trends and Structures of Female Labour Force Participation in Rural and Urban Pakistan." Women in Contemporary India and South Asia. Edited by Alfred D'Souza. New Delhi: Manohar Publications, 1980, pp. 95-123.

Analyses trends in female labor force participation in rural and urban areas of Pakistan. Examines the structural composition of the labor force in terms of occupation, employment status and place of work. Utilizes data from three censuses of Pakistan (1951, 1961, 1972), the Labour Force Surveys, two household level knowledge, attitudes and practice demographic surveys, National Impact Survey--1968 and Pakistan Fertility Survey-1975. Finds that as women in the laborforce obtain more education and acquire varied skills, a diversification of the occupational structure would be expected. One area in which it might be possible to expand job opportunities for women is that of primary school teachers in boys' schools, which is socially permissible but feasible only if the female teachers are not displacing male teachers. Motivations behind work participation vary with the more illiterate women working out of sheer necessity and the highly educated women having high demand for jobs. Concludes that the type of skills as well as cultural constraints related to skill acquisition and utilization can act as behaviors in limiting the potential contributions of females to the laborforce.

Palabrica-Costello, Marilou. "Measurement Issues in the Study of Working Women: A Review of the Philippine Experience."

Women in Development: Perspectives from the Nairobi Conference.
Ottawa: International Development Research Centre, 1986, pp.
166-185.

See item #72

3d.   Philippines

Books and Monographs

894. Paqueo, Vincent B. and Edna S. Angeles. An Analysis of Wife's
Labour Force Participation in the Philippines and the Threshold
Hypothesis. Quezon City: Council for Asian Manpower Studies,
University of the Philippines, 1980. 39 pp. (Discussion Paper
Series no. 80-02)

Estimates the effects of income, education, unemployment level,
fertility, place of residence and migration on married women's
probability of being employed. Using logit analysis, finds that
below some threshold, the effects of additional schooling is
negative, while above it the marginal effect is positive.
Suggests that, unlike most industrialized countries, economic
development in the Philippines is likely to be accompanied by
declining laborforce participation of married women. However,
predicts that decline will taper off and may even rise again as
more families move beyond critical levels of income and
education.

895. Rojas-Aleta, Isabel et al. A Profile of Filipino Women.
Manila: Philippine Business for Social Progress, 1977. 400 pp.

Reports a study of the status of Filipino women sponsored by the
Women in Development Working Group of USAID. Argues that in
precolonial Philippines, women were equal to men, but under
Spanish colonization, women were relegated to inferior roles.
The American occupation brought about social and political
emancipation. Points out that women are socialized both at home
and at school to accept roles as wives and mothers. Within the
Philippines there appears to be equal opportunity in education:
both males and females have the same literacy rates (82
percent), school enrollment and academic performance. There is,
however, sex typing of programs of specialization and in
vocational training. Despite this, the workforce outcomes of
education for women are different than for men. Only one third
of all women work. The only field where women have equality
with men is in education. Women's wages are 44 percent lower
than are males. Recommends that priority be given to vocational
training of women in both agriculture and industrial skills.

Shah, Nasra M. and Peter C. Smith. Nonfamilial Roles of Women and Fertility: Pakistan and the Philippines Compared. Honolulu: The East-West Center, 1981. 47 pp. (Papers of the East-West Population Institute no. 73)

See item #1118

Articles

Encarnacion, J. "Family Income, Educational Level, Labor Force Participation and Fertility." The Philippine Economic Journal 7 (1973): 536-549.

See item #1093

896. Flores, Pura M. "Career Women and Motherhood in a Changing Society." Philippine Educational Forum 14 (1965): 50-56.

Attempts to answer such questions as why do married women seek occupations, who takes care of their children and what difficulties do they have, by examining the responses to open-ended questionnaires gathered from 400 married women with full time jobs in the Philippines. The respondents were all college graduates. 72 percent of the respondents work for financial reasons, 74 percent leave the care of their home and children to servants and 68 percent have problems with family relations. Suggests that young mothers spend a greater portion of their time in close company of their children.

897. Sison, P.S. "The Role of Women in Business and Industry in the Philippines." International Labor Review 87 (1963): 118-132.

Compares the educational and vocational levels of women and men in the Philippines based on the data from the Philippine Survey of Households in 1957. The literacy rate has been consistently higher for men than women, and more males than females are enrolled in all levels of education. There are as many female as male chemists, women outnumber men among dentists, women predominate in pharmacy, nursing and midwifery, but women are absent from most of the engineering profession. The number of women in the workforce is increasing, but the majority are still in agriculture as unpaid family workers, and earnings of male workers are about three times as much as those of female workers.

4.   Latin America and the Caribbean

Books and Monographs

898. Acosta-Balén, Edna (ed.)   The Puerto Rican Woman.   New York: Holt, Rinehart and Winston, 1979. 169 pp.

Focuses on the changing status of Puerto Rican women including their educational and professional status.   Points out that despite the fact that women have educational opportunities equal to those of men, this does not have any effect on women's participation in the workforce.   Women are underrepresented in jobs of power and influence and are paid lower than men with equivalent levels of education and training.   Argues this is because the socialization given in schools emphasizes female stereotypes of wife and mother and does not encourage women to work outside the home once married.

899. Chang, Ligia and María Ducci.   Realidad del Empleo y la Formación Profesional de la Mujer en América Latina. Montevideo: Centro Interaméricano de Investigación y Documentación sobre Formación Profesional, 1977.   124 pp. (Estudios y monograficas, no. 24)

Summarizes women's workforce participation patterns in Latin America.   Focuses on the relation of education to workforce participation rates, the sector of the economy in which women are employed as well as the status of women in the workforce. Reviews the relevant legislation in Latin America affecting women's workforce participation and discusses women and employers' attitudes concerning women's paid labor.

900. Chang, Ligia and María Ducci.   Formación Profesional para la Mujer.   2e ed.   Montevideo: Centro Interaméricano de Investigación y Documentación sobre Formación Professional, 1978. 214 pp.   (Estudios y Monografias, no. 20)

Focuses on women's employment in Latin America and relates women's employment pattern to their training opportunities relative to men.

901. Cisneros, J.   Roles Femininos y Participación Económica de la Mujer en el Contexto Socio Étnico Cultural de Bolivia.   La Paz: Centro de Investigaciones Sociales, 1978.   126 pp.

Focuses on the constraints to women working in Bolivia and the role of education in women's workforce participation.   Surveys over 600 people in 1975 and finds that the higher the level of education, the fewer the family constraints there are to women working. This is especially the case when women are highly educated. Hypothesizes that there is a relation between educational level and the sector of the workforce in which women will be employed. Finds that there is a strong relation between female primary education and women's participation in the agricultural sector of the workforce, secondary education and manufacturing and higher education and women's employment in the service sector of the economy. This relationship changes for women with incomplete primary and incomplete secondary education. Postulates that the reason for this is that receiving some secondary education raises women's expectation of employment but does not give women credentials for employment in manufacturing as it does for women who complete secondary education.

Cisernos, J. et al. Cambio y Tendacias Evaluativas sobre Educación Familiar para la Mujer Trabajadora. La Paz: Centro de Investigaciónes Sociales, 1984. 96 pp.

See item #1128

Confederación Interamericana de Educación Católica. Formación de la Mujer en el Mundo Actual. Bogotá: Secretaria General de la CIEC, 1976. 124 pp.

See item #426

Feijoó, Maria del Carmen. La Mujer, el Desarrollo y las Tendencias de Población en América Latina. Bibliografia Comentada. Buenos Aires: El Centro de Estudios de Estado y Sociedad (CEDES), 1980. 59 pp.

See item #45

902. Filgueira, Nea, et al. La Mujer en el Uruguay: Ayer y Hoy. Montevideo: Ediciones de la Banda Oriental SRL, 1983.

Provides an overview of women's status in Uruguay with special emphasis on women in the workforce. Points out that women are underrepresented in the paid laborforce in part because of cultural pressures that mitigate against their entry into work outside the home and in part because of the demands of childbearing and childrearing in the family. In rural areas women are outside the workforce; in urban areas educated women enter the paid laborforce but are assigned a secondary role there.

903. Henriquez de Paredes, Querubina et al. Participación de la Mujer en el Desarrollo de América Latina y el Caribe. Santiago de Chile: UNICEF, 1975.

Provides an overview of women in Latin America and Caribbean. Data is presented on women in the workforce, urbanization and industrailization, women's participation in politics, fertility rates, mortality rates, and educational pattern. Argues that the expansion of education has had some relation to women's workforce participation as new areas of the workforce open in tourism, public relations, trade and business. The development of parttime work is seen as stimulating further opportunities for women in the workforce.

904.   Luzuriaga C., Carlos.   **Situación de la Mujer en El Ecuador.** Quito: Maurilia   Mendoza   de   Jimenez,   1982.   180   pp.

Focuses on women's roles in the family and in the workforce. Points out that women have long been discriminated against in gaining employment outside the home, distinguishing between barriers to women's employment in urban versus rural areas. Women tend to be clustered in personal service occupations (predominantly as domestics, although highly educated women do become professionals). In 1974 women were 43 percent of all workers in sales and 35 percent of all clerical workers. Literacy rates of women have improved. In 1950 only 51 percent were literate; by 1974 69 percent of all women wre literate. Women were discriminated against in education--they   make   up about 2 percent of all students in higher education and 17 percent of secondary school students. | In higher education, women are clustered in education and social sciences and medical technology, but noticeably absent in medicine, planning and administration.   Argues   that   the   pattern   of   education contributes to women's poverty and explains their workforce participation.

905.   Martorelli, Horacio.   **Mujer y Sociedad.**   Montevideo: Fundación de Cultural Universitaria, 1978.

Discusses women's status in Uruguay with special emphasis on women's workforce participation and their changing educational levels.   Points out that with increasing education, women have begun to enter professional and white collar employment in urban areas, despite the fact that most women do not work for a wage and those who do are concentrated in low level service occupations as domestics and petty traders. Argues that women's status is likely to change only through increasing their educational levels and through development which will open up more job opportunities.

906.   Massiah, Joycelin.   **Women as Heads of Households in the Caribbean Family Structure.**   Paris: UNESCO, 1983.   64pp.

Looks at the poverty associated with women living without partners or with temporary or absent partners. Points out the very limited role of education since close to 90 percent of these women have primary education or less.

907. Pavón González, Ramiro. **El Empleo Femenino en Cuba.** Aspectos Económicos, Demográficos y Socioculturales. Havana: Editorial de Ciencias Sociales, 1977. 104 pp.

Focuses on women and the workforce and presents data on women's workforce participation by economic sector for a number of Latin American countries--Argentina, Bolivia, Chile, Haiti--sometimes in comparison with Cuba, the U.S., Japan and the Soviet Union. There are a few sections on the relation of education to workforce participation. In chapter 1, through Panamanian data from 1971, shows that education has little relation to men's workforce participation, but it has a strong relation to women's: the more education a woman has the more likely she is to participate in the workforce. Chapter 3 focuses solely on Cuba and compares the workforce participation rate of Cuban women with those in Peru and Argentina. The data, which are taken from 1971, show little difference between the three countries in women's laborforce participation rates. Chapter 3 also discusses changes in women's educational level in Cuba in the early 1970s, but it does not relate these changes to the workforce status of Cuban women.

908. Prates, Suzana and Graciela Taglioretti. **Participatión de la Mujer en el Mercado de Trabajo Uruguayo:** Características Básicas y Evolución Reciente. Montevideo: Centro de Informaciones y Estudios del Uruguay (CIESU), 1980.

Focuses on women's workforce participation in Uruguay between 1908 and 1975. Less than 1.3 percent of the female population is employed in wage labor (this figure has remained the same since 1908). Women in urban areas have been employed in handicrafts production, sewing and food preparation. It was only after 1955 when industrialization began that women began to change employment and enter public sector jobs. However, in the face of economic crisis, women have been pushed out of many of these jobs and placed in more marginal positions, despite their increasing educational level.

909. Recchini de Lattes, Zulina. **Dynamics of the Female Labor Force in Argentina.** Paris: UNESCO, 1983. 98 pp.

Studies the relation between women's workforce participation, their fertility levels, socio economic development and education using 1947, 1960 and 1970 census data in Argentina. Finds that differences in educational levels and fertility rates are not related to workforce participation, but marriage is, especially among younger women.

Recchini de Lattes, Zulina and Catalina H. Wainerman. La Medicion del Trabajo Femenino. Buenos Aires: Centro de Estudios de Poblacion, 1981.

See item #60

910. Taglioretti, Graciela. La Participación de la Mujer en el Mercado de Trabajo: Uruguay 1963-1975. Montevideo: CIESU Centro de Informaciones y Estudios del Uruguay, 1981. 86 pp. (Caderno no. 43)

Focuses on women's workforce participation in Uruguay in the context of massive rural/urban migration and the brain drain. Points out that the flow of labor abroad during the economic recession of the 1960s opened opportunities for educated women to enter the Uruguyaian workforce. During the period under study women became urban migrants and government employees. Because of the demand for female labor in the brain drain abroad, women became more educated than men who remained in the country.

911. Torrez P., Hugo. La Mujer Boliviana y sus Características Demográficas en la Fuerza de Trabajo, 1975. La Paz: Centro de Investigaciones Sociales, 1977. 49 pp. (Estudios de Población y Desarrollo no. 12)

Investigates the relation between women's workforce participation and their age, level of education, marital status, fertility rates, urbanization and migration pattern. Shows that over time the educational level of the female workforce has risen: 52 percent of 20 to29 year olds had primary education and 23 percent had secondary education while 74 percent of women over the age of 60 had no schooling at all. Women who had no schooling entered the workforce at an earlier age than women who had primary education and the workforce participation rates were highest among women 15 to 19 years old and among unschooled women. Finds also that workforce participation rates rise with age and educational levels. Close to 48 percent of all women with secondary education aged 30 to 39 years old were in the workforce versus 63 percent of that age cohort who possessed university training.

912. United Nations, UNICEF. Participación Económica y Social de la Mujer Peruana. Lima: UNICEF, 1981. 388 pp.

Focuses on women in the workforce in Peru, arguing that women's participation is in large part dependent upon their educational levels and family situation. Chapter 1 looks at rural women while chapter 2 focuses on urban women. Women in rural areas have little education and have been denied access to agricultural nonformal education programs as well as technical education. Thus, they work as unskilled workers and petty traders. Urban women are better educated than rural women, but they have less education than men and lack vocational skills that will prepare them for work other than as domestics, cooks, petty traders and service workers. Urges that more programs be set up to prepare women for the workforce, but points out that such programs of necessity would be different in urban and rural areas. Surveys in chapters 3 and 4 UNICEF programs designed to improve women's skills and facilitate their entry into the workforce.

Articles

Antrobus, Peggy. "Women in Development: The Issues for the Caribbean." Convergence 13 (1980): 60-63.

See item #749

Bengelsdorf, Carollee and Alice Hageman. "Emerging from Underdevelopment: Women and Work in Cuba." Race and Class 19 (1978): 361-378.

See item #753

Carleton, Robert O. "Labor Force Participation: A Stimulus to Fertility in Puerto Rico?" Demography 2 (1965): 233-239.

See item #1134

Davidson, Maria. "Female Work Status and Fertility in Urban Latin America." Social and Economic Studies 24 (1978): 481-506.

See item #1135

Draper, Elaine. "Women's Work and Development in Latin America." Studies in Comparative International Development 20 (1985): 3-20.

See item #755

913. Elizaga, Juan C. "The Participation of Women in the Labour Force of Latin America: Fertility and Other Factors." International Labour Review 109 (1974): 519-538.

Explores the effect of marital status, education, income and the stage of economic development on women's workforce participation in Latin America. Finds that the workforce participation rates of married women would increase if their educational levels were improved, the economies modernized and fertility rates reduced. Argues also that if fertility rates are to be lowered, women need to be educated since education, as well as economic development, have strong influences on fertility.

Fernández Berdaguer, Maria Leticia. "Educación Universitaria y Desempeño Profesional: El Case de las Mujeres Estudiantes de Ciencias Económicas de la Universidad de Buenos Aires." **Revista Paraguaya de Sociologia** 20 (1983): 75-97.

See item #560

914. Galeano, Luis A. "Las Mujeres como Proveedoras de Fuerza de Trabajo en Paraguay." **Mujer y Trabajo en el Paraguay.** Edited by Luís Galeano. Asunción: Centro Paraguayo de Estudios Sociologicos, 1982, pp. 239-303.

Focuses on women's participation in the workforce of Paraguay and argues that women's low participation rates are due to the limited expansion of industry, the lack of education among women to prepare them for technical and professional work, sex role socialization which defines women's proper place as the household and discrimination in the workforce.

915. Gutierrez de Pineda, Virginia. "Status de la Mujer en la Familia." **La Mujer y el Desarrollo en Colombia.** Edited by Magdalene Leon de Leal. Bogota: Asociación Colombiana para de Estudio de la Población, 1977, pp. 318-394.

Summarizes work on education, fertility patterns and explores the effect of education on entry to the labor market in Colombia. Compares working population by gender over the time span from 1951 to 1970. Looks at types of occupation by gender and education level.

916. Pico de Hernandez, Isabel. "Estudio sobre el Empleo de la Mujer en Puerto Rico." **Revista de Ciencias Sociales** 19 (no. 2, 1975): 141-166.

Describes women's participation in the Puerto Rican workforce, analyzing it by age and educational level. Shows that women are overrepresented in low wage, low skilled jobs such as service industries while they are underrepresented in managerial, technical and professional occupations.

917. Pico de Hernandez, Isabel. "Research Notes: The Quest for Race, Sex and Ethnic Equality in Puerto Rico." **Caribbean Studies** 14 (1975): 127-141.

Looks at the recruitment, hiring, promotions and salaries of women, Blacks and Puerto Rican males and demonstrates a consistent pattern of discrimination against women. Through a survey of 42 major employers, finds that women are segregated into distinct occupations and concentrated in low level, poorly paid work despite their educational levels.

918. Powell, Dorian L. "Female Labour Force Participation and Fertility: An Exploratory Study of Jamaican Women." Social and Economic Studies 25 (1976): 234-258.

Focuses on fertility and its relation to work among Jamaican women. Considers three associated variables of age, education, union/marital status and place of residence, based on the data from the 1970 Population Census of Jamaica. Finds that there is an inverse relationship between employment and fertility and that both marriage and marital fertility contribute significantly to this inverse relationship. Suggests that policy should aim at reducing the traditional attitudes and practices relating to the role of women and at increased educational and skill training facilities for not only women already in the labor force but also nonworking married women in order to absorb and retain women in economic activity.

919. Rosenberg, T.J. "Individual and Regional Influences on the Employment of Colombian Women." Journal of Marriage and The Family 38 (1976): 339-353.

Correlates education, age, marital status and number of children and women's workforce participation rate using a random sample of 10,000 in five regions in Colombia. Finds that the higher a woman's education, the greater her participation in the workforce. However, the presence of young children and high husband's income tend to reduce woman's workforce participation rates. One of the five regions of Colombia studied had markedly lower workforce participation rates of women despite women's educational levels. Explains this in terms of sex role ideology. This region is a ·center for aggressive businessmen who consider nonworking, but educated wives a mark of high status.

920. Silva, Juan Andrés. "Participación de la Mujer en la Fuerza de Trabajo." Revista Paraguaya de Sociologia 13 (May-August 1976): 143-171.

Describes women's laborforce participation in Paraguay for the years 1962 through 1972. Points out that with education, women's workforce participation rates increase: 67 percent of women in the workforce in 1972 had elementary education, 22 percent had high school. Only 10.5 percent of women in the workforce had no education.

921. Sautu, Ruth. "The Female Labor Force in Argentina, Bolivia and Paraguay." Latin American Research Review 15 (1980): 152-161.

Investigates the supply and demand factors affecting both the rates of female participation in the workforce and their pattern of workforce participation. Finds that family composition and educational levels are the major factors affecting whether women enter the labor force and the types of jobs they obtain.

922. Schmidt, Steffen. "Women in Colombia." Women in the World, 1975-1985. The Women's Decade. Edited by Lynne B. Iglitzen and Ruth Ross. Santa Barbara: ABC-CLIO, 1986, pp. 273-304.

Describes women's formal and informal laborforce participation in Colombia. Finds that education and laborforce participation are important basic indicators of women's status and that as education has expanded, so has women's workforce participation. Points out that despite the gains, women in Colombia are concentrated in "female" occupations. This pattern is attributable both to the amount and kind of education women receive as well as outright discrimination by employers.

923. Smith, M.G. "Education and Occupational Choice in Rural Jamaica." Social and Economic Studies 9 (1960): 332-354.

Studies male and female occupational choice among 15 and 24 year olds in rural Jamaica in the 1950s with that of 25 to 39 year olds. Finds that young women aged 15 to 24 aspired to domestic work because, even with education, employment opportunities for women are very limited.

924. Velez, Elizabeth. "Trends Among Puerto Rican Women." Political Affairs 15 (1976): 24-30.

Describes the situation of Puerto Rican women in the United States in terms of their laborforce participation. While the rate of female laborforce participation as a whole is increasing, Puerto Rican women are more and more excluded from the laborforce. Discrimination, the state of economy, lack of educational opportunities, etc. make it more difficult for them to obtain better jobs, and confine them in low wage and typical women's jobs. Contends that a program of action which is collectively organized by all women is needed to improve their situation.

925. Wainerman, Catalina. "Impact of Education on the Female Labor Force in Argentina and Paraguay." Comparative Education Review 24 (1980): S180-S195. (Also in The Education of Women in the Third World: Comparative Perspectives. Edited by Gail P. Kelly and Carolyn M. Elliott. Albany: SUNY Press, 1982, pp. 264-282.

Asks whether education mediates the impact of child bearing and child rearing on women's workforce participation rates in Argentina and Paraguay. Finds that formal education exerts a strong influence on laborforce participation over and beyond that of family situation in both countries. Assumes that highly educated women are more likely to overcome difficulties which inhibit their laborforce participation since education has a close relationship with the class structure. Suggests further research which takes into account the impact of marriage and the family on women's workforce participation.

926. Wainerman, Catalina H. "Las Mujeres Como Proveedoras de Mano de Obra a Los Mercados de Argentina y Paraguay." La Mujer y Trabajo en Paraguay. Edited by Luis Galeano. Asunción, Paraguay: Centro de Estudios Sociologicos, 1982, pp. 441-511.

Studies the relation between educational level, women's marital status, her reproductive characteristics and participation in the Argentinian and Paraguayan workforce. Argues that education, independent of other factors, plays a central role in women's participation in the workforce. Education also affects fertility.

4a.   Brazil

Books and Monographs

927. Cardoso, Irede. Mulher e Trabalho: Discimiações e Barriras no Mercado de Traboho. São Paulo: Cortez Editora, 1980. 104 pp.

Administers a questionnaire developed at Harvard University to a number of women who were working in Sao Paulo in Brazil. The population consisted of women who had secondary and above education. 36.2 percent worked as secretaries or clerical workers, 20.6 percent were secondary school teachers and school directors. Another 43.7 percent were writers and journalists. Most of the women were between 20 and 30 years of age. Finds that women were conscious of discrimination in the workforce but that they all believed that education was the major way in which they could overcome this discrimination. Over half of the women were enrolled in further education courses.

da Silva, Lea Melo. Greater Education Opportunities for Women Related to Population Growth. East Lansing: Michigan State University, Women in International Development, 1982. 18 pp. (Working Paper no. 11)

See item #1129

Rosemberg, Fulvia et al. A Educacao da Mulher no Brazil. Sao Paulo: Global Editora, 1982.

See item #354

928. Saffioti, Heleieth I.B. The Impact of Industrialization on the Structure of Women's Employment. East Lansing: Michigan State

University, Office of Women in International Development, 1983. (Working Paper no. 15)

Reports research on female textile and garment workers in Sao Paulo. Finds that the female workforce is becoming increasingly stratified due to technological advances.

Articles

929. Aranha Bruschini, Maria Cristina. "Sexualização das Ocupações: O Caso Brasileiro." **Cadernos de Pesquisa** 28 (1979): 5-20.

Argues that modernization has depressed women's workforce participation in Brazil. In large part this has meant that women remain clustered in service industries and women have been denied access to manufacturing jobs except in a few sex segregated industries.

Hahner, June E. "Women's Place in Politics and Economics in Brazil Since 1964." **Brazilian Review** 19 (1982): 83-89.

See item #1158.

Leal, Maria Angela. Educação e Desigualdade Economica." Educação e Desigualdade no Brasil. Edited by Henry Levin <u>et al.</u> Petropolis: Editora Vozes, 1984, pp. 173-255.

See item #682

930. Lewin, Helena. "Educação a Forca de Trabalho Feminina no Braszil." **Cadernos da Pesquisa** 32 (Fevereiro 1980): 45-59.

Analyses women's participation in the Brazilian workforce. Focuses on women's distribution by different occupations, wages relative to those of men's and women's college careers. Claims that women's low income and status in the workforce is a function of capitalist social dynamics which exploits women's labor.

931. Oliveira, Zuleika L. Cide et al. "Aspectos Sócio-demográficos do Trabalho Femino nas Áreas Urbanas do Estado de São Paulo: 1970-1976." **Revista Geografica** (Mexico) 97 (1983): 70-82.

Discusses the effect of marital status, age and socioeconomic background on women's workforce participation in Sao Paulo, Brazil. Analyzes four types of women: single, married with children older than one year of age, married with children older than 13 years of age, and separated and widowed women.

Tabak, Fanny. "Women's Roles in the Formulation of Public Policies in Brazil." **Women, Power and Political System.** Edited by Margherita Rendel.   London: Croom Helm, 1981, pp. 66-80.

See item #1164

932. Vasquez de Miranda, Glaura.   "A Educação da Mulher Brasileira e
sua Participação nas Actividades Econômicas en 1970."   Cadernos
da Pesquisa 15 (1975): 21-36.

Argues that level of education, SES, marital status, age and
regional economic development affect women's level of workforce
participation and the occupations in which they work in Brazil.
Paradoxically women's workforce participation is most restricted
in the most industrialized regions of Brazil.

933. Vasques de Miranda, Glaura.   "Women's Labor Force Participation
in a Devloping Society: The Case of Brazil."   Signs: Journal
of Women in Culture and Society 3 (1977): 261-274.

Studies the correlates of women's laborforce participation.
Finds that social class and its strong relation to educational
attainment   has   a   positive   effect   on   women's   laborforce
participation rates.   Women with little or no education tend not
to join the paid laborforce because their wage earning capacity
does not offset the costs of their labor in the household.
Women with secondary and higher education have higher levels of
workforce participation because they hire labor to do household
work.   Also   looks   at   changes   in   women's   labor   force
participation rates in Brazil over time (from 1940 to 1960) and
finds that as the agricultural sector modernizes, there is an
increase in agricultural unemployment and men displace women in
agricultural work.   Women in developed urban areas tend to
become employed in crafts and in the service sector.

4b.   Chile

Books and Monographs

934. Silva Donoso, Maria de la Luz.   El Empleo Feminino: Algunos
Factores que Inciden en la Participación Femenina en Mercados de
Trabajo Diferenciales.   NP: Organización Internacional de
Trabajo, Programa Regional del Empleo para América Latina y el
Caribe, 1977.   115 pp.

Studies female employment in Chile based on early 1970s census
data.   Shows that working women are more than twice as likely as
men to have secondary education; that higher education leads to
workforce participation (47 percent vs. 30 percent of unmarried
women work who have higher education and 32 percent vs. 10
percent of married women with higher education work); and that
women with four to six years of education constitute 40 percent

of the industrial workforce and 20 percent of the commerce and service sector. Women outnumber men at the highest levels of education because there is more workforce opportunity for men at an earlier age but this educational advantage has occurred only since the late 1950s and has had little effect on job distribution. Women with higher degrees seem limited to employment in education, health and social science.

Articles

935. Barrera, Manuel. "Estructura Educativa de la Fuerza de Trabajo Chilena." **Revista Paraguaya de Sociología** 15 (1978): 57-75.

Describes women's workforce participation in Chile using the 1970 Census. Finds that education in urban areas relates to workforce participation rates. Women's employment is concentrated in commerce, service and female segregated manufacturing industries.

936. Bravo, Rosa and Rosalba Todaro. "Chilean Women and the UN Decade for Women." **Women's Studies International Forum** 8 (1985): 111-116.

Analyses Chilean women's political participation and their role in the laborforce over the UN Decade for Women. Argues that women's increased laborforce participation is not a response to improved opportunities, opened access to schools or more egalitarian treatment, but rather is the consequence of increased male unemployment in lower class families where women enter the workforce to support the family, but in marginal occupational roles.

937. Fucaraccio, Angel. "El Trabajo Femenino en Chile: Un Estudio de Caso de las Areas Urbanas." **Chile: Mujer y Sociedad.** Edited by Paz Covarrubias and Rolando Franco. Santiago: Alfebeta Imp., 1978, pp. 135-160.

Looks at women in the labor market in urban Chile based on 1970 census data. Workforce participation depends on the number of children and marital status. Since educational level is related to fertility rates, and number of children is related to labor force participation, argues that education does affect women's workforce participation rates and their duration within the urban paid laborforce.

Gonzales Cortes, Gerarado. "Desarrollo, Mujer y Fecundidad. Chile 1960-1970." **Chile Mujer y Sociedad.** Edited by Paz Covarrubias and Rolando Franco. Santiago: Alfebeta Imp., 1978, pp. 97-134.

See item #1136

938. Saavedra C., Wilna. "Los Jardines Infantiles y el Trabajo de la Mujer." Chile Mujer y Sociedad. Edited by Paz Covarrubias and Rolando Franco. Santiago: Alfebeta Imp., (1978): 469-79.

Considers the development of attention to the needs of preschool age children in Chile and the relationship of preschool education to the facilitation of women's work. The author was one of the authors of Law 17.301 (April 16, 1970) which created the Junta Nacional de Jardines Infantiles (National Council of Kindergartens). This law is discussed in some detail.

939. Schiefelbein, Ernesto and Joseph P. Farrell. "Women Schooling and Work in Chile: Evidence from a Longitudinal Study." Comparative Education Review 24 (1980): S160-S179. (Also in Women's Education in the Third World: Comparative Perspectives. Edited by Gail P. Kelly and Carolyn M. Elliott. Albany: SUNY Press, 1982, pp. 228-248.)

Investigates why women's educational attainment and workforce participation rates in Chile are higher than those in other developing and most industralized nations. Shows that the rates in Chile are directly traceable to the high quality of education women receive and the status of the schools women attend. Argues that women are attracted to higher quality schools more than are men and stay in school longer because education enables them to overcome discrimination in the labor market.

940. Taborga, Mercedes. "Aspectos Económicos del Trabajo de al Mujer." Chile Mujer y Sociedad. Edited by Paz Covarrubias and Rolando Franco. Santiago: Alfebeta Imp., 1978, pp. 41-66.

Considers the magnitude of the incorporation of women into the workforce and into different economic sectors, examining the decision to work in an economic model and presenting descriptive statistics on the Chilean case. A simple neoclassical model of utility maximization is used to explain labour supply as a function of income (standing for the goods that can be consumed with a given level) and leisure. Part I discusses the model while Part II presents data on workforce participation by age group; urban and rural participation rates; distribution of employment by sector, by occupational group and by occupational category (and percent of women represented); participation by educational level; and changes from 1960 to 1970. Concludes that Chile has a dual labor market structure with different markets for males and for females. Predicts some expansion in the supply of female labor and calls for an increase in demand for female labour.

4c.   Mexico

Books and Monographs

941. Ramones, Jesus. **La Mujer** en el Mercado Laboral de Monterrey.
Monterrey: Centro do Investigaciones Económicas de la
Universidad de Nuevo Leon, 1980. 39 pp.

Draws on census and other material to compare the work situation
of women and men in the decade of the 1970s in Monterrey. Shows
growth of jobs from 90,000 to 150,000 with the greatest
percentage growth for females in commerce (from 14 percent to 24
percent of the total) and government (from 1.3 percent to 3.3
percent). Female service sector jobs were most common but
dropped from 53 percent to 46 percent of the total. Industrial
jobs were stable. Female's share of professional and technical
occupations grew from 11 percent to 18 percent and female sales
workers from 9 percent to 21 percent. Women earned about 10
percent less than men in 1979. Women had slightly more
education than men, with 8.2 years (vs. 7.3 years for men).
Commercial education (with 12,400 men and 7400 women) produced
salary differentials of less than 10 percent ($9049 vs. $8151)
as did university level education (43,500 men and 9900 women)
with a salary differential of $14,117 vs. $13,888. However,
postgraduate study (only 3000 men and 1000 women) showed the
greatest salary differential, $23,229 vs. $14,995.

Articles

942. Arizpe, Lourdes. "Women in the Informal Sector: The Case of
Mexico City." Signs: Journal of Women in Culture and Society 3
(1977): 25-37.

Explores the degree of occupational choice that women have
within the structural margins of employment in Mexico City.
Finds that age and marital status influence the formal or
informal employment opportunities for women. Women represent 26
percent of the Mexican laborforce while 29.7 percent of the
workforce in Mexico City are women. Women are overwhelmingly
employed in the tertiary sector of economy (64 percent in
services); they rarely hold high administrative or professional
posts. Female employment is closely related to their education.

943. Barbieri, M. Teresita de. "Politicas de Población y la Mujer:
Antecedentes para su Estudio." Revista Mexicana de Sociologia
45 (1983): 293-308.

Studies how demographic policies adopted by the Mexican
government in 1974 have affected women's participation in the
workforce and their educational levels.

944. Elu de Leñero, Maria de Carmen. "Educación y Participación de la Mujer en la Población Economicamente Activa (PEA) de México." **Revista de Centro de Estudios Educativos** (Mexico) 7 (1977): 71-83.

Focuses on the relation between education and women's participation in the paid laborforce in Mexico. Points out that level of education, social class and marital status are the most important factors affecting women's entry and maintenance in the workforce. Argues that lack of employment opportunities has led Mexican women who are highly educated to leave the workforce.

945. Gonzalez Salazar, Gloria. "La Mujer: Condiciones Estructurales y Educación." Reforma Educativa y "Apertura Democratica". Edited by Fernando Carmona. Mexico City: Ediciones Nuestro Tiempo, 1972, pp. 106-124.

Studies the sex segregation of women in the workforce in Mexico and argues that women's position in the workforce is shaped by the media, by illiteracy and by prejudice. Claims that education increasingly challenges women's subordination in the Mexican workforce.

946. Gonzalez Salazar, Gloria. "Participación Laboral y Educativa de la Mujer en México." **Boletin Documental sobre las Mujeres** (Cuernavaca) 4 (no. 3, 1974): 14-22.

Focuses on the relation between incrases in women's education and their laborforce participation in Mexico. Despite gains in education, the pattern of women's workforce participation relative to men's has remained the same--women are still clustered in service occupations and are underrepresented in government service, in agriculture, industry and manufacturing. Attributes women's laborforce participation pattern to undereducation, especially lack of access to higher education and to technical education.

947. Mendoza, Guadalupe. "Educación y Capacitación de la Mujer." Participación de la Mujer en la Vida Economica de Pais. México: Instituto Nacional ed Estudios del Trabajo, 1975, pp. 31-39.

Points out the poor position and low pay of women workers and calls for the extension of workers' education to women. Also points to gender bias within the school system, calls for equal treatment, and predicts the natural movement of women into better positions.

Smith, Stanley K. "Determinants of Female Labor Force Participation and Family Size in Mexico City." **Economic Development and Cultural Change** 30 (1981): 129-152.

See item #1139

Srinivasan, Mangalam. "The Impact of Science and Technology and the Role of Women in Science in Mexico." Scientific-Technological Change and the Role of Women in Development. Edited by Pamela d'Onofrio-Flores and Sheila M. Pfafflin. Boulder: Westview Press, 1982, pp. 113-148.

See item #783

5.   The Middle East

Books and Monographs

948. Abu Nasr, Julinda, et al. **Women, Employment and Development in the Arab World.** Berlin: Mouton, 1985. 143 pp.

Looks at laborforce participation in Yemen, Jordan, Lebanon and the Gulf States and presents an overview of educational statistics on literacy levels and school enrollment for the entire region. The last chapter by Abu Nasr and I. Lorfig studies male/female role attitudes in four universities in Lebanon, Kuwait and Egypt using a sample of more than 400 students. Compares mother's and father's education, work experience, student's age, religion and class in school. Mother's education in two cases, work experience in one case and father's education in one case seem to have the most profound effects on liberal role attitudes for women.

949. **The Measurement of Women's Economic Participation: Report of a Study Group.** Giza, Egypt: The Population Council, 1979. 78 pp.

Reports on the study group of specialists on the Measurement of Women's Economic Participation which was held in Egypt in 1979. The papers sought to define women's work, develop methodologies of study based on time budgets, study the impact of education on work. The eight papers printed here focus on women's economic participation in North Yemen, the economic activities of Jordanian women, women in the laborforce of Egypt, cultural and structural obstacles to women's employment in Cuba and studies of part time work and the unacknowledged work of women. Education is at best a tangential subject in these papers.

950. Mernissi, Fatima. **Country Reports on Women in North Africa: Libya, Morocco, Tunisia.** Addis Ababa: African Training and Research Centre for Women, United Nations Economic Commission for Africa, 1978. 42 pp.

Focuses on women's workforce participation, education and legal status in three North African countries. Finds that the labor

force participation rates of Libyan women are very low as
compared to Morocco and Tunisia. Believes this is because the
Libyan government has refused to adopt policies that would raise
women's status and has opposed ILO advice that women be provided
with more education and training that would equip them for
workforce participation. In all three countries illiteracy
rates are quite high. However, government policies in Tunisia
and Morocco which have extended education and modified civil and
religious law, have helped get women into the workforce. In
both countries working women are clustered in traditional
agriculture, domestic work, textile manufacturing and food
services.

951. Molyneux, Maxine. State Policies and the Position of Women
Workers in the Democratic Republic of Yemen, 1967-77. Geneva:
International Labour Office, 1982. 87 pp.

Traces the changes in women's status as a result of the
socialist revolution in 1967 in Yemen. Argues that while the
state has instituted changes in the constitution and law and
encouraged women's education, equity with men has not been
attained. The introduction details legal and constitutional
changes. Chapter 1 focuses on the increasing participation of
women in politics, while the second chapter is on education.
Chapter 3 concentrates on employment and, the final chapter
reports a survey of women factory workers conducted in 1977.
The chapter on education provides a series of enrollment
statistics as well as a summary of post-1967 educational
reforms. The number of girls in primary school has grown
substantially: in 1967 20 percent of girls went to school; by
1977 this had changed to over 54 percent; by 1977 99 percent of
primary school aged boys attended. While women's illiteracy
rates are still quite high, adult education programs have
focused more on women than on men. The chapter on the workforce
illustrates that despite educational expansion, women's
workforce participation lags appreciably behind that of men.
Most women are employed in agriculture, very few are in
manufacturing; those who are segregated into low paying,
semi-skilled labor despite their relatively high educational
levels. Women are segregated into nursing and midwivery and
teaching, much of this is a function of women's education and
the admission of women disproportionately into teacher education
and nursing programs. The fourth chapter which presents the
1977 survey of factory workers details their educational levels,
their employment patterns in sex segregated industries, marriage
and child bearing patterns and attitudes towards work.

Articles

952. Abdelkrin, Rabia. "Les Femmes à la Campagne: Quelle Formation
et Quel(s) Emploi(s)? Exclues du Système de Formation,

Sont-elles des Ménageres ou une Armée active Refoulée." La
Politque de L'Emploi-Formation au Maghreb (1970-1980). Edited
by Chantal Bernard. Paris: CNRS, 1982, pp. 325-343.

Outlines the inequalities between males and females in the
school system of Algeria and the greater disparities betwen the
sexes in rural areas. Women are discriminated against in the
workforce and increasingly, despite gains in education, women
have become a source of free labor working in the household.
When employed, women usually work in agriculture.

953. Baffoun, Alya. "L'Acces des Tunisiennes au Salariat." **Femmes
et Multinationales.** Edited by Andree Michele, et al. Paris:
Editions Karthala, 1981, pp. 227-245.

Focuses on the expansion of education for women in Tunisia and
the ways in which that expansion has opened to women
opportunities for employment in industry. Points out that
increased access to technical and profesional training has meant
a decline in female employment in agriculture and an increase in
manufacturing, often replacing male labor. Women workers are
younger than male workers and more highly educated. Most female
factory workers are single about 25 years old and have a few
years of schooling. They tend to be migrants from the
countryside and use their earnings to support their parents,
particularly in families where their father is unemployed.
Discusses the psychological costs of increased female employment
and education and argues that girls with secondary schooling
have greater problems of adjustment to factory work and its
harsh conditions than do girls with lesser education. Concludes
that Tunisian society "exports" its girls as a kind of tribute
to the factors controlled by international capitalist concerns
via the educational system.

954. Korayen, Korima. "Women and the New International Economic
Order in the Arab World." **Women and Work in the Arab World.**
Edited by Earl L. Sullivan and Korima Korayen. Cairo: Cairo
Papers in Social Science, December 1981, pp. 45-78. (Monograph
no. 4, vol. 1)

Focuses on projecting the effect of the New International
Economic Order, proposed by the United Nations, both on women's
education and women's workforce participation in the Arab world.
Analyses literacy and educational levels for Algeria, Egypt,
Kuwait, Jordan, the Democratic Republic of Yemen, Sudan, Syria
and Tunisia and points out that only in 2 countries of the
Middle East are less than 50 percent of all women illiterate.
In most of the region, 78.3 percent are illiterate versus 50.6
percent of males. Only 6.6 percent of all women have gone to
school and of these only 2.2 percent have secondary education
(she admits that her estimates are based on very scanty data and
may be low). In the Middle East women's labortorce

participation rates are low, averaging 10.4 percent. Argues that the New International Economic Order may not have any effect on women at all since the increases in education and employment projected by the UN will probably benefit men since there are cultural and legal constraints, not to mention attitudinal ones, which prevent women from either going to school or working outside the home.

955. Joekes, Susan. "Working for Lipstick? Male and Female Labor in the Clothing Industry in Morocco." **Women, Work and Ideology in the Third World**. Edited by Haleh Afshar. London: Tavistock, 1985, pp. 183-213.

Explores the ways in which male and female labor are used and rewarded differently by employers in the clothing industry in Morocco. Argues that women's low level of skill and lack of commitment to wage employment largely follow from the way employers use female labor. Analyses the social factors which influence the supply of female labor and the wage at which women work. Emphasizes female labor supply is influenced to a far greater extent than male by household structures and distribution of household types in the population.

956. Mahfoud-Draoui, D. "Formation et Travail des Femmes en Tunisie. Promotion ou Alienation?" **La Politique de l'Emploi-formation au Maghreb (1970-1980)**. Edited by Chantal Bernard et al. Paris: Editions du Centre National de la Recherche Scientifique, 1982, pp. 255-288.

Surveys the workforce participation rates of women in Tunisia and argues that the reason why so few women are in the workforce is because women are undereducated. Most women in Tunisia work either as domestics or as independent employees in the primary sector. In 1972 educational reforms promised to break the pattern of women's undereducation but the government slowed down the pace of educational expansion, disadvantaging women once again. Finds that women have been unable to enter the service sector of the economy despite the increases in their educational levels simply because of government discrimination against hiring women. Does find, however, that in rural areas women do enter the government administration at the lower levels when they receive secondary or better education.

957. Nouacer, Khadidja. "The Changing Status of Women and the Employment of Women in Morocco." **International Social Science Journal** 14 (no. 1 1962): 124-129.

Argues that certain occupations have become respectable for women in Morocco, including teaching, nursing and welfare work. Education plays a strong role in these. Other respectable occupations include skilled traditional work like carpet making. Suggests social class divisions with the skilled working class, shipkeepers, etc. pushing and supporting their daughters in education, while the lower working class stresses traditional values.

958. Talahite-Hakiki, F. "Scolarisation et Formation des Filles en Algérie: Préparation au Salariat ou Production de Menagères Modernes?"   La Politique de l'Emploi-Formation au Maghreb (1970-1980). Edited by Chantel Bernard et al. Paris: Editions du Centre National de la Recherche Scientifique, 1982, pp. 289-323.

Surveys changes in women's education in Algeria since independence from France. Finds, through a detailed analysis of educational enrollment statistics, that there is a great increase in women's educational levels.   However, women's workforce participation has stagnated and current educational ideology reinforces preparation of women for roles in the household rather than in the workforce.

959. Youssef, Nadia.   "Social Sructure and the Female Labor Force: The Case of Women Workers in Muslim Middle Eastern Countries." Demography 8 (1971): 427-439.

Analyses why female participation rates in economic activities outside of agriculture in Middle Eastern countries are low. Five countries are selected for intensive analysis: Chile, Mexico, Egypt, Morocco and Pakistan.   Points out that the low level and particular character of women's involvement in the workforce in the Middle East can be explained by institutional arrangements contingent upon aspects of social structure. Emphasizes the interplay betwen the willful avoidance by women of certain occupational sectors because of social stigma and the prohibition of occupational opportunities imposed by males. Concludes that the combined effects of the tradition of female seclusion and exclusion are confirmed by the analysis of the structure of the nonagricultural laborforce.   Middle Eastern women are absent from occupational and industrial sectors of employment which involve public activity and presuppose contact with males.

Youssef, Nadia H.   "The Status and Fertility Patterns of Muslim Women." Women in the Muslim World. Edited by Lois Beck and Nikki Keddie. Cambridge: Harvard University Press, 1978, pp. 69-99.

See item #1079

5a.   Egypt

Articles

960. Guindi, Fadwa. "The Egyptian Woman: Trends Today, Alternatives Tomorrow." Women in the World, 1975-1985: The Women's Decade. Edited by Lynne B. Iglitzen and Ruth Ross. Santa Barbara: ABC-CLIO, 1986, pp. 225-242.

   Analyses the development of women's status in Egypt in the context of cultural processes. Assesses the contemporary situation of women in the workforce. Finds that there has been a significant decrease in illiteracy and increase in education at every level among working women after the revolution of 1952. Egyptian women tend to be evenly distributed in all coeducational majors. Women are significantly increasing at those levels of employment requiring college education, as the result, male-female ratios are 3.5:1 for technical, managerial, professional, clerical positions combined.

961. Mohsen, Safia K. "New Images, Old Reflections, Working Middle-Class Women in Egypt." Women and the Family in the Middle East. Edited by Elizabeth Warnack Fernea. Austin: University of Texas Press, 1985, pp. 56-71.

   Examines how Middle Eastern women and men react to the new social and political conditions created by rapid development. Focuses on the Egyptian urban working middle class women. Using interview data, finds, among other things, that the open door policy of Egypt has created new job opportunities for upper middle class women, who traditionally have shown an interest in foreign education and a disdain for public education. The open door policy has encouraged private sector and foreign investment, and thus created more demand for language skills and the ability to deal with foreigners. Upper middle class women have these skills and do not have to fight for the privileges of education and employment, due to the current social and economic conditions and public attitudes. Nevertheless, there has been very little change in the traditional views of sex roles and very little adjustment in the nature of family relations and the allocation of domestic responsibilities.

962. Papanek, Hanna. "Class and Gender in Education--Employment Linkages." Comparative Education Review 29 (1985): 317-346.

   Explores the relationship among class, gender, education and employment of women using data from regional studies in Bangladesh and Egypt. The theoretical framework employed focuses on family strategies of survival and social mobility stressing the interplay between family structures and kinship systems and labor markets. Proposes that the continuous interplay between family households and labor markets determines both female educational and laborforce participation through the development of specific family strategies. Discusses the impact of gender differences in the context of class differentiation using the Egyptian population census data for 1976. Finds that family households tend to operate as economic and social collectivities. Strict control over labor deployment has obvious consequences for female participation in education and employmemt, and sex segregation remains an important factor constraining the supply of female labor and shaping its demand.

963. Sullivan, Earl L. "Women and Work in Egypt." **Women and Work in the Arab World.** Edited by Earl L. Sullivan and Korina Korayen. Cairo: Cairo Papers in Social Science, 1981, pp. 1-44. (Vol. 4, Monograph no. 4)

Focuses on women's workforce participation in Egypt. Points out, using national data, that since 1961 the overall workforce participation of women has declined, despite increases in education for women. This was a result of economic development strategies which emphasized urbanization and industrialization. Women's employment in agriculture declined as a result of the overall decline in agricultural employment (despite the fact that women constitute most of the farm labor). Increases in women's employment occurred in manufacturing and in the service industries. This was a direct result of increases in women's education which meant women could find jobs as clerical workers and in the professions. The single largest employer of women is the government, but in the public sector women work predominantly in health and education. In the private sector women cluster in banking and services. Women's entry into white collar work has been accelerated by the shift in men's employment. Educated men have been leaving Egypt to take up work in other parts of the Arab world where they are paid higher wages and women have filled many of the public sector jobs men might otherwise have filled. Points out that employment does not have any effect on women's emancipation: fertility rates have stayed stable and many educated women have taken on the veil.

5b.   Kuwait

Books and Monographs

Al-Sabah, S.M. Development Planning in an Oil Economy and the Role of the Women: The Case of Kuwait. London: Eastlords Publishing Ltd., 1983. 380 pp.

See item #761

Articles

964. Cornell, M. Louise. "The Development of Education for Women in Kuwait." Canadian and International Education 5 (1976): 73-83.

    Traces the development of women's education in Kuwait since the oil boom of the 1950s and 1960s. The expansion of education has resulted in major changes for women despite sex segregation in schooling and the workforce. Educational expansion has not brought equality in the workforce; women become doctors and managers of services provided for women. In Kuwait, women do not become nurses and clerks as is the case in much of the rest of the world.

965. Meleis, Afaf I. et al. "Women, Modernization and Education in Kuwait." Comparative Education Review 23 (1979): 115-124.

    Provides an historical overview of women's education in Kuwait. Widespread education is recent to Kuwait and began shortly after the intensification of oil drilling in 1946. The educational system initially served the children of the Kuwaiti elite. In the case of women, parents saw education only in terms of providing their daughters with an enhanced life of leisure. Most were reluctant to send their daughters overseas for university education and women did not receive higher education until the first Kuwaiti university opened in 1966. Despite the increase in women's education, the relation between education and workforce participation for women is weak. The Kuwaiti workforce is sex segregated and women's employment opportunities, even when women possess advanced degrees, are restricted to professions which serve other women.

966. Nath, Kamla. "Education and Employment among Kuwaiti Women." Women in the Muslim World. Edited by Lois Beck and Nikki Keddie. Cambridge: Harvard University Press, 1978, pp. 172-188.

    Studies workforce participation and related changes among Kuwaiti career women. Based on a survey conducted during early 1970, finds that by 1970 the workforce participation rate of women had gone up to 5.2 percent, among the highest in the Arab Middle East. Behind this statistical change lay a massive increase in the education of women. In 1965-66, nearly 67 percent of the girls in the 5 to 9 age group were attending government schools, where they constituted 41.5 percent of the total student body. In 1968-69, 43 percent of all school students were female. About a thousand girls were attending the University of Kuwait which had been established in 1966. Older women were also pressed into government adult education centers with an attendance of 5215 in 1969. As a result, large numbers of women entered into government service in increasing numbers as civil servants, social welfare workers and teachers. The number of university women graduates increased from 38 in 1966 to 155 in 1968 and 246 in 1970. Of them, the work participation rate is more than 99 percent with the Kuwait government as almost the sole employer and with most of the graduates working in the education sector.

5c.   Turkey

Articles

967. Erkut, Sumru. "Dualism in Values toward Education of Turkish Women." Sex Roles, Family and Community in Turkey. Edited by Cigdem Kagitcibasi and Diane Sunar. Bloomington: Indiana University Press, Turkish Studies 3 1982, pp. 121-132.

Analyses the reasons why relative to men, Turkish women display substantially lower levels of educational attainment; women who go on in school beyond the primary level, show more persistence and achieve greater success, and despite the low levels of educational attainment for women in general, substantial numbers of Turkish women obtain professional degrees and practice in some prestigious occupations. Finds that elite women in Turkey are encouraged to engage in educational pursuits which lead to professional employment outside the home because of the large numbers of nonelite women who have limited educational and therefore occupational opportunities. Concludes that the successes of an elite group of Turkish women is made possible by the lack of opportunities for the majority of uneducated women.

968. Kazgan, Gulten. "Labour Force Participation, Occupational Distribution, Educational Attainment and the Socio-Economic Status of Women in the Turkish Economy." Women in Turkish Society. Edited by Nermin Abadan-Unat. Leiden: E.J. Brill, 1981, pp.131-159.

Discusses female laborforce participation, the occupational distribution of female labor, and the educational attainment of women in the laborforce. Shows that women from better income families enjoy a higher probability of improving their socioeconomic status because they are more likely to receive a better education, and consequently are more likely to be committed to a career. In addition, they are more likely to marry better educated men and the higher income members of their own social class, and to give birth to a small number of children. The same factors tend to accumulate in the opposite direction in the case of low income, rural women and hamper the relative improvement in their socioeconomic status.

969. Ozbay, Ferhunde. "The Impact of Education on Women in Rural and Urban Turkey." **Women in Turkish Society.** Edited by Nermin Abadan-Unat. Leiden: E.J. Brill, 1981, pp. 160-179.

Studies educational inequality, employment and education, laborforce participation in rural areas, limited job opportunities in the nonagricultural sector, jobs towards which females are directed, education and marriage, education and fertility, etc. Shows that the Turkish female laborforce participation rate is very low and consists mainly of women who have not finished any school. It is very difficult for women to work outside their homes even if they do have an education, because they have to take care of their families. About 40 percent of 2322 women sampled thought, 'there is no need for rural/urban women to receive an education.' Professionally oriented education has an effect on increasing social mobility, but very few women have received this kind of education.

970. Ozbay, Ferhunde. "Women's Education in Rural Turkey." **Sex Roles, Family and Community in Turkey.** Edited by Cigdem Kagitcibasi and Diane Sunar. Bloomington: Indiana University Press, 1982, pp. 133-150.

Looks at the relation between educational levels and laborforce participation in four villages in different parts of Turkey. Finds that education by itself does not affect female labor force participation rates, but the way the rural economy is organized does affect women's education.

971. Senyapili, Tansi. "A New Component in Metropolitan Areas: The Gecekondu Women." **Women in Turkish Society.** Edited by Nermin Abadan-Unat. Leiden: E.J. Brill, 1981, pp. 194-214.

Focuses in the problems of Geckondu women as a new workforce in metropolitan areas. In the 1950-70s time period, Gecekondu women performed an important function in urban economies by working in low paying jobs in which unsatisfactory work conditions discourage enthusaism for further work. Suggests that even if the decision to raise women's level of education is realized within the existing framework, low income third world women still will not be able to afford long years of classical education which has no functional relation to their social environment. In the near future with the enlargement of the market and the favorable medium created for women to enter work, the Gecekondu women will join the urban workforce. Women's work conditions should be readjusted considering females' differing socioeconomic backgrounds. If not, the Gecekondu women, as new components in Turkish metropolises, will never be a fully effective part of the laborforce and they will always be subjected to increasing levels of exploitation.

B.   Women in the Professions

1.   General

Books and Monographs

972. Anani, Elma Lititia, et al. **Women and the Mass Media in Africa: Case Studies from Sierra Leon, the Niger and Egypt.** Addis Ababa: United Nations Economic Commission for Africa, African Training and Research Centre for Women, Voluntary Fund for the United Nations Decade for Women, 1981. 29 pp.

Contains three essays on women in the mass media: one by Elma Lititia Anani on Sierra Leone, another on Niger by Alkaly Miriama Keita and a third on Egypt by Awatef Abdel Rahman. These were presented at a Study Visit of Women Journalists held at the United Nations Economic Commission for Africa at Addis Ababa, 24-30, September 1978.   The articles focus on women's image in the press, radio and television.   The papers on Niger and Sierra Leone do focus on training and employment opportunities for women.   They point out that there are few women in the mass media because women are undereducated in these countries and because most training opportunities are dependent on international travel and the largess of bilateral and multilateral agencies.   Women cannot take advantage of such programs because they either lack the educational and work qualifications or because of family responsibilities.   Makes a series of recommendations to improve women's participation in mass media.

Articles

973. Blitz, Rudolph C.   "An International Comparison of Women's Participation in the Professions."   **Journal of Developing Areas** 9 (1975): 499-510.

Compares women in the professions in 49 countries stratified by level of economic development.   Finds that while economic development relates to increases in the proportion of women in the paid laborforce, it does not have the same relation to women in the professions.   The proportion of women in the professions worldwide is generally low.   However, women's representation in the professions is higher in less developed countries than in industralized countries.

2.   Africa

Books and Monographs

Likimani, Muthoni.   Women of Kenya: Fifteen Years of Independence. Nairobi: Likimani, 1979. 76 pp.

See item #715

974. Schuster, Ilsa M. Glazer.   New Women of Lusaka.   Palo Alto, California: Mayfield Publishing Company, 1979.   209 pp.

Studies the lifestyles of educated career women in Lusaka, Zambia. This ethnographic study focuses on women who have had at least nine years of education and were born between 1945 and 1953 and looks at family socialization, schooling, women in the workforce, women and marriage and the family and images of women in society. Finds that these young educated women and the wider society are ambivalent about "emancipated" roles for women. Women are disadvantaged in education and remain disadvantaged relative to boys while in school since they are expected to do housework, serve adults and care for babies. The percentage of women in the modern laborforce is small and the job market in this mining economy is narrower for women than it is for men. In the short run, education has expanded opportunities for women who have managed to get education due to the Zambianization of the laborforce whereby women are expected to replace foreign women in the process of Africanization. Remains pessimistic about the long run employment possibilities for educated women once Africanization has run its course.

975. Van Rooyen, J.   Female Career Commitment (A Life-Span Perspective). Braamfontein, South Africa: National Institute for Personnel Research, September 1981. 307 pp. (CSIR Special Report PERS 327)

Studies 111 white women employed by the South African Council for Scientific and Industrial Research, half of whom have a primarily male sex role identity (as measured by the Bem Sex Role Inventory) and half of whom have a primarily female sex role identity. The population consisted of university educated women. Compares their personalites, marital status, age, work interest and satisfaction with life and finds that women who have primarily male sex role identity have greater need achievement, tend to be more interested in their work and are more able to combine family with work.

Articles

976. Barthel, Diane L.   "The Rise of a Female Professional Elite:
The Case of Senegal." African Studies Review 18 (Dec. 1975):
1-17.

Studies the education, family and work histories of 100 women
university graduates working as professionals, librarians,
social workers and health care providers in Dakar. Points out
that these professional women came from elite families whose
fathers were officials in the colonial government.

977. Butter, Irene.   "Women and Health Care Personnel Planning."
Women, Health and International Development. Edited by Margaret
Aguwa.   East Lansing: International Development and African
Studies Center, Michigan State University, 1982, pp. 21-32.

Presents a broad overview of women in the health system,
pointing out women's low status has led them to occupy only the
lower positions of the formal health care system.   Even when
they become doctors they are rarely in prestigious specialties
or in administrative positions.   In the informal health
system--family nutrition, family care of children--women have
almost total responsibility. Argues improvements in health care
depend on recognition of the waste of human resources and the
female nature of the audience for health provision.

978. "Career Women of West Africa." West Afrian Review (1955):
290-296.

Introduces West African women in various careers with pictures
and captions.   The occupations of the women introduced are,
government officer, radio announcer, teacher, nun, secretary,
hairdresser, doctor, actress, fashion model, politician,
journalist, nurse, librarian, police officer, etc.

979. Gould, Terri F.   "A New Class of Professional Zairian Women."
African Review 7 (nos. 3-4, 1977): 92-105.

Studies the conflicts and problems of Zaire professional women.
The women investigated are university graduates living in urban
Zaire.

980. Gould, Terri F.   "Value Conflict and Development: The Struggle
of Professional Zairian Women." Journal of Modern African
Studies 16 (March 1978): 133-139.

Studies role conflicts among professional women in Zaire.
Points out that in Zaire only 3.2 percent of the women work in
the modern economy and less than 4 percent of women in the
modern sector work in a profession.   Gould conducted interviews
with women in Zaire's third largest city. Most of the women had

postsecondary education.   Most worked as professionals as
nurses, teachers, university assistants, directors of
homemaking schools. Women's segregation into these occupations
was due to harsh sexual stereotypes, legal restrictions (women
had to have their husband's permission to work), the demands of
the polygamous and the traditional extended families, and the
demands of motherhood.

981. Lindsay, Beverly. "Issues Confronting Professional African
Women: Illustrations from Kenya." **Comparative Perspective** of
Third World Women. Edited by Beverly Lindsay. New York:
Praeger, 1980, pp. 78-95.

Studies the socioeconomic and domestic roles of professional
women who have graduated from secondary and higher education in
Kenya. Finds that these women are a small minority and work in
increasingly female segregated fields. Most of them come from
high SES backgrounds and were trained in the humanities,
education, nursing and the arts.

982. Schuster, Ilsa. "Perspective in Development: The Problem of
Nurses and Nursing in Zambia." Journal of Development Studies
17 (1987): 77-97.

Studies the evolution of nursing as a female occupation in
Zambia and the development of nurses' training programs. Points
out that women were trained on the western model and that they
were trained to be subordinate to the male medical
establishment. Traces also the social background
characteristics of nurses and finds that they are predominatly
from urban middle class families and are part of Zambia's new
urban elites.

983. Unterhalter, Beryl. "Discrimination against Women in the South
African Medical Profession." **Social Science and Medicine** 20
(no. 12, 1985): 1253-1258.

Studies women in medicine and finds, despite rising attendance
and graduation from medical schools, women do not achieve high
status in their profession. They remain tied to public health,
kept out of many specializations, and have limited entry to
private practice. Ascribes this to the patriarchial values
present in any private practice organization of medicine.

3.   Asia

Books and Monographs

Baquai, Sabihuddin. Changes in the Status and Roles of Women in Pakistan. Karachi: Department of Sociology, University of Karachi, 1976, pp. 86 pp.

See item #1127

Articles

984. Guerrero, Sylvia H. "An Analysis of Husband-Wife Roles Among Filipino Professionals at U.P. Los Banos Campus." Philippine Sociological Review 13 (1965): 275-281.

Describes the role of the working wife in the family in rapidly changing Filipino society by interviewing 52 professional couples working at the University of the Philippines. Almost half of the respondents answered that the reason for the wife's working was for additional income. Two thirds of the husbands and one third of the wives had a traditional conception of wife's role, but both seemed confused about the role of the wife. Although the wife did most of the housework, all the couples with children had domestic helpers. The analysis shows that modern Filipino women do not entirely subordinate traditional wife-mother roles to that of career, but has growing concern for personal happiness.

Lee, Hie-Sung. "A Case Study on Achievement Motivation of Women Professors in a Women's University in Korea." Challenges for Women: Women's Studies in Korea. Edited by Chung Sei-Wna. Seoul: Ewha Woman's University Press, 1986, pp. 192-229.

See item #534

Mitchell, Edna M. "Women Leaders in Nepal: A Generation Gap." Delta Kappa Gamma Bulletin 44 (1977): 40-51.

See item #535

985. Pongsapich, Amara.   "Female Participation and Industrial Development in Thailand." Women in Development: Perspectives from the Nairobi Conference. Ottawa: International Development Research Centre, 1986, pp. 93-115.

Studies women executives in Thai industries and finds that the proportion of women is smaller than that of men. Argues that the reason women are underrepresented in industry is lack of education, family ties and personal sophistication. Points out

that women are 19 percent of participants in management training
programs organized by the Thai Department of Industrial
Promotion between 1980 and 1984.

986. Sidel, Ruth. "Women in Medicine in China." **Eastern Horizon** 12
(no. 4 1973): 57-60.

Looks at women in the medical profession in China in the 1970s
when women constituted approximately 30 to 40 percent of all
physicians and over 50 percent of all medical school students.
Traces the history of medical training for women in the country.

3a. India

Books and Monographs

987. Blumberg, Rhoda Lois and Leela Dwaraki. **India's Educated Women:
Options and Constraints.** Delhi: Hindustan Publishing
Corporation, 1980.

Studies highly educated professional women from urban middle
class families in Bangalore. The women were 97 graduates and
post graduates who possessed B.A., M.A., medical and law degrees
from Bangalore University. The interviews on which the study is
based were conducted in 1966-67 and in 1977. The 1967
interviews generated data about education, employment and family
situations and about how women viewed the importance of
education in their daily life. The 1977 follow up interviews
concentrated on marital status, children, work history and
salary and problems the women confronted over the 10 year
period. Finds that most of the women retained traditional
values despite their education. Education provided economic
independence for those women as well, although all reported they
suffered from the double burden of household and job and came
into conflict with uneducated female family members.

988. Chaturvedi, Geeta. **Women Administrators of India: A Study of
the Socio-Economic Background and Attitudes of women
Administrators of Rajasthan.** Jaipur: RBSA Publishers, 1985.
328 pp.

Studies 36 women who are government executives and 64 women who
are administrators in education to find out their attitudes to
social change, political modernization, and economic development
and their attitudes and perceptions toward work and the family.
The respondents were all from Rajasthan. Finds that most of
these women were highly educated and came from upper middle
class families where the fathers possessed higher education;
some fathers had graduate degrees. The SES backgrounds of women
who were government executives were higher than those of the

educational   administrators.   Finds,   through   structured
interviews, that the educational administrators tended to be
more conservative than the government executives, although both
groups were modern in their attitudes.   The women all reported
they worked for economic reasons, although the executives tended
to see career enhancement as a very important reason for
working.

989. Chauhan, Indira. **Purdah to Profession (A Case Study of Working
Women in M.P.)** Delhi: B.R. Publishing Corporation, 1986.
292 pp.

Surveys 300 women who had secondary education and above (18
percent had completed high school, 8.67 percent college, 14.67
percent graduate school, 27.33 percent postgraduate and 31.33
medical, law or engineering school).   The women were employed in
Bhopal Vity, Madhhya Pradesh, India.   Most worked as teachers on
the primary, secondary and higher education levels (36 percent)
while 12 percent worked as technicians and 8 percent as doctors
and other professionals.   Finds that most had low income
relative to men were in arranged marriages, lived in nuclear
families and belonged to few organizations.   Most had hired help
but were responsible for the household.   Husbands did help them
with some tasks, mainly in caring for the children, but the
women for the most part had to combine their careers with their
household responsibilities.

990. Liddle, Joanna and Rama Joshi. **Daughters of Independence:
Gender, Caste and Class in India.** London: Zed Books, 1986.
264 pp.

Argues that it has been possible for educated middle class women
in India to move into the professions.   This movement, limited
though it may be, has occurred because India has been moving
from a castestratified to a class stratified society.   Educated
daughters of traditionally privileged groups in India have begun
to enter professions deemed compatible with ideas of female
status and respectibility.   The book is based on interviews
conducted with college educated women who are professional
workers.   The sample consisted of 120 women, aged 22 to 59,
equally divided into four professions: medicine, education, the
civil service and management.   The interveiws reveal the
life histories of the women, how they experienced education, the
views of their fathers, grandfathers and husbands about their
receiving an education and their work and family situations.
Many of the women lived through a period when restrictions on
women's activity were loosened.   They reported that their
parents wanted them to receive education, but if they worked as
a result outside the home, they had to maintain respectability
by working in teaching and in women's occupations like medicine.
Chapter 17 describes some of the problems the women experienced
in obtaining education--sexual harassment, stereotyped female

subjects, discouragement of study on the part of their families, and the insistence on the part of their families that education be a commodity for marriage. Interviews with the women discuss discrimination in employment, the effect of employment on work in the family and the conflicts and contradictions of being professional married women. The book ends with an examination of the ways in which professional women resist male domination.

991. Nayak, Sharada, (ed.) Profiles of Indian women. New Delhi: Educational Resources Center, University of the State of New York, State Education Department, 1977. 56 pp.

Presents biographical sketches of a number of Indian women, including medical doctors, female vendors, teachers and a woman general. The book was developed under the sponsorship of the New York Sate Department of Education to strengthen the teaching of Indian studies in the secondary schools.

992. Rairikar, B.R. et al. Problems of Women Executives. Bombay: Lala Lajpatrai College Research Centre, 1978. 58 pp.

Examines the problems of women executives their jobs. Three questions are asked: what motivates women executives to aspire for managerial positions; are these motivations different from those of men; how are they accepted by their male subordinates, colleagues and bosses. Administers questionnaires to women executives in Bombay and 73 of their male subordinates, colleagues and bosses. All the women had high educational attainments. Finds that the nonmonetary factors have greater significance than monetary factors on the motivation, that these factors are not in any way different from those that motivate men and that three groups of males have favorable attitudes towards women in executive positions.

993. Srinivas, M.N. The Changing Position of Indian Women. Delhi: Oxford University Press, 1978. 30 pp.

Argues that social change for women in India is tied to urbanization and education. In rural areas high status women have not experienced changes in roles. In urban areas, however, high status Hindi women who get education become employed in the modern sector of the economy and in government with much the same status and power as men. However, these urban, educated women represent a very small percent of Indian women. Of urban women, only 40 percent are educated through the primary grades and only 1 percent are university graduates or postgraduates. Of the 900,000 university educated women in India, 50 percent are primary school teachers, 15 percent are secondary school teachers, and 15 percent become clerks and typists. Only 20 percent are doctors, lawyers and administrators. Identifies the following as preconditions to changing women's status: 1) movement to urban areas; 2) education; 3) marriage to a more highly educated man.

Trivedi, Sheela.   Non-Formal Education for Women Officers (Education Department U.P.) Lucknow: Literacy House, 1976.

See item #630

Articles

Agarwal, Bina.   "Exploitative Utilization of Educated Womanpower." Journal of Higher Education 2 (Autumn 1976): 186-195.

See item #546

Bhargava, Gura. "Intra-Professional Marriage: Mate Choices of Medical Students in India." Social Science and Medicine 17 (1983): 413-417.

See item #548

Krishnaraj, Maithreyi. "Research on Women and Career: Issues of Methodology." Economic and Political Weekly 21 (October 25, 1986): WS 67-74.

See item #71

994. Krishnaraj, Maithreyi.   "Women, Work and Science in India." Women's Education in the Third World: Comparative Perspectives. Edited by Gail P. Kelly and Carolyn M. Elliott. Albany: SUNY Press, 1982, pp. 249-263.

Studies role conflict among women scientists in India. Interviews were conducted with 400 women scientists, 80 percent of whom were Hindus, 8 percent Christians and 2 percent Muslims. Over 60 percent were married. Finds that women were content with their jobs, even though they believed that they were discriminated against in employment and job advancement. They were pleased to have a job in their field of study, given high underemployment rates in India. In addition, the women scientists tended to compartmentalize their scientific beliefs and confine them to the workplace. Concludes that science educated women have traditional values because the family is the major institution in society through which individuals gain their identity. A scientific education's impact on women's values is limited because science in India still confers status within the existing social structure rather than changes the social structure.

995. Strivastava, Vinita. "Professional Education and Attitudes to Female Employment: A Study of Married Working Women in Chandiagarh." **Social Action** 27 (1977): 19-30.

Studies 150 working women and a matched sample of housewives to find out whether professional education develops favorable attitudes to employment and insures job satisfaction. Finds that number of years of education is more significant than the type of education women receive in changing women's attitudes toward work. College educated women in the laborforce have attitudes supportive of women's employment and are more able to juggle occupational and family demands.

4.   Latin America and the Caribbean

Books and Monographs

996. Andradi, Esther and Ana Maria Portugal. **Ser Mujer en el Perú.** Lima: Tokapu Editores S.A., 1979.

Presents the life histories of 17 Peruvian women about the relationship between their roles as wives and mothers and their professions.

997. Bruschini, M.C. Aranha. "Mulher e Trabalho: Engenheiras, Enfermeiras e Professoras." **Cadernos de Pesquisa,** 27 (1978): 3-17.

Studies women in the professions, particularly in engineering, medicine and teaching in higher education. Special attention is given to socioeconomic background, ethnic origin, mother's occupation, socialization patterns and to number of children and marital status.

Articles

998. Cohen, Lucy M. "Women's Entry to the Professions in Colombia: Selected Characteristics." **Journal of Marriage and the Family** 35 (1973): 322-329.

Interviews 100 professional women who graduated from Colombian universities between 1940 and 1955. Examines their career experiences and life in the family. Finds family members, teachers or significant others encourage these women's professional lives and that their husbands support their wives careers.

Fernández Berdaguer, Maria Leticia. "Educación Universitaria y Desempeño Profesional: El Case de la Mujeres Estudiantes de Ciencias Económicas de la Universidad de Buenos Aires." Revista Paraguaya de Sociologia 20 (1983): 75-97.

See item #560

999. Kinzer, Nora Scott. "Women Professionals in Buenos Aires." Female and Male in Latin America. Edited by Ann Pescatello. Pittsburgh: University of Pittsburgh Press, 1973, pp. 159-190.

Interviews 125 professional women residents of Buenos Aires, Argentina working in masculine or neuter professions. Describes their background, the education and SES of the subjects' fathers and husbands, the subjects' religious affiliation and marital status. Describes how these women cope in a machismo society where male superiority is carried to the extreme.

1000. Kinzer, Nora Scott. "Sociocultural Factors Mitigating Role Conflict of Buenos Aires Professional Women." Women Cross-Culturally: Change and Challenge. Edited by Ruby Rohrlich-Leavitt. The Hague: Mouton, 1975, pp. 181-198.

Studies 125 professional women employed full time in Buenos Aires, Argentina, to look at role conflict. Finds that role conflict is affected by societal norms and legal constraints, social class background, job role relationship, attitude of spouse and attitudes of children.

1001. Miller, Beth and Alfonso Gonzales. 26 Autoras del México Actual. México: B. Costa-Amie, 1978. 463 pp.

Looks at women's impact on the national cultural and intellectual life. Contains brief biographies, including education background, of 26 female authors followed by a personal interview. The interviews attempt to trace intellectual roots and to comment on the current period's intellectual trends. The list of women include those who live in Mexico not necessarily those born there.

1002. Moses, Yolanda. "What Price Education: The Working Women of Montserrat." Anthropology and Education Quarterly 6 (August 1975): 13-16.

Argues that middle class, professionally educated married women have a strong place in the family. Women will follow their husbands' careers but decisions are made jointly. Professional unmarried women have little place in society. Less educated married women were under the control of the husbands. Less educated unmarried women have the greatest freedom; supported by female kin, they have few restrictions in terms of child bearing, work schedules, etc.

5.   The Middle East

Books and Monograph

1003. Abadan-Unat, Nermin. **Women in the Developing World: Evidence from Turkey.** Denver: University of Denver School of International Studies, 1986. 199 pp. (Monograph Series in World Affairs no. 22)

Provides a collection of essays Abadan-Unat has written about Turkish women, many of which have been published earlier. The articles in Part I ask whether the changes in women's legal status, increases in educational opportunity and increases in workforce participation have resulted in equality. Finds that since the 1920s a professional elite has arisen in Turkey with greater authority and in greater numbers than in Western Europe. Education has not liberated women. In large part the author speculates that this is because women persist in attitudes about their roles that place the family and the role of mother and wife first. While Turkey has developed a large female professional elite, the illiteracy rates in the country remain high. In the workforce women are segregated into discrete occupations. Most women are employed in agriculture as they traditionally have been. Highly educated women concentrate in government employment and administrative positions in education, social services, tourism and information. Cites surveys of professional women that show they stress family over work.

Articles

1004. Oncu, Ayse. "Turkish Women in the Professions: Why So Many?" **Women in Turkish Society.** Edited by Nermin Abadan-Unat. London: E.J. Brill, 1981, pp. 181-193.

Focuses on the question of why there are so many Turkish women in the prestigious professions—law and medicine. One in every five practicing lawyers in Turkey is female, and one in every six practicing doctors is again female. Concludes in Turkey, the range of work opportunities in the professional labor market for women is wider than in the most industrialized societies of the West. There are high proportions of women in professional schools and also in the professional labor market. Law, medicine and dentistry constitute a "cluster" of occupations that appear as women's options. Those women in the highest ranking professions are predominantly drawn from urban, professional or civil service backgrounds.

1005. Howard-Merriam, Kathleen. "Women, Education and the Professions in Egypt." **Comparative Education Review** 23 (1979): 256-270.

Describes post 1952 Egyptian government attempts to increase the number of women entering the professions. Points out that despite these measures, university education is still limited to urban upper and middle class women due to the government's failure to provide primary and secondary education in rural areas. Women's professional equality has been hindered by uneven economic development and an oversupply in some professions for university graduates.

XII. WOMEN'S EDUCATION AND THE FAMILY

The research studies listed here focus on the impact of women's education on life in the family. Such studies look at the impact of women's schooling on marriage patterns, on maternal behavior, on children's schooling and school achievement and on childhood nutrition and health care. Many of these studies lack a feminist orientation: they ask about women's roles as wives and mothers in patriarchial families and presume woman's role as child bearer and child rearer, guardian of her family's health and nutrition. Few if any studies ask whether education changes power relations within the family.

We have separated studies of women's education and fertility from those relating women's schooling to the family. Fertility studies are listed in secion XIII of this bibliography.

1. General

Books and Monographs

Paolucci, Beatrice et al. **Women, Families and Non-Formal Learning Programs.** East Lansing: Institute for International Studies in Education, Michigan State University, Program of Studies in Non-Formal Education, 1976. 102 pp. (Supplementary Paper no. 6)

See item #580

Weeks-Vagliani, Winifred and Bernard Grossat. **Women in Development: At The Right Time for the Right Reasons.** Paris: Development Centre of the Organization for Economic Cooperation and Development, 1980. 330 pp.

See item #671

Smock, Audrey Chapman. **Women's Education in Developing Countries: Opportunities and Outcomes.** New York: Praeger, 1981. 292 pp.

See item #374

Articles

1006. "A Report from UNICEF--Perspective 1983. State of the World's Children." UN Chronicle (February 1983): 57-71.

Focuses on the nutritional, health and educational status of children world-wide, particularly in the third world. Finds that although visible malnutrition and starvation have declined, they have been replaced by a less visible form of malnutrition. Finds also that 60 percent of mothers did not recongize malnutrition in their children. Urges that maternal education in health matters be instituted.

1007. Caldwell, J.C. "Maternal Education as a Factor in Child Mortality." World Health Forum 2 (no. 1, 1981): 75-78.

Cites several articles that show higher maternal education levels are related to lower child mortality. Argues this results from educated women's willingness to break from tradition and to take a less fatalistic attitude.

1008. Chen, Lincoln C. "Child Survival: Levels, Trends and Determinants." Determinants of Fertility in Developing Countries. Edited by Rodolfo A. Bulatao and Ronald D. Lee. New York: Academic Press, 1983, pp. 199-232.

Reviews childhood mortality levels, trends and patterns in the major developing regions of the world. Presents a conceptual framework that delineates the proximate variables of child mortality. These variables include paternal and maternal education, nutrition and diet, infectious disease and childcare. Concludes with a review of current hypotheses regarding the impact of mortality control policies and health intervention programs.

Finegan, T.A. "Participation of Married Women in the Labour Force." Sex Discrimination and the Division of Labour. Edited by Cynthia B. Lloyd et al. New York: Columbia University Press, 1975, pp. 27-60.

See item #809

1009. Kakar, D.N. "Planning Culturally Relevant Nutrition Education Programmes: What Can Anthropologists Do?" Journal of Family Welfare 23 (September 1976): 45-53.

Examines the state of nutrition education in India and finds it lacking. Argues that social scientists can increase the effectiveness of nutrition education programs by providing information on how to communicate, what to communicate, the structure of communities and the knowledge of local food and nutrition resources. Urges the social science community to share research techniques to aid nutrition experts in planning cultural relevant nutrition programs for women.

1010. LeVine, R.A. "Influences of Women's Schooling on Maternal Behavior in the Third World." Comparative Education Review 24 (1980): S78–S105. (Also in Women's Education in the Third World: Comparative Perspectives. Edited by Gail P. Kelly and Carolyn M. Elliott. Albany: SUNY Press, 1982, pp. 283–310.)

Asks whether better educated women make better mothers in that a) their children are better nourished; b) their children do better in school. Reviews the data from Latin America and Africa and finds that, given the fragmentary nature of current data, it is difficult to sort out the effect of education from family income, urban residence and media exposure. Concludes that while no clearcut relation can be identified between education and maternal behavior, there is evidence to indicate that maternal behavior is different among educated women lesser educated women and that the children of educated women do better on school tests.

1011. Safilios-Rothschild, Constantina. "A Cross-Cultural Examination of Women's Marital, Educational and Occupational Option." Acta Sociologica 14 (1971): 96–113.

Examines women's marital, educational and occupational options in a number of countries. Finds that there is no linear relation between level of economic development and women's options to marry, pursue a career and obtain education. Finds also increasing chances for married women to combine family and work and that these options are often greater in developing than in industralized societies.

2.   Africa

Books and Monographs

1012. Buvinić, Mayra et al. Individual and Family Choices for Child Survival and Development: A Framework for Research in Sub-Saharan Africa. Washington, D.C.: International Center for Research on Women. 1987. 82 pp.

Examines the factors that influence parental decision making and child rearing practices in Africa focusing on women. The purpose of the paper is to respond to the concern of development agencies to encourage families to invest in child development by exploring what factors affect women's acceptance and continued use of newly introduced child survival and development services and practices. The second chapter presents the conceptual model with a brief review of concepts from different disciplines. The third chapter reviews the community, household and individual factors affecting women's choices to utilize certain child rearing practices and services in the African context. The section on women's education asks how variations in women's education affect child development outcomes. Suggests that education affects both women's ability and motivational variables and therefore encourage women to adopt new childrearing strategies by increasing their beliefs of internal control and their risk taking preferences. The last chapter presents questions and hypotheses for the design of policy relevant research derived from the model and the review of the literature.

1013. Oppong, Christine and Katherine Abu. **The Changing Maternal Role of Ghanaian Women: Impacts of Education, Migration and Employment.** Geneva: World Employment Programme, 1984. 184 pp. (Population and Labour Policies Programme, Working Paper no. 143.)

Reports on an in depth survey project using extensive biographical research technique. Looks at women from different ethnic groups in Ghana. Includes a sample of 60 women who received comparable levels of education depending on age and area. Almost all strove for an occupational role and received high satisfaction from it. Most attempted to change family and kin relations (although most felt frustrated in this aspect of their lives). Contains very individualized and complex portraits of women's lives.

Weinrich, A.K.H. **Women and Racial Discrimination in Rhodesia.** Paris: UNESCO, 1979. 143 pp.

See item #131

Articles

1014. Barrow, R. Nata. "Women in the Front Line of Health Care." **Convergence** 15 (1982): 82-84.

Reports on the Sixth Commonwealth Health Ministers' Conference held in Tanzania in 1980 which focused on women in health. The meeting was attended by 40 women from 36 countries. Argues that rural women need education on hygiene, safe water and nutrition, given the fact that these women have great responsibility for their families. Sees rural women's education as key to improved health status in the countryside of third world nations.

Butter, Irene. Women and Health Care Personnel Planning." **Women: Health and International Development.**   Edited by Margaret Aguwa.   East Lansing: International Development and

African Studies Center, Michigan State University, 1982, pp. 21-32.

See item #977

1015. Caldwell, J.C. "Education as a Factor in Mortality Decline: An Examination of Nigerian Data." Population Studies 33 (1979): 395-413.

Examines the relation between women's education and lower child mortality rates using two samples of women (6606 in one and 1499 in the second) in Nigeria. Finds a that woman's education, along with father's occupation, area of residence, family planning practices and other variables were associated with lowered child mortality rates, but that mother's education was the most significant. Explains the effect of women's education in terms of the effect of education on women's knowledge about food and nutrition, on women's sense of efficacy, on women's awareness of modern medicine, and on improved women's self-concept and enhanced power to demand needs of children be given priority.

1016. Lewis, Barbara C. "Economic Activity and Marriage among Ivoirian Urban Women." Sexual Stratification: A Cross-Cultural View. Edited by Alice Schlegal et al. New York: Columbia University Press, 1977, pp. 161-191.

Explores education's effect on women's laborforce participation, earnings and marriage based on surveys, interviews and observations of 800 women, aged 20 to 44 years, in Abidjan, Ivory Coast. Despite the long tradition of women's laborforce participation in the Ivory Coast and women's economic independence, men are still crucial in determining the economic status of women. This occurs despite the increases in women's educational attainment. Education tends to be used to gain a woman a well educated husband who can find her a salaried position in the modern sector of the economy. Educated women are seen as more desirable mates than uneducated women because their earning potential is higher, despite the fact that women still earn less than similarly educated men.

1017. Oppong, Christine. "Women's Roles and Conjugal Family Systems in Ghana." The Changing Position of Women in Family and Society. Edited by Eugen Lupri. Leiden: E.J. Brill, 1983, pp. 331-343.

Discusses women and the family in Ghana comparing with other regions of the world to look for potential consequences for women of their economic participation in different types of women's roles in the family. Explains four kinds of conjugal family role systems according to family type and the conjugal division of labor and points out that while many wives prefer open/joint type family, educated women in Ghana are facing the growing difficulty in combining household chores, child care and a profession. Contends that collective action of women is needed in order to challenge the deteriorating position of women in West Africa.

1018. Orubuloye, I.O. Education and Socio-Demographic Change in Nigeria: The Western Nigerian Experience." Education and Modernization of the Family in West Africa. Edited by Helen Ware. Canberra: Department of Demography, Australian National University, 1981, pp. 22-41. (Changing African Family Project Series Monograph no. 7)

Examines the extent to which education has influenced socio-demographic changes, such as the individual life style, age at marriage, polygyny, and fertility in Western Nigeria. Based on the data from Nigerian survey, argues that rising age at marriage is closely associated with extended education, that the increasing cost of raising children has stronger effect on the diminution of polygyny than education, and that extended education has a significant impact on fertility decline especially in urban areas. Concludes that education will continue to play in important role in these changes, but that it will depend on the size of school intakes at both the secondary and tertiary levels of education.

1019. Tardits, Claude. "Reflexions sur le Problème de la Scolarisation des Filles au Dahomey." Cahiers des Études Africaines 3 (1962): 266-281.

Contrasts attitudes of educated versus uneducated women in Dahomey and finds that educated women chose their own husbands and are more imdependent than are their uneducated peers. Educated women tend to share housework and child care more with their husbands. Most women, regardless of educational levels, want their daughters to become government functionaries and not become traders, which is a traditionally female occupation. Argues one reason for the undereducation of girls in Dahomey is the belief that educated girls are a "menace" to traditional values. Another reason is the conflict between school and girls' economic activities.

3.   Asia

Books and Monographs

Chaudhury, Rafiqul Huda. Married Women in Urban Occupations of Bangladesh: Some Problems and Issues. Dacca: Bangladesh

Institute of Development Studies, 1976.   92 pp.   (Research
Report Series, New Series no. 22)

See item #842

Hafeez, Sabeeha.   The Metropolitan Women in Pakistan: Studies.
Karachi: Royal Book Company, 1981.   406 pp.

See item #889

Tomeh, Aida K.   Familial Sex Role Attitudes among College
Students in Korea.   East Lansing: Office of Women in
International Development, Michigan State University, 1982.   23
pp.   (Working Paper no. 12)

See item #526

Articles

1020. DaVanzo, Julie and Jean-Pierre Habicht.   "Infant Mortality
Decline in Malaysia, 1946-1975:   The Roles of Changes in
Variables and Changes in the Structure of Relationships."
Demography 23 (1986): 143-160.

Assesses the role of some factors that may have affected infant
mortality in Malaysia, focusing on mother's education, household
water and sanitation, breastfeeding, length of preceding birth
interval and mother's ethnicity.   Using data from Malaysian
Family Life Survey, shows that mother's education and
improvements in water and sanitation contributed to the infant
mortality decline, that the substantial reduction in
breastfeeding has kept the infant mortality rate from declining
as rapidly as it would have otherwise and that birth interval
has had little effect.

Korson, J. Henry.   "Career Constraints among Women Graduate
Students in a Developing Society: West Pakistan."   Women in
Family and Economy: An International Comparative Survey.
Edited by George Kurian and Ratna Ghosh.   Westport, Conn.:
Greenwood Press, 1981, pp. 393-411.

See item #891

1021. Kok-Hautlee.   "Age at First Marriage in Peninsular Malaysia."
Journal of Marriage and the Family 44 (1982): 785-798.

Examines the socioeconomic determinants of age at first marriage
among ever-married women aged 25 and above in 1974 in peninsular
Malaysia.   Investigates both interage and intra-age components
of the variation in age at first marriage within a causal
structural framework employing standard path analysis and
hierarchial analysis of covariance.   Finds that there is a basic

temporal increase in age at first marriage; that education, ethnicity and premarital work duration have the strongest impact on marriage postponement while premarital occupational status and premarital work status have lesser effects.

1022. Manderson, Lenore. "Bottle Feeding and Ideology in Colonial Malaya: The Production of Change." International Journal of Health Services 12 (1982): 597–616.

Traces the development of maternal and child health services in colonial Malaya and shows how the media, industry and the medical profession promoted bottle feeding rather than breast feeding.

1023. Wong, Aline. "Maternal Employment, Education and Changing Family Values in Singapore." Journal of Economic Development and Social Change 6 (1976): 23–40.

Investigates the effect of material employment and education on decision-making in the family. Surveys 900 Chinese Singaporean women who had between 1 and 3 children. Finds that with increasing female education and workforce participation, more egalitarian patterns of household decision making have evolved. Women who have more education and who are in the workforce, as compared with nonworking women with lesser amounts of education, tend to be more "modern" in their attitudes.

1024. Salaff, Janet W. "The Status of Unmarried Hong Kong Women and the Social Factors Contributing to their Delayed Marriage." Population Studies 30 (1976): 391–412.

Interviews 28 working women aged 18 to 29 in Hong Kong over a three year period to look at the reasons for delayed marriage. Finds that women's obligation to support their parents and to repay education debts is related to delayed marriage as well as women's reluctance to take on the double load of work and marriage.

1025. Sjafri, Aida. "Socio-Economic Aspects of Food Consumption in Rural Java." The Endless Day: Some Case Material on Asian Rural Women. Edited by T. Scarlett Epstein and Rosemary A. Watts. New York: Pergamon Press, 1981, pp. 107–127.

Discusses food consumption in Javanese rural households by examining the role of women in access to food and in intra household food distribution. The hypothesis suggested by the data obained from the Applied Nutrition Programme and others, that employment, education, income and food habits are the most important factors that influence food consumption by villagers, is tested by describing profiles of five households in rural Indonesia.

3a.   India

Books and Monographs

Blumberg, Rhoda Lois and Leela Dwaraki. **India's Educated Women: Options and Constraints.** Delhi: Hindustan   Publishing Corporation, 1980.

See item #987

Devi, Lalitha U. **Status and Employment of Women in India.** Delhi: B.R. Publishing Corp., 1982. 186 pp.

See item #857

Goldstein, Rhoda L. **Indian women in Transition: A Bangalore Case Study.** Metuchen: Scarecrow Press, 1972. 172 pp.

See item #541

Jesudason, Victor et al (ed.) **Non-Formal Education for Rural Women to Promote the Development of the Young Child.** New Delhi: Allied Publishers, 1982. 419 pp.

See item #626

1026. Kapadia. K.M. **Marriage and Family in India.** Delhi: Oxford University Press, 1966. 387 pp.

Focuses on Hindu and Muslim views of the family and discusses polyandray, polygyny, age at marriage, the family in an urban setting, and the erosion of the Hindu joint family. Chapter 11, which focuses on the status of women, includes educational statistics for 1930/31 through 1960. Argues that modernization, urbanization and education have put strains on the Indian family structure and has led to the development of the conjugal family with more egalitarian relations.

Kapur, Promilla. **The Changing Status of the Working Woman in India.** Delhi: Vikas Publishing House, Ltd., 1974. 178 pp.

See item #860

Liddle, Joanna and Rama Joshi. **Daughters of Independence: Gender, Caste and Class in India.** London: Zed Books, 1986. 264 pp.

See item #990

Mehta, Rama. The Western Educated Hindu Woman. Bombay: Asia
Publishing House, 1970.

See item #543

1027. Mies, Maria. Indian Women and Patriarchy: Conflicts and
      Dilemmas of Students and Working Women. Delhi: Concept
      Publishing, 1973. 266 pp.

      Focuses on role conflict among female students and women in the
      workforce in India, with particular emphasis on the strains that
      work outside the household place on women. The study begins
      with an analysis of the structure of the Indian family and how
      intra-family relations determine women's roles. Role conflicts
      were studied via 15 biographies taken on women in Poona and
      Bombay in 1966-67 and follow-up interviews with the same women
      conducted in 1970. Despite the role conflicts these women
      experience, concludes that educated women do deviate from the
      ideology of women's roles among upper caste women.

1028. Roy, Shibani. Status of Muslim Women in North India. Delhi:
      B.R. Publishing, 1979. 241 pp.

      Reports a field survey of 300 Muslim women, 150 from Delhi and
      150 from Lucknow. The survey was conducted in 1970-72. The
      sample consisted of three generations: 55.92 percent were aged
      15 to 34 years, 25.33 percent aged 35-49 years and 18.75 percent
      over age 50. Asks what the impact of modern secular education
      is on attitudes and values of Muslim women. Begins by tracing
      women's educational backgrounds and attitudes toward education.
      Finds that all the women could read Arabic and most could read
      Urdu as well. A large proportion of the older generation was
      educated solely in the home in traditional Koranic traditions.
      They did learn Urdu and several passed school examinations,
      tutored in secret by their male relatives. Most women in the
      older two generations reported parental opposition to their
      education outside the home. However, the data indicate over
      time women have increasingly gone to school, but their formal
      education has tended to be in Muslim state-subsidized single-sex
      schools close to home. Finds that more upper class women tend
      to go to school longer in all three generations than lower class
      women; lower class women tend to be home-educated. Educated
      women tend to be married to more educated men and tend to be
      more supportive of their daughter's education. Surveys the role
      of education in marriage and the family. Finds that women's
      roles in the family did shift over time. Educated women tended
      to take on more educational roles within the household and have
      different relations with their husbands. Educated women do tend
      to marry later and their sphere of activity in the household has
      broadened. Despite this, they are still subordinate to their
      husbands and confined to the private domestic sphere. Education
      has not changed these women's roles in the workforce.

Ramanamma, A.   Graduate Employed Women in an Urban Setting.
Poona: Dastane Ramchandra and Company, 1979. 159 pp.

See item #863

Srivastava, Vinita.   Employment of Educated Married Women in
India (Its Causes and Consequences). New Delhi: National
Publishing House, 1978. 192 pp.

See item, #867

Talwar, Usha. Social Profile of Working Women.   Jodhpur, India:
Jain Brothers, 1984. 252 pp.

See item #868

Articles

1029. Ahmad, Shabans.   "Education and Purdah Nuances: A Note on
Muslim Women in Aligarh." Social Action 27 (no. 1, 1977):
45-52.

Inquires as to whether educated women observe purdah.   Finds
that over one fourth of the secondary educated women continued
to observe purdah in varying degrees. Finds also that women's
education is valued as a means of finding a well educated,
middle class husband.

Bhargava, Gura.   "Intra-Professional Marriage: Mate Choices of
Medical Students in India."   Social Science and Medicine 17
(1983): 413-417.

See item #548

1030. Conklin, George H.   "Cultural Determinants of Power for Women
within the Family: A Neglected Aspect of Family Research."
Women in the Family and the Economy: An International
Comparative Survey.   Edited by George Kurian and Ratna Ghosh.
Westport, Conn.: Greenwood Press, 1981, pp. 9-27.

Examines power differences within the household between husband
and wife in a non-Western setting and compares the findings with
those of the previous studies in the United States. Argues that
unlike in the United States where competence was found to be the
strongest predictor, both culture and competence are important
in determining conjugal power in India, and that increased
education leads to increased power for women which is correlated
with kinship accommodation instead of kinship exclusion.

D'Souza, Alfred.   "Women in India and South Asia: An
Introduction."   Women in Contemporary India and South Asia.

Edited by Alfred D'Souza. New Delhi: Moa Manohar
Publications, 1980, pp. 1-29.

See item #875

1031. Gopaldes, Tara et al.   "Nutritional Impact of Anti-Parasitic
      Drugs.   Prophylatic Vitamin A and Iron-Folic Acid on
      Underprivileged School Girls in India." **Nutritional Research** 3
      (1983): 831-844.

      Determines the most widely prevalent nutritional and related
      public health disorders among underprivileged school girls and
      assesses the feasibility, efficiency, impact and cost of
      delivering different packages of health/nutrient inputs.
      Samples utilized are 170 school girls aged 5-13 years who were
      not participants of the midday meal program and who manifested
      nutritional anaemia, mixed parasitic infestations and vitamin A
      deficiency.   Confirms previous reports of wide prevalence of
      nutritional anaemia and higher than average prevalence of
      vitamin A deficiency among school children.

1032. Gulati, Subhash Chander.   "Impact of Literacy, Urbanization and
      Sex-Ratio on Age at Marriage in India."   Artha Vijriana 11
      (1969): 685-697.

      Examines the impact of overall education, urbanization and sex
      ratio on age at marriage for both sexes at the state level in
      India, based on the data from the 1961 census and other sources.
      Finds that the overall spread of education is more conducive to
      late marriages than the level of urbanization and more effective
      among females than males, and that lower sex ratios induce males
      to marry early and females to marry late. As a whole it is the
      literacy level which has the most significant effect on the late
      marriage for both sexes.

      Jhabvala, Renana and Pratima Sinba.   "Between School and
      Marriage--A Delhi Sample."   Indian **Women**.   Edited by Devabe
      Jain.   New Delhi: Publications Division, Ministry of
      Information and Broadcasting, Government of India, 1975,
      pp. 283-287.

See item #552

1033. Kale, B.D.   "Education and Age at Marriage of Female in India."
      Journal of Institute of Economic Research 4 (1969): 59-74.

      Examines the relationship of education with age at marriage.
      Finds out that the greater the number of years a girl spends in
      the school, the more likely it is that she would be married at
      an older age. Concludes that education explains to a very great
      and satisfactory extent the regional variations in age at
      marriage in India, especially in urban India.   Points out that

greater efforts to encourage female education would indirectly work towards raising the age of marriage. Suggests that policy makers and planners should consider whether the age of compulsory education can be enforced at nothing less than 13 or 14 years in the urban areas, and that more facilities in the middle school and higher secondary stage in the form of free tuition, free books, free uniform should be provided for the purpose of attracting a large number of students.

Kurian, George and Mariam John. "Attitudes of Women Towards Certain Selected Cultural Practices in Kerala State, India." **Women in the Family and Economy:** An International Comparative Survey. Edited by George Kurian and Ratna Ghosh. Westport, Conn.: Greenwood Press, 1981, pp. 131-142.

See item #401

1034. Minturn, et al. "Increased Maternal Power Status, Changes in Socialization in a Restudy of Rajput Mothers of Khalapur, India." **Journal of Cross-Cultural Psychology** 9 (1978): 483-498.

Presents a follow-up investigation of 38 mothers who came from the families of 24 women previously studied in a 1954 survey. Finds that increase in education has gained daughters greater status and power in the family than lesser educated mothers had. The women included in the 1975 study reported here were more assertive and had greater privacy than did the 1954 sample.

1035. Prasad, M.B. et al. "Perception of Parental Expectations and Need Achievement." **Journal of Social Psychology** 109 (1979): 301-302.

Correlates the need achievement scores of 260 second year college students in South Bihar, India, with parental encouragement and discouragement. Finds that high need achievement scores correlated with fathers being the key parent offering support while low need achievement scores correlated with mother as the source of suppprt and encouragement.

1036. Vijayaraghavan, K. et al. "India Population Project, Karnataka: Evaluation of Nutritional Activities." **Hygie: Revue Internationale d'Education pour Sante** 1 (no. 3-4, 1982): 9-14.

Shows significant gains from health education programs on nutrition, immunization and prevention of disease with about 50 percent of mothers attending sessions taking positive action. Knowledge reaches a low proportion of those not attending and the authors decry even their 50 percent success--urging more activity in this area since it can be shown to work.

3b.   Philippines

Articles

Flores, Pura M.   "Carer Women and Motherhood in a Changing Society."   Philippine Educational Forum 14 (1965): 50-56.

See item #896

Guerrero, Sylvia H.   "An Analysis of Husband-Wife Roles Among Filipino Professionals at U.P. Los Banos Campus."   Philippine Sociological Review 13 (1965): 275-281.

See item #984

1037. Maglangit, Virginia R.   "The Maranao Woman: Growing Up, Education, Courtship and Marriage."   Solidarity 9 (1975): 36-42.

Describes the life of Maranao women in the Philippines.   The Maranaos, who are Muslims, have long isolated themselves from other parts of the Philippines and have not been exposed to modern influences until the early 1960s.   Only a few rural families send their children to school out of fear of their being Christianized, while in the urban areas attitudes toward education and social mores have undergone changes.   Urban Maranao women can go to coeducational school.   Most of those who go to college become teachers, but few become physicians, nurses, engineers and lawyers.   Some go to Arabic schools which are coeducational and require lower tuition fees and expenses. The Maranao women, especially educated women, do not approve of polygamy.   Contends that Islam has given the Maranao women equality, but that there is still a necessity to eliminate the customs and values that impede the progress of Maranao society while preserving good customs and identity.

1038. Smith, Peter C.   "Age at Marriage: Recent Trends and Prospects."   Philippine Sociological Review 16 (1968): 1-16.

Estimates the level and the trend of age at marriage in the Philippines in recent years by examining three types of data on marriage patterns.   The level of age at marriage can be set at about 20 years for females and 22.5 for males.   The age at marriage is higher for urban women than for rural women and for persons of higher educational and economic status levels.

Suggests that the recent rise in age at marriage is too small to have any effect on Philippine fertility.

1039. Tagumpay-Castillo, Gelia and Sylvia Hilomen-Guerrero. "The Filipino Woman: A Study in Multiple Roles." Journal of Asian and African Studies 4 (1969): 18-29.

Looks at the multiple roles of educated Filipino women in the Tagalog region, focusing on women's role in decision making in the family, the use of household help, their roles as wives and their role in family finances.

1040. Youngblood, R.L. "Female Dominance and Adolescent Filipino Attitude Orientations and School Achievement." Journal of Asian and African Studies 13 (1978): 65-80.

Asks how female headed households affect a child's political attitudes and behavior as well as the scholastic achievement of adolescents. The study was conducted in Manila in 1970 via questionnaires administered to 127 high school students ranging in age from 13 to 21 years old. Finds that female dominance (either where women are heads of household or are the major breadwinner) does affect childhood socialization patterns and attitudes. There were more identity conflicts in families where mothers were the major breadwinners and lower academic achievement among students from such families.

3c.   Taiwan

Articles

1041. Diamond, Norma. "The Middle Class Family Model in Taiwan: Women's Place is in the Home." Asian Survey 13 (1973): 853-872.

Explores changes in women's status in Taiwan and finds that it has deteriorated. Attributes the deterioration to the following: 1) women's entry into low paid jobs prior to marriage; 2) women's allocation into domestic labor, despite educational levels, after marriage; 3) the social isolation of women in urban Taiwan. Points out that higher education has done little to change this trend, since the ideology underlying female higher education is preparation for motherhood.

1042. Diamond, Norma. "The Status of Women in Taiwan: One Step Forward, Two Steps Back." Woman in China: Studies in Social Change and Feminism. Edited by Marilyn Young. Ann Arbor: Center for Chinese Studies, 1973, pp. 211-242. (Michigan Papers in Chinese Studies no. 15)

Describes women's status in Taiwan, in particular in various social, economic and cultural spheres which determine their position, and how it is degraded to a second class level in society. A brief period of advance in feminist ideology has retreated. Though there are more educated women than ever before, most of them have no choice but to become nonworking housewives which is held both as an ideal and a status symbol of a middle class family.

1043. Marsh, Robert and Albert O'Hara. "Attitudes toward Marriage and the Family in Taiwan." American Journal of Sociology 67 (1961): 1-8.

Examines the attitudes of undergraduates in Taiwan toward marriage and the family. A questionnaire was administered to 651 undergraduates in Taipei and 238 American undergraduates at the University of Michigan. Finds that important changes in non-kinship subsystems have begun to gain momentum in Taiwan due to the declining proportion of farmers in the laborforce, to increasing industralization and urbanization and the decline of the traditional monopoly of formal education by males.

1044. O'Hara, Albert R. "Changing Attitudes toward Marriage and Family in Free China." Journal of the China Society 2 (1962): 57-67.

Tests the changes that have taken place in university students' attitudes towards marriage and family life. Administers questionnaires to 651 Taiwanese students and 238 students at University of Michigan in the U.S. Finds Chinese and American students are nearly equally modern in respect to love as basis of choice of mate, the desire to choose one's mate independently, preference for the new (Western) style of marriage, interaction between the sexes at social gatherings, coeducation at the primary school and university level and engagement before marriage.

Olsen, Nancy J. "Changing Family Attitudes of Taiwanese Youth." in Value Change in Chinese Society. Edited by Richard W. Wilson et al. New York: Praeger Publishers, 1979, pp. 171-184.

See item #489

1045. Zhang, Shiao-chun. "The Role Played by Urban Housewives in Modern Society." The Institute of Ethnology Academia Sinica (Taipei) 37 (1974): 39-82.

Looks at the attitudes of educated housewives in Yenping and Daan Districts of the city of Taipei. Administers a questionnaire to a sample of 300 women and finds that most have modern attitudes and share decision making in the household.

4.   Latin America

Books and Monographs

Andradi, Esther and Ana Maria Portugal. Ser Mujer en el Perú.
Lima: Tokapu Editores S.A., 1979.

See item #996

1046. Barrig, Maruja. Cinturón de Castidad: La Mujer de Clase en el
Perú. San Isidro: Musca Azul Editores, 1982. 210 pp.

Focuses on women's roles in Peru and argues that the extension
of education has changed both societal expectations of women's
roles and middle class women's attitudes and expectations of
life in the family and the workforce.

Cisneros, Antonio J. Roles Femininos y Participación Económica
de la Mujer en el Contexto Socio Étnico Cultural de Bolivia. La
Paz: Centro de Investigaciones Sociales, 1978. 126 pp.

See item #901

Luzuriaga C., Carlos. Situación de la Mujer en El Ecuador.
Quito: Maurilia Mendoza de Jimenez, 1982. 180 pp.

See item #904

Articles

1047. Behrman, Jere R. and Barbara L. Wolfe. "More Evidence on
Nutrition: Income Seems Overrated and Women's Schooling
Underemphasized." Journal of Development Economics 14 (1984):
105-128.

Examines the importance of income, household size and women's
schooling in the determination of nutrient intakes, using the
data from 3726 household samples from Nicaraugua in 1977-1978.
Suggests that the elasticity for women's schooling is larger
than those for income or household size and the childhood
background of women is one of the significant factors. The
results also suggest that placing a strong emphasis on income
improvements is misleading.

1048. Bender, Deborah. "Women as Promoters of Health in the
Developing World." Women, Health and International Development.
Edited by Margaret I. Aguwa. East Lansing: Office of Women in
International Development and African Studies Center, Michigan
State University, 1982, pp. 7-20.

Describes a project in Bolivia which sought to improve the nutritional status of low income women and their children through food distribution and health education. The program failed because it did not use educational methods traditional to the Aymara people to whom the program was directed. A new program was constructed and run through mothers' clubs. It was based on interviews with the women. Argues that successful programs can only be built on the basis of existing interactions. Makes a series of recommendations for health programs.

Cohen, Lucy M. "Women's Entry to the Professions in Colombia: Selected Characteristics." Journal of Marriage and the Family 35 (1973): 322-329.

See item #998

1049. Gonzalez, Victoria Durant. "The Realm of Female Familial Responsibility." Women and the Family. Women in the Caribbean Project, Vol. 2. Edited by Joycelin Massiah. Cavehill, Barbados: Institute of Social and Economic Research, University of West Indies, 1982, pp. 1-27.

Discusses women's responsbility for child rearing and child caring in the English speaking Caribbean, based on the first phase of a long term, female centered research, Women in the Caribbean Project and the pilot study of 27 interviews. The concepts, sources of livelihood, power and authority and emotional support systems are used as the analytical devices to examine women and family, politics and work. Summarizes that a majority of Caribbean women are caught and bounced around in a set of conflicting cultural, economic and social forces which work both toward and against women's self interest.

Kinzer, Nora Scott. "Sociocultural Factors Mitigating Role Conflict of Buenos Aires Professional Women." Women Cross-Culturally: Change and Challenge. Edited by Ruby Rohrlich-Leavitt. The Hague: Mouton, 1975, pp. 181-198.

See item #1000

Moses, Yolanda. "What Price Education: The Working Women of Montserrat." Anthropology and Education Quareterly 6 (August 1975): 13-16.

See item #1002

1050. Rosen, Bernard C. and Anita L. LaRaia. "Modernity in Women: An Index of Social Change in Brazil." Journal of Marriage and the Family 34 (1972): 353-360.

Examines the relationship between industralization and some family linked attitudes and behavior of women in Brazil. Five communities were selected to represent points of the rural—urban—industrial continuum and 816 married women were interviewed. Finds that women in industrial communities have a greater sense of personal efficacy, participate more in family decision making as well as in activities outside the home and place a greater emphasis on independence and achievement in the socialization of their children than women in nonindustrial communities. These attitudes and behavior patterns are positively related to a woman's level of education, work experience, membership in voluntary associations and inversely related to her preferred and actual family size.

Thiret, Michele and Ann—Marie Coutrot. "L'Éducation aux Isles: Parents et Enfants de Guadeloupe." L'École des Parents 7 (1976): 50—59.

See item #652

5.   The Middle East

Articles

1051. Adams, Leah D. et al.   "Implications for Education and Child-Rearing: The Role of Women in the Middle East." School Psychology International 5 (1984): 167—174.

Traces changes in women's status and roles in the Middle East and argues that these changes will affect their children's school achievement.

1052. Al-Isi, Ismail, et al.   "Formal Education of Mothers and their Nutritional Behavior." Journal of Nutrition Education 7 (January—March 1975): 22—24.

Studies 60 mothers in Beirut, Lebanon, stratified by four levels of education (the top level was completion of grades 7 through 9). Measures nutritional knowledge by a standard test and by growth pattern of children. Finds superior knowledge of nutrition correlated with more education.

1053. Bach, Rebecca et al.   "Mothers' Influence on Daughters' Orientations Toward Education: An Egyptian Case Study." Comparative Education Review 29 (1985): 375—384.

Focuses on the impact of mothers' education on daughters' educational level, marriage age and expected careers. Data were gathered in 1980—1982 through interviews with approximately 800 girls enrolled in Cairo's public schools. The average age of students was 15 while mothers' age averaged 44. Concludes that the more education women receive, the later they will marry, the more likely they are to marry men with high status occupations, the fewer the number of children they will have and the more education their daughters will obtain.

1054. Kagitcibasi, Cigdem. "Status of Women in Turkey: Cross-Cultural Perspectives." International Journal of Middle East Studies 18 (1986): 485-499.

Examines women's intrafamily statuses in Turkey from a comparative perspective. Focuses on family dynamics and interaction patterns as well as the place of women in the family. Finds out that the greater gains in women's intrafamily status are achieved through development and that the formal structural changes and the legal institutional reforms have a greater impact on some groups of women than others. Stresses that the change in women's intrafamily status is an inherent part of a pattern of change involving decreased filial loyalties and some preference and this pattern reflects a substantial shift from a male-centered and male-dominated family culture to one of more egalitarian relationships. This pattern is facilitated by urban employment of women in jobs which require education.

1055. Moracco, John C. and Arpy Mouses. "Relationship of Armenian School Children's Attitude toward School, Their Sex, Age, and Mother's Authoritarianism." International Journal of Sociology of the Family 7 (July-December 1977): 135-141.

Investigates the relationship of age, sex and mother's authoritarianism to elementary school children's attitude toward school. The sample included 96 randomly selected Armenian children in Beirut, Lebanon, in equal numbers of boys and girls. Measuring instruments utilized are the Semantic Differential (SD) for students and the authoritarian F-scale for their mothers. Finds that Armenian girls have more positive attitude towards school in general, but concepts dealing with personal concerns are scored more negatively than boys. Shows that the greater the mother's authoritarianism, the less positive are boys' attitudes toward school. For girls, the relationship is just the reverse. Age differences play no part in the relationship.

1056. Tezcan, Sahabat. "Health Problems of Turkish Women." Women in Turkish Society. Edited by Nermin Abadan-Unat. Leiden: Brill, 1981, pp. 96-106.

Studies the health problems of women ages 15 to 44 in Etimesgut. Finds the proportion of women with gynecological disorders rose as the number of pregnancies increased and that the proportion of women with induced abortions rose with women's educational level. Women who live in cities and/or who have a higher educational level are more motivated to limit family size than women living in rural areas and who have low educational levels.

XIII. WOMEN'S EDUCATION AND FERTILITY

The articles, book chapters, monographs and books included here focus almost exclusively on the impact of education on the number of children women bear. Some of these studies relate fertility to education via the relation between women's education and access to the workforce. Others see fertility reduction as the key to national economic development and thus see women's contribution to development in terms of contraception and limiting population growth.

1.   General

Books and Monographs

1057. Ali, Mohamed Adham. **Education, Fertility and Development: An Overview.** Khartom, Sudan: Economic and Social Research Council, National Council for Research, 1984. 36 pp. (Bulletin 11)

Reviews the research literature on education, fertility and development, including some feminist critiques of the women and development literature. Argues that education brings women into development via entry into production and through fertility regulation. There are several glaring inaccuracies in the citations.

1058. Cain, Mead. **Women's Status and Fertility in Developing Countries: Son Preference and Economic Security.** Washington, D.C.: The World Bank, 1984. 68 pp.

Examines the relationship between women's status, defined by the degree to which they are economically dependent on men, and fertility in developing countries. The first part of the book presents the theoretical point of view regarding fertility determinants and focuses on the value of children as security assets in developing country settings. The second part looks at women's status and fertility in terms of women's economic dependence and son preference. Argues that in societies where women are more dependent on men, sons will have greater preference and the fertility level will be considerably higher than in societies where women have greater economic independence and son preference is weaker. The final part presents a cross-national empirical analysis of women's status, patriarchial structure and fertility using the data from World Fertility Survey. Concludes that patriarchial structure and women's economic dependence are important mediators of fertility transition in the developing countries.

1059. Cochrane, Susan H. **Fertility and Education: What Do We Really Know?** Baltimore: Johns Hopkins University Press, 1979. 175 pp.

Explores the apparent inverse relationship between the level of educational attainment and fertility. Formulates a model which emphasizes such variables as age at the time of marriage, desired family size and contraceptive knowledge. Considers individual women's attitudes and education as determinants of family size as well as those of men along with community attitudes and level of education. Postulates that areas with low female literacy rates experience an increase in live births and child survival when education expands as a result of better health and nutritional conditions engendered. Education also may serve to decrease the use of traditional patterns of birth control such as lactation and abstinence. The critical point in the education and fertility relationship occurs when, due to the decrease in miscarriages and infant mortality rates, large numbers of pregnancies are no longer desired by either men, women or the communitites in which they live. Calls for additional research in the relation between education and women's marriage age and education, workforce participation and fertility.

1060. Repetto, Robert. **Economic Equality and Fertility in Developing Countries.** Baltimore: Johns Hopkins University Press, 1979. 186 pp.

Studies the relation between income distribution and fertility reduction and argues that economic development in and of itself does not mean that population growth will slow; rather declining gaps between rich and poor predict population decline, independent of the spread of education. Points out in the case study of Korea presented in chapter 4 that increasing women's levels of education, when matched with decreasing income differentials, does dramatically reduce population growth. Presents case studies of India (looking at the effect of land reform on population growth) and Puerto Rico (where increases in women's education does bear a nonlinear relation to reduced population growth) as well.

1061. Safilios-Rothschild, Constantina. **The Status of Women and Fertility in the Third World in the 1970-1980 Decade.** New York: Center for Policy Studies, the Population Council, 1985. 49 pp. (Working Paper no. 118)

Examines the relation between women's status, participation in paid workforce, access to schools and fertility based on data collected from 75 developing countries. Finds that women's economic activity rate has little relation to fertility rates and that in countries where fertility rates declined during the decade under study, women's status increased. Finds also that women's increased access to education and paid employment was related to declines in fertility rates.

Smock, Audrey Chapman. **Women's Education in Developing Countries: Opportunities and Outcomes.** New York: Praeger, 1981. 292 pp.

See item #374

1062. Ward, Kathryn B. **Toward A New Model of Fertility: The Effects of the World Economic System and the Status of Women on Fertility Behavior.** East Lansing: Michigan State University, Women in International Development, 1983. 32 pp. (Working Paper no. 20)

Argues that family planning programs are ineffective if they fail to take into account the effect of the world economic system and of the declining status of women which accompanies international market participation in third world countries. Points out that international markets have introduced goods that compete directly with women's products in third world countries. Women therefore withdraw from the economy and thereby lose status. With loss of status comes increases in fertility rates. Conducts a regression analysis for 1975 for all third world countries betwen fertility, women's status (including education) and their income generating powers to prove the point.

1063. Ware, Helen. **Women, Demography and Development.** Canberra: Australian National University, Development Studies Center, 1981. 242 pp. (Demography Teaching Notes no. 3)

Focuses on demographic aspects of development. Argues that women's status declines as a result of development and that this decline is most clearly seen in demographic terms. Women are treated in general throughout the third world less well than men. Develops the concept of underinvestment in women. Women are less well fed than are men, have less health care and little education. Chapter 3 focuses on fertility and education and points out that conceptualizing this relationship implies that control of fertility is the sole educational outcome for women (or ought to be) and that this is women's major contribution to development. Argues that such a view is oppressive. In Chapter 3 discusses the general finding that with increases in women's education levels, fertility rates decline in general, but this is not the pattern in the poorest of the LDCs. Lists the following as issues research has left unresolved: 1) the conditions under which education does not depress fertility; 2) the relative contributions of women's versus men's education to fertility rate decline; 3) why education makes a contribution to fertilty decline; 4) the relative cost of education versus other means of fertility control; 5) the effect of quality of education on fertility.

Weeks Vagliani, Winifred and Bernard Grossat. **Women in Development: At the Right Time for the Right Reasons.** Paris: Development Centre of the Organization for Economic Cooperation and Development, 1980. 330 pp.

See item #671

Women and Industrialization in Developing Countries. Vienna: United Nations Industrial Development Organization, 1981. 81 pp.

See item #673

1064. **Women, Population and Development.** New York: United Nations Fund for Population Activities, 1977.   47 pp.

Discuses the issues on women, population and development as a response of United Nations Fund for Population Activities (UNFPA) to the Action Plan of the International Women's Year Conference of 1975. Points out the following problems: there has been a bias against women in demographic studies and population and population programs regarding women's work and fertility; development activities have often had adverse impact on women by replacing women with men and machines; technological advancement and industralization do not really touch women's lives or provide them with either economic or social benefits. Maintains that progress towards the demographic goals of governments will be promoted by raising the status of women and by ensuring their full participation in setting economic, social and political goals to meet women's needs. The latter half of the book lists the Guidelines set by the Task Force to suggest how UNFPA activities should respond to women's special needs and requirements to achieve equal status and choice in such areas as data collection and analysis, information, education and communication, family planning and training.

Articles

1065. Calixto, Julia. "Education of Women in Developing Countries and Population Avalanche." **Science Review** 10 (1969): 20-26.

Examines the historical background and present factors of population growth in developing countries. Finds that the education of women and the eradication of illiteracy is one of

the foremost problems in developing countries and argues that
educational demands must be viewed in terms of labor power
specialities and skills. Points out that literacy and education
are mutually related with aspects of modernization and that
countries which are educationally behind will gain most by wise
application of their resources to education.

1066. Calixto, Julia. "The Education of Women in Developing Countries
and Population Avalanche." The Educational Dilemma of Women in
Asia. Edited by Alma de Jesus Viardo. Manila: Philippine
Women's University, 1969, pp. 1-18.

Analyses population growth trends and discusses the relation
betwen food supplies and population expansion. Argues that
women's education is directly related to population control and
urges its expansion as part of national plans to curb population
growth.

1067. Cochrane, Susan. "The Relationship between Education and
Fertility." Education and Modernization of the Family in West
Africa. Edited by Helen Ware. Canberra: Department of
Demography, Australian National University, 1981, pp. 154-178.
(Changing African Family Project Series Monograph no. 7)

Summarizes the relationship between education and fertility
based on the data from the author's books on education and
fertility. Points out that the frequent finding of the inverse
relationship between education and fertility is not likely
observed in the poorest societies, that education in the poorest
regions may increase fertility in the short run, but in the long
run adjustments to new circumstances may bring about a decline
in fertility. Suggests that more studies be done on education
and age adjusted fertility, the effect of education on several
variables which are important in determining fertility, the
channels through which education effects fertility and the
various results of education which are important in reducing
fertility. Concludes that education does not always lead to an
automatic reduction in fertility, but that increases in female
education versus male education and education in urban areas and
in the more literate countries are more likely to reduce
fertility, and that education might have strong effects in
minimizing the time lag between the factors increasing fertility
and countervailing forces which reduce it.

1068. Cochrane, Susan H. "Effects of Education and Urbanization on
Fertility." Determinants of Fertility in Developing Countries.
Vol. 2. Edited by Rodolf A. Bulatao and Ronald D. Lee. New
York: Academic Press, 1983, pp. 587-626.

Reviews the impact of education and urban residence on
fertility. Among the findings are the following: 1) the
effects of education on fertility vary as to whether male or

female education is considered; 2) female education is more often inversely related to fertility than is male education; 3) the effect of female education on depressing fertility rates is primarily through increasing age at marriage; 4) the differences in fertility rates between urban and rural populations are smaller than between the least and most educated populations and 5) the ways through which residence effects fertility are less understood than the ways in which education affects fertility.

1069. Colclough, Christopher. "The Impact of Primary Schooling on Economic Development: A Review of the Evidence." World Development 10 (1982): 167-185.

Examines the contribution of primary schooling to economic development. Argues that primary schooling increases labor productivity in both urban and rural sectors and that the economic returns to such investment are high. Discusses female education in terms of noneconomic effect of education. Finds that the amount of schooling received by females indirectly affects their fertility in three ways: 1) it offers the "biological supply" of children, 2) the demand for children tends to reduce with schooling, 3) the knowledge of how to regulate fertility through contraception increases with schooling. Also finds that infant and child mortality rates are lower the higher the mother's level of schooling and that a wife's education has a larger total effect on mortality than that of her husband.

1070. De Tray, Dennis N. "Population Growth and Educational Policies: An Economic Perspective." Population and Development. Edited by Ronald G. Ridker. Baltimore: The Johns Hopkins University Press, 1976, pp. 182-209.

Discuses the major features, assumptions and critiques of the household production model and reviews the role that education plays when this model is used to study the determinants of family size. Makes a number of specific recommendations concerning educational policy and outlines a research program to illuminate better the relation betwen education and fertility reduction.

1071. Dixon, Ruth B. "Education and Employment: Keys to Smaller Families." Journal of Family Welfare 22 (December 1975): 38-49.

Examines the relation between women's education, employment and ability to control the number and timing of her children. Points out that while there is a relationship, causation is unknown. Urbanization, for example, has a strong impact on fertility rates, so does employment (although some forms of employment have a stronger effect than do others). Concludes that more reliable models predicting the effect of education and employment on fertility rates need to be developed.

1072. Espenshade, T.   "The Value and Cost of Children."   Population
Bulletin 32 (April 1977): 49.

Summarizes the literature on the costs and benefits of children
world wide, including the U.S. and developing countries.   Argues
that parental perceptions of the value of children, coupled with
intensive empirical study will lead to the development of more
effective government policies.

1073. Holsinger, Donald and John D. Kasarda.   "Education and Human
Fertility: Sociological   Perspectives."   Population   and
Development.   Edited by Ronald G. Ridker, Baltimore: Johns
Hopkins University Press, (1976): 154-181.

Analyses the relationship betwen education and human fertility.
Points out that schooling influences fertility in three ways: a)
the influence of the environment, curriculum, and content of
schooling in shaping attitudes, values and beliefs toward
preferences concerning family size; b) the effect of education
on age at marriage, female laborforce participation, social
mobility, husband-wife communication, exposure to contraceptive
information and material and mortality and morbidity or children
and c) schooling may operate jointly with other independent
variables to have an interactive effect on fertility.   Concludes
that greater exposure to schooling will ultimately result in
declining fertility.   Points out that compulsory education is
not a practical policy solution in the less developed countries
because educational places are so severely limited in these
countries that more than an elementary education may never be
acquired by a majority of people.

1074. Jain, Anrudh K.   "The Effect of Female Education on Fertility:
A Simple Explanation."   Demography 18 (1981):   577-595.

Examines quantitatively the structure of the relationship
between women's education and fertility, based on data published
in First Country Reports of the World Fertility Surveys for
eleven   countries--Costa   Rica,   Colombia,   Dominican Republic,
Panama, Fiji, Korea, Malayasia, Pakistan, Sri Lanka, Thailand
and Indonesia.   Shows that educated women are relatively more
homogenous across nations than are women with no education in
terms of their average cumulative marital fertility.   A lack of
uniformity in the relationship between education and fertility
observed   cross   nationally   is   shown   to   be   due to   marked
differences among countries in the average fertility of women
with no education rather than to the differences in the average
fertility of educated women.   The structure of the relationship
is   similar   across   several   developing   countries.   Suggests that
advancement of women's education might be more influential in
reducing fertility than an increase in women's participation in
economic activities outside the home.   Hypothesizes that primary
education, by providing basic skills of numeracy and literacy,

enhances women's status within and outside their families and increases their access to information through printed materials. This brings changes in their general behavior including breast feeding, use of contraceptives and fertility.

1075. Menard, Scott. "Inequality and Fertility." Studies in Comparative International Development 20 (1985): 83-95.

Focuses on the relationship between inequality and fertility with empirical analysis of direct influences and tries to clarify the issues of the measurement of inequality. Using the data on 65 less developed countries, points out that a measure of the relative educational status of women emerges as one of three important predictors of fertility.

1076. Menard, Scott. "Fertility, Family Planning, and Development: Indirect Influences." Studies in Comparative International Development 21 (1986): 32-47.

Focuses on the indirect influences on changing fertility and on the direct and indirect influences of family planning efforts. Based on the data from 65 less developed countries, tries to clarify the relationships among fertility, family planning effort and development. Concludes that education, besides family planning effort, may play a more crucial role than is obvious in fertility reduction in less developed countries.

1077. Standing, Guy. "Women's Work Activity and Fertility." Determinants of Fertility in Developing Countries. Edited by Rodolfo A. Bulatao and Ronald D. Lee. New York: Academic Press, 1983, pp. 517-546.

Concludes that the influence of work activity on fertility remains unclear, whether type of employment, motivation, or area of employment is considered. Argues that schooling is the only variable with a significant and negative impact on desired fertility; employment as a separate variable was statistically insignificant and that economic activity exerts a tenuous influence on fertility--schooling and associated nondomestic employment may raise the expected age at which women first become pregnant, in turn lowering fertility.

1078. Timur, Serim. "Demographic Correlates of Women's Education." International Population Conference 3 (1977): 463-493.

Investigates the relationships between women's education, fertility and age at marriage. Reviews empirical evidence from different societies at varying stages of development and with varying family systems. Finds that although education is associated with fertility at the individual level, a particular educational level can not affect fertility at the same rate across countries nor between urban and rural areas even within the same country. In a number of high fertility countries, there is an indeterminate association between fertility and educational attainment. In number of developing countries, there is a clear-cut inverse association between female education and fertility. In some Western European countries, the inverse relationship previously existing between female educational achievement and family size has given way to a flat U-shaped relationship with the highest fertility rate occurring among the least and among the most educated groups. While literacy is strongly correlated with the time of female marriage, the differences in marrige age may be due to other factors which are largely determined by family systems that set the norms of "socially acceptable" age at marriage.

1079. Youssef, Nadia H. "The Status and Fertility Patterns of Muslim Women." **Women in the Muslim World.** Edited by Lois Beck and Nikki Keddie. Cambridge: Harvard University Press, 1978, pp. 69-99.

Relates available information on the fertility patterns of Muslims in North America, the Middle East and Asia to the status and position of women in Muslim social structures. Relies on the census data of 1974, United Nations publications and sample surveys conducted in the countries concerned. Deals with topics of women's fertility, status, pronatalism in Islamic doctrine, fertility and women's education and employment. In discussing education related issues, finds that women's literacy rate makes the greatest contribution to fertility levels. Higher female education is accompanied by considerably reduced fertility and a relatively high proportion of employment in professional jobs. The most relevant aspects of education for fertility regulation are delaying marriage and increasing the probability of nonmarriage; reducing desired family size by creating aspirations for higher levels of living and stimulating women's interest and involvement in extrafamilial activities; and exposing women to knowledge, attitudes and practices favorable to birth control communication.

2.   Africa

Books and Monographs

1080. Dow, Thomas E., Jr. and Linda H. Werner. **A Note on Modern, Transitional and Traditional Demographic and Contraceptive Patterns Among Kenyan Women's: 1977-78.** Nairobi: Population and Research Institute, University of Nairobi, 1981. 35 pp.

Studies more than 4000 ever married women and more than 1500 never married women and creates a four cell analysis on contraception practice (use or non-use) and family size (more than six children labeled traditional, less than six modern). Two thirds of ever married women were traditional on both dimensions. Uses variables of age, education (women's and spouse's), occupation, urbanization and family pattern (nuclear families).   All indices of modernization cut traditional attitudes sharply--more than 9 years of female education did so by more than 50 percent. However, the focus of the article is how to better establish family training programs--here the need is seen for a wide scale approach to help those who want to limit fertility but do not use or plan to use modern methods (20 percent of the sample) and those who want traditional families but would prefer to space them more conveniently.

1081. Molnos, Angela. Atitudes Toward Family Planning in East Africa. Munchen: Weltforum Verlag, 1968. 414 pp.

Surveys the attitudes toward family size among 2648 East Africans in 1965 through 1968. Subjects were students in Kenya, Tanzania and Uganda in the 7th and 10th year of schooling whose age ranged from 10 to 22 years. Argues that population growth is related to women's status. Finds that there are no significant differences between males and females on ideal family size, but there are differences by grade levels. The more education an individual receives, the fewer children are desired. However, finds also that women have no status unless they are mothers despite women's education and their ability to get a high paying job. Men, however, do gain status through increasing educational levels and through occupation irregardless of whether they have children.

1082. Petit, J.J. Integrated Family Life Education Project: A Project of the Ethiopian Women's Association.   Project Assessment. Washington, D.C.: World Education, 1977. 98 pp.

Evaluates a population education project initiated in Ethiopia in 1973. Focuses on how resource materials were developed and participatory teaching methods were used to create an effective learning environment. Concludes that integrated curricula which incorporate health, nutrition, agriculture and population planning are most effective in changing attitudes toward family size.

Articles

1083. Arowolo, Oladele. "Plural Marriage, Fertility and the Problem of Multiple Causation."   Education and Modernization of the Family in West Africa.   Edited by Helen Ware.   Canberra: Department of Demography, Australian National University, 1981, pp. 112-133. (Changing African Family Project Series Monograph no. 7)

Examines the relationship between polygyny and fertility, using data from the interviews with 957 women in Ibadan, Nigeria, in 1974. The factors examined are age, type of marriage, position among wives, place of birth and conjugal mobility, duration of marriage and years of formal education. When all these factors are considered jointly, women in monogamous unions are slightly less fertile than women in polygynous unions, but the variance is very small. Finds it is difficult to guage the influence of education on the fertility of polygynously married women because of the lack of highly educated women in polygynous unions. Concludes that even though monogamy tends to depress fertility, the pattern of variations in fertility among Yoruba women in Ibadan has little to do with polygyny.

1084. Erasmus, G.   "Decision-Making in Regard to the Use of Contraceptives after Confinement: A Study among Urban Black Women." South African Journal of Sociology 15 (1984): 94-97.

Analyses factors which may have an influence on decision making in regard to the acceptance of modern contraception after confinement.   The study was conducted in South Africa. Schedules were used to gather data during interviews with 250 black women in an urban community shortly before the birth of their babies and again three months after the birth.   By using multivariate analaysis techniques, it was found that the family planning program, status, demographic, educational level and other background variables had little influence on the decision making process.   The only variable to show a significant association was the attitudes of the man towards his wife using contraception.

1085. Ketkar, Suhas L.   "Female Education and Fertility: Some Evidence from Sierra Leone." Journal of Developing Areas 13 (1978): 23-33.

Explores the reasons for the observed U-shape relationship between female education and fertility in developing countries. The available data from a small West African country--Sierra Leone--were used for this purpose.   The estimated regression equation for the entire sample of 1999 western area housewives is reported.   While the first five years of school have the effect of increasing fertility, only female educational attainment beyond five years has a depressing effect on the number of children born.   Discusses specifically the reasons for the impact of female education on fertility.   The major contribution of this study relates to the development of an extended version of the household model of fertility.

1086. Koenig, Dolores B.   "Education and Fertility Among Cameroonian Working women." Education and Modernization of the Family in West Africa. Edited by Helen Ware. Canberra: Department of

Demography, Australian National University, 1981, pp. 134-153. (Changing African Family Project Series Monograph no. 7)

Examines the impact of education on fertility in economic and psychosocial perspectives. Data were collected by interviewing three groups of working women defined by occupational and educational level (plantation workers, bank clerks and elite women) in Cameroon in 1975 to 1976. Elite women were found to have the largest number of living children and plantation workers the least. Argues that the educated women continue to have relatively larger families than their uneducated counterparts because, while considerations related to both traditional values and to government policy lead women to want to have large families, the economic constraints on educated women are not strong enough for them to limit the size of their families.

1087. Lewis, Barbara. "Fertility and Employment: An Assessment of Role Incompatibility among African Urban Women." Women and Work in Africa. Edited by Edna G. Bay. Boulder, Colorado: Westview Press, 1982, pp. 249-276.

Examines the relationship between employment and fertility behavior among women in the Ivory Coast. Eight hundred and eighty working and nonworking women from three areas with differing socioeconomic characteristics were interviewed in 1973-74. Finds that fertility does not keep women from working and that insufficient employment opportunities rather than lack of childcare have the negative effect on women's laborforce participation. Contends that the popular concept of role incompatibility is plausible but of limited usefulness and that the availability and cost of childcare should be a research focus.

1088. Mitchell, J. Clyde. "Differential Fertility amongst Urban Africans in Zambia." Rhodes-Livingstone Journal 37 (June 1965): 1-25.

Notes slight increase in fertility among the educated and middle class, but fertility measure included survival rates and the effect is attributed to greater survival rather than a higher birth rate.

Orubuloye, I.O. "Education and Socio-Demographic Change in Nigeria: The Western Nigerian Experience." Education and Modernization of the Family in West Africa. Edited by Helen Ware. Canberra: Department of Demography, Australian National University, 1981, pp. 22-41. (Changing African Family Project Series Monograph no. 7)

See item #1018

3.   Asia

Books and Monographs

Chung, Betty Jamie. The Status of Women and Fertility in Southeast and East Asia: A Bibliography. Singapore: Institute of Southeast Asia Studies, 1977. 167 pp.

See item #30

1089. Fawcett, James T. (ed.)   The Satisfactions and Costs of Children: Theories, Concepts, Methods. Honolulu, Hawaii: The East-West Center, 1972. 324 pp.

Contains the proceedings of the Workshop on Assessment of the Satisfactions and Costs of Children held in Honolulu in April 1972. The purpose of the workshop was to develop a broad theoretical framework for studying the satisfactions and costs of children and their relationships to understanding fertility behavior. Papers were presented by scholars from the U.S. as well as from Asian nations. The papers represented a number of disciplinary orientations. All, however, view children as functional for their parents or for the sociocultural system. Several papers in the book focus on methodology. Concludes that research on the satisfactions and costs of children has implications for population policies, family planning communications programs and understanding and predicting fertility behavior. Recommends that both macro and micro level studies which use diverse techniques and which are longitudinal and cross-national be conducted to further knowledge of fertility behavior.

1090. Harrison, David S. The Effects of Education and Wages on Fertility: Some Evidence from Malaysia. Clayton: Monash University, 1981. 50 pp. (Department of Economics Seminar Paper no. 15/81)

Uses the Malaysian Family Life Survey which interviewed 1262 households on fertility, education and income. Major finding is that raising women's wage levels do not decrease fertilty when education level is held constant, i.e. more education does lead to higher wages. More education does reduce fertilty. Time delay for marriage attributable to education and knowledge of contraception gained in education account for 40 percent of the reduction.

1091. Paqueo, Vincente B. and Joseph Fernandez.   An Empirical Analysis of A Disequilibrium Model of Fertility Behavior and the Threshold Hypothesis. 1973 Philippines. Quezon City: Council for Asian Manpower Studies, University of the Philippines, 1980. 36 pp. (Discussion Paper Series no. 80-01)

Examines a model of fertility behavior which posits that some
women have excess capacity to bear children, while others have
excess demand. Finds that life expectancy appears to have an
insignificant effect on fertilty of women with less than
completed elementary education and and family income of under
2500 Philippine dollars in 1973. However, life expectancy at
birth does effect fertility among higher income and more
educated women. The study was conducted among Philippino women
in 1973.

1092. Pernia, Prabowo and E.M. Pernia. An Empirical Analysis of the
Effects of Income and Education on Fertility in Indonesia.
Quezon City: Council for Asian Manpower Studies, 1982.   28 pp.
(Discussion Paper Series no. 82-12)

Examines the impact of family income and wife's education on
fertility in Indonesia. Posits both affect fertility positively
in families below subsistence level but negatively in families
above subsistence level. Data are derived from the 1976
Intercensal Population Survey of Indonesia. Finds, except in
rural Java and in Bali, that increased family income and wife's
education depress fertility rates in families below subsistence.
However, in rural Java and Bali, increases in family income and
women's education consistently depress birth rates, even in
families living above subsistence. Finds also that wife's
education has a more significant effect on fertility reduction
than family income level.

Articles

1093. Encarnacion, J. "Family Income, Educational Level, Labor Force
Participation and Fertility." The Philippine Economic Journal 7
(1973): 536-549.

Examines the effects of family income and educational level on
fertility and laborforce participation of married women in the
Philippines based on the data from the 1968 National Demographic
Survey which covers 7237 households. Finds that the effects of
the two variables are positive or negative depending on whether
these variables fall below certain levels. Concludes that
unless large scale family planning programs are carried out,
birthrates are likely to be higher before they get lower during
the earlier stages of economic development.

1094. Fernando, D.F.S. "Female Educational Attainment and Fertility."
Journal of Biosocial Science 9 (1977): 339-351.

Finds that education is strongly related to decline in fertility
rates in a sample drawn from the 1971 Sri Lankan census. In
both rural and urban areas, fertility rates begin to decline
among those with at least a fourth grade education. The

steepest decline in fertility rates occurs among those who have completed grade 10. This effect is in part explained because education delays marriage age and also because single women are more common among educated women than uneducated women.

1095. Gans, Lydia P. and Corinne Shear Wood. "Brief Communications." Human Organization 44 (1985): 228-233.

Studies receptivity to family planning among women in Western Samoa. Interviews 90 women and finds that there exists a wide spectrum of beliefs concerning fertility regulation and that the role of education in forming such beliefs is intertwined with other social and cultural factors.

1096. Han, Suyin. "Family Planning in China." Japan Quarterly 17 (1970): 433-442.

Describes the course of education in planned parenthood and the various phases of this movement in China from 1956 to 1970. Stresses that the essential feature of the continuing Chinese revolution since 1949 is the speed of change and this also applies to all activities including family planning. Affirms the significance of government policies and the spread of education in planned parenthood.

1097. Hawkins, John N. "Family Planning Education and Health Care Delivery in the People's Republic of China: Implications for Educational Alternatives." Comparative Education Review 20 (1976): 151-164.

Describes programs that have led to effective population control in China which worked through women's organizations. Points out that family limitation programs have widened women's opportunities for gainful employment.

1098. Kim, Ik Ki. "A Multilevel Analysis of Fertility Behavior in Korea." Studies in Comparative International Development 22 (1985): 65-91.

Traces the effect of education and childhood residence on fertility in Korea based on data from National Fertility Survey. Focuses on the micro(individual)- macro (social settings) nexus of fertility behavior. Concludes that childhood residence interactively played a role in explaining the fertility measures, but, unlike the common finding, women's education in general did not work either additively or interactively.

1099. Kim, Soung-Yee and W.F. Stinner. "Social Origins, Educational Attainment and the Timing of Marriage and First Birth among Korean Women." Journal of Marriage and the Family 42 (1980): 671-679.

Studies 988 Korean women between 30 and 44 years old to look at
the impact of social origins, educational attainment, age at
marriage and first birth on fertility rates. Finds that the
effects of education on fertility reduction is diminishing.

1100. Mueller, Eva. "Economic Motives for Family Limitation: A Study
Conducted in Taiwan." Population Studies 26 (1972): 383-403.

Examines the linkages between economic motivations and fertility
change at the family level in Taiwan. Based on the data from a
survey in 1969, finds that economic considerations have a
significant bearing on fertility decisions. Parents' views
regarding the economics of family size are affected by rising
educational and income levels, exposure to mass media and the
availability of new consumer goods. Suggests that policies in
Taiwan should focus on continuing efforts to raise educational
levels, attempts to popularize the small family concept by mass
media, educational assistance for children and the enhancement
of the economic self-reliance of parents, and that it is
necessary to bring questions of population growth to the fore in
economic policy decisions.

1101. Nelson, Merwyn. "Level of Living and Fertility among a Rural
Population of the Philippines." Studies in Comparative
International Development 20 (1985): 31-45.

Examines whether the relationship of fertility to three measures
of economic resources, e.g. income, quality of housing and
provision of schooling to children, is different at lower income
levels than at higher levels in rural Philippines. Finds that
household per capita income has a positive effect on fertility
in the low income group but no effect in the higher income
group, that housing quality has also a positive effect on
fertility in the low income group but negative in the higher
income group and that education of the children was not related
to fertility in this model.

1102. Wang, Virginia Li. "Application of Social Science Theories to
Family Planning Health Education in the People's Republic of
China." American Journal of Public Health 66 (May 1976):
440-445.

Describes the organization of family planning campaigns in
China. Discusses rewards, group and leader approval, public
announcement of acceptance of the program and group pressure to
spread involvement.

3a.   Bangladesh

Books and Monographs

1103. Mabud, Mohammed A. **Women's Development, Income and Fertility.**
       Dhaka: The External Unit, Planning Commission and Canadian
       International Development Agency, 1985.   180 pp.

       Investigates the impact of vocational training on women with
       respect to their income and contraceptive and reproductive
       behavior by comparing the reproductive behavior of women in
       vocational training programs with village women who are not in
       such programs. The evaluation is based on data collected in
       Bangladesh in 1979 obtained from 520 women who had completed
       vocational training, 655 women currently enrolled in the program
       and 312 women who remained untouched by the program. Included
       also were data from the 1976 Bangladesh Fertility Survey and the
       1979 Bangladesh Contraceptive Prevalence Survey. Finds that
       women who entered vocational training programs had higher status
       due in large part to the income they could earn. Vocational
       training, however, did not relate to family size or
       contraceptive use. Fertility control was more strongly
       associated with number of living children, age at first marriage
       and duration of marriage.

1104. Noman, Ayesha. **Status of Women and Fertility in Bangladesh.**
       Dhaka: University Press, Ltd. 1983. 91 pp.

       Argues that women's education has a strong impact on fertility
       reduction since education tends to postpone marriage,
       improves husband-wife communication, encourages women to enter
       the workforce and changes women's attitudes. Maintains that
       increasing women's education will serve to promote national
       development since it will depress fertility rates. In chapter
       1, which is on women's status, discusses Bangladesh's first and
       second five year plan which emphasize extending education to
       women.

Articles

1105. Chaudhury, R.H. "Female Status and Fertility Behavior in a
       Metropolitan Urban Area of Bangladesh."   **Population Studies** 32
       (1978): 261-273.

       Analyses work experience, education, husband-wife communication
       in regard to using contraception and fertility rates using a
       matched sample of 500 working and nonworking women in
       Bangladesh. Finds that the higher the level of education, the
       greater the use of contraceptives and the lower the number of
       children women had.   Husband-wife communication also was

significantly related between contraception use while there was
little relationship to contraceptive use and work. Despite
this, working uneducated women had lower fertility rates than
all the groups sampled.

1106. Chaudhury, Rafiqul Huda. "Female Status and Fertility Behavior
in a Metropolitan Urban Area of Bangladesh." Women and
Development: Perspectives from South and Southeast Asia.
Edited by Rounaq Jahan and Hanna Papanek. Dacca: The
Bangladesh Institute of Law and International Affairs, 1979,
pp. 319-351.

Examines the relationship between three aspects of status of
married women (employment status, education status and conjugal
role relationship) and the use of contraception and fertility
behavior in urban Bangladesh. Data were collected from a survey
of 1130 married women in Dacca in 1974. It was found that
education had the strongest positive relationship to the use of
contraception and had an inverse relationship to fertility.
Conjugal role relationship had the second strongest correlation.
Working experience had very little or no effect on contraception
use and fertility behavior, especially among the highly educated
women. Among the lesser educated women, work experience brought
higher use of contraception and lower ferility rates. Suggests
that women's status, particularly education and decision making
power in the family, be improved.

1107. Chaudhury, R.H. "The Influence of Female Education, Labor Force
Participation and Age at Marriage on Fertility Behavior in
Bangladesh." Social Biology 31 (1984): 59-74.

Studies the relationship between three aspects of female status
(education, work experience and age at marriage) and the use of
contraception and fertility in Bangladesh. These relationships
are examined separately for rural and urban areas, using data
collected by the Bangladesh Fertility Survey of 1975. Finds
that education is the variable most strongly correlated with use
of contraception and is also one of the significant variables
explaining fertility behavior. The most important factor
explaining fertility behavior is age at marriage (the higher the
age at marriage, the lower the fertility). Work experience has
very little or no effect on use of contraception and fertility.
Suggests the importance of providing more girls' schools, an
effective form of nonformal education, and adequate employment
opportunities for women, in order to reduce future fertility.

Elahi, K. Maudood. Anthropogeographic Approach to Population
Studies: Indepth Survey Guidelines for Bangladesh. Dacca:
Center for Population Studies, 1981, pp. 32. (Occasional Paper
no. 2)

See item #59

1108. Teel, Howard and Rammohan Ragade.   "Simulation Modeling Perspectives of the Bangladesh Family Planning and Female Education System." **Behavioral Science** 29 (1984): 145-161.

Finds that the increased participation of females in formal and nonformal education is a key means for controlling rapid population growth.

3b.   India *

Books and Monographs

1109. Jain, Anrudh K. and Moni Nag.   **Female Primary Education and Fertility Reduction in India.**   New York: The Population Council, Center for Policy Studies, 1985.   57 pp.   (Working Paper no. 114)

Reviews the relation between increases in female education and fertility reduction in India.   Finds that the relation is complex: increases in educational levels sometimes lead to a rise in the fertility rate; but this increase is the case for women who have incomplete primary education.   Fertility rates decline for women who have secondary and higher education or who complete primary school.   The reduction in fertility with women's education results from increases in the use of contraception among educated women and a rise in the marriage age.   Urges that primary education be universalized for women as a means of controlling fertility.

Jesudason, Victor et al. (ed.)   **Non-Formal Education for Rural Women to Promote the Development of the Young Child.**   New Delhi: Allied Publishers, 1981.   419 pp.

See item #626

1110. Singh, K.P.   **Status of Women and Population Growth in India.**   New Delhi: Munshiram Manoharlal Publishers, 1979.   165 pp.

Investigates the relation between Indian women's status and their fertility.   Social status was measured by educational and occupational attainment levels.   Samples 311 married women, 20 years of age and over.   Finds that the higher the social status, the lower the fertility rate.   Education was an important factor: educated women had a mean of 2.6 children while lesser educated women had 4.5 children.

Articles

Chhabra, Rami. "Establishing Linkage between Women's Literacy Programmes, Status Issues and Access to Family Planning." Indian Journal of Adult Education 41 (no. 4, 1980): 6-9, 24.

See item #632

1111. D'Souza, A. "Women in India: Fertility and Occupational Patterns in a Sex-Segregated Less Developed Society." Social Action 26 (1976): 66-79.

Focuses on the relation between fertility and women's status in India. Argues that women's education and urbanization will raise women's status since it will help women enter the workforce and therefore depress fertility rates. Maintains that women's status is lowered by confinement to the role of wife and mother and that high fertility rates keep women status low. Believes that further government policies are necessary to accommodate women in the workforce. Among these are flexible time and day care.

1112. Jain, Anrudh K. and Moni Nag. "Importance of Female Primary Education for Fertility Reduction in India." Economic and Political Weekly 21 (1986): 1602-1608.

Examines the relationship between female education and fertility in India to find effective strategies for fertility reduction. Argues that female education has a significant impact in that it increases use of contraception and age at marriage. Suggests that the educational policy makers give high priority to increasing female primary education and to reducing high repetition and dropout rates from primary schools.

1113. Jain, Anrudh K. and Moni Nag. "Importance of Female Primary Education for Fertility Reduction in India." Education and the Process of Change. Edited by Ratna Ghosh and Mathew Zachariah. New Delhi: Sage Publications, 1987, pp. 157-177.

Examines the relationship between female education and fertility in India. Based on the data from national surveys, argues that the positive effect of education on fertility that operates through fecundity variables is compensated by the negative effect that operates through the use of contraception and age at marriage. Contends that educational policy in India should give high priority to increasing female primary education in order to reduce fertility.

1114. Mulay, Sumati. "Literacy and Family Planning Behavior of Rural Women." Indian Journal of Adult Education 37 (1976): 9-10.

Evaluates the role education plays in family planning by interviewing 200 Indian women, 100 literate and 100 illiterate, in rural areas. Finds that 57 percent of the illiterates and 59 percent of the literate women knew of the existence of family planning programs. Literate women tended to have a broader understanding of family planning techniques, tended to use birth control more than their illiterate sisters and were aware of the social and personal advantages of family planning.

1115. Rao, Kamala G. "Status of Women: Factors Affecting Status of Women in India." Sub-regional Seminar on Status and Role of Women. Bangkok: International Labour Organization, 1978, pp. 1-60.

Consists of a background paper for an ILO seminar which was held in Dacca in 1977. Argues that education is an enabling condition of equality and traces the enrollment patterns of women in India. Low educational levels mean low workforce participation rates. A majority of working women were unskilled laborers in 1969; 10 percent were professional, technical or managerial workers (including school teachers). Reviews the pattern of workforce participation and argues that it will improved only if there is more schooling. Sees education also key to fertility control and spends the majority of the paper discussing this.

1116. Rosenzweig, Mark and Robert Evenson. "Fertility, Schooling, and the Economic Contribution of Children in Rural India: An Economic Analysis." Econometrica 45 (1977): 1065-1079.

Applies a household time allocation model which explicitly takes into account the economic contribution of children in agricultural areas of less developed countries, to direct level data pertaining to the rural population of India. Examines empirically joint family decisions concerning fertility and the allocation of male and female child time to schooling.

3c.   Pakistan

Books and Monographs

1117. Baquai, Sabihuddin. Changes in the Status and Roles of Women in Pakistan. Karachi: Department of Sociology, University of Karachi, 1976. 86 pp.

Investigates the relation between changes in the status and roles of women and fertility. Surveys 200 career women and 225 women who were not in the workforce in Karachi. Finds that women with higher education tend to marry later and have few children. Women with higher education value children's education more than lesser educated women. Concludes that the success of family planning programs largely depends on raising women's educational levels and occupational status.

1118. Shah, Nasra M. and Peter C. Smith. Nonfamilial Roles of Women and Fertility: Pakistan and the Philippines Compared. Honolulu: East-West Center, 1981. 47 pp. (Papers of the East-West Population Institute no. 73)

Examines the relationship between workforce participation and fertility behavior of women in Pakistan and the Philippines based on the data from the 1975 Pakistan Fertility Survey and the 1973 National Demographic Survey of the Philippines. Three measures of work participation (working versus nonworking, place of work and type of occupation) and three measures of fertility (recent fertility, child ever born and desire for another child) were used. In the case of Pakistan, none of the work variables had a significant effect on fertility, while in the Philippines, work participation had a significant negative effect on fertility behavior except on desire for another child, which needs further investigation. The different effect of work participation on fertility seems to arise from the different occupational structures in the two countries. The occupational structure of the Filipino women was more diverse than that of the Pakistani women. Many more of the Filipino women worked outside home than the Pakistani women. In urban areas, the working women were less educated than the nonworking women and tended to concentrate in low status occupations in Pakistan, whereas in the Philippines the working women were more educated than the nonworking women and more Filipino women than Pakistani women were engaged in professional occupations.

Articles

1119. Khan, M.A. and I. Sirageldin. "Education, Income and Fertility in Pakistan." Economic Development and Cultural Change 27 (1979): 519-547.

Asks how income and education effect desired and real family size in Pakistan. Surveys 2910 married women and interviews a number of women and their spouses. Finds that income has a positive influence on fertility rates in rural Pakistan while it has a negative influence in urban areas; in rural areas educational levels of both husbands and wives have a negative effect on family size and that the greater the number of sons, the lower the probability of a couple wanting additional children despite educational levels.

1120. Shah, Nasra M. "Female Labour Force Participation and Fertility Desires in Pakistan: An Empirical Investigation." The Pakistan Development Review 14 (1975): 185-206.

Asks whether female laborforce participation is negatively associated with fertility if other relevant factors are controlled. Data for the study were drawn from Pakistani women from the National Impact Survey in 1968-69. Factors examined are husbands' and wives' educational and employment status, number of living children and sons, family type, age of wife, and wife's work status. Finds that demographic variables such as the age of wife and the number of living sons, are far more important than the socioeconomic factors. Points out that the relatively weak relationshp between female work status and fertility may be due to the nature of jobs most women hold. Concludes that policies for increasing female employment cannot be expected to have a significant negative effect on fertility except for specific jobs in some subgroups.

1121. Shah, Nasra M. "Ferility of Working vs. Non-working Women in Pakistan, 1973." Women and Development: Perspectives from South and Southeast Asia. Edited by Rounaq Jahan and Hanna Papanek. Dacca: The Bangladesh Institute of Law and International Affairs, 1979, pp. 275-318.

Analyzes the rates and structure of female laborforce participation and fertility differentials between working and nonworking women in Pakistan, based on the data from the 1973 Housing, Demographic and Economic survey. Finds that about 9 percent of the women age ten or more were in the laborforce in 1973, 33 percent of urban working women were classified professional and technical occupations and there was a positive relationship between education and employment in urban areas. Concludes that, although the fertility rates of working women were slightly lower than those of nonworking women, it is not clear whether this was caused by employment itself, by some other variable like education, or by the interaction among several variables.

3d.   Thailand

Books and Monographs

1122. Buripakdi, Chalio. The Value of Children: A Cross-National Study of Thailand. Honolulu: East West Center, 1977.

Studies how Thai parents value children and how those values relate to population control. Interviews 360 married couples from three socioeconomic groups in Bangkok in 1973. Urban middle class respondents had an average educational attainment of a little less than two years of college while urban lower class respondents had completed less than six years of school. Rural respondents' educational attainment was slightly over four years. Findings related to education include: 1) female roles are defined in terms of having children and having children is viewed as an informal education process; 2) parents want to limit family size so that they can afford educational costs; 3) family size is affected by gender of children already born and parental aspirations for those children; 4) parents with higher education tend to want small families and approve of the use of contraceptives.

1123. Navawongs, Tippan. Career Plans and Fertility Expectations of College Women in Bangkok, Thailand. Singapore: Southeast Asia Population Research Awards Program, Institute of Southeast Asian Studies, 1980. 96 pp. (Research Report no. 71)

Investigates the relation between women's career plans and the number of children desired among 360 firstyear female students at Chulalongkorn University in Thailand. Finds that women who plan to have a career desire a lower number of children than women who plan to combine career with family or to become homemakers. Finds also that women in the sciences desire fewer children than women in the social sciences; women who have higher grades in college also desire fewer children. SES does not have a direct relation to number of children desired, although students from low SES backgrounds as well as those from very high SES backgrounds tend to want fewer children than women students from middle SES backgrounds.

Articles

1124. Goldstein, Sidney. "The Influence of Labour Force Participation and Education on Fertility in Thailand." Population Studies 26 (1972): 419-435.

Tests the relationship between fertility, laborforce participation of women and education in Thailand. Finds a differential relation between laborforce participation and fertility in rural, agricultural areas and the urban center of Bangkok. Women engaged in farming have on an average a larger number of children than those in other occupations and that education is inversely related to fertility level. Concludes that education plays a key role as an instrument of fertility reduction. Argues that policies directed at fostering high rates of educational enrollment of women, greater participation in the nonagricultural laborforce and greater exposure to the urban way of life should be considered as part of any program designed to achieve reductions in fertility.

1125. Krannich, Caryl Rae and Ronald L. Krannich. "Family Planning Policy and Community-Based Innovations in Thailand." Asian Survey 20 (1980): 1023-1037.

Explains the role of community based family planning strategies on family planning success in Thailand. Argues that the overall success of the national family planning program is due to strong and dynamic leadership, the cooperative efforts of both public and private organizations, the effectiveness of community based activities and the continuity of communication and education. Suggests that through experimentation, family planning and other public policy problems can be better understood, resolved and communicated to other developing nations.

4.   Latin America and the Caribbean

Books and Monographs

1126. Brody, Eugene B.   Sex, Contraception, and Motherhood in Jamaica. Cambridge: Harvard University Press, 1981. 278 pp.

Studies the use of contraceptives and fertility among working class men and women in Jamaica. Argues that education is highly related to the use of contraception, especially among women. The relation drawn is that education changes attitudes of both men and women and provides women with more modern attitudes, including beliefs in their own efficacy and in women's autonomy. Education also is related to greater communication between males and females which, in turn, is related to declining fertility rates. The study is based on statistical/survey data as well as private biography.

1127. Conning, Arthur M. and Albert M. Marckwardt. Analysis of WFS Data in Colombia, Panama, Paraguay and Peru: Highlights from the CELADE Research and Training Seminar. London: World Fertility Survey, October, 1982. 34 pp.

Presents abstracts of papers prepared at a seminar held at the Latin American Demographic Center (CELADE) from April to December 1980 in Colombia. Participants were from Colombia, Panama, Paraguay and Peru and analyzed the World Fertility Survey data. Provides abstracts of papers. Edgar Baldion's (Colombia) associates education with declines in infant mortality rates. Else Gomez's on female workforce participation and family formation points out that educational level and occupation affect timing of children and family size. Other papers focus on fertility and laborforce participation in Paraguay and Peru, on women's attitudes toward fertility in Peru, infant mortality and mother's education in Panama and Peru.

1128. Cisneros, Antonio J. et al.   Cambio y Tendancias Evaluativas sobre Educacion Familiar para la Mujer Trabajadora.   La Paz: Centro de Investigaciones Sociales, 1984.   96 pp.

Describes and to some degrees evaluates a program of birth control education.   Uses a sample of 300 women, the great majority with secondary education and shows most had one or two children, but the second largest group had seven or more children.   Those finishing the program demonstrated a wide knowledge and use of all forms of birth control devices and pratices.

1129. da Silva, Lea Melo.   Greater Education Opportunities for Women Related to Population Growtrh.   East Lansing: Michigan State University, Women in International Develolpment, 1982.   18 pp. (Working Paper no. 11)

Reports a survey of 2445 households with 8079 individuals in Belo Horizonte, Brazil that focuses on the relation between education and fertility.   Argues that the relation is complex and does not operate at the same intensity for all levels of education.   The greatest impact on family size reduction is completed primary and secondary education.   Post-secondary education's impact is marginal.   Finds also that in low income groups an increase in education may increase fertility rates since there is a relation between increasing women's education and a declining child mortality rates.   Workforce entry also exerts a force on fertility reduction because the roles of mother and work are in compatability and women perceive having more children as an economic disadvantage.

Henriquez de Paredes, Querubina et al.   Participación de la Mujer en el Desarrollo de América Latina y el Caribe.   Santiago de Chile: UNICEF, 1975.

See item #903

1130. Plantelides, Edith A.   Las Mujeres de Alta Fecundidad en la Argentina Pasado y Future.   Buenos Aires: CENEP, 1982.   58 pp. (Cuaderno del Centro de Estudios de Población no.23)

Tests fecundity against factors of age, education, place of origin, economic activity using census data over time.   Shows most of the usual relationships but with some surprizes, such as foreign born women have higher birth rates than native Argentinians.   Clearly education level reduces the birth rate--more than 30 percent of those educated to at least the incomplete secondary level (highest level given) had only two children while the average for uneducated women was twice as high (all figures from the 1970 census).   However, looking over time all education levels have dropped substantially to one third of previous rates.   Further, with women of high fertility (five or more children) education does not seem to demonstrate any differences between having five or, for example, eight children.

Recchini de Lattes, Zulina. Dynamics of the Female Labor Force in Argentina. Paris: UNESCO, 1983. 98 pp.

See item #909

Articles

1131. Barbieri, M. Teresita de. "Politicas de Población y la Mujer: Antecedentes para su Estudio." Revista Mexicana de Sociologia 45 (1983): 293-308.

Focuses on government population policies in Mexico and the way in which these policies have redefined women's roles. Argues that while there are increasing educational levels among women and changing marriage patterns, unless barriers to women's participation in the workforce are removed, further reduction in fertility rates will be difficult to achieve.

1132. Bouvier, Leon F. and John J. Macisco, Jr. "Education of Husband and Wife and Fertility in Puerto Rico, 1960." Social and Economic Studies 17 (1968): 49-59.

Analyses the effects on fertility of the education of both the wife and husband based on data from the 1960 Census for Puerto Rico. Finds that wife's education has stronger inverse relationship with fertility than does husband's education, fertility declines within all categories with the increased education of the husband, especially at the college level. Maintains that not only education but also other variables such as rural living or rural to urban migration should be examined for fertility studies.

1133. Brody, E.B. et al. "Early Sex Education in Relationship to Later Coital and Reproductive Behavior: Evidence from Jamaican Women." American Journal of Psychiatry 133 (1976): 969-972.

Studies a sample of 100 birth control users and 50 birth control nonusers in Jamaica to ascertain the relationship between sex education and reproductive behavior. Finds that women who had no sex education had a larger number of sexual partners and pregnancies than women who were informed by their mothers about sex. Level of education had a positive relationship to contraceptive use and to lowered number of pregnancies.

1134. Carleton, Robert O. "Labor Force Participation: A Stimulus to Fertility in Puerto Rico?" Demography 2 (1965): 233-239.

Explores the relationships among women's laborforce participation, level of education and their fertility. Data are 1960 census cards collected in Puerto Rico by the Puerto Rico Planning Board and the U.S. Bureau of the Census. Finds that proportionally, very few women with little education are economically active. As educational levels increase economic activity increases. Finds there is very little difference in fertility roles between high school graduates and women with at least some higher education in some age groups; it is however large with others. Several hypothetical explanations are given for the phenomena. Concludes that studies on a larger scale and from the historical perspective will be more helpful to decide if this is a new trend.

1135. Davidson, Maria. "Female Work Status and Fertility in Urban Latin America." Social and Economic Studies 24 (1978): 481-506.

Examines the relation between work status of wife, additional desired number of children, age at marriage, education and occupation of wife, husband's occupation and fertility. Uses data obtained from fertility surveys conducted by CELADE during 1963-1964, and for Guatemala City during 1965. Finds that among married women in the eight cities considered, working wives had lower fertility rates than nonworking wives. Among working wives, those working outside the home had lower fertility rates than those working in the home. Women who worked in nonmanual occupations had lower fertility rates than those in manual occupations. Husband's occupational status had less influence on fertility rates than wives' occupational status. Concludes that the most important factors affecting fertility are age at marriage of wife and her education, and these two factors are related.

Elizaga, Juan C. "The Participation of Women in the Labour Force of Latin America: Fertility and Other Factors." International Labour Review 109 (1974): 519-538.

See item #913

Fucaraccio, Angel. "El Trabajo Femenino en Chile: Un Estudio de Caso de las Areas Urbanas." Chile: Mujer y Sociedad. Edited by Paz Covarrubias and Rolando Franco. Santiago: Alfebeta Imp., 1978, pp. 135-160.

See item #937

1136. Gonzales Cortes, Gerarado. "Desarrollo, Mujer y Fecundidad. Chile 1960-1970." Chile Mujer y Sociedad. Edited by Paz Covarrubias and Rolando Franco. Santiago: Alfebeta Imp. 1978, pp. 97-134.

Studies three interrelated aspects of the social development of Chile: women's increased access to technical and university education; women's participation in the labor market, particularly in modern sector employment requiring high qualification; and the observed decline in fertility in Chile. The theoretical discussion and model suggest that a sophisticated treatment of data will be necessary to understand these interrelationships. However, based on the aggregate data available from the Chilean censuses, the analysis in this paper is restricted to cross-tabulations which illustrate aspects of the model. The data available illustrate the complex interactions among education, laborforce participation and fertility which are affected by social class, age, etc. Overall women's laborforce particiption did not increase notably in Chile between 1960 and 1970 censuses but changes were apparent especially for women with professional qualification.

Guierrez de Pineda, Virginia. "Status de la Mujer en la Familia." La Mujer y el Desarrollo en Colombia. Edited by Magdalena Leon de Leal. Bogotá: Asociación Colombiana para el Estudio de la Población, 1977, pp. 318-394.

See item #915

1137. Pardo Tellez, Franz. "Condiciones de Salud de la Mujer." La Mujer y el Desarrollo en Colombia. Edited by Magdalena Leon de Leal. Bogotá: Asociación Colombiana para el Estudio de la Población, 1977, pp. 123-182.

Uses education as a background variable matched against region to analyze fertility patterns. Shows that urban-rural differences are as important as changing educational levels. Rural women have more children at each education level, but the higher the level of education, the lower the birth rate. However, the higher the education level, the lower the rate of abortions. All data is from 1964-65.

Powell, Dorian L. "Female Labour Force Participation and Fertility: An Exploratory Study of Jamaican Women." Social and Economic Studies 25 (1976): 234-258.

See item #918

1138. Roberts, G.W., et al. "Knowledge and Use of Birth Control in Barbados." Demography 4 (no. 2, 1967): 576-600.

Finds that education, at least, to the level of functional literacy (four years of primary education) seems necessary before the knowledge and use of contraception occurs.

1139. Smith, Stanley K.   "Determinants of Female Labor Force Participation and Family Size in Mexico City."   Economic Development and Cultural Change 30 (1981): 129-152.

Focuses on the effects of explanatory variables on family size and female laborforce participation in Mexico City, particularly on the effect of the wife's potential wage on female laborforce participation and family size.   Based on the data from 800 women, finds that the wife's potential wage is found to have a negative effect on work that can be done simultaneously with childcare (traditional sector), a positive effect on work that cannot be done (modern sector), and a negative effect on family size.   Concludes that attempts to affect fertility rates through female employment in developing countries must take into account not only target levels of female employment but also the nature of the employment.

1140. Stycos, J.M.   "Recent Trends in Latin American Fertility." Population Studies 32 (1978): 407-415.

Focuses on the relation of education to drops in fertility in Barbados, Chile, Costa Rica, El Salvador, Guatemala, Jamaica, Panama, Puerto Rico, Trinidad and Venezuela.   Family planning education appears to be related to fertility declines in Barbados and Puerto Rico and rising levels of female literacy in Costa Rica seems to be associated with fertility rates. However, in Chile and Trinidad there appears to be an inverse relation between educational and literacy levels and fertility.

1141. Tienda, Marta.   "Community Characteristics, Women's Education, and Fertility in Peru."   Studies in Family Planning 15 (July-August 1984): 162-169.

Examines how community characteristics influence completed fertility in Peru using data from the World Fertility Survey of 1977-78.   Shows that community characteristics do not interact with mother's education in determining completed fertility. Rather the effects of community characteristics are best described by a threshold model, which posits that below or above critical points, the effects on fertility of community (or individual) characteristics will diminish or increase. Empirical results showed that residence in communities with higher levels of access to the benefits of development decreased completed fertility beyond what one would have predicted on the basis of women's characteristics alone, and this effect was further amplified with increasing levels of development.

1142. Wolfe, Barbara and Jere R. Behrman.   "Child Quantity and Quality in a Developing Country, Family Background, Endogenous Taste, and Biological Factors."   Economic Development and Cultural Change 34 (1986): 703-720.

Explores empirically some of the different implications of two models ("Chicago-Columbia" economic model of fertility and "Pennsylvania" economic analysis of fertility) for the determination of child quantity and quality. Uses data collected on adult women siblings in Nicaragua. Finds that increased female schooling and better labor market alternatives for women may have less impact on fertility in the developing world than the World Bank, Colcough and others have maintained, that the recent drop in fertility may be due in no small part to changing tastes, which imply much more ambiguous private welfare effects than the Chicago-Columbia interpretation suggests.

5.   The Middle East

Articles

1143. Aghajanian, Akbar. "Fertilty and Family Economy in the Iranian Rural Communities." **Women in the Family and Economy:** An International Comparative Survey. Edited by George Kurian and Ratna Ghosh. Westport, Conn.: Greenwood Press, 1981, pp. 297-305.

Examines the fertility differences across families in rural communities in Iran. 550 rural couples in 25 villages of a rural area in Fars Ostan province comprise the sample. Finds that farmers have higher fertility rates than nonfarmers and that large landholders have the highest rates of fertility among the farmers. The effect of wife's economic activity on fertility of rural couples is negligible. Husband's education is important for its indirect effect on fertility as it leads to a change in the occupation of the husband from farmer to nonfarmer. Concludes that in agrarian communities where the family is the major economic unit, the positive relation between family size and size of farm may be interpreted as showing the demand for children for their productive services.

1144. Al-Kadhi, Ann Bradgon. "Women's Education and its Relation to Fertility: Report from Baghdad." **Women and the Family in the Middle East.** Edited by Elizabeth Warnock Fernea. Austin: University of Texas Press, 1985, pp. 145-47.

Reports a field study conducted in 1975-76 which focused on education and fertility. The author distributed a questionnaire to middle school girls which elicited information regarding mothers' educational levels and number of children in the family. Finds that education relates to fertility rates in Iraq: women with no education had the largest number of children. Concludes that education has a strong effect on family size and life style.

1145. Darbai, Katherine. "Education and Fertility in Iran."
Community Development Journal 11 (April 1976): 141-148.

Focuses on the relation between literacy and education in
Tehran, Iran, sampling military families who use birth control
clinics. Suggests that given early marriage, low levels of
literacy, absence of outside work available to women and other
cultural factors, that the relation between literacy and
fertility found elsewhere does not hold.

1146. Kohli, K.L. "Regional Variations of Fertility in Iraq and
Factors Affecting It." Journal of Biosocial Science 9 (1977):
175-182.

Compares fertility in Iraq by region based on 1965 census data.
Finds that neither literacy nor urbanization could account for
regional variations. Finds that female age of marriage, the
number of unmarried women and the ratio of men to women were
statistically significantly related to fertility rates.

1147. Suchindran, C.M., and A.L. Adlakha. "Effect of Infant Mortality
on Subsequent Fertility of Women in Jordan: A Life Table
Analysis." Journal of Biosocial Sciences 16 (1984): 219-229.

Asks how infant mortality influences subsequent fertility of
women in Jordan. Data were gathered in the Jordan Fertility
Survey, undertaken by the Department of Statistics of the
Government of Jordan in 1979. Pregnancy history data were
obtained from 3610 ever-married women aged 15-49. Finds that
the fertility of women with low education is consistently high,
but fertilty of women in the highest education category is
relatively low. Women in the highest education category tend to
breast feed their children for a shorter period and tend to use
contraception more often. The low fertiltiy in the highest
education category can be attributed mainly to the use of
contraception, and increase in the probability of a birth among
highly educated women after a child's death can be regarded as a
result of the motivation to replace the lost child.

5a.   Turkey

Articles

1148. Farooq, Ghazi M. and Baran Tuncer. "Fertility and Economic and
Social Development in Turkey: A Cross-Sectional and Time Series
Study." Population Studies 28 (1974): 263-276.

Examines the longterm effects of economic and social advancement
on fertility in Turkey between 1935 and 1965. Based on the data
from the quinquennial population censuses, shows that female

literacy (or education) is the strongest factor that negatively influences fertility, followed by a lower marital rate. Contends that continuing modernization and the concomitant spread of female education should result in a continuing decline in the fertilty rate.

1149. Fisek, Nusret and K. Sumbuloglu. "The Effects of Husband and Wife Education on Family Planning in Rural Turkey." Studies in Family Planning 9 (October-November 1978): 280-285.

Presents a control sample study of two types of family planning education; the first directed at husbands and wives, the second at wives only. The control group had over a 60 percent use of contraceptives, wives only reached 75 percent, husband and wives together over 80 percent. Argues for the joint approach because with high levels of use it is hard to achieve even higher usage.

1150. Kagitcibasi, Cigdem. "Sex Roles, Value of Children and Fertility." Sex Roles, Family and Community in Turkey. Edited by Cigdem Kagitcibasi and Diane Sunar. Bloomington: Indiana University Press, 1982, pp. 151-180. (Turkish Studies no. 3)

Interviews 2305 married people (1762 females and 543 males) to ascertain the values attributed to children and their relation to fertility in Turkey. Finds that the value of children is affected by socioeconomic class, family dynamics and level of education (the economic value of children, for example, declines among more highly educated parents).

1151. Kagitcibasi, Cigdem. "Value of Children, Women's Role and Fertility in Turkey." Women in Turkish Society. Edited by Nermin Abadan-Unat. Leiden: E.J. Brill, 1981, pp. 74-95.

Reports the Value of Children Project (VOC). The VOC Project is a nine-country comparative social psychological study which aims to throw some light on the relationship between the attitudinal and behavioral correlates of fertility in the context of women's intra-and extra-familial roles. The Turkey project started in 1974 with an exploratory pilot study conducted with a selected sample of 189 married respondents. Shows that women who have less education, less media exposure, less decision making power within the family and greater belief in external control emerge as more 'traditional' than men. Educational programs and communications designed to increase women's status by lowering fertility could utilize effectively the knowledge of women's child related values.

Tezcan, Sahabat. "Health Problems of Turkish Women." Women in Turkish Society. Edited by Nermin Abadan-Unat. Leiden: Brill, 1981, pp. 96-106.

See item #1056

XIV. WOMEN'S EDUCATION AND POLITICS

Amazingly, very little has been written about women's education and politics. The works we have listed here cover studies of women's political socialization and attitudes, women in political leadership, women's roles in public policy and women as political elites. Most of these studies use education as a background variable.

The meager research literature listed here on women and politics is divided into two sections. The first contains general studies of women in the political system. The second is devoted to women's organizations, which increasingly have become the route for women's entry into politics.

A. Women's Education and Politics

Books and Monographs

Agnew, Vijay. **Elite Women in Indian Politics.** New Delhi: Vikas Publishing House, 1979. 163 pp.

See item #242

1152. Delcroix, Catherine. **Espoirs et Réalités de la Femme Arabe: Algérie-Egypte.** Paris: Editions L'Harmattan, 1986. 236 pp.

Studies the place of women in the Arab world by interviewing a sample of 100 Algerian women and 100 Egyptian women, stratified by age and educational level. Asks whether there are differences in women's political consciousness and participation between the two countries. Finds that although education tends to increase women's consciousness and ends their isolation in the household, in a revolutionary society like Algeria, there is greater political consciousness of 20 to 50 year old women than in Egypt despite the fact that in Algeria the government has done less to promote women's rights than in Egypt.

1153. Diarra, Abdramane. **Politische Sozialisation und Rolle der Frau in Mali.** Aachen: Rader Verlag, 1986. 243 pp.

Studies political socialization in Mali with formal education being only a small part of the process. Men outnumber women by two to one at all levels of education, and over 80 percent of the men and women receiving education are only receiving the first four years of primary school. Concentrates mainly on the Islamic heritage and its limitations, but includes the changes wrought by French colonialism which altered economic, political and social roles in such a way as to push continuing informal socialization toward political involvement.

1154. Hirschmann, David. **Women, Planning and Policy in Malawi.** Addis Ababa: United Nations Economic Commission for Africa. 1984. 54 pp.

Discusses women's participation in planning and policy making in Malawi and the government plans, policies and practices affecting women. Data are collected through official documents, interviews, questionnaires and workshop. Part I describes basic features of Malawi's economy and the role of women. 92.6 percent of all women live in rural areas and 80 percent of them are illiterate. Women are employed almost exclusively in agriculture and have inferior status in society. Part II examines women's participation in planning and policy making, indicating a marked increase of women representation in Parliament, a stronger participation at district levels and a lower percentage of women members in local councils. In the formal civil service planning machinery, women's participation is negligible. Problems of women participation are discussed and suggestions are made for strengthening the participation. Part III reviews plans in the planning documents and policies of ministries relating to women. Data show that few references are made in planning documents to women and these few are almost restricted to home economics and health, while in practice women's issues receive more attention. A survey of ministries' policies is presented. Part IV offers a list of recommendations for government departments to heighten consciousness about women, strengthen the information base for policy making and to increase women's participation at all levels.

1155. Tabak, Fanny (ed.) **A Mulher como Objecto de Estudio.** Serie Estudios-PUC/RJ no. 11. Rio de Janeiro: Pontificia Universidade Católica do Rio de Janeiro, Centro de Ciencias Socials, 1982. 146 pp.

Represents a beginning study of women in politics in Brazil and particularly in Rio de Janeiro. Includes the study of party position, delineation of women's groups, voting records, etc. with little social science analysis of why women vote. Education is mentioned only in terms of the demand for child care and in the biographical review of a dozen women elected to parliament--over half of these responded to strong pressures from organized women school teachers and fought for specific issues in education or served on education committees.

1156. Vandevelde-Daillière, Hélène. **Femmes Algériennes à Travers la Condition Féminine dans le Constantinois Depuis L'Indépendance.** Alger: Office des Publications Universitaires, 1980. 496 pp.

Studies women's attitudes towards and participation in politics since the gaining of independence in Algeria. Administers a questionnaire to 1300 individuals, including a subsample of women with higher education, women with secondary education and women who are currently students. Finds that the higher the education a woman has, the more likely she is to reject traditional women's roles, work outside the household and participate in politics. Concludes that education plays a strong role in overcoming sex segregation imposed by the household in Algeria and contributes to women's consciousness of being female in a patriarchial society.

Articles

Bravo, Rosa and Rosalba Todaro. "Chilean Women and the UN Decade for Women." Women's Studies International Forum 8 (1985): 111-116.

See item #936

Camp, Roderic A. "Women and Political Leadership in Mexico: A Comparative Study of Female and Male Political Elites." Journal of Politics 41 (1979): 417-441.

See item #567

1157. Devon, Toniak. "Up from the Harem? The Effects of Class and Sex on Political Life in Northern India." **Comparative Perspectives of Third World Women.** Edited by Beverly Lindsay. New York: Praeger, 1980, pp. 123-142.

Examines the process of political socialization among working class women. The research consisted of interviews conducted in 1971 with 80 housewives and factory workers in Faridabad in Haryana and Modinagar in Uttar Pradesh, both in Northern India. Finds that despite their inferior education, these women possess a great deal of political information. Their sources are newspapers, their children who share information gained in school, other family members and neighbors. The single greatest source of political information for housewives are the schools and the radio. Educated housewives and women factory workers employed in male-dominated industries have a high degree of political awareness and are conscious of their status as women. Concludes that females who remain in school for several years are more likely to participate in politics than females who have little or no schooling.

1158. Hahner, June E. "Women's Place in Politics and Economics in Brazil Since 1964." Brazilian Review 19 (1982): 83-89.

Examines women's economic and political roles in Brazil since the military coup. Surveys women's workforce participation and finds that only 6 percent of women were employed in industry versus 19.3 percent of men. Most of the women employed in industry worked in bureaucratic and clerical rather than productive positions. Domestic service was the major employer of women and, as a result, women earned one third the salaries of men. Points out that while education, particularly higher education has opened considerably for women, less than 1 percent of Brazilian women hold university degrees. Women are almost invisible in politics despite the fact that women entered electoral politics in 1932. They are absent from leadership and policy positions in Brazil's political parties and in most professional organizations as well.

1159. Howard-Merriam, Kathleen. "Egypt's Other Political Elite." Western Political Quarterly 34 (1981): 174-187.

Focuses on the character of the post-1952 female public leadership, the successors to feminist Hodo Sha'rawi. Interviews were conducted with forty five women, including Madame Sadat, who either belong to the governing elite or who have become leaders among and for women. Examines these women's backgrounds, personalities, and the environmental factors contributing to their assumption of public service roles. Finds that the contemporary Egyptian female leadership comprises those who have assumed public roles by virtue of 1) their social feminism as developed by their own ambition and their familial situation, or 2) their political feminism as developed by their experiences in pursuing professional careers or engaging in social work. All three women who have served in the Cabinet come from academe. Argues that their qualities of independence and formal training made them stronger figures than their male colleagues who were appointed not for their formal training and experience.

1160. Howard-Merriam, Kathleen. "Women's Political Participation in Morocco's Development: How Much and for Whom?" The Maghreb Review 9 (1984): 12-25.

Focuses on the role of elite Moroccan women in women's organizations, in government and in political organizations. Although women are noticeably absent from positions of power and authority in the country, their presence in the bureaucracy has grown. Many elite women head welfare oriented organizations and are from upper class highly educated backgrounds.

1161. Katzenstein, Mary Fainsod. "Towards Equality? Cause and Consequence of the Political Prominence of Women in India." Asian Survey 78 (1978): 473-486.

Examines the anomaly of women's position in Indian politics from three perspectives: by identifying the extent to which women occupy elite positions in Indian politics; by evaluating possible explanations for women's prominence in elite positions and by exploring the impact which women's participation in politics has for the social and economic position of women in Indian society at large. Concludes that in a society where women are subordinated to men to a serious degree, the prominence of women in Indian politics is due more to the visibility of a few women than to the participation of any significant numbers.

1162. O'Brien, Mary. "Feminism and the Politics of Education." Interchange 17 (Summer 1986): 91-105.

Analyses education in the context of conservatism, liberalism and socialism, and criticizes them as being patriarchial and thus radically conservative in terms of gender. Argues that the goal of a feminist education is the abolition of gender as an oppressive cultural reality, and not equality in knowledge, power and wealth, and that an integrative curriculum must abolish gender.

1163. Schuster, Ilsa. "Constraints and Opportunities in Political Participation: The Case of Zambian Women." Geneve-Afrique 21 (1983): 7-37.

Examines the participation of women in the formal, extradomestic political process of Zambian society from precolonial times through 1974, a decade after independence. Argues that colonialism, introduced to the country where matriliny had predominated among precolonial tribes, a gap between women and men in access to education, employment and political functions and reduced the leadership potential for women. Points out that nationalist movement and the post independence government utilized women for their activities but did not represent women's interests, which caused the disinterest of women in politics.

1164. Tabak, Fanny. "Women's Role in the Formulation of Public Policies in Brazil." Women, Power and Political System. Edited by Magherita Rendel. London: Croom Helm, 1981, pp. 66-80.

Examines the role of employment and education in relation to the political participation of women in Brazil. Discusses the distribution of women in the occupational structure, taking into account the main changes in late 1970s and some results of the introduction of new areas of learning and professional training.

Also examines the degree of participation of Brazilian women in
high level decision making in the public agencies responsible
for the formulation of three types of crucial public
policy—housing, urban planning and prices. General hypotheses
are proposed about women's participation in some crucial sectors
of national development in order to evaluate possible changes in
their role in Brazilian society. The low rates of female
participation in economic activity are presented to indicate
that the number of new opportunities for female employment
brought about by economic growth is much lower than the number
of women enlarging the urban population every year. Data on
female professionals show that women are still a minority in
professions and hold positions of minor importance, that women
concentrate in "female" careers like humanities and nursing and
that proportion of women members of academic/scientific
associations has increased only recently. As for the
formulation of public policies, women have held higher-level
positions only in education and social welfare. Discussion is
made of the low political participation of women in elected
assemblies either before 1964 or since 1979.

B. Women's Organizations

Books and Monographs

1165. Everett, Jana M. **Women and Social Change in India.** New York:
St. Martin's Press, 1979. 233 pp.

Compares the women's movement in India with that of the United
Kingdom. Points out that one of the major concerns of the
Indian woman's movement has been the extension of educational
opportunities. Criticizes the Indian women's movement for
ignoring the needs of poor and illiterate women.

Kader, Soha Abdel. **Egyptian Women in a Changing Society,
1899-1987.** Boulder and London: Lynne Rienner Publishers, 1987.
163 pp.

See item #295

ISIS Women's International Information and Communication
Service. **Women in Development: A Resource Guide for
Organization and Action.** Philadelphia: New Society Publishers,
1984. 225 pp.

See item #665

1166. Nimer, Kamal K. The Role of Women's Organizations in Eradicating Illiteracy in Jordon. Washington: Abbe Publishers Association, 1986. 247 pp.

Focuses on adult literacy in Jordan and the role of the Women's Association for Combatting Illiteracy. Points out that the government's efforts have been directed toward men and that without the Women's Association, female illiteracy would be greater than it currently is (50 percent). Studies barriers to women's participation in literacy programs and the reasons for the high dropout rate (over 30 percent in 1980). Finds that women's work in the home, their family responsibilities, transport problems, child care, work in the fields and the lack of curricular relevance are identified most by women as the causes of the high dropout rates. Urges more government support for the women's associations' efforts to spread literacy.

1167. Organisation des Femmes de l'Union Nationale Camerounaises. Integration de la Femme Camerounaise dans le Processus de Développement Économique. Yoaunde: OFUNC, WCNU, 1982. 181 pp.

Presents the program of the Women's Wing of the Cameroon National Union Party. Discusses the various government programs to train women as rural animators and to provide women with high school and vocational training. Presents interviews with a number of distinguished women who are senior officials in the Cameroon government. This publication is bilingual and is an agit-prop piece for the Cameroon National Union Party.

1168. Otra Sociedad, Otra Mujer. Bogotá: Comité Femenino del Nuevo Liberalismo, 1982. 128 pp.

Consist of a political statement by feminists within the liberal party of Columbia. Includes a statement by 1982 presidential candidate Lois Carlos Galan. Calls for the organization and official recognition of women in all levels of governance to fulfill the 1981 equal rights law and for further action on abortion, family law and access to and role within the work force. Specifically in education, calls for a wider range of sex education, greater concern for life styles of rural and native women in education, full equality of education and attention to the media as an educative organ which produces negative sex role stereotypes from both domestic and foreign sources.

1169. Seetharamu, A.S. Women in Organized Movements. New Delhi: Ambika Publications, 1981. 144 pp.

Examines the nature and extent of elite women's participation in organized movements in India. Data were collected by

interviewing 175 employed women in Bangalore city.   Chapter one
(Introduction) briefly explains the plight of women in India and
the role which elite women could play in improving women's
status by participating in their professional union activities.
Chapter two through chapter six describe the participation of
women advocates in their two associations, the participation of
women doctors in the Indian Medical Association, the
participation of women senior civil servants in the IAS
Association, the participation of women engineers in the
Institution of Engineers and the participation of female college
and university teachers in their associations, respectively.
Points out that only women advocates and female teachers, to a
certain extent, show a minimum level of awareness and
understanding of the need and significance of participation, and
others, especially doctors, gave a disappointing picture.   The
last chapter analyzes this inadequate participation of women in
organizational activities in terms of socialization, male
domination, caste-class background, etc., and calls for a deeper
study of the problem in a comparative setting.

The Role of Women in Development: The Indonesian Experience.
Jakarta: KOWANI (Indonesian Women's Congress), 1980.   35 pp.

See item #724

United Nations, Economic Commission for Africa.   Séminaire sur
les Mécanismes Nationaux en Faveur de l'Intégration des Femmes
au Procesus de Développement Tenu au 6 Septembre 1979.   Adddis
Ababa: Nations Unies Commission Economique pour l'Afrique,
1981.   26 pp.

See item #703

1170. World Congress of Women, Documents of the World Congress of
Women--Equality, National Independence, Peace.   Prague, CSSR,
8-13 October 1981.   Berlin, GDR: Secretariat of the Women's
International Democratic Federation, 1981.   168 pp.

Reprints speeches made at the 1981 World Congress of Women
meeting in Prague.   Several of the speeches mention women and
development.   Contains the reports of the Congress Secretariat,
most of which call for peace and disarmament.

Articles

1171. Corkery, Mary.   "Subversion: Chilean Women Learning for
Changes."   The Decade for Women.   Edited by Aisla Thomson.
Toronto: Canadian Congress for Learning Opportunities for
Women, 1986, pp. 133-140.

Describes the Movement of Shantytown Women in Chile which is organized by Chilean women to resist against hunger and misery that are part of their every day lives. The primary goal of the movement is to end the dictatorship and bring back democracy in the country. The movement provides nonformal education to women through its activities, helps raising women's political consciousness and sets up ways for women to learn what they need to know to survive and change their environment.

1172. Enabulele, Arlene Bene. "The Role of Women's Associations in Nigeria's Development: Social Welfare Perspective." **Women in Nigeria Today.** Edited by Editorial Committee, Women in Nigeria. London: Zed Books, 1985, pp. 187-194.

Provides background on women's associations in Nigeria which have played an active role in Nigeria's development. Presents information on data from random sample of 50 women's associations in Benin City which are known as bands, committees, groups, clubs, guilds, unions or societies ranging from very informal to formal, with 5 to over 500 members. Describes the multiple roles and general objectives of these volunteer associations. Describes their important contributions to health, education and social areas of life. Points out contributions to education as being to foster the need for female education for national development, provide scholarships and funds, establish and maintain day care and nursery schools. Suggests issuing an annual updated directory listing women's organizations and information which could be used by those who would consult associations for advice and assistance.

Hahner, June E. "Feminism, Women's Rights, and the Suffrage Movement in Brazil, 1850-1932." **Latin American Research Review** 15 (1980): 65-111.

See item #280

McCall, Cecelia. "Women and Literacy: The Cuban Experience." **Journal of Reading** 30 (1987): 318-324.

See item #650

1173. Lee, Wendy. "Women's Groups in Papua New Guinea: Shedding the Legacy of Drop Scones and Embroidered Pillowcases." **Community Development Journal** 20 (1985): 222-236.

Outlines recent government policies concerning women in Papua New Guinea. Examines whether women's groups have the potential to mobilize women against the processes of marginalization. Presents an overview of some of the main issues and difficulties associated with special projects for women. Concluded that women's inferior social status has not been altered since the government has been unable or unwilling to take the step further and make the link between women's poverty and men's power.

Ravindran, Sundari. "Confronting Gender, Poverty and Powerlessness: An Orientation Programme for and by Rural Change Agents." Community Development Journal 20 (1985): 213-221.

See item*#639

1174. Southard, Barbara. "Bengal Women's Education League: Pressure Group and Professional Association." Modern Asian Studies 18 (1984): 55-88.

Discusses the goals and activities of Bengal Women's Education League in Bengal, India. Questions examined are: Who were these women? For whom did they speak? What were their educational and social backgrounds? Finds that the League pressed for the inclusion of girls in schemes of compulsory primary education and adequate representation of women on administrative boards supervising education. The League was almost entirely composed of women educators. Top leaders of the League are from the upper castes. The League supports the key demands of the national education movement for rapid introduction of UPE and more extensive use of the vernacular. Stresses on Indian cultural values and more vocational and practical training in the schools. The success of the League was limited.

1175. Tandon, Kalpana and V. Rukmini Rao. "Learning from and about Women's Organizations: An Exploratory Analysis in the Indian Context." Convergence 13 (1980): 124-134.

Describes the significant characteristics and problems of women's organizations and discusses some strategies for building new organizations and helping existing ones by looking at two such organizations in India. Suggests that focus be in the direction for change towards the building of a nonhierarchial organization that functions effectively by considering the particular characteristics of women's organizations.

1176. Wipper, Audrey. "The Maendeleo Ya Wanawake Organization: The Co-optation of Leadership." African Studies Review 18 (December 1975): 99-120.

Provides a critical study of a major philanthropic women's organization which formerly aimed at rural development projects and education. Traces the rise of dominance of urban educated women within the organization who have been coopted by the government and its promises. Urges a reassertion of values and education goals.

XV. WOMEN'S STUDIES

Women's Studies is a relatively new phenomenon and we end thi
bibliography with a list of works that chart the development o
women's studies as an educational program as well as a research are
in the third world.

Books and Monographs

1177. Bonder, Gloria and Cristina Zurutuza. Seminario Regional
Latinoaméricano y del Caribe Sobre el Desarrollo de Curricula y
Preparación de Materiales de Ensenanza en Estudios de la Mujer
para la Educación Superior en América Latina y el Caribe.
Buenos Aires: Centro de Estudios de la Mujer, 1986.

Presents a women's studies curricula for higher education in
Latin America and provides a research guide to the literature on
women in Latin American on women and work, women and politics,
culture and female identity formation which would be appropriate
for women's studies courses.

Papanek, Hanna. Women in Development and Women's Studies:
Agenda for the Future. East Lansing: Office of Women in
International Development, Michigan State University, 1984.   18
pp. (Working Paper no. 55)

See item #668

1178. Report of the National Conference on Women's Studies, April
20-24, 1981. Bombay: Shreemati Nathibai Damodar Thackersey
Women's University, 1981.

Indicates a broad criticism and research agenda for women's
studies in India. Includes demands for research on the dropout
rate of women in Indian education and concern for middle class
domination of education to foster its own interest. Comments on
survey research on curriculum, particularly at the university

level, and demands broad consideration of women's roles in
agriculture and vocational education where they are grossly
ignored.

Articles

1179. Bonder, Gloria. "Los Estudios de la Mujer y la Critica
Epistemologica a los Paradigmas de las Ciencias Humanas."
Estudios Sobre Desarrollo Economica 13 (January 1984): 25-39.

Discusses the challenges of feminsim to the social sciences and
traces the beginning of such challenges in Latin America to
1970. Critiques history, sociology, anthroplogy and psychology
and discusses the development of women's studies and its
paradigms.

1180. Chung, Sei-wha and Jin-sook Park. "Women's Studies at Ewha
Woman's University." Challenges for Women: Women's Studies in
Korea. Edited by Chung Sei-wha. Seoul: Ewha Woman's
University Press, 1986, pp. 282-319.

Traces how women's studies was started and developed as a formal
curriculum in a women's university in Korea by describing its
administrative organization and the contents of the program in
both graduate and undergraduate schools. Since women's studies
is taught as a major discipline only in graduate school with a
master's degree program and students come from various academic
backgrounds, it is difficult to advise them how to link their
earlier training to women's studies. Points out that it is
important to develop the theory, methodology and approach of the
field from the Korean perspective.

1181. Faulkner, Constance. "Women's Studies in the Muslim Middle
East." The Journal of Ethnic Studies 8 (1980): 67-76.

Reviews the history of women's studies in the Middle East.
Describes the position of Muslim women, stressing that the
tenacity of religious rule over family and personal matters is
well demonstrated among most of the populations and that a more
conservative attitude towards women is asserted in the
societies. Points out that despite stated national goals to the
contrary, women in Middle Eastern Muslim culture are worse off
today than women in any other part of the world—fewer women are
educated, the gap between male and female levels of educational
attainment is growing; the percent of women working in
nonagricultural jobs is the smallest in the world; the birth
rate is the highest and laws governing family and personal life
are among the world's most oppressive. Concludes that Islamic

values in Muslim families are reinforced by and in turn reinforce
the relatively low status of women.

1182. Glenn, Evelyn. "As Ciencias Humanas e a Situação da Mulher."
Cadernos de Pesquisa no. 24 (1978): 15-21.

Traces the development of the study of women and women's studies
in Brazil. Argues that most of the social science disciplines
discriminate against women and use theories which reinforce
patriarchial relations. Urges the development of women's
studies and greater emphasis on the cross cultural study of
women.

1183. Kashif-Badri, Hagga. "The History, Development, Organization
and Position of Women's Studies in the Sudan." Social Science
Research and Women in the Arab World. Edited by UNESCO. London
and Dover, New Hampshire: Pinter, 1984, pp. 94-105.

Reviews the history of women's studies in the Sudan, stressing
that women's studies in the modern scientific sense began in the
Sudan at the beginning of the second half of this century.
During the 1950s, women's studies dealt with educational and
health questions as they affected women, with the question of
women's work and their opportunities for training and
specialization and their social and political rights. In the
period from the mid-1960s to the mid-1970s women's studies
concentrated on political studies.

Kim, Okgill. "The Place of Women's Colleges: The Korean
Experience, Ewha University." New Frontiers in Education 8
(1978): 47-56.

See item #533

1184. Messiah, Joycelin. "Establishing a Programme of Women and
Development Studies in the University of the West Indies."
Social and Economic Studies 35 (no. 1, 1986): 151-197.

Reports the background and progress made towards the
establishment of a Women and Development Studies Program at the
University of the West Indies. Discusses regional activity
concerning women, United Nations activity, the position of women
in the Caribbean, contradictions, the University of West Indies
and Programs related to women, traditional stereotypes,
teaching, research, the Women in the Caribbean Project, Outreach
(linking the University to the Wider Community), links between
UWI programs and other regional programs, how the program is
envisaged, an outline of how the program should be integrated,
principles of the program, structure and funding.

1185. Mazumdar, Vina and Kumud Sharma. "Women's Studies: New Perceptions and the Challenges." Economic and Political Weekly 14 (January 20, 1979): 113-120.

Surveys women's studies in India. Points out the role of half the population is being ignored in economic developmenmt. Urges organization of pressure groups, organizations in the state to focus on women's needs, the organization and training of cadres with a broad feminist perspective and special preference for women in vocational training.

1186. Rendel, Margherita. "A Worldwide Panorama of Research and Teaching Related to Women." Cultures 8 (no. 3, 1982): 105-125.

Surveys teaching and research related to women. Shows some aspects common to the geocultural regions, among which the most striking difference between the third world and some of the western countries is the lack of women's studies teaching in the majority of third world countries. Points out that women's studies research is undertaken in the overwhelming majority of countries throughout the world and attributes this development to the policy and the financial support by international organizations.

1187. Spender, Dale. "Learning to Create Our Own Knowledge." Convergence 13 (1980): 14-22.

Argues for women's studies programs that are controlled by women and autonomous. Urges that adult education programs include women's studies in order to help transform women's subordination to liberation. While women's studies should be a major part of adult education, advocates that women's studies should not be confined to adult education. Advocates the construction of women centered knowledge.

1188. Tabak, Fanny. "UN Decade and Women's Studies in Latin America." Women's Studies International Forum 8 (no. 2 1985): 103-106.

Examines the significance of UN's Women Decade to the advancement of women's studies in Latin America. By early 1980s women's studies in this part of the world was still in its early stages and few regular programs had been really implemented. One of these was the Center for Women's Studies at the Pontifical Catholic University of Rio de Janeiro in early 1981. A Regional Seminar on Women's Studies in South America and the Caribbean was held at the University in late 1981 to evaluate the situation of teaching and research in 11 countries and concluded that much still needed to be done in that field.

Yossundara, Chintana.   "Viable Programs in Higher Education for
Women in Development in Southeast Asia."   The Role of Women in
Development: Seminar Papers and Statements.   Edited by Leonardo
Z. Legaspi.   Manila: University of San Tomas Press, 1976,
pp. 182-186.

See item #540

Aalami, Schahrus
297
Abadan-Unat, Nermin
763, 1003
Abbasi, M.B.
139
Abbott, Susan
716
Addelkrin, Rabia
952
Abeille, Barbara
312
Abramovich, Fanny
561
Abu, Katherine
1013
Abu-Laban, Baha
365, 576
Abu-Laban, Sharon McIrvin
365
Abu Nasr, Julinda
948
Acharya, Meena
104
Acker, Sandra
62,75
Acosta-Belén, Edna
898
Adams, Leah D.
1051
Adams, Lois
215
Adams, Milton N.
313, 316
Adlakha, A. L.
1147
African Training and
Research Center for Women
593, 769, 772
Agarwal, Bina
546, 871
Aggarwal, J. C.
38
Aggarwal, Yash
555

Aghajarian, Akbar
886, 1143
Agheyisi, Rachel Uwa
828
Agnes, Vijay
242
Agrawal, Mamta
739
Ahmad, Anis
524
Ahmad, Karuna
241, 547, 872
Ahmad, Manzoor
579
Ahmad, Shabans
1029
Ahmad, Shadbano
420
Ahmed, Nilufer Raihan
141
Ahooja-Patel, Krishna
773
Akandr, Bolanle E.
479
Alamsir, Susan Fuller
105
Al-Bassam, Ibtissam A.
570
Alexander, L.
476
Al-Hariri, Rafeda
430
Al-Hatimy, Said Abdullah Seif
405
Ali, Mohamed Adham
1057
Ali, Parveen Shaukat
117
Al-Isi, Ismail
1052
Al-Kadhi, Ann Bradgon
1144
Allaghi, Farida
63

Almana, Aisha
    63
Al-Nouri, Q. N.
    571
Al-Qazzaz, A.
    53, 57
Alrabaa, Sami
    446
Al-Sabah, S. M.
    761
Al-Sa'Dawi, Nawal
    433
Al-Sanabary, Nagat
    366
Altorki, Soraya
    196
Alvarez, Alberto Miguel Correa
    746
Amoroso, M.
    559
Anani, Elma Lititia
    972
Anant, Suchitra
    39
Anderson, C. A.
    303
Anderson, G. M.
    375
Andiappan, P.
    856
Andors, Phyllis
    157
Andradi, Esther
    996
Angeles, Edna S.
    894
Antrobus, Peggy
    750, 751
Appleton, Sheldon
    485
Aragonés, Maria
    558
Arittin, Rohana
    148
Arizpe, Lourdes
    942
Arnand, Anita
    674
Arosemena de Tejeira, Otilia
    432

Arowolo, Oladele
    1083
Asayehgn, Desta
    824
Ashby, A. Jacqueline
    399
Atkiewicz, Susan
    22
Attir, Mustafa O.
    298
Awanohara, Susumu
    266
Awosida, Keziah
    829
Aziz, Nov Laily
    721
Baali, Fuad
    572
Bach, Rebecca
    1053
Báez, Clara
    110
Baffoun, Alya
    953
Ballou, Patricia K.
    1
Bam, Brigalia H.
    407, 740
Bangladesh, Ministry of Education
    324
Bangun, Masliana
    612
Baquai, Sabihuddin
    1117
Barazangi, Ni'mat Hafez
    367
Barber, Elinor G.
    376
Barbieri, M. Teresita de
    943, 1131
Barbin, Christina
    752
Bardouille, Raj
    704
Barrera, Manuel
    935
Barrig, Maruja
    1046

Barroso, Carmen L. M.
    434, 562
Barrow, R. Nata
    1014
Barthel, Diane
    216, 976
Bay, Edna G.
    83
Bazante, Julia
    185
Beachy, Debra
    566
Beck, Lois
    102
Beckett, Paul A.
    519
Beekman, E. M.
    267
Behrman, Jere R.
    1047, 1142
Belhachmi, Zakia
    764
Belloncie, Guy
    581, 691
Bender, Deborah
    1048
Benería, Louredes
    806
Bengelsdorf, Carollee
    753
Benitez, Helena
    527
Bennett, Lynn
    140
Beran, Janice Ann
    447
Bernard, Anne K.
    582
Bernstein-Tarrow, Norma
    160
Bhandari, R. K.
    251, 341
Bhansali, Kamalini
    345
Bhargava, Gura
    548, 549
Bhasin, Kamala
    346, 631
Bhatt, R. V.
    550

Bhatty, Zarina
    400
Biaggio, Angela Maria
    492
Bickner, Mei Liang
    2
Biraimah, Karen
    456, 457, 458, 459, 520
Bird, Edris
    644
Blake, Myrna
    847
Blau, Francine D.
    807
Blaug, Mark
    830
Blitz, Rudolph C.
    973
Blumberg, Rae Lesser
    849
Blumberg, Rhoda Lois
    987
Bocquet-Siek, Margaret
    231
Bonder, Gloria
    1177, 1179
Bonilla de Ramos, Elssy
    353
Bonnell, Susanne
    528
Boothbody, Roger A.
    462
Borges, Wanda Rose
    270
Borthwick, Meredith
    243, 252
Bose, Ashish
    108
Boserup, Ester
    658, 873
Boulding, Elsie
    675
Bouvier, Leon F.
    1132
Bowman, Mary Jean
    303
Bradshaw, Sue
    238
Braslavsky, Cecilia
    94

Bravo, Rosa
    936
Brey, Kathleen Healy
    641
Briones, Jose M.
    504
Brody, Eugene B.
    1126, 1133
Brown, Lagage
    594
Brown, M.
    559
Browner, C. H.
    657
Bruchhaus, Eva-Maria
    314
Bruschini, M. Aranha
    929, 997
Bryson, C. Judy
    692
Bryson, Hugh
    230
Burga, Terersa
    111
Buripakdi, Chalio
    1122
Butter, Irene
    977
Butterfield, Cynthia
    825
Buvinic, Mayra
    3, 850, 1012
Byrne, Pamela R.
    4

Cain, Mead
    1058
Caldwell, J. C.
    1007, 1015
Calixto, Julia
    1065, 1066
Callaway, Barbara J.
    411, 412
Callaway, Helen
    224, 676
Camp, Roderic A.
    567
Campbell, Penelope
    217

Canlas, Dante B.
    883
Cardoso E. Silva, Maria Luisa
    705
Cardoso, Irede
    927
Carleton, Robert O.
    1134
Carmen Regueiro, Maria del
    173
Casal, Lourdes
    192
Cathelat, Marie-France
    111
Cebotarev, Eleonora A.
    645, 808
Centro de Estudios de Poblacion y
Desarrollo
    112
Cha, Itty
    237
Chang, Ligia
    899, 900
Channey, Elsa M.
    754
Chapman, Bruce J.
    884
Chapman, David W.
    462
Charlton, Sue Ellen M.
    659
Chaten, Jeanne H.
    791
Chaturvedi, Geeta
    988
Chaudhury, Rafiqul Huda
    141, 842, 1105, 1106, 1107
Chauhan, Indira
    989
Chaui, Marilena
    448
Chemli, M.
    654
Chen, F. K. Y.
    725
Chen, Lincoln C.
    1008
Cheng, Soik Hwa
    325, 848

Chesterfield, Ray
651
Cheung, Paul P. L.
340
Chhabra, Rami
632
Chiang, Lan-hung Nora
142
Cho, Hyoung
849
Chung, Betty Jamie
30
Chung, Sei-wha
435, 1180
Cismaresco, Françoise
5
Cisneros, Antinio
1128
Cisneros, J.
901
Clark, Noreen
660
Clason, Carla
677
Clemente, Ursula Uichanco
529
Clignet, Remi
831
Cochrane, Susan H.
1059, 1067, 1068
Cohen, Lucy M.
998
Cohen-Stuart, Bertie A.
44
Cohn, Steven
792
Colclough, Christopher
1069
Cole, Jane
595
Cole, Johnnetta
193
Cole, Joyce
275
Collazo-Collazo, Jenaro
354
Colson, Elizabeth
379
Comhaire-Sylvain, S.
317

Comision Interamericana de
Mujeres
95
Conde, Maryse
186
Confederacion Interamericana
de Educación Católica
426
Conklin, Goerge H.
1030
Conning, Arthur M.
1127
Cooksey, Brian
318
Coombs, Philip H.
579
Corkery, Mary
1171
Cornell, M. Louise
964
Correas, E.
276
Cosar, Fatman Mansur
203
Coutrot, Ann-Marie
652
Covarrubias, Paz
96
Crocombe, Marjorie Tuainekore
530
Croll, Elisabeth
158, 161
Crone, c.
609, 610
Cross, Malcolm
393
Csapo, Marg.
413
Curtin, Leslie B.
803
Cutler, Virginia F.
661
Cutrufelli, Maria Rosa
213

Danforth, Sandra C.
6, 18
Dann, Graham M. S.
49

Darbai, Katherine
    1145
Daro, B.
    333
Das Dupta, Kalpana
    40
DaVanzo, Julie
    1020
Davidson, Maria
    1135
Davies, Lynn
    64, 505
Davis, Fanny
    291
Dawit, T.
    596
Deole, Isabelle
    300, 853
DeBopp, Marianne O.
    514
de Carvalho, Abilio
    218
DeGallo, Maria Gowland
    277
Delcroix, Catherine
    1152
Derryck, Vivian L.
    662
Desai, Chitrakum
    342
Desai, Neera
    168, 551
de Silva, Lea Melo
    1129
De Tray, Dennis N.
    1070
Devendra, Kiran
    244
Devi, Lalitha U.
    857
Devon, Toniak
    1157
Diamond, Norma
    1041, 1042
Diarra, Abdramane
    1153
Dichie, Virginia
    856
Dixon, Ruth B.
    1071

Dodd, Peter C.
    431, 497
Doeriat, F.
    383
Don, Fatimah Hamid
    149, 334
D'Onofrio-Flores, Pamela M.
    770, 774
Doraiswami, S. S.
    858
Doublas, Ray
    160
Draper, Elaine
    755
Drayton, K. B.
    187, 278
Droegkamp, Janis
    663
D'Souza, Alfred
    86, 874, 1111
D'Souza, Stan
    66
D'Souza, Victor S.
    875
DuBois, Ellen Carol
    58
Ducci, María
    899, 900
Due, Jean M.
    706
Dupont, Beatrice
    442
Durno, Janet
    621
Dwaraki, Leela
    987

Eichelbaum de Babini, Ana M.
    355
Eisen, Arlene
    143
Ejiogu, Aloy M.
    506
Elahi, K. Maudood
    59
El Guindi, Fadwa
    573
Eliou, Marie
    304, 319

Elizaga, Juan C.
   913
Elliott, Carolyn M.
   78, 305, 742
Ellis, Pat
   67, 646
Elsasser, Nan
   647
Elu de Leñero, Maria de Carmen
   944
Enabulele, Arlene Bene
   1172
Encarnacion, J.
   1093
Endagama, Malari
   326
Engle, Patricia L.
   463
Erasmus, G.
   1084
Erkut, Sumru
   967
Escudero, Christina Maria
   642
Eskamp, C.
   7
Espenshade, T.
   1072
Evans, David R.
   478, 480
Evenson, Robert
   1116
Everett, Jana M.
   1165

Fan, Kok-sim
   31
Fapohunda, Eleanor R.
   517
Farooq, Ghazi M.
   1148
Farrell, Joseph P.
   120, 939
Fasheh, Munir
   854
Faulkner, Costanie
   1181
Fawcett, James T.
   1089

Feijoó, Maria del Carmen
   45
Feinberg, Renee
   19
Fernandez, Joseph
   1091
Fernández Berdaguer, Maria
Leticia
   560
Fernando, D. F. S.
   1094
Fernea, Elizabeth Warnock
   103
Ferree, Myra Marx
   859
Ferretti, C. J.
   563
Filgueira, Nea
   902
Finegan, T. A.
   809
Finn, J. D.
   306, 464
Fiore, Kyle
   647
Fisek, Nusret
   1149
Fisher, Marguerite J.
   531
Fisher, Michael M. J.
   204
Flora, Cornelia Butler
   795
Flores, Pura
   335, 896
Fonseca, Claudia
   597
Forbes, Geraldine H.
   253
Forde, Norma
   97, 174
Fortmann, Louise
   23, 693
Fox, Greer Litton
   765
Foz y Foz, Pilar
   271
Frances, Jeanne
   726

Franco, Rolando
    96
Franco, Zoila
    194
Freedman, Marion
    604
Friderich, Nicole
    307
Fry, Gerald W.
    32
Fucaraccio, Angel
    937
Fundação, Carlos Chagas
    46
Fundação Instituto Brasileiro
de Geografia e Estatística
    114
Furst, Alduild
    197
Futehally, Laeeq
    87

Galadanci, Alhasi S. A.
    414
Galal, Salma
    292
Galeano, Luis A.
    914
Gallin, Rita S.
    843
Gálvez Barrera, Ana M.
    279
Gama, Elizabeth Maria Pinheiro
    564
Gans, Lydia P.
    1095
Garfield, Richard
    532
Garmon, Martha
    521
Gayfer, Margaret
    582, 583
George, Igoche
    598
Gérard, Renée
    619
Germain, Adrienne
    734

German Foundation for
Developing Countries
    694
Ghimire, Durga
    727
Ghosh, Ratna
    388, 389
Ghosh, Srabashi
    254
Giele, Janet Z.
    68, 76
Glazer, Daphne
    380
Glenn, Evelyn
    1182
Golstein, Rhoda L.
    541
Golstein, Sidney
    1124
Gonzales, Alfonso
    1001
Gonzales Cortes, Gerarado
    1136
Gonzalez Salazar, Gloria
    945, 946
Gonzalez, Victoria Durant
    1049
Gopaldes, Tara
    1031
Gordon, Joanna
    599
Gorwaney, Naintara
    542
Gould, Ketayun
    347
Gould, Terri F.
    979, 980
Graciano, Marilia
    436
Grande, Humberto
    175
Green, Justin J.
    728
Greenhalgh, Susan
    398
Greenstreet, Miranda
    133, 832
Grogan, D.
    472

Grossat, Bernard
671
Guarín de Vizcaya, Delina
188
Guerra-Cunningham, Lucia
98
Guerrero, Sylvia H.
984, 1039
Gugler, Josef
859
Guindi, Fadwa
960
Gulati, Saroj
245
Gulati, Subhash Chander
1032
Gupta, Anirudha
132
Gutierrez de Pineda, Virginia
915

Habicht, Jean-Pierre
1020
Hafeez, Sabeeha
889
Hafkin, Nancy
24, 83
Hageman, Alice
753
Hahner, June E.
280, 1158
Halim, Fatimah
885
Hall, Marjorie
125
Hamilton, Marlene
356, 465, 466
Han, Suyin
1096
Hansen, Karen Tranberg
833
Haque, Adhila
633, 634
Haque, Rezaul
623
Harding, J. Ros
884
Harfoush, Samira
368

Hariani, Kamala
486
Harlen, Wynne
467
Harnisch, Delwyn L.
468
Harper, J.
834
Harrison, David S.
1090
Hassan, Iftikhar N.
399
Hassan, Soad Hussein
574
Hawkins, John N.
1097
Hayani, I.
205
Heggade, Ideyar D.
741
Henriquez de Paredes, Querubina
903
Herbert, Suzanne
796
Hermalin, Albert I.
384
Hernández de Alba, Guillermo
281
Herrmann, Eleanor Krohn
282
Higgins, Kathleen Mansfield
600
Hinderstein, Cora
849
Hironaka, Kazuhiko
255
Hirschman, C.
336, 886
Hirschmann, David
1154
Holsinger, Donald
1073
Hooper, Beverley
729
Hoque, N.
620
Howard-Merriam, Kathleen
1005, 1159, 1160
Hull, Valerie
854

Hunter, Carman St. John
    648
Hussain, Ghulam
    613
Huston, Perdita
    664
Hwa, Cheng Soik
    150
Hyder, Qurratulain
    421

Ihromi T. Omas
    151
India, Ministry of Education
and Social Welfare
    625
Ingrams, Doreen
    198
International Labour
Organization
    611
Irfan, Mohammad
    890
ISIS Women's International
Information and Communication
Service
    665
Islam, Mahmuda
    33, 735
Islam, Shamima
    327, 622
Ismail, Bakhita Amin
    125

Jacobs, Sue Ellen
    9
Jacobson, Doranne
    743
Jahan, Mehraj
    256
Jahan, Rounaq
    88
Jahoda, Gustav
    481
Jain, Anrudh K.
    1074, 1109, 1112, 1113
Jaquette, Jane S.
    679
Jarial, Gurpal Singh
    469

Jayaweera, Swarna
    385, 640
Jaynes, G.
    206
Jenkins, Janet
    584
Jerez Alvarado, Rafael
    350
Jesudason, Victor
    626
Jesus-Viardo, Alma de
    89
Jahabvala, Renana
    552
Jiagge, Justice Annie
    601, 797
Jiménez de Vega, Mercedes
    176
Joekes, Susan
    955
John, Mariam
    401
Johnson, Cheryl
    225
Jones, Connie A.
    169
Jones, Garvin W.
    850
Jones, Marie T.
    369
Joshi, Rama
    990
Joshi, Vibha
    65
Joyner, C. C.
    680
Joyner, Nancy D.
    680
Junge, Barbara Jackson
    602, 614
Jusenius, Carol L.
    807, 810
Jusuf, Naftuchah
    337
Jys, J. M.
    136

Kader, Soha Abdel
    295
Kagitcibasi, Cigdem
    1054, 1150, 1151
Kakar, D. N.
    1009
Kakar, Sudhir
    437
Kale, B. B.
    1033
Kalia, N. N.
    443, 444, 449
Kamat, A. R.
    348
Kamikamica, Esiteri
    338
Kannagara, Imogen
    851
Kapadia, K. M.
    1026
Kappoor, B. L.
    319, 1034
Kapur, Promilla
    860
Karanja, Wambui Wa
    835
Karl, Marilee
    798
Karlekar, Malavika
    257
Kasarda, D. John
    1073
Kashif-Badri, Hagga
    1183
Katiyar, P. C.
    469
Katyal, F. C.
    41
Katzenstein, Mary Fainsod
    1161
Kazgan, Gulten
    968
Keddie, Nikki
    102
Keeves, John
    470
Kelly, Alison
    471, 775
Kelly, David H.
    10, 20, 21

Kelly, Gail P.
    10, 20, 21, 69, 77, 78,
    305, 308, 377, 378
Kelly, Maria Patricia
    Fernández
    649, 681
Kerina J. M.
    28
Ketkar, Suhos L.
    1085
Khalid, Ruhi
    424
Khan, M. A.
    ·1119
Khan, M. W.
    487
Khan, Nighat Said
    152, 627
Khatun, Sharifa
    736
Khawaja, Sarfraz
    328
Khiang, Mi Mi
    144
Kight, Howard R.
    496
Kim, Chu-suk
    153
Kim, Ik Ki
    1098
Kim, Okgill
    533
Kim, Soung-Yee
    1099
Kindervatter, Suzanne
    615, 660
King, Ursula
    406, 408
Kinyanjui, Kabiru
    836, 837
Kinzer, Nora Scott
    999, 1000
Kishwar, Madhu
    258
Klimpel, Felicitas
    177
Klineberg, Stephen L.
    498, 766
Knabe, Erika
    417

Knaster, Meri
    47, 51
Knauss, Peter R.
    296
Koenig, Dolores B.
    1086
Koh, Hesung Chun
    34
Kohen, A. I.
    11
Kohli, K. L.
    1146
Kok-Huatlee
    1021
Kokuhirwa, Hilda
    838
Korayen, Korima
    954
Korson, J. Henry
    891
Kotwal, Marilyn
    309
Krannich, Caryl Rae
    1125
Krannich, Ronald
    1125
Krishnaraj, Maithreyi
    70, 776, 876, 994
Kruppenbach, Susan E.
    313, 316
Ku, Yenlin
    142
Kumerloeve, Arnd D.
    329
Kurian, George
    401
Kutner, Nancy G.
    472

Labadie, Gastón J.
    557
Lafosse, Violta Sara
    178
Lamba, Isaac C.
    219
Langley, Philip
    695
Langmore, D.
    232

LaRaia, Anita L.
    1050
Lavalle Urbina, Maria
    568
Lazo, Lucita
    844
Leal, Maria Angela
    682
Lebner, Dietlinde
    199
Lebra, Joyce
    861
Lee, Hie-sung
    534
Lee, Hyo Chae
    153
Lee, Wendy
    1173
Leet, Mildred Robbins
    777
Legaspi, Leonardo Z.
    90
Leghorn, Lisa
    667
Lemsine, Aicha
    428
Lao-Rhynie, Elsa
    356
Leonard, Karen
    71, 170
Leon de Leal, M.
    52
Levine, R. L.
    565, 1010
Lewin, Helena
    930
Lewis, Barbara C.
    1016, 1087
Lewis, Shelby F.
    707
Liddle, Joanna
    990
Likimani, Muthoni
    715
Lindsay, Beverly
    79, 121, 482, 483, 717,
    981
Link, Beulah M.
    162

Lipeovich de Querol, Tamara
189
Little, Cynthia Jeffress
283
Liu, Mei Ching
239
Llano Cifuentes, Carlos
569
Lobo, Francisco Bruno
284
Lodgesdon, Martha
450
Luguga, Lucy
590
Luseno, D.
718
Luz, Madel T.
99
Luzuriaga C., Carlos
904
Lynch, Enid
357

Mabud, Mohammed A.
1103
MacDonald, John Stuart
811
MacDonald, Leatrice
811
Macisco, John J.
1132
Macy, Joanna
722
Maglangit, Virginia R.
1037
Mahadevan, Meera
877
Mahajani, Usha
730
Maher, Vanessa
200, 207
Mahfoud-Draoui, D.
956
Mahmud, Satnam
616
Mair, Lucille
585, 586
Malta Campos, Maria M.
402

Manderson, Lenore
233, 1022
Mann, Kristin
226
Marckwardt, Albert M.
1127
Marsh, Robert
1043
Martha, H.
598
Martin, Luis
272
Marin-Liao, Tienchi
235
Martorelli, Horacio
905
Mascarenhas, Ophelia
25
Masermann, Vandra
460
Maskiell, Michelle
246, 259, 418
Massiah, Joycelin
48, 906, 1184
Mathur, Anita
635
Mathur, Y.B.
247
Matsepe, Ivy
839
Mauras, Marta
179
Mauricio, Rufino
32
Max-Forson, Margaret
126
May, Joan
826
Mazumdar, Vina
553, 744, 745, 1185
Mbilinyi, Marjorie J.
25, 320, 381, 394, 395,
522, 708
Mburu, F.M.
709
McCall, Cerelia
650
McGrath, Patricia L.
301

McKenzie, Hermione
358
McSweeney, Brenda Gael
603, 604
Mead, Margaret
122
Meesook, Kanitta M.
845
Meghdessian, Samira Rafidi
54
Meghji, Zakia
605
Mehryar, A.H.
499
Mehta, Rana
543
Mehta, Sushila
165
Mehta, Vimla
544
Meleis, Afaf I.
574, 965
Melo Cardona, Ligia A.
351
Menard, Scott
1075, 1076
Mendoza, Guadalupe
947
Menon, Geeta
65
Menon, M. Indu
422
Mernissi, Fatima
950
Meyer, V.I.
359
Mies, Maria
1027
Miller, Beth
1001
Miller, Errol L.
493
Miller, Linda
501, 508
Minai, Naila
429
Minattur, Joseph
171
Mincer, J.
812

Minces, Juliette
208
Minturn, L.D. Boyd
1034
Misra, Lakshmi
248
Mitchell, Edna M.
535
Mitchell, J. Clyde
1088
Mitchnik, D.A.
591
Mitra, Asok
106, 862
Mohammed, Patricia
360
Mohsen, Safia K.
961
Molla, M.K.U.
260
Molyneux, Maxine
123, 124, 209, 951
Moorman, P.
370
Moracco, John C.
1055
Morrow, S.
220
Moses, Yolanda
1022
Mouses, Arpy
1055
Muchena, Olivia N.
827
Mueller, Eva
1100
Mujahid, Ghazy
299
Mukerjee, A.K.
41
Mukerjee, S.N.
261
Mulay, Sumati
1114
Munger, F.
663
Muni, Anuradha
731
Muni, S.D.
731

Muntemba, M. Shimwaayi
22
Mustaffa-Kedah, O.
371, 655
Mutua, Rosalind
719
Myin, Marie Antionette
710
Myntti, C.
762

Naciones Unidas. Comision
Economica para America Latina
y el Caribe
180
Nag, Moni
1009, 1112, 1113
Naidu, Usha S.
390
Naik, Chitra
636, 637
Naik, J.P.
343
Namo de Mello, Guiomar
438, 562
Nanda, B.R.
91
Nash, June
100
Nashif, Rwadah Z.
513
Nasir, Rohany
887
Nath, Kamla
966
National Commission on the
Role of Filipino Women
445
Navawongs, Tippan
1123
Nayak, Sharada
991
Neher, Clark D.
154
Nelso, Nici
683
Nelson, Cynthia
423
Nelson, Merwyn
1101

Newland, Kathleen
118
Newman, Jeanne S.
127
Ngean, Ng See
488
Niemi, Albert W. Jr.
813
Nimer, Kamal K.
1166
Nischol, K.
451
Nizza da Silva, Maria Beatriz
285
Noman, Ayesha
1104
Noor, Yetty R.
732
Nouacer, Khadidja
957
Nwanosike, Eugene
12
Nxumalo, Simanga
606

Obbo, Christine
134
O'Brien, Leslie N.
536
O'Brien, Mary
1162
Ochoa Nuñez, Hernado
361
O'Connell, James
519
O'Donnell, Carol
814
Oduyaye, Mercy Ambo
415
Oey, Mayling
852, 853
Oglesby, K.L.
587
O'Hara, Albert
1043, 1044
Okonkwo, Rina
227
Oleksy-Ojikuta, A.E.
473

Oliveira, Zulieka L. Cide
    931
Olsen, Nancy J.
    489
Oncu, Ayse
    1004
Onibokun, Yemi
    484
Ontiveros, Suzanne R.
    4
Oppong, Christine
    1013, 1017
Organisation des Femmes de
l'Union Nationale
Camerounaises
    1167
Orubuloye, I.O.
    1018
Osborne, R.J.
    607
O'Shaughnessey, T.J.
    372
Ossandon, Josefina
    179
Otto, Ingeborg
    55
Ozbay, Ferhunde
    969, 970

Pakizegi, Behaaz
    210
Pala, Achola
    84
Palabrica-Costello, Marilou
    72
Palmer, Ingrid
    684
Palmier, Leslie
    537
Pampel, Fred
    815
Pandit, Harshida
    43
Paolucci, Beatrice
    580
Papanek, Hanna
    73, 88, 668, 892, 972
Paqueo, Vincent B.
    894, 1091

Pardo Tellez, Franz
    1137
Park, Jin-sook
    1180
Parker, Betty June
    13
Parker, F.
    13
Parker, Katherine
    667
Pascual, Noemi
    115
Passow, A.H.
    461
Patel, N.F.
    550
Patel, Tara
    344
Pavón Gonzalez, Ramiro
    907
Pearson, Gail
    262
Pellow, Deborah
    696
Penders, L.M.
    268
Peralta, Maria Cid
    538
Perez, Magaly
    115
Perez Pelaez, Liria
    502
Perez-Venero, Mirna M.
    286
Peters, Joan Hellen
    685
Petit, J.J.
    1082
Pfafflin, Sheila M.
    770, 778
Phadke, Sindhu
    1263
Pico de Hernandez, Isabel
    916, 917
Pimpley, P.N.
    391
Plantelides, Edith A.
    1130
Polacek, S.
    812

Pongsapich, Amara
  985
Portugal, Ana Maria
  996
Potter, Robert B.
  49
Powdermaker, Hortense
  128
Powell, Dorian L.
  494, 918
Pernia, E.M.
  1092
Pernia, Prabowo
  1092
Prasad, M.B.
  1035
Prates, Suzana
  908
Pratima, Asthana
  264
Pratima, Sinba
  552
Preston, Rosemary
  403
Prevelou, Clio
  779
Pugazhenthi, G.
  638

Qadir, Sayeda Rowshan
  737
Qayyum, Shah Abdul
  211

Raccagni, Michelle
  56
Radicliffe, David
  855
Raharjo, Yulfita
  854
Raina, M.K.
  490
Rairikar, B.R.
  992
Rajeswari
  790
Rakowski, Cathy A.
  15
Ram, Rati
  816

Rama, Germán W.
  181
Ramanamma, A.
  863
Rammohan, Rgade
  1108
Ramones, Jesus
  941
Ramos, Ana
  195
Rana, Kamal
  109
Rani, Kala
  864
Rao, Amba U.
  554
Rao, N.J. Usha
  878
Rao, Kamala G.
  1115
Rao, V. Rukmini
  1175
Rashedi, Khorram
  201
Ravindran, Sundari
  639
Raza, Moonis
  555
Razak, Mohd
  883
Razik, Taher A.
  496
Rebecca, Summary
  706
Recchini de Lattes, Zulina
  60, 909
Reddly, A. Venkata Rami
  474
Reddy, Balakrishna
  474
Reejad, Pushkar Raj
  723
Rendel, Margerita
  1186
Repetto, Robert
  1060
Rhim, Soon Man
  92
Richter-Dridi, Irmhild
  293

Rihani, M.
    14
Rivero, Enedia B.
    452
Rizika, Jill
    800
Roberts, G.W.
    1138
Robertson, Claire
    129, 321, 322, 608, 711,
    840
Robinson, Jean C.
    163
Rogers, Barbra
    787
Rojas-Aleta, Isabel
    895
Romero San Martin, Esther
    189
Roodkowsky, Mary
    686
Rosales, Sara Elisa
    182
Rosemberg, Fulvia
    352, 362
Rosen, Bernard C.
    1050
Rosenberg, T.J.
    919
Rosenzweig, Mark
    1116
Rousseau, Ida Faye
    135
Rousseau-Mukenge, Ida
    523
Roy, Shibani
    1028
Ruddle, Kenneth
    651
Ruiz, Macario
    509
Russell-Wood, A.J.R.
    287

Saavedra C., Wilma
    938
Sabri, Marie Aziz
    294
Sackey, J.A.
    495

Sackey, T.E.
    495
Safa, Helen I.
    100
Saffioti, Heleieth I.B.
    928
Safilios-Rothschild, Constantina
    1011, 1051
Sahai, S.N.
    42
Sajjad, Muslim
    524
Sajogyo, P.
    617
Salaff, Janet W.
    1024
Salili, Farideh
    500
Sara-Lafosse, Violeta
    190
Sarkar, Lotika
    740
Saulniers, Suzanne Smith
    15
Saunders, Fays E.
    439
Sautu, Ruth
    921
Savigliano, Mauta
    74
Saxena, Rajendra K.
    249
Schiefelbein, Ernesto
    363, 939
Schimmel, Gordon L.
    478
Schmidt, Steffen
    922
Schmidt-Dumont, Marianne
    55
Schmink, Marianne
    754
Schmukler, Beatriz
    74
Schurubsole, A.C.
    510
Schuster, Ilsa
    697, 974, 982, 1163
Schwartzbaum, Allan M.
    393

Scudder, Thayer
379
Seeetharamu, A.S.
1169
Sejourne, Laurette
191
Selassie, Alesebu Gebre
26
Selowsky, Marcelo
515
Seminaire Operationnel Regional
d'Alphabetisation
Fonctonnelle, Banfora,
Haute-Volt
698
Seminar on the Status of Women
865
Sen, Arun K.
167
Sen, N.B.
93
Senyapili, Tansi
971
Sethi, R.M.
669, 866
Seward, Georgene H.
477
Shafii, Forough
404
Shah, Madhuri R.
349
Shah, Makhdoom A.
893
Shah, Nasra M.
893, 1118, 1120, 1121
Shalinsky, Audrey C.
440
Sharma, M.L.
382
Sharma, Radha Krishna
250
Sharma, Savitri
545
Sharma, Sumedha
511
Shaw, Kathryn
756
Shea, J.
525

Sheehan, Glen
804
Shelley, Nancy
475
Shields, N.G.
817
Shresta, Shashi M.
614
Shrestha, Gajendra Man
386
Shrestha, Neeru
846
Siann, Gerda
424
Sievent, Maria Teresa
183
Sidel, Ruth
986
Silva, Juan Andrés
920
Silva Donoso, Maria de la Luz
934
Silver, P.
818
Simmons, Donita Vasiti
35
Simmons, Emmy B.
699
Simmons, J.
476
Singh, K.P.
819, 1110
Singhal, Sushila
879
Sirageldin, I.
1119
Siraj-ul-Haq, Mahmud
107
Siriwardena, Subadra
339
Sison, P.S.
898
Sjafri, Aida
1025
Smith, D.R.
516
Smith, Jane I.
409
Smith, Mary Ann
618

Smith, M.G.
    923
Smith, Peter C.
    340, 1038, 1118
Smith, Stanley K.
    1139
Smock, Audrey Chapman
    76, 374, 820
Smucker, Jacqueline Nowak
    747
Soffan, Linda Usra
    202
Soni, I.M.
    550
Soriano, Liceria Brillantes
    234
Sosa de Newton, Lily
    273
Southard, Barbara
    1174
Spade, Beatrice
    240
Spender, Dale
    1187
Srinivas, M.N.
    172, 993
Srinivasan, Mangalam
    783
Srivastava, Vinita
    867, 880, 995
Ssenkoloto, G.M.
    702
Standing, Guy
    804, 821, 1077
Staudt, Kathleen A.
    472
Steyn, Anna F.
    136
Stichter, Sharon
    841
Still, Kathy
    525
Stinner, W.F.
    1099
Strange, Hether
    145, 888
Strobel, Margaret
    214
Stycos, J.M.
    1140

Suchindran, C.M.
    1147
Sudarkasa, Niara
    137, 712
Sullivan, Earl L.
    963
Sumbuloglu, K.
    1149
Sundaram, K.
    881
Suryochondro, Sukanti
    155
Susto, Juan Antonio
    274
Sutherland, Margaret B.
    310
Swain, Margaret B.
    757
Szanton, M. Christina Blanc
    156

Taamallah, Lemouria
    373
Tabak, Fanny
    1155, 1164, 1188
Taborga, Mercedes
    940
Tadesse, Zenebeworke
    781
Taglioretti, Graciela
    908, 910
Tagumpay-Castillo, Gelia
    1039
Talahite-Hakiki, F.
    958
Talesra, Hem Lata
    556
Tall, Penda Sidibe
    700
Talwar, Usha
    868
Tan, Nalla
    733
Tanaka, Kazuko
    815
Tandon, Kalpana
    1175
Tandon, Rajesh
    635

Tan-Willman, C.
    512
Tardits, Claude
    1019
Tashakkor, G.A.
    499
Taylor, Jean
    269
Teel, Howard
    1108
Tegegne, D.
    602
Tellis-Nayak, Jessie B.
    628, 629
Tessler, Mark A.
    212
Tezcan, Sahaba
    1056
Thapa, Krishna B.
    146
Thiret, Michele
    652
Thom, Betsy
    801
Thomas, E. Jr.
    1080
Thomson, Aisla
    80
Thomson, Marilyn
    184
Tibenderana, Peter Kazenga
    228
Tierda, Marta
    1141
Timm, K.
    297
Timur, Serim
    1078
Tinker, Irene
    16, 713
Todaro, Rosalba
    936
Tomeh, Aida K.
    526, 577, 578
Torki, Mostafa A.
    575
Torrez, P. Hugo
    911
Triuedi, Sheela
    630

Tuncer, Baran
    1148
Turner, June H.
    748

Umea Universitet Pedagogiska
    Institutionen Weed-Projectet
    61
UNESCO
    50, 670, 749
UNESCO, Division on Statistics
    on Education
    302
United Nations. UNICEF
    912
United States. Department of
    Commerce
    119
Unterhalter, Beryl
    983
Urdang, Stephanie
    130
Ursha Rao, N.J.
    166

Van Allen, Judith
    138
Van Esterik, John
    507
Van Rooyen, J.
    975
Vander Voet, Susan McCrae
    311
Vandevelde-Daillière, Hélène
    1156
Vasquez de Miranda, Glaura
    932, 933
Vats, Arunima
    490
Vaughan, Mary K.
    288
Vazques, Josefina Zoraida
    289
Velez, Elizabeth
    924
Verghese, Valsa
    687
Verma, Lokesh
    511

Verma, Margaret
   453
Viezzer, Moema
   643
Vijayaraghavan, K.
   1036
Visaria, Pravin
   882
Vohra, Roopa
   167

Wadhera, Kiron
   869
Wadsworth, Gail M.
   27
Wainerman, Catalina H.
   60, 101, 925, 926
Wallace, Tina
   382
Wang, Bee-lan Chan
   164, 387
Wang, Virginia Li
   1102
Ward, Barbara E.
   785
Ward, Colleen
   441
Ward, Kathryn B.
   1062
Ware, Helen
   85, 1063
Watkins, D.
   491
Watson-Franke, María-Barbara
   653, 758
Weekes-Vagliani, Winifred
   671
Wei, Karen T.
   36
Weinrich, A.K.H.
   131
Weis, Anita
   419
Weis, Lois
   323
Wellesley Editorial Committee
   87
Werner, Linda H.
   1080

Wessels, Dinah M.
   518
West, L.
   565
Westergaard, Kirsten
   738
Westfall, Gloria D.
   29
White, Elizabeth H.
   410
White, Pauline
   147
Whitehead, Clive
   221
Whiting, B.B.
   588
Whyte, Robert Orr
   147
Wickterich, Christa
   672
Wickramasinghe, Shanti
   855
Wiesinger, Rita
   767
Williamson, Kay M.
   454
Williamson, Robert C.
   477
Wilson, Flona
   765
Wipper, Audrey
   1176
Wolfe, Barbara L.
   1047, 1142
Wolfe, Margery
   159
Wong, Aline
   1023
Wood, Corinne Shear
   1095
Woodcroft-Lee, Carlien Patricia
   425
Woodhall, Maureen
   689, 822
World Congress of Women
   1170
World Education
   724

Yao, Esther S. Lee
    236
Yates, Barbara
    222, 223
Yeager, Gertrude M.
    290
Yee, Sin Jran
    35
Yeld, Rachel
    229
Yossundara, Chintana
    540
Youngblood, R.L.
    1040
Youngman, Frank
    592
Youseff, Nadia H.
    768, 802, 959, 1079

Za'rour, George
    513
Zeidenstein, G.
    690
Zeidenstein, Sondra
    760
Zhang, Shiao-Chun
    1045
Ziogas, Marylin Godoy
    427
Zouadi, Mustafa
    455
Zurutuza, Cristina
    1177

GEOGRAPHIC INDEX BY ENTRY NUMBER

Afghanistan
    417, 440
Africa (General)
    12, 15, 23, 24, 27, 82, 83,
    85, 126-128, 137, 138, 213,
    217, 218, 221, 227, 313, 316,
    319, 322, 510, 523, 591, 596,
    601, 607, 694, 695, 698,
    701-703, 706-708, 708,
    711-714, 769, 772, 788, 797,
    800, 835, 839, 841, 972, 977,
    978, 1012, 1014, 1081, 1176.
Algeria
    199, 296, 952, 958, 1152, 1156
Angola
    705
Argentina
    273, 276, 283, 355, 560, 642,
    909, 925, 926, 999, 1000, 1130
Asia (General)
    30-32, 35, 37, 66, 73, 86-90,
    92, 147, 385, 527, 531, 539,
    611, 730, 789, 844, 847, 850,
    874, 1089

Bahamas
    647
Bangladesh
    33, 59, 105, 141, 324, 327,
    332, 397, 619-624, 734-738,
    842, 1103-1108
Barbados
    97, 174, 275, 278, 357, 495,
    1138
Belize
    282
Bolivia
    901, 911, 921, 1048, 1128
Botswana
    592, 600
Brazil
    99, 114, 175, 270, 280, 284,
    285, 287, 352, 362, 402, 434,

    436, 438, 448, 492, 501, 508,
    559, 561-565, 648, 927,
    928-933, 997, 1050, 1129,
    1155, 1158, 1164, 1182
Burma
    144, 784

Cameroon
    318, 692, 831, 1086, 1167
Chile
    96, 177, 277, 290, 363, 558,
    677, 934-940, 1136, 1171
China
    36, 157-164, 235-240, 532,
    729, 986, 1096, 1097, 1102
Colombia
    188, 281, 353, 361, 502, 503,
    653, 915, 919, 922, 998, 1127,
    1137, 1168
Congo
    215
Costa Rica
    756, 790
Cuba
    115, 191, 192-195, 650, 753

Dahomey
    1019
Dominican Republic
    110, 351, 643
Ecuador
    95, 176, 185, 403, 904
Egypt
    211, 292, 295, 297, 423, 433,
    497, 573, 960-963, 972, 1005,
    1053, 1152, 1159
El Salvador
    184
Ethiopia
    26, 589, 602, 830, 1082

Fiji
    338, 530

Ghana
    129, 133, 321, 323, 460, 481,
    595, 599, 608, 661, 696, 831,
    840, 1013, 1017
Guatemala
    463
Guinea-Bissau
    130

Haiti
    747
Honduras
    182, 350
Hong Kong
    745, 1024

India
    38-43, 65, 66, 71, 73, 86, 91,
    93, 106, 108, 165-172,
    241-265, 332, 341-349,
    388-392, 400, 401, 420-422,
    437, 443, 444, 449, 451, 453,
    469, 474, 486, 487, 490, 511,
    540-556, 625-641, 669,
    739-745, 776, 780, 865-882,
    987-995, 1026-1036, 1060,
    1109-1116, 1157, 1161, 1165,
    1169, 1174, 1175, 1178, 1185
Indonesia
    151, 155, 231, 266-269, 337,
    383, 425, 450, 537, 612, 617,
    724, 732, 852-854, 1025, 1092
Iran
    201, 204, 206, 210, 404, 499,
    500, 656, 767, 1143, 1145
Iraq
    198, 572, 1143, 1146
Ivory Coast
    319, 700, 831, 1016, 1087

Jamaica
    356, 465, 466, 493, 494, 918,
    923, 1126, 1133
Japan
    34, 256
Jordan
    513, 1147, 1166

Kenya
    84, 132, 214, 482, 483, 521,
    609, 660, 715-720, 790, 825,
    836, 837, 981, 10180
Korea
    34, 153, 435, 526, 533, 534,
    849, 1060, 1098, 1099, 1180
Kuwait
    964-966

Latin America (General)
    15, 44-52, 60, 94, 98, 100,
    101, 179-181, 183, 186, 187,
    358, 426, 427, 432, 642, 645,
    646, 652, 748-750, 752, 754,
    755, 759, 760, 786, 899, 900,
    903, 906, 907, 913, 1002,
    1049, 1127, 1135, 1140, 1177,
    1179, 1188
Lebanon
    294, 431, 576-578, 1052, 1055
Liberia
    462
Libya
    298, 571, 950

Malawi
    219, 1154
Malaysia
    145, 148, 149, 230, 233, 334,
    336, 387, 441, 488, 536, 721,
    883-888, 1020-1022, 1090
Mali
    700, 1153
Mauritania
    312
Mexico
    103, 173, 271, 288, 289, 359,
    566-569, 657, 746, 783,
    941-947, 1001, 1131, 1139
Middle East (General)
    53-57, 63, 102, 103, 117, 197,
    208, 365-368, 371, 372, 428,
    429, 574, 575, 655, 761, 768,
    948-950, 954, 959, 1051, 1181
Morocco
    200, 207, 764, 950, 955, 957,
    1160

Nepal
    104, 109, 140, 146, 330, 332,
    386, 399, 535, 614, 677, 723,
    727, 731, 846
Nicaragua
    1047, 1142
Niger
    691, 972
Nigeria
    29, 224-226, 228, 229, 380,
    411-415, 454, 457, 473, 479,
    484, 506, 517, 519, 520, 594,
    598, 699, 828, 829, 1015,
    1018, 1083, 1172

Oman
    364, 496

Pakistan
    107, 139, 152, 246, 328, 331,
    332, 416, 418, 419, 424, 613,
    616, 889-893, 1117-1121
Panama
    274, 286, 1127
Papua New Guinea
    232, 333, 525, 528, 1173
Paraguay
    914, 920, 921, 925, 926, 1127
Peru
    111, 112, 178, 189, 190, 272,
    279, 912, 996, 1046, 1127,
    1141
Puerto Rico
    354, 452, 898, 916, 917, 924,
    1060, 1132, 1134
Philippines
    154, 156, 234, 335, 340, 445,
    447, 491, 504, 509, 512, 529,
    538, 609, 610, 618, 660, 726,
    728, 730, 894-897, 984,
    1037-1040, 1091, 1093, 1101

Rwanda
    396

Saudi Arabia
    196, 299, 370, 430, 570
Senegal
    216, 319, 700, 976

Sierra Leone
    135, 972, 1085
Singapore
    150, 325, 733, 848, 1023
Somalia
    315
South Africa
    136, 518, 975, 983, 1084
Sri Lanka
    326, 339, 722, 731, 851, 855,
    1094
Sudan
    125, 1183
Swaziland
    606
Syria
    205, 446, 497

Taiwan
    142, 384, 398, 485, 489, 843,
    1041-1045, 1100
Tanzania
    25, 320, 381, 394, 395, 522,
    590, 605, 693, 708, 710, 824,
    838
Thailand
    329, 507, 615, 845, 985,
    1122-1125
Togo
    317, 456, 458, 459
Trinidad-Tobago
    116, 360, 393
Tunisia
    212, 293, 369, 373, 455, 498,
    654, 766, 950, 953, 956
Turkey
    203, 291, 669, 763, 765, 866,
    967-971, 1003, 1004, 1054,
    1056, 1148-1151

Uganda
    131, 134, 382, 478, 480
United Arab Emirates
    202
Upper Volta (Burkina Faso)
    314, 319, 597, 603, 604, 677
Uruguay
    557, 902, 905, 908, 910

Venezuela
     651, 653, 758
Vietnam
     143

West Indies
     559, 644, 751, 1184
Western Somoa
     1095
Worldwide (General)
     1-21, 58, 61, 62, 64, 67-70,
     72, 74-81, 118-124, 300-311,
     374-378, 405-410, 439, 442,
     461, 464, 467, 468, 470-472,
     475-477, 505, 514-516, 524,
     579, 580-588, 658-660,
     662-668, 670-690, 769-771,
     773-775, 777-779, 781, 782,
     785, 787, 789, 791-796,
     798-823, 973, 1006-1011,
     1057-1079, 1162, 1170, 1186,
     1187.

Yeman Arab Republic
     209, 762
Yeman, Democratic Republic of
     951

Zaire
     135, 215, 222, 223, 979, 980
Zambia
     22, 131, 220, 379, 697, 704,
     833, 974, 982, 1088, 1163
Zimbabwe
     826, 827